VOICE AND DICTION HANDBOOK

Robert G. King
Eleanor M. DiMichael

Prospect Heights, Illinois

For information about this book, write or call:

Waveland Press, Inc.
P.O. Box 400
Prospect Heights, Illinois 60070
(708) 634-0081

ISBN 0-88133-585-1

Printed in the United States of America

7 6 5 4 3 2 1

Contents

Preface

The result of our third collaboration is this textbook, *Voice and Diction Handbook*. This is not a revision of our book *Articulation and Voice*, but we have used some exercises from it. Although this entire book is a product of genuine co-labor, Robert King is primarily responsible for the material on articulation, and Eleanor DiMichael is primarily responsible for the material on voice. One chapter, Chapter 21, ''Body Readiness,'' was prepared by Carmelita Tillotson.

This book is grounded in sound communication theory and linguistics, but it is not theoretical in its approach. This is a *handbook*. We have tried to limit ourselves to providing only the information students really need to know to improve their voice and articulation skills. This drillbook should help you, the student, identify your articulation and voice problems and provide you with exercises designed to help you solve those problems. The exercises are real speech, not contrived. They are average daily living language rather than artificial, mechanistic tongue-twisters.

We have aimed for a book that is practical, written in a style that is clear and comprehensible, but not condescending. Our pragmatic approach focuses on the accumulated reinforcement of learned skills. You will be encouraged to ''carry over'' corrected deviations to all new material being presented.

Unlike most other books in the field, our book begins with articulation rather than voice. This order is not accidental. Our years of teaching experience have led us to conclude that this approach is more effective. We believe that a sound program of articulation improvement provides a good basis for voice improvement. Noticeable changes will take place in the sound of your voice when you learn to produce sounds clearly and precisely. Improved articulation is basic and necessary to a successful program of voice improvement.

We have attempted to organize the material in a step-by-step approach. In the Foreword, we introduce you to the "payoffs" you can expect and the benefits you can derive from this course. We also discuss the focus of the book, its rationale. We think of ourselves as part of a team with you and the instructor. We want this book to work for *you*, to help you accomplish *your* goals.

In Part I, we deal with the sounds of the American English language in isolation and in combinations. Here we use a three-fold structure to organize the content: Principles, Problems, and Pragmatics. In this way, you can understand the principles involved in correct production, the problems or pitfalls you face in achieving correct production, and exercises to help you master the skills needed to accomplish your objectives. We have attempted to make the exercises specific, useful, and fun. In Part I, we also have chapters on sounds in context, on pronunciation of words, and on rhythm and melody. Your instructor may or may not use these three chapters in your particular program of speech improvement. We conclude Part I with a chapter on special English problems—those encountered by speakers whose first language is not English.

In Part II, we begin with consideration of basic principles of voice, body readiness (yes, it's very important!), and vocal processes. Then we address the four elements or characteristics of voice: quality, loudness, pitch, and rate. Here again we have taken the practical approach. We are teaching skills, and this is a how-to approach. We find it works!

This handbook is not a book on speech pathology for speech pathologists. We think speech pathologists would find our explanations accurate, but elementary. In this book, we have tried to be as specific as possible with regard to voice problems, and we have provided you with practical, usable, and effective voice improvement exercises. These exercises have come out of years of experience (don't ask *exactly how many*) in classroom teaching and private practice in speech improvement.

From our students and colleagues over the years, we have learned much, and we acknowledge that debt. To Tom Andrian, Frank Harland, John Monaghan, Dr. Irwin Ronson, Carol Rowe, Neil Rowe, Phyllis Seigal, and especially to Dr. Laurence Powell and Dr. Salvatore DiMichael we are grateful.

R.G.K.
E.M.D.

Foreword

Introduction

To The Student

What Is Voice and Diction?

We have written this handbook to help you improve your oral (spoken) communication skills. We assume you have begun a systematic program of speech improvement. We do not know how you arrived at this point. You may be a college or university student, and required to take a course in Voice and Diction; you may be an executive whose company urged you to see a speech consultant; you may be an acting student taking a course to sharpen the skills you will need; you may be a professional taking a short workshop; or you may have learned another language before you learned English and want to learn to speak American English more clearly and correctly.

Whoever you are, if you really want to improve the way you speak and are willing to work toward that goal, this handbook is for you. The course (or workshop) you have started may be called Voice and Diction or Voice and Articulation. Either way, you have a right to know what's in store for you.

Voice is a common word, so you know what that means. A course in voice and diction, or a program of voice improvement (or therapy), will help you overcome any problems you may have with your speaking voice. *Diction* is not a common word; it means speaking clearly, speaking distinctly. *Articulation* means producing speech sounds. In a program of articulation improvement (diction), you would learn to make all the sounds of a language correctly and clearly. Whether the course or workshop is called Diction or Articulation, it will focus on helping you make speech sounds clearly and distinctly—both for yourself *and* for your listeners.

The goal of any (speaking) voice program is not just a "beautiful" voice, and the goal of any articulation/diction program is not just making the clear, isolated sounds of a language. The purpose is to help you communicate more effectively with other human beings. The purpose is to help you, through your speech, achieve your own personal goals and objectives.

Improving the way you speak is not easy, but it is certainly possible. You already can speak, sending messages out loud. Maybe you can speak more than one language. We will work on your oral communication in just one language: American English. *And* we will concentrate on one dialect (variety) of American English: the dialect spoken by business and professional people in the United States. Sometimes that dialect is called "the Standard Dialect"; sometimes it is called "the Status Dialect" or "the Prestige Dialect" because it is spoken by those with status and power. Of all the many dialects of American English spoken in the United States, it is the one given the greatest prestige. The ability to speak that dialect enables you to convey a more impressive image. Being able to speak that dialect helps you get the attention and respect your ideas deserve.

If you do not now speak "the Standard Dialect" of American English, you may want to learn to speak it all the time. Or, you may want to add it to the dialect or dialects you already speak, to be used when you need it. Either way, the choice is yours. We do want you to know, right from the start, that is the dialect we are focusing on (teaching), and we assume it is the dialect you want to learn to speak. Whether you decide to speak it on all occasions or only on certain occasions is entirely up to you.

Why Learn New Patterns?

Most authorities on communication agree that you learned to speak the way you do now. You can learn to speak in other ways too. As we said, that task is not an easy one, but it certainly is possible! Naturally, it will take some training and some effort. It took time and effort to develop your present speech patterns (although you have probably forgotten how much effort it was). It will require some time, some motivation, and considerable practice to develop new speech patterns to add to or to replace the old ones.

Let us face a problem at the outset: you may resist learning new speech patterns. How often have we heard students say, "But the way I talk now seems natural to me. Why should I learn another way of talking?" We have already given you half the answer. There are no "natural" speech patterns. You did not get your present speech patterns automatically. You *learned* them. "Why should I learn another way of talking?'' must still be answered. Unfortunately (or fortunately) you are the only one who can really answer that question.

To answer it, you must first take a good, honest, critical, analytical look at the way you talk now. You may have taken your speech patterns so much for granted that you have never analyzed them at all. If you are going to answer the ''Why?'' question, you must. You may have to use a tape recorder—audio and/or video—and get a speech teacher or therapist to help you with this analysis. We have included in the book both articulation and voice forms to use as guidelines in this analysis.

After you have taken this good, hard look at your present speech patterns (the way you talk now), you will then have to decide whether those patterns suit your present and future purposes and needs well. You have to ask yourself whether the speech patterns you have now will help you achieve your long-range goals in your personal life and in your career. And that means thinking through what your purposes and needs are.

What kind of job, business, or profession are you in or are you planning to enter? How are people in those jobs, businesses, or professions expected to speak? What kind of social status do you want for yourself and your family? What kind of people will you be socializing with, working with, working for? What people will you be trying to influence? How do these people speak, and what kind of speech patterns do they respect?

If you do not know what kind of speech patterns you will need in the situations and positions you expect (or aspire) to be in, find out. Consult people in those positions and in those fields. It may be that the way you speak now will serve your purposes well. If those patterns and skills suit *all* of your purposes, goals, and needs, then there is no reason to learn any new ones. *But*, if your present speech patterns will *not* suit all the communication situations you will face socially and professionally, then you *do* need to learn new ones.

The decision on whether you should learn new ways of speaking is your own. No one else can make it for you. Unless you are motivated and willing to put out the effort needed, you will probably not learn new speech patterns anyway. Before you decide, let us share some of our experiences.

The inability to speak the Standard (or Status) Dialect can be a serious handicap to your career plans, an obstacle to your professional advancement.

One of our students graduated in Accounting with an excellent academic record. He was well-trained; he was intelligent; he was ambitious; and he was eager to work. He went to the personnel office of United Parcel Service in New York City to apply for a position in their accounting department. When he asked at the personnel office for an application and an interview, he was told, ''They're hiring truck drivers down the hall.'' The problem was not how he dressed (he was quite neat in jacket and tie), but how he spoke. He said only a couple of sentences, but those few sentences impressed the personnel representative as the speech of a truck driver, not that of an accountant. That's a prejudice, you say. Yes, it is. But we must recognize that people have expectations about how professionals sound and how they speak. You will judged and evaluated based on those expectations.

An executive with a large corporation recently began an intensive speech improvement program. He is in mid-career and ready to move to the highest level in his company. He is brilliant; he is invaluable to his corporation and highly respected. He has advanced because of his incomparable knowledge, abilities, and talents. *But* the corporate leadership decided he could not advance further unless he learned speech patterns appropriate for his position. Until this point, he had not realized how much his non-standard speech stood out and what a handicap it was. Now he is working hard to remedy the speech deficits and to move up.

The inability to speak the Standard Dialect of American English can be an obstacle to your ''social mobility,'' to your ability to fit into the larger, mainstream social fabric.

One of our students many years ago was a bright pre-med student from a small, insulated neighborhood in Brooklyn. He spoke the dialect characteristic of that tiny neighborhood. Many of his speech sounds were different from the way most Americans would produce them. And the rhythms and melodies of his sentences would strike most Americans as ''foreign.'' When he entered Columbia College of Columbia University, he found (for the first time in his life) that he did not speak like the people with whom he lived and socialized. Everyone who met him and heard him speak noticed his ''strange'' patterns. Most people found his speech patterns distracting, and some found them annoying. This young man discovered that his speech patterns interfered with his interpersonal communication (communication with other human beings) in his new social environment. He had to decide whether to learn new patterns in order to ''fit in.'' The decision was difficult for him. Everyone he had known and loved all his life spoke the familiar (non-standard) patterns. He decided to learn the Standard Dialect, the national patterns, because he knew the rest of his social and professional life would not be confined to the small neighborhood from which he had come. He also decided that learning to fit in with, and speak like, the larger society did not mean rejecting the smaller society or unlearning its dialect. He decided there were reasons—social reasons—for learning another way of speaking.

Another student we remember vividly was a woman in her middle thirties who lived her formative years in a country where English was not the national language. She spoke English, but with a heavy ''accent.'' She had no motivation to improve her English speaking patterns until recently. Her children were growing up; they spoke English well, and they associated with people who spoke American English well. She decided there were social reasons to improve her own speech patterns. And she did!

How Can You Learn New Patterns?

You have been practicing your old speech habits for a long time. Those patterns have been reinforced by repetition. Whether you want to replace the present habits or merely add to them, you will have to work at the process. If you see the need to learn new patterns and if you are willing to work to learn them, you *can* overcome the obstacles.

To establish a new speech habit requires three steps: (1) awareness of the problem (or difficulty or deficit), (2) development of new skills, and (3) transfer of the new skills into everyday use. In this handbook, we try to make you aware of specific problems you may need to work on, to tell you simply and clearly how to develop the new skill by providing a progressive, cumulative plan to correct the deficit, and to give you interesting, realistic practice materials to make the change habitual. Using these practice materials should help you establish the new habits and transfer them into your daily speech.

When we said that we would provide "a progressive, cumulative plan" to correct a deficit, we had two things in mind. First, our approach focuses on the cumulative reinforcement of learned skills. We encourage our students to "carry over" skills already learned to new material being presented. Second, we build new skills on those already mastered. You must be "ready" to learn some speech skills. You use the speech skills you have already acquired to learn others. You will see how our plan for speech improvement works as you go through the book.

We will work on two types of problems, so the handbook is divided into two major parts. Unlike many books on the subject, we take up articulation before we deal with voice. That is no accident; we have done it deliberately. We believe that this order creates a more logical and systematic program of speech improvement.

In Part II, "Articulation," you will work on the process of producing the sounds of the language. Our goal is to help you make each of those sounds in the customary way (in the United States) and in a clear and distinct way. To do that, we will have to work to get good oral (mouth cavity), pharyngeal (throat cavity), and nasal (nose cavity) resonance (amplification) on those sounds. All of this work on sound production will affect your voice; it should improve the balance of resonance in your voice.

In Part III, "Voice," we build on the work you have already started in your program of articulation improvement. We take advantage of the diction skills you have already acquired, or at least have begun acquiring. It has been our experience that control of your articulators encourages increased vocal resonance. It bears repeating that resonance is not only a characteristic of voice but is a necessary component of a well produced voice. Articulation is basic to improved vocal quality.

What Is the Focus?

Every time you speak, you reveal an image of yourself to others. People form impressions about you—not just from *what* you say, but from *how* you say it. They judge you on the basis of your speech skills and speech patterns.

It is through speech that one's inner self does barter with the outside world. Through speech, you project an image of your self to the other human beings with whom you communicate. What image do you project by your speech patterns? Is it the image you *want* to project? Are others getting the impression you want them to get? If not, where do the problems lie? What changes must you make in your speech patterns to convey the impression you want to convey? What changes must you make in your diction, voice, and language usage in order for others to see you as you want to be seen? What principles must you learn, what skills must you master, what deficits must you correct to project *your* image of your self? If you see yourself as intelligent, educated, competent, professional, how do you portray/convey that self to the world? You must identify the image-breakers, learn the accepted and expected voice, speech, and language patterns, and practice to develop them.

This, then, is the focus of this handbook: Speech as Self Projection. You *will* project some image of yourself. The only question is what image you will project. You *can* project a better, more accurate, more acceptable image, because you can improve your diction, voice, and language patterns.

What Are the Payoffs?

Since this program of speech (and language) improvement is going to be a lot of work, you certainly have the right to ask, "What's in it for me?" or "What specifically do I get out of it?" And the answer is rather simple: *power*! By getting new knowledge, new awareness, and new skills, you will gain more power and control. You will gain:

1. Power to recognize deficits (image-breakers).
2. Power to accept the fact that you have speech and language deficits.

3. Power to recognize medical, physical, and emotional factors (or conditions) that can affect your voice and diction.
4. Power to work toward your speech goals efficiently and effectively.
5. Power to correct deficits (image-breakers).
6. Power to take care of your voice.
7. Power to use your voice efficiently and dynamically.
8. Power to convey your ideas, intentions, attitudes, and feelings more accurately.
9. Power to control or manipulate (in a good sense, of course) the image you project.
10. Power to use your voice as an extension of the image you want to project.
11. Power to choose what dialect(s) * to speak.
12. Power to choose among speaking styles (functional varieties).*
13. Power to speak clearly, distinctly, and effectively.
14. Power to improve pronunciation and language usage.

Well, that is the bottom line. These are the payoffs from this program of speech improvement. These benefits make you more powerful because they give you more control over the most important tool of interpersonal communication—your voice, diction, and language usage.

One final explanation: We have referred to language usage several times in this chapter, even though this is not a "language" book. We have done so because the proper use of this handbook and this program will have a significant impact on developing linguistic (language) skills. You will be exposed to some new words, so your vocabulary will grow. You will develop some new concepts (categories of ideas) as you acquire new meanings. And your use of English grammar should improve as you formulate your own words and sentences based on the exercises in the handbook.

More power to you!

* This concept will be explained in Chapter 1, "Basic Principles of Articulation."

Part I

Articulation

Articulation Glossary

Abutting consonants: Two different, adjacent consonants; one ends (terminates) the first syllable and the other starts (initiates) the following syllable.

Addition: An articulation error, in which a sound is added or inserted that does not belong.

Affricate: A single consonant phoneme produced by combining the articulations for a stop and a fricative.

Allomorph: A variation (variant form) of a morpheme.

Allophone: A variant form of a phoneme; there are two kinds of allophones of a phoneme: those that can be used interchangeably without affecting meaning and those that appear only in certain contexts.

Alphabet: A set of written letters that tries to represent the phonemes (the speech sounds) of the language; the English alphabet has twenty-six letters to represent forty-two phonemes.

Alveolar ridge: The gum ridge behind the upper front teeth.

Articulation: Obstruction (either partial or complete) of the outgoing air stream by the lips, teeth, tongue, palate, velum, and glottis.

Aspiration: Release of a sound with a puff of air.

Assimilation: A change in a sound caused by the influence of a neighboring sound.

Bilabial: Articulated by the two lips.

Centralizing (centering): Centralization is a distortion of a sound caused by raising the tongue in the center of the mouth instead of the front or the back.

Cognate: One of a pair of sounds, articulated in the same place and released in the same manner, but distinguished from each other by the presence or absence of vocal fold vibration.

Compound consonant: A group of two or more consonants that serve to initiate or terminate a syllable.

Consonant: A speech sound characterized by obstruction, either partial or complete, of the outgoing air stream.

Continuant: A consonant on which the air stream is impeded, but not completely stopped; a sustainable consonant; a consonant that can be continued (held on to).

Contour: The pitch pattern (melody) of a phrase; each contour contains at least two pitch levels and a phrase terminal.

Dentalization: Distortion of a sound by placing the tongue on the teeth.

Devoicing: Weakening of vocal vibration on a voiced consonant because of the influence of a neighboring voiceless sound or the pause following the sound.

Diacritical marks: Modifying marks used by dictionaries, in combination with letters of the alphabet, to represent pronunciation.

Dialect: A variation of a language spoken by a regional or social group.

Digraph: A combination of two written letters representing one speech sound: for example, *th* in *thing*, *ph* in *phony*, and *ng* in *ring*.

Diphthong: A blend of two vowels, the first of which is fairly strong and the second of which is relatively weak.

Dissimilation: A sound change in which one of two similar or repeated sounds is altered to become less like the other one.

Distortion: An articulation error, in which a sound is changed by being produced in an unusual way.

Enunciation: How clear and understandable speech is; how precise the articulation is.

Etymology: The study of the derivation of words; etymology is a division of lexicology.

Foot: A rhythmic group made up of a single strongly stressed syllable alone or a few syllables grouped around a single strongly stressed syllable.

Form words: Words that do not usually carry main ideas, but are necessary for the form (grammar) of our sentences; form words have a strongly stressed form and a weakly stressed form (the more commonly used of the two forms).

Fricative: A consonant on which the air stream is emitted with audible friction because the air is forced out between two articulators.

Fronting: Distortion of a sound by arching the tongue near the front of the mouth rather than at the back or center of the mouth.

Functional varieties: Those varieties of an idiolect that differ in degree of formality or informality.

Glide: A consonant on which the articulators move from one position to another.

Glottal stop: A stop sound made at the glottis.

Glottis: The space between the vocal folds.

Grammar: The study (descriptive, not prescriptive) of the patterns used in forming words and sentences.

Haplology: Omission, in speech, of one or two repeated consecutive sounds or syllables.

Homonym: A word written like and pronounced like another word of the same language, but different in meaning.

Homophone: A word pronounced like another word of the same language, but different in spelling and meaning.

Homorganic sounds: Sounds articulated at the same place; for example, /t/ and /l/ are homorganic because both are articulated by the tongue tip on the alveolar ridge.

Idiolect: An individual's personal variety of a language.

International Phonetic Alphabet (IPA): A symbol system devised by the International Phonetic Association to represent the sounds of the principal languages of the world; each symbol represents one sound—no matter what the language.

Interpersonal: Between persons; person to person.

Intonation: Melodies that result from pitch changes and pitch differences in phrases.

Intrapersonal: Inside a person; within one human being.
Labiodental: Articulated by the lips and teeth.
Lateral: The consonant on which the air is emitted over the sides of the tongue.
Lexicology: The study of words as the expressions of ideas.
Lingua-alveolar: Articulated by the tongue and the alveolar (upper gum) ridge.
Lingua-dental: Articulated by the tongue and teeth.
Lingua-palatal: Articulated by the tongue and the palate.
Lingua-postalveolar: Articulated by the tongue and the area just behind the alveolar ridge.
Lingua-velar: Articulated by the tongue and the velum.
Melody: The "tune" of a phrase, created by the varying pitches used in its utterance.
Metathesis: Reversal of sounds.
Morpheme: The smallest meaningful unit in a language; a meaning unit from which words are made; a root, a prefix, or a suffix.
Morphology: The study of word formation.
Nasalization: A distortion caused by nasal resonance on non-nasal sounds.
Nasals: Consonants on which the air is emitted through and resonated in the nose.
Nonphonemic diphthong: Blend of two vowels, each of which retains its phonemic identity.
Nonstandard dialects: Varieties of a language that differ from the variety spoken by those in positions of power and prestige.
Nonverbal: Without words; not in words.
Occlusion: The bringing of the edges of the inner surfaces of the upper front teeth and the edges of the outer surfaces of the lower front teeth together.
Omission: An articulation error, in which a sound is left out (omitted) in the pronunciation of a word.
Oral: Made by, or related to, the mouth.
Phonation: The vibratory process by which sound is produced at the vocal folds.
Phone: A speech sound.
Phoneme: A significant sound; a sound that may distinguish one word from another word; a group of phonetically related or similar sounds (phones) that function as one sound in a given language; a minimum unit of distinctive sound features; the smallest significant sound class; a family of sounds (phones) that are phonetically similar and that may be used interchangeably without affecting the meaning.
Phonemic diphthong: A blend of two vowels that functions in the language as a single sound; a blend of two inseparable vowels that have lost their separate phonemic identity—the blend itself functioning as a distinctive phoneme.
Phonemics: The study of the significantly different sounds (phonemes) of a language.
Phonetics: The study of sounds (phones).
Phrase: A thought group, a sense group, a unified idea that can hang together; a succession of syllables uttered on one stream of outgoing breath; a breath group.
Phrase terminal: The use of rising, falling, or level pitch at the ends of phrases.

Pitch levels: Four significant, relative pitch ranges used in American English intonation.
Prestige Dialect: The variety of a language spoken by the people in positions of power or prestige. (Also called Status Dialect and Standard Dialect).
Pronunciation: The uttering of words; pronunciation involves selecting sounds and syllabic stress.
Raising: Distortion of a sound by elevating (raising) the tongue from the usual position for forming the sound.
Resonation: The process by which sound generated at the vocal folds is amplified in the cavities of the head and chest.
Respiration: The process of breathing, which forms the motor force of speech; we speak on the exhaled air stream.
Retracting: Distortion of a sound by placing the tongue in back of the usual position for forming the sound.
Rhythm: The pattern of pulses or beats created by variations in duration and intensity of syllables.
Semantics: The study of the meaning of words.
Sibilants: The high-frequency sounds characterized by hissing: /s/, /z/, /ʃ/, (sh), /ʒ/, (zh), /tʃ/, (ch), and /dʒ/ (j); the s family of sounds.
Simple consonant: A single consonant that serves to initiate (start) or terminate (end) a syllable.
Standard dialect: See Prestige Dialect.
Status dialect: See Prestige Dialect.
Stop: A consonant on which the air stream is completely obstructed (stopped).
Stress: Various degrees of prominence given to a syllable, usually by varying duration, intensity (force or volume), and pitch.
Substitution: An articulation error in which one sound is replaced by another.
Syllable: A sound or group of sounds uttered on one chest pulse, a pulse of air created by slight contraction of the intercostal muscles of the chest.
Syntax: The study of sentence formation.
Unvoicing: Distortion of a voiced consonant by turning it into its voiceless cognate.
Velum: The soft palate.
Verbal: Related to, or using, words.
Vocal: Related to, or produced by, the human voice.
Voiced consonant: A consonant on which the vocal folds vibrate.
Voiceless consonant: A consonant on which the vocal folds do not vibrate.
Vowel: A speech sound on which the air stream is emitted with relatively little obstruction and that is formed by modifying resonance in the mouth.

1

Basic Principles

Before we begin your program of speech improvement, we must make clear some basic concepts and provide some essential definitions. You will find these words throughout this handbook, so it is very important that we agree at the very beginning on their meanings. If you do not know and understand these basic principles and the vocabulary we are using, your use of this handbook and its program of speech improvement will be severely limited. We will not use technical words that you do not need, but an understanding of basic terms is essential to the program.

Communication

In its broadest sense, the word *communication* refers to a process in which a response is evoked (elicited or induced) by a message sent and received. In that broad sense, flipping a switch to turn on a lamp, pushing a button to ring a bell, and the thermostat turning on a furnace are all examples of communication. A message was sent; a message was received; the receiver reacted to the message. Communication occurred.

Some of the lower animals can communicate. Bees do a kind of dance, and the other bees know where to find the food supply. Mama hogs can tell the difference between baby pigs' squeals for "I'm hurt" and "I'm hungry." The messages may be simple, but there are messages sent, received, and responded to. It is clearly communication in the broadest sense of the word.

Human communication, a narrower term, refers to communication in which a human being is involved as sender, receiver, or both. We are concerned in this handbook only with communication within and between human beings. We are limiting our attention here to human communication where the message sender and the message receiver are both human.

If the communication is within one human being (*intrapersonal communication*), the same human being is both sender and receiver of the message. Thinking is one example of intrapersonal communication.

If the communication is between human beings (*interpersonal communication*), the two persons send messages to and receive messages from each other. Because the two persons both send and receive at the same time, and because the two persons are sending and receiving continuously and simultaneously, we human beings are said to be *transceivers*.

Our definition of human communication is receiver-oriented. For communication to take place, someone must receive a message and react to it. Another common definition also focuses on the receiver: Communication occurs when a human being attaches significance (meaning) to something perceived. When you say to yourself, "Aha! That (whatever *that* is) means something"—communication has taken place.

This receiver-oriented definition of communication has very important implications. We are reminded that talking is not a synonym for communication. We must speak so our listeners can and will listen and respond. We must consider and adjust to the listener's beliefs, values, and attitudes to get the response we want.

The implications for the student of Voice and Diction are enormous. Remember that our receivers' reactions are at the heart of communication. Remember also that *how* we speak has a significant effect on the response our spoken messages receive. We put in all this effort to have a better chance of eliciting the responses we want.

In interpersonal communication, we strive for *efficient* and *effective* communication. Communication is efficient if the receiver understands the sender's message accurately (or as accurately as humanly possible). Communication is effective if the receiver responds as the sender intended.

Interpersonal communication succeeds (is efficient) only if the receiver receives the message the sender intends to send. That should be obvious on the face of it. So the speaker must talk in such a way that the receiver can understand the message. That should be obvious too. That is why diction (clarity of utterance) is so important. Your speech must be intelligible. Doesn't it logically follow, then, that anything in the sender's speech patterns that interferes with the listener's understanding of the intended message must be analyzed, overcome, and (if possible) eliminated?

Are you an efficient interpersonal communicator? If not, what barriers to efficient communication do your speech patterns present? How is the way you speak hindering you from getting across the messages you want to transmit? The diction and voice improvement program presented in this handbook should help you overcome the barriers to efficient interpersonal communication your present speech patterns may impose.

When you send a spoken message, you have a purpose in mind, a goal to achieve. We send messages to get particular reactions. To be effective (to get the desired response), a speaker must adapt the message to the beliefs, values, attitudes, expectations, purposes, and background of the listener(s). And you must adapt not only *what* you say (content) and the verbal style you use (choice of words), you must also adapt your transmission (diction and voice).

Just as you faced potential barriers to efficiency in your transmission, you also face potential barriers to effectiveness in the way you speak. If there are any aspects of your speech patterns that interfere with getting the responses you want from listeners, you should face those problems and undertake a systematic program to overcome them.

Speech

We have used the words *speech* and *speak* many times in this book already. Both are everyday words. To speak is to talk, and a person's speech is his/her way of talking. Dictionaries have defined speech as "vocal utterance," "spoken sounds that mean something," "making communicative sounds," and "to utter words with the human voice."

All the definitions of the words *speak* and *speech* make it clear that speaking is something that people *do*. It is an action; it is an activity. That action involves something our bodies do (so there is a physiological factor), something produced that can be heard (so there is an acoustic factor), and something seen (so there is a visible factor). We need to remember that speech is an action—it involves motor skills, and those skills can be developed and improved.

We believe there are three distinct *elements* in speech communication:

(1) vocal—the use of the human voice;
(2) verbal—use of words (spoken symbols) to represent ideas;
(3) physical (physical from the point of view of the sender; visible from the point of view of the receiver)—the use of the entire body, including posture, movement, and facial expression.

The vocal element of speech communication is also called *paralanguage* (or *paralinguistic features*). The vocal element includes four aspects of the use of voice:

(1) *voice characteristics*, variations of:

pitch
rate
loudness
quality

(2) *vocal holders* (non-fluencies meant to hold the listener's attention, such as *um, uh, er, and er ah*)

(3) *vocal signals* (such as *sh* for "silence," *sss* for disapproval, *ssst* for "come here," *unh-unh* for "no," and *un-huh* for "yes")

(4) *vocal reflectors* (such as groans, moans, sighs, yawns, belches, whines, throat clearings, and snoring)

Note that two out of the three elements of speech communication are non-verbal (not-word) communication: the use of the voice and the use of the body. Part I of this book will deal primarily with the verbal element of speech communication, and Part II will deal primarily with vocal and physical elements. In that section, too, we will show that the two elements are related.

Speech Production Processes

When we human beings speak, we turn our bodies into transmitters. We send out communicative signals by activating, monitoring, and controlling certain movements in the body. There are six related, but separate, processes involved in the transmission of speech communication:

(1) innervation

(2) respiration

(3) phonation

(4) resonation

(5) articulation

(6) audition

Since we will refer to these processes throughout the book, we will explain each of them briefly now. We will look at them in more detail, and from a slightly different angle, in Chapter 22.

All sound-making instruments or devices must contain two parts: something that will vibrate, which we call the *vibrator*, and some source of energy or power, which we call the *motor*. Because sound *is* vibration, you can see that we need something that will vibrate and something that will start the vibration. These two parts are the absolute minimum. Most sound-making instruments also have a third part: something that will amplify, reinforce, or resonate the vibration. We call this the *resonator*.

In a guitar, the strings are the vibrator, the fingers of some human being are the motor, and the curvaceous box is the resonator. In a clarinet, the mouthpiece has a reed that serves as the vibrator, the player's breath stream is the motor, and the entire tube of the instrument itself is the resonator.

We said earlier that human beings use their bodies as transmitters. We are sound-making instruments. Our bodies have all the necessary ingredients: the vocal cords in the larynx are the vibrator, the exhaled breath stream is the motor, and the cavities of the laryngeal pharynx, oral pharynx, and nasal pharynx are the main resonators. We also have articulators, which we will explain soon. We human beings stimulate and control and monitor our transmission through innervation and audition.

Let's look at each of the six processes briefly:

Innervation

Your "transmitter" has to be controlled, directed, and coordinated. The Central Nervous System performs this function for us. Through a complicated communication system inside our bodies, we stimulate speech activity. (See chapter 22 for a more complete explanation.)

Respiration

The source of power for speech is the stream of air coming from the lungs as we exhale. Of course, we have to breathe to stay alive. Breathing for speech is slightly different from breathing for life. In breathing for speech, we must *control* the exhaled breath—deliberately and voluntarily—so it will fit our speech communication needs. Respiration, with directions for developing proper control, is explained in detail on pp. 436-443.

Phonation

In breathing for life, the inhaled and exhaled breath streams pass between the vocal cords with no noticeable sound. To produce voiced sounds, the exhaled breath stream must vibrate. Sometimes we do this unintentionally when we snore. When we speak, we deliberately vibrate the exhaled breath stream as it passes between the vocal cords which are inside the larynx (commonly called the voice box). The vocal cords generate a complex pattern of vibrations, consisting of a fundamental tone and several overtones (harmonics) when voiced sounds are produced. These vibrations set up sound waves (a tiny buzz, really) that pass outward through the vocal tract. This vibratory process of creating sound waves in the larynx is called phonation. We explain this process in more detail in the voice section.

Resonation

The tones generated by the vocal cords are tiny and weak. They must be enlarged and strengthened, reinforced, amplified—resonated.

The word *resonation* means "the process of sounding again": re + son + ation. That is exactly what happens in this process. The tones produced by the vocal cords are selectively echoed in the pharynx, nose, mouth, and larynx. We can modify these cavities (changing the echoing chambers slightly) and thus alter the resonance. We can make the cavities longer or shorter, wider or narrower. We can make their walls softer or harder. We can even shut off cavities, making it possible to resonate sounds in one, two, or all three of the cavities. This process of resonation takes the tiny tones produced by the vocal cords and, by sympathetic vibration, amplifies and enriches the sound. For a more detailed explanation of this process, see the voice section.

Articulation

Articulation is the process by which the outgoing air stream is divided into distinguishable speech sounds. The word *articulation* comes from a Latin word for *joint*, a place where two things come together. In the process of articulation, we "joint" the outgoing air stream to make individual, recognizable speech sounds. When we articulate, we bring two things together (either completely or partially) to modify the expelled breath. The articulators we use are the lips, teeth, tongue, hard palate, soft palate, and vocal cords. These articulators chop the air stream up into individual speech sounds.

Audition

Feedback is defined as "a response that affects the transmission." We need feedback to be able to modify our speech transmission as we send out the messages. We use other people's reactions for feedback, of course. We also *monitor* ourselves. *Audition* (hearing and listening) involves paying attention to the outgoing message so we can adapt that message as we speak. That adaptation can change what we say *and* how we say it. See the voice section for more discussion of this concept.

Codes: Nonverbal and Verbal

Nonverbal

We human beings take in information (receive messages) through the five senses: sight, hearing, smell, taste, and touch. You can readily see, then, that many messages we receive are not packaged (coded) in language at all. We attach significance to many stimuli other than words. This communication without words or apart from words has been labeled *nonverbal communication*.

Words are not the only means of human communication, and any study of speech communication is incomplete without some attention to nonverbal elements.

When discussing speech earlier, we noted that two of the three elements of speech are nonverbal—the use of voice (apart from words) and the use of the body. Both convey meanings to our listeners whether we intend them to or not.

Vocal holders, vocal signals, and vocal reflectors (See p. 10.) are meaningful, but we will not give much attention to them in this handbook. We must remind you, however, that we *learn* the meanings to attach to nonverbal messages. The meanings attached vary from culture to culture. For example, hissing is a sign of disapproval in the United States, but a mark of approval in Europe. When an audience whistles in America, it is demonstrating its enthusiasm *for* a performance, but whistling has the opposite meaning in Europe. If you come from another country, you must learn a new nonverbal code as well as a new verbal one to communicate efficiently and effectively in America. When Americans go abroad, they must remember that the nonverbals they have learned may not get the same response in the changed environment.

We will concentrate on voice characteristics (variations of quality, loudness, pitch and rate) in this handbook. (See Chapters 23, 24, 25, and 26.) When a person speaks, that person utters words (made out of individual speech sounds); that, of course, is verbal communication. But a person's voice can vary in many ways and still be saying the same word. Those nonverbal variations are a major means for a listener to guess our meanings, attitudes, intentions, and feelings.

If you and I have a conversation, will somebody who was *not* present know what was expressed through reading a typed manuscript of the words of the conversation? Of course not, you say. There might be ambiguities. Besides, tones and feelings are not conveyed in a written transcript. You're right. We get part of the meaning—maybe *much* of the meaning—from hearing the voices of people as they speak words. Having an audio tape recording would be much better than having a written transcript. It would add the *vocal* element to the *verbal* element. Even with the audio tape recording, would that third person get *all* the possible meanings transmitted by the two of us in our conversation? The answer is no, again. There is still an element missing. Give that person a videotape of our conversation, and the missing element is added: the *visual* component of speech communication.

Your body posture (or stance), your body movements and gestures, and your facial expressions will all provide *metacommunication* (extra messages about the main, verbal message, giving hints about how to interpret the main message). These extra, nonverbal messages provide the listener with invaluable information about the speaker's physical and emotional state. Again, however, we need to be reminded that we have *learned* how to use these nonverbal physical cues, and we have *learned* how to interpret them. They are not universal—the same all over the world.

One final reminder about nonverbal communication: We can receive (and respond to) several different nonverbal (vocal *and* visual) messages at the same time. That fact makes nonverbal cues all the more influential and important.

Verbal

As important as nonverbal messages are, words carry the heaviest freight of meaning. The two nonverbal elements of human speech communication (the speaker's use of voice and the speaker's use of body) do convey messages about the speaker's emotions. But *idea* messages—abstract concepts—are carried by the verbal element of human speech communication: **language**.

Words are verbal symbols. When we talk about the verbal symbols of the human race collectively, we call that abstract collection *language*. Language is an abstraction in the same way that law, medicine, and painting are abstractions. Law refers to that area of knowledge dealing with rules governing human conduct; medicine refers to the art or science of preserving or restoring health; painting refers to the art of those who make visual representations (paintings). Like the other three words, *language* refers to a concept. Language refers to the use of words to stand for things, actions, relationships, and ideas. *Verbal communication* utilizes language; it represents ideas with words (spoken symbols).

We can talk not only about language in the abstract sense, we can talk about *languages* in a very specific sense. We can talk about languages—just as we can talk about laws, medicines, and paintings. Laws are specific regulations; medicines are specific remedies; paintings are specific products of a painter's skill. *A language* is a specific verbal code. A code is a system of signs or symbols.

Each language in the world is a separate code. The language we are concerned with in this handbook is American English.

The systematic study of language is the field of *linguistics*. Linguists study how language in general or a language in particular works. The basic branch of linguistics is *descriptive linguistics*, which constructs comprehensive theories about the systems of specific languages. *Historical linguistics* deals with the changes in a language over time, and *comparative linguistics* compares and contrasts the features of two or more languages.

Subdisciplines of linguistics are phonetics, morphology, syntax, and lexicology. *Phonetics* is the study of the sounds of languages; *morphology* is the study of word patterns of languages; *syntax* is the study of sentence patterns of languages; and *lexicology* is the study of words as expressions of ideas. There are two divisions of the study we call lexicology: (1) *etymology*, the study of the origin and history of words, and (2) *semantics*, the study of the meaning of words. Etymology traces the evolution of words; semantics studies definitions. Traditionally, the word *grammar* was used to encompass morphology and syntax. More recently, grammar has been thought to include phonology as well as morphology and syntax.

4 Elements of a Language

All languages—no matter how complicated (such as Navajo) or how simple (such as English)—have four basic elements:

(1) Phonology—a set of sound families, called phonemes;
(2) Morphology—patterns for making words;
(3) Syntax—patterns for making sentences; and
(4) A Lexicon or Vocabulary—a collection of words.

If we are to understand the nature of a language, we must look at each of these four elements in more detail.

Phonemes

Every language uses a set of sound families. Almost all speakers of a language think of those sound families as single sounds, even though that is not technically correct. There are variations of each "sound" called *allophones*. The sound class or sound family is called a *phoneme*.

This concept is not as complicated or difficult to understand as it sounds. Every language has its own set of phonemes. American English has about forty-two; Spanish uses approximately thirty-two. Phonemes are features of a particular language and are not relevant to any other language. If you are going to learn any language, you have to learn its own set of phonemes (sound families).

We have some phonemes in English that the Spanish language does not have—the vowel sounds in the words *shut* and *book*, for example. And Spanish has some phonemes we do not have in English—the trilled sound of *rr* in such words as *perro*, for example. If your first language is English and you are trying to learn another language, you cannot just transfer over the phonemes of English to the new language and have them work. On the other hand, if you learned a language other than English first, you cannot just use the phonemes of your first language in English either. You must learn the phonemes of each language.

At the risk of confusing you, we must contrast the words *phone* and *phoneme*. A phone is a sound—any sound. A phoneme is a sound class or category, and that group or family of sounds (that native speakers think of as a single "sound") has certain characteristics. A phoneme is a class of sounds which (l) are phonetically similar, (2) are significantly different from all other phonemes of the same language, and (3) show characteristic patterns of distribution in words of the language. Let us look at each of these points in turn.

The allophones (variations) of a phoneme are phonetically similar. For example, the /k/ in *key*, *ski*, and *cop* are not exactly alike. There are variations in their production, but they are similar enough to be grouped together into the same phoneme. The /h/ in *half* and *behalf* are not exactly alike either, but they are similar—alike enough to be the same phoneme in English.

Each phoneme is significantly different from all other phonemes of the same language. When we say that each phoneme is "significantly different," we mean that it is different enough to change the meaning of a word. A phoneme can distinguish one word from another word. (A phoneme does not *have* meaning; it does not *convey* meaning; but it can *change* meaning.) Think of the words *hill* and *hell*. Both start with /h/ and end with /l/; each has a vowel in the middle. Are those two vowel sounds (phones) the same phoneme in English? No. They cannot be substituted for each other without changing the meaning of the word. You can see why it is essential to learn the phonemes of a language and learn to produce them in the conventional ways.

We have already said that many phonemes have several differing varieties (called *allophones*, based on the Greek words for *other* and *sound*). These allophones show characteristic patterns of distribution. In other words, they appear in words in a regular and predictable pattern. Let us prove it to you. We have a /t/ phoneme in American English, but we Americans do not produce /t/ exactly the same way in every context. The /t/ allophones in *top*, *stop*, *pot*, *city*, and *hit them* are not exactly the same. Try the words out loud and see. You might put a candle about four inches away from your mouth when you say the first three words. Is there the same amount of explosion on the /t/ in each of those three words? No. Americans produce the first with a lot of aspiration (air release), the second with a little aspiration, and the third with no aspiration at all. The context is different: the first at the beginning of a word, the second after /s/, and the third at the end of a word. Would you expect the same kind of distribution with the /k/ and /p/ phonemes? If you said yes, you are quite right. The /t/ in *city* is different from the others, because it is between vowels and begins an unstressed syllable. The /t/ in *hit them* is made on the teeth rather than on the gum ridge (as the other allophones are) because it comes before a *th* sound.

Even though we often think of one phoneme (sound family) as one sound, it has several different variations (allophones). To master a language fully, you must master not only all the phonemes of the language, you must learn the allophones of each phoneme and which allophone to use when.

Remember that we are talking about *speaking* American English—not writing it. You must learn to think of the sounds of the language—not letters of the alphabet. As we shall see later, our spelling system does not represent the (spoken) language very well. Look at the following words. Note how they are spelled, and then count the number of phonemes in each word:

1. though	________	5. gnaw	________
2. thought	________	6. limb	________
3. cough	________	7. ring	________
4. knee	________	8. phone	________

Check your answers. Here are the correct number of phonemes for the eight words: 2, 3, 3, 2, 2, 3, 3, 3. Did you identify the number of phonemes in each word? Did the spelling mislead you? Did saying the words out loud help? We must tune up our ears and sharpen our consciousness to focus on the sounds we utter.

Morphology

Morphology, the study of word formation, gets its name from the word *morpheme*. Morphemes are the meaning-units from which words are made. Phonemes, you remember, do not mean anything; they can *change* meaning, but they do not *convey* meaning. Morphemes are units that do convey meaning. They are the building blocks we put together to form words. You may think of them as roots, prefixes, and suffixes. The word *previewer* is made up of three meaning units or building blocks: *pre* (which means "before"), *view* (which means "to look at"), and *er* (which means "one who"). A previewer, therefore, is "one who looks at (something) before." The root or base of the word is *view*; *pre* is a prefix (because it is put in front of roots), and *er* is a suffix (because it is attached after roots).

You have to know word patterns to construct words. If you know that *-er* means "one who" and that it can be attached after any verb (the pattern), you can make up words you have never heard before. If you know the verb *teach*, you can build the word *teacher*—whether you have been taught that particular word or not.

However, you must be careful. Remember that morphemes have to do with meaning—not with spelling. An *actor* is "one who acts," even though the *-er* is spelled with an *o*. Too, words that look alike may not be built alike. The word *singer* is made up of two morphemes (sing + er), but *finger* is made up of only one morpheme. The word finger is indivisible; a *finger* is not "one who fings." The word *finger* was not constructed of *fing* + *er*. *Fing* does not mean anything, so it is not a morpheme. Or, put another way, the *er* in *finger* is a completely different *er* from the *er* in *singer*.

Remember that morphemes and syllables are not the same. A syllable is a sound or group of sounds uttered on one beat or chest pulse. Syllables are related to rhythm, not to meaning. Syllables, of themselves, do not mean anything. Syllables do not represent meaning; morphemes do. A morpheme is the smallest unit of meaning, and it may be one or more syllables long.

Here are some words. On the first line, tell how many morphemes the word contains. On the second line, divide the word into its morphemes to show how the word was built. Use this example as a guide:

4	unmercifully	un + mercy + full + ly
________	quick	________________
________	thoughtless	________________
________	unpredictable	________________
________	disproportionate	________________
________	inconvenient	________________
________	disrespectful	________________
________	smarter	________________
________	defrost	________________
________	uneducated	________________
________	professor	________________
________	frightened	________________
________	flowers	________________
________	valuable	________________
________	flying	________________
________	disgusting	________________
________	paintings	________________

A morpheme, then, is the smallest unit in a language that has meaning. Just as phonemes had variations called allophones, morphemes have variations called *allomorphs*. You must learn all the variations (allomorphs) and learn which one to use in what instance.

Let us look at one example. What do all the following words have in common?

inappropriate	irresistible
unacceptable	impenetrable
illogical	atypical

You are right. They all have the same pattern: a prefix + an adjective. Did you notice anything else? Do all the prefixes mean the same thing? Yes, we hear you saying, they all mean *not*. They are all allomorphs (variations) of the negative prefix in English. So there are at least six allomorphs of that morpheme. Can you figure out which allomorph to use when?

Here are a few adjectives. Fill in the correct allomorph of the negative prefix for each:

________	certain	________	reverent
________	active	________	perfect
________	religious	________	effective
________	possible	________	attractive
________	theistic	________	legible
________	legal	________	sexual

There are some interesting subtleties in English. This exercise reminds us of one. The words *amoral* and *immoral* both use allomorphs of the negative prefix, but they do not represent exactly the same idea. What is the difference?

We will look at four other very important morphemes in English to illustrate the concept and to be sure you are using the correct allophones in each case. All are suffixes. The first is the plural morpheme, the second is the possessive morpheme, the third is the third person singular of the present tense of verbs, and the fourth is the past tense morpheme.

Pronounce these pairs of words out loud:

rope	ropes
robe	robes
rose	roses

The first word in each pair, of course, was the singular of the noun, and the second word in each pair was the plural. The plural words look a lot alike when written, but the ending we add to the noun to indicate "more than one" is different in each case when spoken. If you pronounced these words in the customary American way, you added an /s/ to the word *rope* to make it plural. But you added a /z/ to the word *robe* to make it plural. And what did you add to the word *rose* to make it *roses*? If you are not sure, say the word *rose* by itself first and then say the word *roses*. In *roses*, the allomorph is different from the other two. This time the ending was two sounds: /ɪz/. So there are at least three allomorphs of the plural morpheme in English. Have you figured out the pattern of which variation (allomorph) to use when?

This plural morphemic system in English is regular and predictable. After voiceless sounds (on which the vocal cords are not vibrated), the allophone is /s/ (which is also voiceless). After voiced sounds (on which the vocal cords are vibrated), the allophone is /z/ (which is also vibrated). And after one of the six sibilant sounds (see Chapter 6), the hissing consonants in English, the allophone is /ɪz/.

Here is a list of a few nouns. Indicate which plural ending (allomorph) each would take:

sack	________	lash	________
mat	________	floor	________
match	________	rug	________
road	________	room	________

garage	________	wing	________
cliff	________	wave	________
judge	________	berth	________

There are, of course, some nouns that do not follow the regular pattern. Here are just a few examples. What is the plural?

leaf	________	knife	________
wife	________	basis	________
sheep	________	phenomenon	________
mouse	________	medium	________
deer	________	child	________

The possessive morpheme and the third person singular of the present tense of verbs both follow the same pattern as the plural morpheme in forming their allomorphs. Both add /s/, /z/, or /ɪz/.

In the blank, tell whether the possessive ending is /s/, /z/, or /ɪz/:

boss's	________	cat's	________
Ann's	________	job's	________
Mary's	________	ridge's	________
Mr. Krock's	________	cliff's	________
church's	________	women's	________

In the blank, tell whether the present tense verb ending is /s/, /z/, or /ɪz/:

laughs	________	fights	________
smiles	________	judges	________
watches	________	creeps	________
roars	________	kills	________
passes	________	owes	________

The last of the morphemes we will examine here is the past tense ending for English verbs. We have a morpheme that indicates the action of the verb has already past. This morpheme also has three allomorphs. Pronounce the following words out loud:

hopped robbed faded

The *-ed* we write does not reveal the allomorphs we use when we speak. *Hopped* added a /t/ to the verb *hop; robbed* added a /d/ to the verb *rob*; and *faded* added /ɪd/ to the verb *fade*. Again, can you figure out the allomorphic distribution? There is a system at work here. Which allomorph do you add when? It depends on the last sound in the root verb. If the verb ends in a voiceless sound, the allomorph is /t/; if the verb ends in a voiced sound, the allomorph is /d/; but if the verb ends in /t/ or /d/, we insert a vowel to make pronunciation easier and add ɪd/.

Here are some verbs in the past tense. In the blank, tell whether the past tense ending is /t/, /d/, or /ɪd/:

buzzed	________	heeded	________
wished	________	breathed	________
voted	________	hated	________
forced	________	kicked	________
owed	________	loaned	________

As we have learned from these examples, we must know the allomorphs of English morphemes and when to them. To construct words, you must know word patterns, morphemes, and allomorphs.

Syntax

Syntax is the study of sentence formation. The word comes from a Greek word that means "to put together in order" or "to draw (soldiers) up in line in battle order." Syntax refers to the patterns for making sentences in a particular language. We put words "together in order" to construct our sentences.

English has certain patterns for sentences. Other languages may have completely different patterns. Let us contrast the patterns in English and Spanish for representing exactly the same content. In English, the pattern is **Subject - Verb - Object** (indirect objects, direct objects). In Spanish, the pattern is different: **Subject - Object - Verb**. In English, then, you would say, "I told her." In Spanish, you would say, "*Yo le dije.*" ("I her told.")

You cannot transfer a pattern from one language to another. If you do, it may not make any sense in the other language, even though you are using all the correct words. If I say, "Yo dije le," to Spanish speakers, they only look bewildered. The words are right, but the order is wrong, and the sentence makes no sense.

We have heard people say, "Where he went?" or "What she said?" The words were all English words, but they were not English sentences. They were using Spanish syntax, not English syntax. Those people spoke standard Spanish and understood the customary patterns for sentence construction in Spanish. Unfortunately, they did not know that the English pattern for expressing such questions is quite different. To represent that same idea in English, we use the pattern, "Where did he go?' and "What did she say?"

Recently, a friend said, "Remind me. I must buy paper toilet at the grocery." Again, he was using English words and Spanish syntax (word order). In English, we put the adjective before the noun; in Spanish, the adjective is put after the noun. In English, a "paper toilet" would be a toilet made *out of* paper, while "toilet paper" would be paper made *for* the toilet. To construct sentences in any language, you must know the syntax, the patterns for making sentences, of that language.

Vocabulary

Words are spoken symbols. They stand for ideas. Every language has a collection of words. The name for that total stock of words in a given language is *lexicon*; it comes from the Greek word for *word*. That is why the *lexicology* is the name of the study of words as expressions of ideas. The people who compile dictionaries are called *lexicographers*.

All people who speak a language put together their own personal *lexicon* or collection of words—their *vocabulary*. We hope that you will expand your vocabulary in this program of speech improvement. Whenever you come to a word you do not know in the text or in the exercises, look it up in a good dictionary. Stretch the collection of words you can use.

Dialect

A language is spoken by a group of people, but you know that not all speakers of a language talk alike. There are variations of languages spoken by subgroups. These variations of languages are called *dialects*. Dialects differ enough from each other to be noticeable, but they do not differ enough from each other to be called different languages.

The distinction between a different dialect and a different language is not always clear. Sometimes the distinction is based as much on political and national considerations as on more linguistic and scientific ones. Are Danish and Swedish different languages or merely different dialects of the same language? Well, a Dane could talk to a Swede, each using their own language, and they would probably understand each other's meaning. Both would, however, assure you with nationalistic fervor that they are speaking separate and distinct languages. Citizens of Denmark speak Danish, and citizens of Sweden speak Swedish! In fact, however, the languages are separated less by phonology, morphology, syntax, and vocabulary than by national boundaries.

We see exactly the reverse situation in China. Chinese people from different regions in China *cannot* understand each other. Still, they are said to speak different *dialects* of the Chinese language, not different *languages*. An interesting fact: translators are necessary at national conferences and congresses to provide simultaneous translation from one "dialect" to another.

All languages, you remember, have four basic elements:

(1) a set of significant sounds families, called phonemes;
(2) regular patterns for constructing words;
(3) regular patterns for constructing sentences; and
(4) a collection of words, called vocabulary.

Dialects also differ from each other in four ways:

(1) they may use different sounds (*phones*);
(2) they may use different morphological patterns;
(3) they may use different syntactical patterns;
(4) they may use different words to represent the same thing.

Speakers of different dialects of American English may use different sounds. Some native speakers of American English pronounce the word *greasy* to rhyme with *easy*; others pronounce it to rhyme with *fleecy*. This sound difference is dialectal. In general, speakers from below the Mason-Dixon Line (Southerners) pronounce the word with /z/, Northerners pronounce the word with /s/.

People from the northern portion of the United States may pronounce the words *hoarse* and *horse* alike; people from the South make a clear distinction by pronouncing the word *hoarse* with a "long O" vowel. Do you pronounce *oar* and *or* differently or the same? It is a matter of what dialect of American English you speak.

What vowel sound do you use in the following words?

log hog talk on

Again, the Mason-Dixon Line serves as a dialectal line on these words. Southerners still are likely to use a vowel in the "aw" family on these words.

Not only may speakers of different dialects use different sounds, they may also use different morphological or syntactic patterns. Often, these differences mark the difference between the Standard or Status Dialect and a non-standard dialect of American English.

If you heard one of your fellow students say, "I bought two book for that class," you would notice that the speaker did not add the plural morpheme to the word *book*. Or suppose you ask another student in one of your classes whether the instructor takes attendance in every class, and the other student says, "No, she don't." To which another student responds, "Yes, she do. She surely do!" You would understand the two students, but you would probably notice that both students used the verb form *do* where most speakers of American English would use the verb form *does*. That dialectal difference is typical of a number of non-standard dialects.

We are sure you can think of many other grammatical image-breakers, patterns that indicate the speaker is using a non-standard dialect of the language. Did *ain't*, the non-standard contraction for *am not*, and double negatives, such as "I didn't do nothing" come to your mind? You might even have thought of triple and quadruple negatives, which are marks of a non-standard dialect also. For example, "I don't never do nothing," and "I don't never do nothing to nobody!" just pile up the negatives.

Speakers of different dialects use different words for things. What do you call drinks like Pepsi, Coke, Seven-Up, and Dr. Pepper? If you are a New Yorker, you call them soda. If you are a Southerner, you probably call them soft drinks. Or you may call them tonic, pop, or soda pop. These dialectal differences are vocabulary differences.

People who live in the same section of the country, people who come from the same ethnic background, or people who belong to the same social or economic group may tend to associate with one another and, therefore, to develop common customs. These people also develop language customs. These customs, peculiar to the subgroup, are the basis of a language's dialects. A dialect is a variety of the same language spoken by a regional or social group.

Dialectal differences may cause confusion and communication problems, but we can often clear up the misunderstandings. If a Southerner thought a Northerner said, "I'm a little horse today," he could saddle the fellow with clarifying questions. In the same way, if a New Yorker stopped in a Georgia grocery store, asked for soda, and received a box of bicarbonate of soda, the New Yorker could hand it back and patiently explain that sodas are beverages. Sooner or later, the Yankee would get the refreshment he wanted.

Regional dialects are weakening in the United States, perhaps because of the strong influence of television. There is strong evidence, however, that social dialects are not dying out. We must give attention to the Standard Dialect and non-standard dialects.

Standard Dialect, Status Dialect, or Prestige Dialect

One language is as good as another, of course. A language is a tool used for communicating. If both speaker and listener know, understand, and react to a language in an essentially similar manner, that language works for them. In the same way, one dialect is as good as another if it works to accomplish the purposes of the speaker and the listener.

It is equally true, however, that not all dialects have the same status or prestige. There is a dialect of American English that is sometimes called the "Standard Dialect" or the "Status Dialect" or the "Prestige Dialect." That variety of American English is accorded more status and prestige than the other dialects. This dialect gets more respect because it is spoken by the people with the greatest status and prestige in American society. This dialect is spoken by the upper-middle and upper classes. For that reason, it has been called the Business and Professional Dialect. Some have called it the Career Dialect.

As we have indicated, there is nothing sacred about the Standard Dialect. If the people in power spoke a different variety of the language, then that variety would be the Standard Dialect.

Other languages also have standard dialects. If you were a French student studying the pronunciation of French in France, you could check your pronunciation of the language against the standards set by the French Academy. Spain also has an Academy of scholars to define and describe the standard dialect for Spanish pronunciation. In Great Britain, there is a preferred standard of pronunciation, but it is not laid down by any official agency or organization of scholars. Rather, it is the dialect that distinguishes the elite, educated class from the lower social classes. This dialect is called "Received British Pronunciation" because it is the kind of language spoken by the people received (entertained) in the homes of those in the highest social stratum. (The "Received British" wipes out regional patterns and sets a nationally uniform pattern for the upper class. See a production of G. B. Shaw's play *Pygmalion* or of the musical *My Fair Lady* for an enjoyable comment on Received British.)

There is no official agency in the United States to prescribe what is "standard" and what is not in the pronunciation of American English. Nor is there *one* nationally uniform standard ("received") dialect taught in the influential schools and universities of this country. However, even *without* an official standardizing agency or Academy and with acceptable regional variations in pronunciation, we can talk about a standard dialect of American English.

"Standard" speech patterns, like good manners in general and table manners in particular, are not prescribed by law, codified in any statute, or decreed by any binding authority. Rather, they consist of socially accepted (and respected) customs, usually established by the practice of the social leaders of our communities.

There is nothing in the Status Dialect (or Standard Dialect) itself—the sounds, grammatical patterns, or words used in it—that makes it better than any other dialect of American English. The fact that it is the dialect spoken by the people in power—the style setters, the fashion leaders, and the taste makers—gives this dialect its status and prestige. If the people in power spoke a different way, that way would be "standard."

Whether the Status Dialect is *better* than other dialects of the language is really irrelevant. Because this dialect is spoken by those in status positions, the dialect itself is given respect. In turn, those people who can speak the Status Dialect are given more respect than those who cannot. Perhaps that should not be true, but it *is* true, and we must deal with reality. The Status (or Standard) Dialect is the dialect used—and expected—in education, business, and the professions. It is the dialect we will teach you in this book.

We mentioned that there are acceptable regional variations of the Standard Dialect in the United States. You should know, however, that those variations are quite minor and the regional variations are diminishing. The mass media of communication (television, especially) have helped reduce regional differences. In addition, Americans frequently move from one region of the country to another. At least one family in five will move this year. Our constant mobility is helping to melt the regional variations. An executive of IBM told us a few years ago that IBM stands for "I'll be moved!" His company had stationed him in many parts of the United States, but his speech patterns were standard and would be recognized as the Status Dialect whether he was in Atlanta, Boston, New York, Cleveland, Houston, or San Francisco.

Nonstandard Dialects

Nonstandard dialects are those that differ noticeably from the Standard Dialect. Who would notice? Speakers of the Standard Dialect. What would they notice? Major differences in the four elements of a language: sounds, morphology, syntax and vocabulary.

Speakers of Standard American English would notice if someone said "Git out!" instead of "Get out!" or described Vanna White as "purty" (pretty). They certainly would be aware of the differences if someone said, "Dese are de once" for "These are the ones," or "axed" for "asked," or "She kep' it up" for "She kept it up," or "oncet" for "once." These *sound* differences would be recognized anywhere in the United States as nonstandard.

Arthur Bronstein and Beatrice Jacoby prefer the labels "cultivated and educated forms" and "uncultivated and uneducated forms"* to the terms *standard* and *nonstandard*. But the principle remains the same. They agree that "cultivated, educated speakers" would look askance if someone said, "We don't never do it" or "I ain't got it." All over the United States, these *grammatical* differences would be recognized as nonstandard.

There are vocabulary differences, too, between the Status Dialect and nonstatus (or nonstandard) dialects. Words that are taboo in the Standard Dialect may be commonly used in some nonstandard dialects of American English. Many of the taboo words are very old, and every one knows them. They are simply not uttered by "cultivated, educated speakers,"—at least not in polite society! The acceptable words for many body parts and body functions are Latin root words, such as anus and defecate. The Anglo Saxon (English) words for the same things are taboo—unacceptable. Any speaker of the Standard Dialect will certainly notice if someone violates these *word*, or *vocabulary*, taboos.

Of course, any language is constantly changing. The only languages that are not undergoing change are the ones no longer spoken. A language is a social custom, and all social customs change over a period of time. We cannot tell you what will be standard or nonstandard fifty or a hundred years from now. Our job is to describe accurately what is standard and nonstandard now.

*Arthur J. Bronstein and Beatrice Jacoby, *Your Speech and Voice* (New York: Random House, 1967).

Idiolect

Everyone who speaks American English speaks a dialect (regional or social variety) of that language. That same person also has distinctive speech patterns all his or her own. We call those individual varieties idiolects. The word *idiolect* may be new to you, but you have seen *idio* before. Idiosyncrasies are mannerisms characteristic of one person. An *idiom* is a way of saying something peculiar to one language. An *idiolect*, then, is one person's individual variety of a language.

Many different influences have helped shape the way each of us speaks. We put those elements together in a unique and personal way. You will become more conscious of your own idiolect; you will have to analyze it; you will want to evaluate it; and you may want to modify it or add to it.

Functional Varieties Of An Idiolect

Even a person who always speaks in the Standard or Status Dialect will not always speak in exactly the same way. That person will adjust his or her speech style to the formality of the situation and to his or her relationship to the listeners. We speak in many different kinds of social situations, and we must adapt our speaking style accordingly.

Do you speak the same way at a party with your close friends as you do in the classroom? Do you speak the same way in the classroom as you would in a formal public speech? If you speak with the same degree of informality at a job interview as at home, you may not get the job!

It is important to keep in mind that formal is not a synonym for standard, and informal is not the same as nonstandard. These functional (or situational) varieties exist within the Standard Dialect. "Cultivated, educated speakers" vary their speaking styles between two extremes: careful, precise formal forms and casual, simple, informal forms. The speaker fits the speech to the situation: public, formal, and impersonal at one extreme and private, informal, and intimate at the other. Any given situation may fall somewhere between the two extremes, and the functional variety of speech chosen will fall somewhere between the two extremes as well.

The most formal variety (within the Standard Dialect) is marked by careful control: precision in the production of sounds, care in the construction of sentences (few, if any contractions such as I'll or can't, for example), and caution in the choice of words (avoiding slang and colloquial expressions). When using this variety, a speaker also demonstrates greater control of his or her voice—avoiding extremes of pitch, loudness, rate, and quality.

The most informal variety (within the Standard Dialect) is casual and relaxed. Although articulation of the sounds is clear, it is less perniciously precise than in the most formal variety. Sentence structure includes contractions and more informal, popular constructions (even Winston Churchill said, "It's me," on informal occasions). Although outright taboo words are still avoided, slang and colloquial expressions are included. (In the formal variety, you would call him your "fiance," but in the informal variety, you might refer to him as "the guy I'm going with"). When using the informal variety, a speaker will be more relaxed and "natural" in the use of his or her voice letting the variations in pitch, volume, rate, and quality express attitudes and emotions more openly.

As we have said, informal varieties are not necessarily nonstandard. You must learn which informal varieties are within the Standard/ Status Dialect and which ones *are* nonstandard. You must also develop enough sensitivity to be able to select the appropriate functional variety for different situations.

Representation of Sounds

The language is what we speak; what we write is an attempt to represent the language (what we speak). The little flecks and specks of ink on this page are not words; they stand for words because words are *spoken* symbols. We need to look at our writing system and the problems it presents and decide on some satisfactory way of representing the sounds of our language. If we are going to help you work on your production of sounds, we must have some consistent method of symbolizing those sounds on paper.

There are three kinds of writing systems in use to represent languages: (1) ideographic writing, (2) syllabic writing, and (3) alphabetic writing. The Chinese and Japanese still use ideographic symbols in their writing. Each symbol (sign) stands for a whole idea or word, without reference to the sounds in the word. Highway and traffic signs around the world are being changed from alphabetic to ideographic. No matter what language you speak, the sign will mean something to you. If the sign has a curved arrow pointing to the right with a straight line across the arrow, the idea is "No Right Turn," regardless of the language you think those words in or what sounds you use to stand for those ideas. Syllabic writing uses written characters that represent spoken syllables rather than separate sounds. Alphabetic writing uses letters (written symbols) to represent sounds of the language.

About three thousand years ago, the Phoenicians developed an alphabet, with individual letters representing sounds. That alphabet was incomplete; it had symbols for the consonants, but none for vowels. The reader had to guess the vowels to complete the word; it was an ancient form of Speed Writing. The Hebrews developed their alphabet some time after the Phoenicians, but they too devised letters only for the consonants. (It was many centuries later that scholars invented a system for indicating vowels in Hebrew script.) When the Greeks took over the Phoenician alphabet, they made a significant change. The Greek language had fewer consonant sounds than the Phoenician language, so the Greeks had some Phoenician symbols left over. The extra symbols were used to represent vowels. When the Romans came along, they took from both the Greek and Phoenician alphabets to make their own. The Pax Romana (and, later, Roman missionaries) spread the Roman alphabet throughout Western Europe.

How English Spelling Got That Way

English is basically a Germanic language. The Angles, Saxons, and Jutes invaded and took control of the British Isles in the fifth century A.D. They were Germanic tribes who brought their dialects of German with them. In the sixth century, Christian missionaries from Rome arrived, bringing the Latin language and alphabet. The sounds of Old English (Anglo Saxon) were different from the sounds of Latin, so the sounds (phonemes) of English and the Roman alphabet never did match up perfectly. From the beginning, the alphabet we have used in English (the Roman alphabet) has not been completely phonetic.

Later developments gave our poor alphabet even more problems. In 1066 William the Conqueror, Duke of Normandy, invaded and conquered the British Isles. After his victory, William brought Normans from the continent to settle in Britain. The Normans, a French people, spoke Norman French, which became the language of the upper class—the nobility and businessmen. The masses continued to speak English, but many French words were incorporated into the language. In a couple of centuries, the use of French declined, but French had made an indelible mark on the English language.

In more modern times English ''borrowed'' words from many other languages. Usually the borrowed words kept their original spellings. Some of the borrowed words changed in pronunciation from that of the original language, and some did not. Because each of the languages had different phonemic systems (and different writing systems to represent the sounds), spelling in English became even more inconsistent.

Well, there it is in brief: Take a basically Germanic language and add some Latin, add a lot of French (at least twenty five per cent), add large pinches of Greek, Italian, Spanish, and assorted other languages; and then represent the mixture with a Latin (Roman) alphabet. Stir in the fact that pronunciations tend to change while spelling vigorously resists change, and you have a recipe for our inconsistent spelling system in English.

Problems With English Spelling

Anyone who has tried to learn to read and write English knows there are irritating obstacles in our spelling system. We might as well face the problems and learn to cope with them. English has successfully resisted most efforts to simplify and regularize its erratic spelling. There are no signs of relief on the way.

If our spelling were phonetic, each symbol would represent one sound consistently. We know that is not the case! We have some forty-two phonemes in American English (give or take a couple, depending on your dialect), and we have an alphabet with twenty-six letters. Already we are in trouble. It is impossible to match one letter with one sound and come out even.

The spelling problem, however, is even worse. Three of the twenty-six letters are useless, duplicating tasks already taken.The three useless letters are C, X, and Q.

(1) C is either a K or an S. Look at the word *accent*. The first C is pronounced like a K, and the second C is pronounced like an S.

(2) X is either a KS or a GZ. In the word *extra*, the X is pronounced as KS. In the word *exact*, the X is pronounced as GZ.

(3) Q is pronounced as KW. Notice how Q is pronounced in the words *quiet*, *quick*, and *queen*.

We really have only twenty-three letters to represent forty-two sounds. Four basic problems result:

1. One spelling may represent more than one sound.
2. More than one spelling may represent the same sound.
3. Two or more letters may represent one sound.
4. Some letters are "silent" and represent no sound in the word at all.

Let's look at each of these problems with English spelling.

1. ***One spelling may represent more than one sound***. We will give you a list of examples. This list is not complete, but it should give you an idea of the scope of the problem. In the left-hand column, we have placed a letter of the alphabet. In the right-hand column, beside those letters, we have listed words in which the same letter or letters is pronounced in a different way *in each word*. Read the lists out loud. You will see what we mean. If you are not sure of the pronunciation of a word, look it up in your dictionary.

Spelling	Different Sounds Represented
a	fate, fat, calm, walk
e	beg, sergeant, tete-a-tete
i	sight, fit, elite
o	no, hot, hog, woman, women, come
u	cup, full, rule, bury, busy
ai	laid, said, plaid
ea	meal, steak, breakfast, hearth
ei	veil, deceive, heifer
oa	road, broad
oe	doe, does (verb)
ou	troupe, out, fought, couple, curious
ough	though, through, thorough, rough, cough, bough, hiccough
ow	row (a line), bow (to bend the body)
s	bus, his, sugar, pleasure
sc	scarf, scent
th	then, thin, thyme
wh	which, who

2. ***More than one spelling may represent the same sound.*** Spelling problem number 2 is nearly the reverse of problem number 1. There are forty-two phonemes in American English, and each of them is represented by more than one spelling. Granted, we have not yet discussed the individual sounds of the language and have not yet taught a consistent writing system to represent the sounds. We believe, however, you can follow this list. In the left-hand column is the sound's symbol from the International Phonetic Alphabet (IPA), which will be discussed later in this chapter. In the next column is the symbol for the sound (diacritical marks) found in the paperback edition of the American Heritage Dictionary (with slight modifications). In the third column from the left are various ways of spelling that sound, and in the fourth column are word examples to illustrate each of the spelling variations.

IPA	Dictionary	Spelling	Word-Example
1. p	p	p	pump
		pp	supper
		gh	hiccough
2. b	b	b	bed
		bb	rubber

IPA	Dictionary	Spelling	Word-Example
3. t	t	t	time
		tt	bottom
		th	thyme
		ght	right
		ed	missed
4. d	d	d	did
		dd	muddy
		ed	planned
5. k	k	c	cold
		cc	accord
		cch	Bacchus
		ch	chord
		ck	pick
		cq	acquaint
		cu	biscuit
		k	kiss
		q	quick
		qu	liquor
		que	antique
6. g	g	g	gun
		gg	egg
		gu	guess
		gue	dialogue
		gh	ghost
7. l	l	l	let
		ll	tell
8. ʍ	hw	wh	why
9. f	f	f	feel
		ff	off
		gh	rough
		ph	phone
10. v	v	v	vest
		vv	savvy
		f	of
		ph	Stephen
11. θ	th	th	thin
12. ð	*th*	th	then
13. h	h	h	he

IPA	Dictionary	Spelling	Word-Example
		wh	who
14. s	s	s	so
		sc	science
		sch	schism
		ss	pass
		c	cent
		ce	lace
		se	case
15. z	z	z	zero
		zz	buzzer
		ze	prize
		s	easy
		se	rise
		ss	scissors
		x	Xerox
16. ʃ	sh	ce	ocean
		ch	chic
		chsi	fuchsia
		ci	vicious
		s	sure
		sc	Fascist
		sch	Scheherazade
		sci	conscious
		sh	shine
		shi	fashion
		si	pension
		ss	tissue
		ssi	passion
		ti	lotion
		psh	pshaw
17. ʒ	zh	g	protégé
		ge	corsage
		j	bijou
		s	pleasure
		si	evasion
		z	seizure
		zi	glazier
18. tʃ	ch	c	cello
		ch	child

IPA	Dictionary	Spelling	Word-Example
		che	luncheon
		t	factual
		tch	catch
		te	righteous
		ti	question
		tu	future
19. dʒ	j	d	gradual
		dg	judgment
		dge	lodge
		di	soldier
		dj	adjective
		g	gym
		ge	surgeon
		gg	exaggerate
		j	job
20. m	m	m	me
		mm	hammer
		gm	phlegm
		lm	palm
		mb	limb
		mn	autumn
21. n	n	n	not
		nn	tunnel
		gn	gnaw
		kn	knot
		pn	pneumonia
		mn	mnemonics
22. ŋ	ng	n	sink
		ng	sing
		ngue	tongue
23. w	w	w	win
		o	choir
		u	quiz
24. j	y	y	yes
		i	onion
		j	hallelujah
		g	monsignor
		u	unite
		eu	Europe

IPA	Dictionary	Spelling	Word-Example
		ew	Ewing
25. r	r	r	red
		rr	berry
		rh	rhyme
		wr	wreck
26. i	ē	e	be
		ee	see
		ea	seat
		ae	Caesar
		i	marine
		ie	piece
		ei	receive
		eo	people
		oe	amoeba
		ey	monkey
		y	ready
		uay	quay
27. ɪ	i	e	English
		ee	been
		ei	forfeit
		i	fit
		ie	sieve
		o	women
		u	busy
		ui	guild
		y	lyric
28. e	ā	a	ate
		ai	aid
		au	gauge
		ay	say
		ea	break
		ee	fiancée
		ei	neighbor
		et	cachet
		ey	obey
		ao	gaol (British)
29. ɛ	e	a	any
		ae	aesthetic
		ai	said

IPA	Dictionary	Spelling	Word-Example
		ay	says
		e	red
		ea	read (past tense of verb *read* [rid]
		ei	heifer
		eo	leopard
		ie	friend
		oe	Oedipus
		u	bury
30. æ	a	a	glad
		ai	plaid
		au	laugh
31. ɑ	ä	a	arm
		aa	salaam
		e	sergeant
		ea	heart
		o	odd
		ow	knowledge
32. ɔ	ô	a	call
		ah	Utah
		au	launder
		augh	fraught
		aw	law
		o	off
		oa	broad
		ou	cough
		ough	bought
33. o	ō	o	obey
		oa	road
		oe	doe
		oh	Oh!
		oo	brooch
		ou	soul
		ough	dough
		ow	grow
		au	haute
		eau	beau
		eo	yeoman
		ew	sew

IPA	Dictionary	Spelling	Word-Example
34. ʊ	oo	o	wolf
		oo	wood
		ou	would
		u	put
35. u	o͞o	eau	beautiful
		eu	leukemia
		ew	grew
		ieu	lieutenant
		o	move
		oe	canoe
		oo	food
		ou	group
		ough	through
		u	rude
		ue	blue
		ui	fruit
36. ʌ	u	o	done
		oe	does
		oo	flood
		ou	double
		u	cut
37. ə	ə	a	above
		aa	Canaan
		ae	Michael
		ai	captain
		au	authority
		e	listen
		ea	sergeant
		eo	dungeon
		eou	gorgeous
		i	beautiful
		ia	parliament
		ie	conscience
		io	region
		iou	vicious
		o	bishop
		oi	porpoise
		ou	furious
		u	cranium
		y	analysis

IPA	Dictionary	Spelling	Word-Example
38. ɝ	ûr	ear	heard
		er	herd
		ir	fir
		olo	colonel
		or	word
		our	courage
		ur	fur
		yr	Myrtle
		yrrh	myrrh
39. ɚ	ər	ar	liar
		er	other
		ir	nadir
		or	actor
		oar	cupboard
		r	car
		uo	languor
		ur	femur
		ure	failure
		re	theatre
		yr	martyr
		our	favour (British)
40. ɑʊ	ou	ou	bout
		ough	bough
		ow	town
41. ɑɪ	ī	ais	aisle
		ay	bayou
		eigh	sleight
		eye	eye
		i	ice
		ie	pie
		igh	right
		ui	guile
		uy	buy
		y	sky
		ye	dye
42. ɔɪ	oi	oi	toil
		oy	joy

Remember, the lists in the "spelling" column represent various ways to spell *one* phoneme. Is there a single phoneme in American English that is spelled consistently one way?

3. ***Two or more letters may represent just one sound.***
It is obvious that, if you have forty or so phonemes and only twenty-three useful letters in your alphabet, you must "double up" in some way. Some letters will have to be used more than once if all the sounds are going to be represented. Add to that the needlessly doubled letters and some other inconsistencies, and you have spelling problem number 3. Here is a brief, suggestive list to illustrate the problem. In the left-hand column are letters, each group representing only one sound; a sample word appears in the right-hand column.

bb	bubble	tt	cotton
cc	account	zz	muzzle
dd	ladder	ch	chorus
ff	muffler	sch	schism
gg	egg	sch	Schick
ll	tall	dge	bridge
mm	hammer	tch	watch
nn	thinner	ng	hang
oo	food	ngue	tongue
oo	foot	th	ether
pp	puppy	th	either
rr	arrow	ea	steal
ss	mission	aw	law

4. ***Some letters are "silent" and represent no sound in the word at all.***
The silent letters in English words are especially troublesome for those who have learned English after learning another language. The problem is that these letters sometimes represent sounds in words and sometimes they do not. You just have to learn the spellings of the words containing the useless letters. You must be careful not to be tricked by the spelling into adding sounds when you pronounce these words. (There are some rules to help guide you on some of these spellings; we will highlight them in special warnings throughout this handbook.) For the moment, we will list some of these words to illustrate the point. In the left-hand column are listed the silent letters. In the right-hand column are some of the words containing that letter in their spelling. Pronounce the words out loud.

Check to be sure you do not insert a sound just because the (silent) letter is there.

Silent Letter (s)	**Sample Words**
b	lamb, climb, dumb, limb, numb, thumb, plumb, plumber, debt, subtle, doubt, subpoena
ch	yacht
e	dime, sake, rode, done
g	design, reign, phlegm, diaphragm, gnarl, gnash, gnat, gnaw, gnome, Gnostic, gnu
gh	night, light, right, weight, caught
h	rhythm, ghost, heir, honest, honor, hour
k	knee, knew, knife, knight, knock, knot, know, knowledge, knuckle
l	palm, calm, psalm, half, calf, talk, chalk, walk, almond, Lincoln
n	column, hymn, kiln
p	pneumatic, pneumonia, pshaw! (Maybe someone still says it!), ptomaine, receipt, cupboard
ps	corps
t	often, soften, hasten, listen, moisten, whistle
th	clothes
w	wrench, wrist, writ, write, wrong, wrestle, wretch, sword

All right, we hear you saying, we know the problem. What is the solution? Your question leads us into a brief discussion of the IPA (the International Phonetic Alphabet) and then into a brief discussion on the diacritical marking systems used in our dictionaries.

Two Ways to Represent the Sounds of American English

When somebody asks you about a word, do you think of the written "word" first? If we should ask you how many sounds there are in the word *though*, would you think first of the letters in the written "word"? Well, check yourself. How many sounds does that word have? We hope you answered "Two." If not, were you thrown off by the six letters we use to spell the word?

Do you find it difficult to think in terms of *sounds* in words, rather than *letters*? That is natural, because your teachers have emphasized the written form for so many years. We want you to begin your program of speech improvement by closing your eyes to the letters used in spelling and opening your ears to the *sounds* spoken in words. At first, you will have to concentrate to think in terms of sounds, but with practice it should come more easily. Surely we have proved to you that spelling is unreliable as a guide to pronunciation! Your ears—once trained—will be a much more dependable guide.

Let's test your ears for a moment. Say the word *many* and then the word *penny*. As you say them, you can hear four sounds for both words. The first sound in the word *many* is an /m/, and the first sound in the word *penny* is a /p/. But are the second sounds—the vowels—in each word the same sound or different sounds? Try the words out loud again just to be sure. Were you thrown off by the spelling? The second sound in both words is the same sound—although we spell one with *a* and one with *e*. Test your ears again. Are the first sounds in the words *honest* and *home* the same sounds? Or are the first sounds in the words *one* and *only* the same sounds? If you said yes to either of these questions, your ears need more training.

When we discuss the sounds of American English with you in this book, or when you concentrate on various sounds of the language in your class, a clear and consistent system for representing the sounds in writing is needed. We need a symbol system that will identify each sound precisely to avoid ambiguity and confusion. To accomplish this goal, we need a writing system that has one symbol for each sound and only one sound for each symbol.

In 1888 an international group of scholars designed such an alphabet for the sounds of English, and the International Phonetic Alphabet was born. In the years since, the International Phonetic Association has expanded and modified the International Phonetic Alphabet into a system with enough different characters to represent the sounds of the world's principal languages. This sound representation system has three advantages: (1) Each IPA symbol stands for one sound; that symbol always stands for the same sound—regardless of regular spelling of the word; and that sound is never represented by a different symbol. (2) Because IPA symbols represent sounds, they can be used to record accurately how a speaker actually pronounces a word or phrase. The IPA makes it possible to represent differences in pronunciation of words or phrases. (3) Each IPA symbol stands for the same sound—no matter what the language. In this hook, we will use only the symbols for the sounds heard in American English, but with these symbols and others of the IPA you could pronounce words from other languages; IPA symbols are the same for all languages. The IPA could help you in learning to pronounce any language correctly.

We will use IPA in this book as a means of identifying sounds. You will probably use IPA in your class for this purpose also. It is a useful tool. Of course, learning the IPA symbols for sounds is not an end in itself; it is a means to an end. Your instructor will probably have you learn the IPA symbols as soon as possible to aid you in your program of speech improvement.

The only dictionary of American English words that uses the IPA symbols is Kenyon and Knott's *Pronouncing Dictionary of American English*, published by Merriam-Webster. This dictionary does not give definitions for words, only pronunciations. Although it needs to be updated, it is still a very useful reference guide.

All other dictionaries use a system called diacritical markings to represent sounds. Diacritical marks are a code of dots and lines; dictionary editors use them to indicate pronunciation. For the most part, these marks are added to letters used in regular spelling. There are three major problems associated with diacritical markings: (1) Different dictionaries use different markings to represent the same sounds, so it is necessary to study the explanation each dictionary provides for its marking system, if you are to use it intelligently. (2) The diacritical marks are added to regular letters of the alphabet, and it is easy to get confused by similar symbols. (3) Some dictionaries use more than one symbol for the same sound—primarily the result of an attempt to stay as close as possible to the original spelling of the word.

Of course, there are some advantages to becoming familiar with and learning to use diacritical markings. The dictionaries that are the most widely available and the most widely used indicate pronunciations in diacritics. Also, you should be familiar with diacritics from your past experience using dictionaries, so you already have that tool for identifying sounds. Because using diacritics builds on what you already know and prepares you for future everyday pronunciation checking, many teachers prefer to use a system of diacritical markings in teaching articulation and voice.

In this book, therefore, we will include both systems for representing the sounds of American English. When identifying a sound in this book, we will use both the IPA symbol and the diacritic symbol for the sound.

In American English, there are forty two phonemes (as we count them): twenty five consonants, fourteen vowels, and three phonemic diphthongs. They are presented here with a key word containing the sound, the IPA symbol, and the symbol from the *American Heritage Dictionary of the English Language*:

Key Word	IPA Symbol	*American Heritage Dictionary* Symbol
Consonants:		
1. pill	p	p
2. box	b	b
3. tool	t	t
4. do	d	d
5. king	k	k
6. good	g	g
7. whee	ʍ	hw
8. feel	f	f

9. veal	v	v
10. thigh	θ	th
11. thy	ð	*th*
12. sue	s	s
13. zoo	z	z
14. show	ʃ	sh
15. mirage	ʒ	zh
16. chick	tʃ	ch
17. jerk	dʒ	j
18. hand	h	h
19. let	l	l
20. me	m	m
21. not	n	n
22. sing	ŋ	ng
23. we	w	w
24. right	r	r
25. young	j	y

Vowels:

1. each	i	ē
2. itch	ɪ	i
3. age	e	ā
4. edge	ɛ	e
5. add, am	æ	a
6. odd, alms	ɑ	o, ä
7. awe	ɔ	ô
8. owe	o	ō
9. full	ʊ	oo
10. fool	u	o͞o
11. up	ʌ	u
12. *a*bout	ə	ə
13. earn	ɝ	ûr
14. mother	ɚ	ər

Phonemic Diphthongs

1. ice	ɑɪ	ī
2. out	ɑʊ	ou
3. oink	ɔɪ	oi

Looking over this chart of symbols, you may have the impression that they are weird and that learning them will be difficult. Actually, the IPA symbols are not as new and strange as they appear at first glance. You already know sixteen of the twenty five consonant symbols. Check it out: count up the ones you already use. Granted, in regular spelling we use them to stand for several different sounds, and the IPA uses them to stand for only one sound each, but you do know the symbols. The other nine IPA symbols for consonants are not so difficult either. Number 25 is a familiar letter used in a slightly new way. In IPA, the /j/ stands for what we think of as the y sound. Think of the "j" sound in the word "hallelujah." Numbers 10 and 11 are not totally new to you. If you have studied much math, you have used the Greek letter *theta* (θ); the name of the letter starts with the /θ/ sound. Number 11 is an Old English letter named "ethe." You have seen it before. Does it look more familiar to you in these contexts?

We ȝe People   ȝe Olde Taverne

The "ethe" (ð) is not a *y* and never was; it is the symbol for the voiced "th." Consonant number 7, as you see, is simply the *w* letter turned upside down. It represents the sound many Americans still say (your authors included) as the first sound of such words as *whee*, *why*, and *what*. Otherwise, those words sound like *we*, *Y*, and *Watt*. Speakers of Standard American English who do not use the /ʍ/ sound, of course, have only twenty-four consonant phonemes in their idiolects.

It is not as easy to make associations with the IPA symbols for the vowels and phonemic diphthongs. (Diphthongs are blends of two vowels. We have other diphthongs in the language, but these three function as single sounds—hence, as phonemes. All but two of the other diphthongs are simply combinations of two vowel phonemes. Those two are [oʊ] and [eɪ], which are allophones—variations—of the phonemes /o/ and /e/.) You will find it difficult to associate the IPA vowel symbols with regular spelling, because our spelling is so inconsistent. The simplest thing to do is just memorize the seventeen vowel and phonemic diphthong symbols by writing each of them over and over as you pronounce the sound out loud.

Some authors omit the symbols /ʌ/ and /ɝ/ from their list of vowel phonemes. They argue that the only difference between /ʌ/ and /ə/ and also between /ɝ/ and /ɚ/ is duration (or length, or stress). They believe the difference is insignificant. If there is no significant contrast, they argue, /ʌ/ and /ə/ and also /ɝ/ and /ɚ/ are not separate phonemes but allophones of the same sound. They use the /ə/ symbol for both /ʌ/ and /ə/; they use the /ɚ/ symbol for both /ɝ/ and /ɚ/. The issue is not settled. Until it is, we will follow the IPA custom and use separate symbols and list them as separate sounds.

We have listed for you the significant sounds of American English, and we have given you two alternative ways of representing those sounds. Your instructor will tell you which of the systems (or both) you will be using in your class. Learn the symbol system(s) right away. It will facilitate communication between your instructor and you, your classmates and you, and these writers and you when discussing sounds.

2

Consonants

We turn our attention now to the forty-two phonemes of American English. We will discuss these sounds as separate entities in connected speech. When you say a phrase or sentence, you do not speak a sound at a time, one after another. You speak in a continuous flow of movements from the beginning to the end of each phrase. In that continuous flow, each sound is modified by the sounds around it.

Each phoneme, in daily speech, undergoes a wide variety of modifications or changes. Different people will produce the same phoneme in many different ways in differing contexts. We can talk about individual phonemes because each phoneme has a group of distinctive features (characteristics that distinguish that phoneme from all other phonemes of the language). However much a phoneme may vary, each phoneme has a number of characteristics (distinctive features or components) by which it is identified.

Do you have difficulty producing some of the sounds of American English? Have you ever been told that your production of some sound is not standard or ''correct?'' You probably have a problem with some of the distinctive features of that phoneme. Have you ever been told that you speak with a ''foreign accent?'' Although you may also be having difficulty with American English rhythm and intonation (See Chapter 18), your problems are doubtless related to the basic characteristics of some phonemes of American English. Perhaps there is a problem with only one of the distinctive features of some phonemes. In any case, it is important for you to learn the basic characteristics of the phonemes, how they are produced, where they are placed, and how they sound.

Speech sounds are divided into two groups: consonants and vowels. These two groups of sounds differ in two ways: (1) how they are produced, and (2) how they are used.

You can check out the first difference between consonants and vowels by looking in a mirror and making a few speech sounds. While looking in the mirror, say the sounds (not the names of the letters, but the sounds themselves): /t/, /k/, /f/ on a continuous breath—if you can. Then, while still looking in the mirror, say, "Ah, oh, aye," on a continuous breath. Did you notice that the first set of sounds had the air stream checked, or impeded, on the way out? Did you also notice that your mouth was partly open and the air came out without much interference on the second set of sounds? That is a major difference between consonants and vowels. To produce consonants, the outgoing breath stream is either completely stopped or is markedly impeded (constricted). In consonants, the air flow is partly or completely blocked. To produce vowels, the outgoing air stream is relatively unobstructed. Vowels are relatively "open" sounds, produced by modifying the resonance in the mouth.

Another major distinction between consonants and vowels is that they serve two different functions in our syllables. A syllable is a sound or group of sounds uttered on one chest pulse. "Don't" is a one-syllable word, uttered on one pulse. "Worry" is a two-syllable word, uttered on two pulses (or beats); the first syllable is stronger, or stressed, and the second is weaker, or unstressed. Consonants serve the function, generally, of starting and stopping our syllables. Another way of saying the same thing is to say that consonants either initiate (or release) a syllable or terminate (or end) a syllable. Vowels, on the other hand, provide a specific quality or form the nucleus (or peak) of a syllable.

Let's try some syllables to see if we can make the separate functions of consonants and vowels clearer. Say the word *oh* out loud. That syllable has a peak, a nucleus; that is, it has a vowel. A syllable is somewhat like a cell. It has a nucleus, and, maybe, a cell wall. The nucleus around which a syllable centers is the vowel. The cell wall—front and/or back—is made up of consonants. The vowel provides the carrying power for the syllable; the vowel is the peak of sonority in the syllable. The syllable *oh* contains only a vowel; there is no consonant before or after the vowel.

If you pronounce the word *ho*, however, you will see that your syllable is started by a sound *before* the vowel. That sound before the vowel, starting the syllable, is a consonant. Now pronounce the word *oak*. This syllable does not have a consonant to start it (the open /o/ vowel is the beginning), but it does have a consonant to close (or terminate) the syllable.

What happens when you pronounce the word *Coke*? That syllable contains the same vowel (peak/nucleus), but it has a consonant to initiate it and one to terminate it. Consonants serve to start or arrest syllables. Of course, there may be more than one consonant at the beginning or end of a syllable. The words *gloat* and *gold* are good examples. We are sure you can see that vowels and consonants serve different functions in our syllables.

We begin your program of speech and voice improvement with consonants. So we must first address this question: What characteristics distinguish one consonant phoneme from another in American English? In other words, what features of American English consonants matter?

Distinctive Features: Classification of Consonants

Every phoneme in our language can be identified (set off from all the other sounds of the language) on the basis of a group of distinctive characteristics (or features or components). Consonants are distinguished from each other on the basis of three classes of features:

(1) the presence or absence of voicing (vibration of the vocal folds);
(2) the place of articulation; and
(3) the manner in which the sound is emitted.

If you note all three of these features about a consonant, you have identified it and separated it from all the other consonants of American English.

Let us look at an example. If you want to identify the consonant at the beginning of the word *bold*, you would identify its three distinctive features. /b/ is:

(1) voiced, because it is made with the vocal folds vibrating;
(2) bilabial (two-lips), because it is articulated by bringing the two lips together; and
(3) a stop, because the air stream is completely stopped in its emission.

Therefore, /b/ is a *voiced bilabial stop*. These three descriptions (or features) classify the /b/ consonant phoneme of American English. We will look at each of the three classes of distinctive features separately.

Voicing

One essential way of telling consonants apart is by determining whether they are voiced or voiceless. That is, we must first find out if the vocal cords are vibrating while the sound is made.

Put your hand over your larynx (''voice box'' or ''Adam's apple'') and make the sound /v/, the sound that begins the word *vine*. Did you feel a vibration, a buzzing, coming from the larynx? /v/ is a voiced (vibrated) sound and you should have felt a vibration. Now put your hand over your larynx and make the sound /f/, the sound that begins the word *fine*. Did you feel a vibration this time? Since /f/ is a voiceless consonant, you should not have noticed any vibration.

There are twenty-five consonants in American English. Fifteen of them are voiced, and ten are voiceless.

The first consonant in the following words is *voiced*. The IPA symbol and the dictionary symbol for each of the fifteen voiced consonants follows the word.

Word	IPA Symbol	Dictionary Symbol
bare	b	b
dare	d	d
get	g	g
vet	v	v
then	ð	*th*
Zen	z	z
azure	ʒ	zh
meal	m	m
need	n	n
angle	ŋ	ng
low	l	l
woe	w	w
rude	r	r
you	y	y
June	dʒ	j

There are ten consonants in American English made without vocal vibration. These ten consonants are classified as *voiceless* consonants. These consonants are the initial (beginning) sounds in the following words:

Word	IPA Symbol	Dictionary Symbol
pie	p	p
tie	t	t
key	k	k
why	ʍ	hw

Word	IPA Symbol	Dictionary Symbol
fight	f	f
thigh	θ	th
sigh	s	s
shy	ʃ	sh
hide	h	h
chide	tʃ	ch

Some of the consonants (eighteen, in fact) can be grouped into pairs called cognates. Each of the two sounds in the pair is articulated in the same place and released in essentially the same manner. They differ in that one is voiced and the other is voiceless. Another difference, although not nearly as important, is that a voiceless consonant tends to have greater aspiration—more breath released—in its emission than a voiced consonant does. Following is a list of the cognates (sound pairs), illustrated by the first consonant in the following words:

	Voiceless			Voiced	
Word	**IPA**	**Dictionary**	**Word**	**IPA**	**Dictionary**
peer	p	p	beer	b	b
toe	t	t	dough	d	d
kill	k	k	gill	g	g
whee	ʍ	hw	we	w	w
fear	f	f	veer	v	v
thigh	θ	th	thy	ð	*th*
sue	s	s	zoo	z	z
assure	ʃ	sh	azure	ʒ	zh
chin	tʃ	ch	gin	dʒ	j

A consonant chart appears later in this chapter and lists the twenty-five consonants of American English according to their distinctive features. On the chart, cognates are found side-by-side with the symbol for the voiceless consonant on the left and the symbol for the voiced consonant on the right. There is one exception. On the chart, /ʍ/ and /w/ are listed separately. /ʍ/ is included in the fricatives, and /w/ is included in the glides.

Place of Articulation

To form consonants, the outgoing air stream is obstructed at some point along the route by the articulators—the lips, teeth, tongue, hard palate, velum, (soft palate), and vocal cords. The closure (obstruction) can be complete or partial. To impede the exhaled air column and articulate a sound, bring together your two lips, the lips and teeth, the tongue and teeth, the tongue and upper gum ridge, the tongue and hard palate, or the tongue and velum. One sound, the /h/, is made by impeding the air at the vocal cords. (Since the space between the vocal folds is called the *glottis*, the /h/—articulated by the vocal cords—is a glottal consonant.)

You remember we said earlier in this handbook that articulation means making a joint (bringing two things together) to hinder the outgoing air. One distinctive feature of every consonant in American English is *where* the articulation takes place—that is, what articulators are brought together to obstruct the breath stream. As you can see on the Consonant Chart (pp. 50-51), there are eight "places of articulation" in American English.

CONSONANT

	Place of Articulation:							
Manner of Emission:	Two Lips (Bilabial)		Lip-Teeth (Labio-Dental)		Tongue-Teeth (Lingua-Dental)		Tongue Tip-Gum Ridge (Lingua-Alveolar)	
	Voiceless	Voiced	Voiceless	Voiced	Voiceless	Voiced	Voiceless	Voiced
Stops	p pie	b bare					t tie	d dare
Fricatives	ʍ *why*		f *fie*	v vet	θ *thigh*	ð *then*	s sign	z Zen
Affricates								
Nasals		m meal						n kneel
Lateral								l low
Glides		w *woe*						

CHART

Place of Articulation:								
Tongue Blade-Back of Gum Ridge (Lingua-Post Alveolar)		Tongue Blade-Hard Palate (Lingua-Palatal)		Tongue Blade-Soft Palate (Lingua-Velar)		Vocal Folds (Glottal)		Manner of Emission:
Voiceless	Voiced	Voiceless	Voiced	Voiceless	Voiced	Voiceless	Voiced	
				k *kite*	g *get*			Stops
ʃ *shy*	ʒ *azure*					h *high*		Fricatives
tʃ *chide*	dʒ *June*							Affricates
					ŋ *angle*			Nasals
								Lateral
	r *rue*		j *you*					Glides

Manner of Emission

Another characteristic feature of every consonant is how it sounds (its acoustic properties) or how the air comes out.

Pronounce the word *pick* and check on the way the /p/ comes out. Did you notice that for an instant, while the two lips were completely closed, the air stream was blocked and *nothing* came out at all? Did you then notice that when the lips were opened to release the /p/ sound there was a little explosion of air?

Pronounce the word *pin* and note how the /n/ sound is emitted. There was no explosion this time, was there? Instead, the air was blocked off by the tongue up on the gum ridge and hummed up through the nose. The air was emitted nasally.

Next pronounce the word *live* and hold on to the last sound for a moment or two. How is the /v/ sound emitted? How does it sound? Is it different from the other two consonants we have examined so far? Well, it does not stop and explode, and it does not come out through the nose. Does it sound like a kind of friction noise to you?

Say the word *bowl* out loud and hold on to the last sound for a little while. Note the final /l/ as you pronounce the word again. If you placed your tongue tip in the conventional position for the /l/ (the same place used for the /n/), you blocked the air from coming out of the middle of the mouth. And if you made the /l/ in the customary way, the air came out on both sides of the tongue. That's right. The air came out of the two sides of the mouth.

Finally, look in the mirror as you say the word *wake*. Did your lips move as you said the /w/? Did the sound change as you made it, as the lips were moving?

Each of these sounds—/p/, /n/, /v/, /l/, and /w/—is released in a different way. Each would be classified differently, based on its manner of emission. The way the air is emitted on a consonant is one of a consonant's distinctive features. Based on this characteristic, consonants are divided into six classes:

(1) stops—sounds on which the air is stopped completely;
(2) fricatives—friction noises with the air squeezed between two articulators;
(3) affricates—combinations of a stop and fricative into a single phoneme;
(4) nasals—sounds emitted with nasal resonance;
(5) lateral—a sound emitted with the air coming over the sides of the tongue; and
(6) glides—sounds on which there is continuous movement of the articulators from one position to another.

The stop consonants are sometimes called plosives or stop plosives because they often are released in a little plosion (or explosion or puff of air). In the production of these sounds, the air stream is *always* completely stopped, but it is not always exploded on release. Therefore, we have called these sounds stops rather than plosives. The other consonants are sometimes grouped into a division called continuants because, unlike stops, they can be continued—or their release extended. The designation *continuant* is of no real use in describing distinctive features because the narrower terms—fricatives, affricates, nasals, lateral, and glides—must be used to distinguish individual consonants from each other.

The Consonant Chart should clarify the way we use the three classes of distinctive features to classify or identify any consonant of American English.

3

Stops

Stops are consonants produced by momentarily blocking the outgoing air stream completely. Often, in the production of these six sounds, the air stream is completely blocked, air pressure is built up at the place where the air is blocked, and the built-up breath is then released in a little explosion. For that reason, these stop sounds are also called plosives. Because the air stream is *always* stopped and only sometimes exploded, we think *stops* is a more accurate name for this group of phonemes.

There are six stops in American English—three pairs of cognates. They are /p/ and /b/, /t/ and /d/, and /k/ and /g/. The first of each pair is voiceless and the second is voiced.

There are some characteristics that all stops have in common. First and most important, the two articulators brought together to make the sound must have firm contact. There must be complete closure so the outgoing air stream is totally blocked. Without firm, complete closure, stops are not stops.

Another common characteristic is that the voiceless stops are aspirated more than the voiced stops. That is, more breath is released; they are "breathier" than their voiced cognate partners.

Even in the same phoneme, the amount of aspiration (breath released) varies, depending on the position of the stop in the syllable and on the neighboring sounds. Generally, a stop will be more explosive at the beginning of a syllable and most explosive at the beginning of a stressed syllable. In American English, stops are not exploded at all at the end of a word or phrase. If you learned another language before English, it is especially important that you note these allophonic differences of the stop phonemes.

If a word ends with a stop/plosive and the next word in the phrase begins with a vowel, the words are linked together. We join the words by making the last sound in the first word (the stop) the first sound in the next syllable. This linking is called *elision*. Try the following examples out loud. Use the final stop sound in the first word to hook the words together:

Stop it!	paid out
rub oil	Look out!
Fight on!	Big Apple

The syllables do not divide at the word divisions. As a result, the stops at the ends of these words exploded rather than imploded. Note the contrast when the stop ends the last word in a phrase:

Stop!	paid
Cab!	Look!
Fight!	big

On these words, the stops at the end of the words do not explode, but they *do* stop, and the three voiced sounds (/b/, /d/, and /g/) are vibrated.

There are also other characteristics common to all the stops. If a stop is doubled (doubled in sounds, not just in spelling), we do not make the stop twice. We do not block the air, build up the pressure, release it, then block the air again, build up pressure, and release it again. Instead, we make the stop once and indicate the doubling by holding the closure longer than usual before the release. The closure for the /t/ in the word *lasting* should be only half as long as the closure for the /t/ in *last time*, which must represent the final /t/ in *last* and the initial /t/ in *time*. This slight difference affects the rhythm of your speech. If you do not make this distinction, others may think your speech "sloppy" or may conclude you have an "accent." Try these contrasts out loud:

One Stop:	**"Doubled" Stop:**
stopper	stop paying
robin	rob Betty
shutter	shut Tony's Bar
madder	mad dog
booking	bookcase
bigger	big group

A similar characteristic of stops in American English occurs when two *different* stops come together in the same word or in consecutive words. In such an instance, the first stop sound is stopped, but not exploded; the second is stopped *and* exploded. If you ask for a *hot dog*, you would not explode both the /t/ and /d/ stops. The /t/ must stop—firmly closed—but it is the /d/ only that explodes. Pronounce *hot dog* out loud to be sure. Then try these examples out loud:

back down	cupcake
step down	stopgap
ribcage	bad plan

In each of these instances of successive stops, then, both stops stop, but only the second is released in an explosion. (See pp. 206-209 for further explanation and exercises.)

One other aspect of stops should be noted. Sometimes they are followed by the /l/ sound or by a nasal sound. In these cases, the air is released in a different way.

When a stop is followed by /l/ in the same syllable, the stop is firmly closed, but the explosion-release is over the sides of the tongue. Pronounce these words out loud:

apple	huddle
bubble	buckle
mental	eagle

(See pp. 213-216 for further explanation and exercises.)

When a stop is followed by a nasal sound, the stop is formed, but the explosion-release is through the nose. Notice what happens when you pronounce the word *button*. The second syllable is /tn/. There is no vowel between the /t/ and /n/, so the /t/ does not explode in the usual way. Instead, the air closes off completely for the /t/, but the plosive release occurs through the nose. The same thing occurs on words with /dn/ such as *sudden*. (See pp. 210-213.)

Pronounce these words out loud. They all contain a stop plus a nasal sound.

happen	burden
ribbon	sicken
rotten	wagon

There are six stop phonemes in American English. We will discuss them in three pairs of cognates: /p/ and /b/; /t/ and /d/; and /k/ and /g/.

/p/ and /b/

Principles

Production

If you raise the velum (soft palate) so no air can escape up through the nose, close the two lips firmly to block the outgoing breath stream completely, build up air pressure by holding the lips closed for a moment, and then release the compressed air by quickly opening the two lips, you will produce a bilabial (two lip) stop. There are two bilabial stops in English. One is voiceless (it is produced without the vocal cords vibrating) and is represented in both IPA and the dictionaries by /p/. The other bilabial stop is voiced (there is vibration of the vocal cords) and is represented in both IPA and the dictionaries by /b/.

Precautions

There are three spellings for /p/:

p as in *pump*
pp as in *supper*
gh as in *hiccough*

There are two spellings for /b/:

b as in *bed*
bb as in *rubber*

Sometimes the letter *p* appears in the spelling of a word, but is not pronounced. *p*, then, can be a "silent letter."

1. If *p* comes before *n* at the beginning of a word, the *p* is silent. Note these examples:

   pneumonia, pneumatic, pneumococcus, Pnom Penh, Pnyx

2. If *p* comes before *s* at the beginning of a word, the *p* is silent. Note these examples:

   psalm, pseudo-, psychic, psychosis, psychology

3. If *p* comes before *t* at the beginning of a word, the *p* is silent. Note these examples:

   ptomaine, Ptolemy, ptyalin

4. If *p* comes before *b* in the middle of a word, the *p* may be silent. (But note that in *upbraid*, the *p* is not silent.) Here are two examples:

   cupboard, clapboard

Sometimes the letter *b* appears in the spelling of a word, but is not pronounced. *b* can be a silent letter also.

1. If *b* comes after *m* at the end of a word, the *b* is silent. Note these examples:

   aplomb, comb, climb, dumb, lamb, limb, plumb, thumb, tomb

2. If a suffix is added to a word ending in *mb*, the *b* is silent. (In a word like *limber*, however, the *b* is pronounced, because *limber* was not made out of *limb* + the suffix *er*.) Note these examples of silent *b* in the middle of words:

   climbing, combing, dumber, plumber

Problems

There are six common problems associated with these two phonemes. As we look at each of these deviations, check to see if you have that problem with these sounds.

▶ *Problem 1:* Incomplete closure

Incomplete closure of the articulators on stop sounds results in sloppy, indistinct speech. If your lips are too stiff or too lazy to close completely for the /p/ and /b/, the sounds will not be clear and crisp. You must close the two lips firmly and completely to produce standard /p/ and /b/ phonemes in American English. The temptation to slacken the articulation on these sounds is especially great if they are followed by other consonants. Check to be sure that your stop is complete and the lips are *firmly* pressed together for /p/ and /b/ in these examples:

obvious	flapjacks
capful	caps
cabs	abduction
subsidize	substitute
substantial	hopefully
optimum	upgrade

Here are a few sentences containing a /p/ or /b/ before a consonant. Practice reading them aloud, being sure to make firm stops. If English is not your first language, you must give special attention to this problem. Incomplete closure will not only make your speech more difficult to understand, it will also affect the rhythm and contribute to an "accent."

It's what's up front that counts.
Top value is what I want.
The club fought the regulation.
Prime rib should be well done.
The ship struck a reef.
It was stuffed with crab meat.
The cop did not arrest me.
The cab would not stop for me.

▶ *Problem 2:* Omission

Some speakers do not stop at articulating /p/ and /b/ sloppily; they omit the sounds altogether. Some speakers omit these sounds when they occur at the ends of words—especially if the /p/ or /b/ comes after a consonant. Check your pronunciation of these words to be sure the final stop sounds are not dropped:

wasp	grasp	clasp	crisp
pulp	help	bulb	curb

Remember that the /p/ and /b/ do not always explode, but the air stream must be stopped by the two lips or the sound has not be articulated. Many people omit these sounds after an /m/. The /b/ especially suffers omission after /m/. Check your pronunciation of these words to see if you face that problem.

ample	amble	rumple	rumble
simple	symbol	limper	limber
scamper	amber	simper	ember
hamper	number	amplitude	combination
contemptible	cucumber	bumper	September

The /p/ and /b/ are in danger of being omitted if the preceding syllable contains a /p/ or /b/. Check your pronunciation of these words:

capable	capably	probably	unstoppable
grabbable	proposition	preposition	unflappable

► ***Problem 3:*** Overaspiration

The amount of air released on the /p/ varies, and the amount of force with which /b/ is released also varies. This variation depends on the position of the sound in the syllable and on the sound that comes before or after it. But you should be careful not to *over*-explode /p/ and /b/.

► ***Problem 4:*** Substitution of a voiced bilabial fricative

Some languages have a phoneme that is a voiced fricative sound formed by the two lips. The two lips are puckered, but never completely, firmly pressed together. The sound produced is not a stop/plosive, but a friction noise. If your first language is one with such a phoneme, it is possible you are using that sound to substitute for the English /b/. (You may also be using it to substitute for the English /v/, but we will deal with that later.) You may be especially likely to use this substitution in the middle of words or phrases. Check your pronunciation of the following words to be sure you firmly press your two lips together and release the /b/ in a little plosion:

hobby	habit	rabbit	flabby
table	rubber	bubble	babbling
cabbage	rubbish	webbing	rumble

▶ *Problem 5:* Substitution of a voiceless labiodental fricative

If English is not your first language, you may confuse the /p/ and /f/ phonemes in English. This confusion, of course, probably results from the phonemic structure of your first language. We have both Bengali and Filipino friends who have had this problem. Pronounce these pairs of words out loud. Do you make a clear distinction between them? Is the /p/ always fully stopped by the two lips? Is the /f/ made by placing the edges of the upper teeth on the lower lip?

/p/	**/f/**	**/p/**	**/f/**
peel	feel	pit	fit
pain	feign	pan	fan
pun	fun	pour	four
pine	fine	pound	found
pool	fool	pond	fond
leap	leaf	clip	cliff
pup	puff	wipe	wife
lap	laugh	hoop	hoof
lope	loaf	cup	cuff
cheap	chief	gap	gaffe
append	offend	apply	a fly
a pair	a fair	a pyre	a fire
appealed	a field	appear	a fear
Tupper	tougher	appealing	a feeling

▶ *Problem 6:* Substitution of labiodental stops

If /p/ and /b/ occur before /f/ or /v/, there is a temptation to make the /p/ or /b/ in the same place as the following sound. That would mean that, instead of being articulated by the two lips, the /p/ or /b/ would be articulated by the upper teeth and the lower lip (as the /f/ and /v/ are). Some modification of the /p/ and /b/ will be made in preparation for the next sound, but the articulation should still be made by the two lips and should clearly be a stop sound. Check your pronunciation of these examples:

/pf/	**/pv/**
cu*pf*ul	to*p* *value*
*capf*ul	dee*p* *v*ault
mo*p* *f*loors	si*p* *v*odka
sto*p* *f*ighting	chea*p* *v*acation

/bf/	**/bv/**
tub*f*ul	ob*v*ious
gab*f*est (slang)	ob*v*erse
Bob *f*easts.	sub*v*ersion
Barb *f*asts.	a drab *v*oice

▶ ***Problem 7:*** Unvoicing of /b/

Before voiceless sounds and as the final sound in a phrase, /b/ may be slightly devoiced. That is, vocal vibration may decrease before the sound is finished. But the /b/ should not be completely *un*voiced. The word *tribe*, for example, should not sound like *tripe*, and *Abe* should not be turned into *ape*. Check your pronunciation of these pairs of words. Be certain that the final /b/ sound is a voiced sound.

/b/	**/p/**
cab	cap
mob	mop
gab (slang for talk)	gap
Gabe	gape

▶ ***Problem 8:*** Voicing of /p/

If your first language is not English, you may find it difficult to tell the difference between voiceless and voiced cognates such as /p/ and /b/. Some speakers of Oriental languages may be inclined to voice the /p/ so that it sounds almost like /b/. Read the following pairs of words aloud, and be sure that the /p/ is voiceless (just a puff of air, no buzz at the voice box) and the /b/ is voiced.

/p/	**/b/**
pea	bee
pit	bit
pout	bout
pie	buy
pat	bat
pod	bod (slang for *body*)
pay	bay
peg	beg
pump	bump
pond	bond

Pragmatics

Review the instructions on how to produce the /p/ and /b/ on pp. 56-57. Those instructions tell you how to make the sounds by themselves. If you have any problem(s) with producing these sounds correctly and clearly with complete, firm stops, you must practice making them in the customary way until it becomes a habit. Then transfer the new pronunciation into your everyday speech.

In these "Pragmatics" sections, we will provide you with practice materials to help you develop your articulation skills. We will give you words, phrases, and sentences for practice. The sentences have the target sounds in them, but we believe tongue-twisters do more harm than good. You will not find a sentence here like, "Peter Piper picked a peck of pickled peppers." We hope you will find the words, phrases, and sentences challenging, practical, reasonable, and fun.

Readiness Exercises

For some especially difficult sounds and sound combinations, we will provide "Readiness Exercises" to prepare you for effective practice. These warm-up practice materials will draw on skills you have already mastered to make it easier for you to produce the new target sound(s).

Since we are at the very beginning of your speech improvement program, we will not have any Readiness Exercises for /p/ and /b/.

Reinforcement Exercises

Practice Words for /p/ and /b/

Beginning		**Middle**		**End**	
/p/	**/b/**	**/p/**	**/b/**	**/p/**	**/b/**
peat	beat	happy	abbey	cup	cub
pin	bin	staple	stable	rope	robe
pay	bay	ample	amble	rip	rib
peg	beg	rupee	Ruby	gap	gab
pad	bad	rapid	rabid	cap	cab
pole	bowl	crumple	crumble	lope	lobe
pump	bump	Harper	harbor	slap	slab
peach	beach	dappled	dabbled	tripe	tribe
pill	Bill	a pound	abound	slop	slob

Practice Phrases for /p/ and /b/

a bad person
my poor bank book

proud of Boston
beef and potatoes
a plastic ribbon
a better position
a perfect cabin at the beach
a peach, a pear, and a banana
a bad repair shop
a pretty ebony table
an appropriate blessing
asleep in the bio lab
grabbing the unwrapped presents
a group of responsible laborers
a pleasant neighborhood in the Bronx
ebbing into hopeless repression
purchasing fabulous global trips

Practice Sentences for /p/ and /b/

1. Never buy a pig in a poke. (Southern expression)
2. The patient has a throbbing headache.
3. The robe fits poorly.
4. The president was impeached because of bias.
5. The symbolism in the play is far from simple.
6. People are never absolutely beyond help.
7. Step up to the batter's box.
8. Perhaps you could bend the rules to make me happy.
9. I got into trouble by reaping what I sowed.
10. Bob, a diabetic, apologized for eating cup cakes.

Practice Sentences for /p/ and /b/ (More Challenging)

1. I have not been robbed—except by a couple of brilliant cab drivers.
2. Our president was quite unhappy over the bad publicity we received.
3. It was obvious to everybody present that the baby was absolutely unbearable.
4. The bride will probably be willing to love and honor, but not to obey.
5. Do you believe corporal punishment should be used in the public schools?

6. In my opinion, capital punishment is barbaric.
7. A performer becomes addicted to applause.
8. Urban planners are responsible for this blemish on the city.
9. His bizarre behavior was a cheap trick to grab the parking space.
10. I promise I will practice these materials and become a better speaker.

Practice Sentences for /p/ and /b/ (Most Challenging)

1. Everybody believes in ''Power to the People.'' Everybody disagrees about what powers to which people!
2. Stopgap measures may bring temporary respite, but remember that long-term planning is best.
3. A government's power lies in its ability to decide which people will pay and which people will collect.
4. Bob voted in the last election, but his habit of picking losers is unbroken.
5. You can probably bribe Vince, but don't stoop to blackmail.
6. The promise was not explicit, but maybe he will parole the whole bunch.
7. Is Rap Music appalling or appealing? Bewildered parents are begging for answers.
8. The president made deep cuts in the budget, but was unable to kill the program.
9. If you want to travel abroad, you must obtain a passport and produce it upon demand.
10. Tennis fans, it's triple break point for Becker!

/t/ and /d/

Principles

Production

If you raise the velum to prevent the air from escaping through the nose, block the air stream at the front by pressing the tip of the tongue against the gum ridge, and then release the air by quickly dropping the tongue tip, you will produce a lingua-alveolar (tongue-gum ridge) stop. There are two lingua-alveolar stops in American English. One is voiceless (produced without vocal cord vibration); it is represented in both IPA and the dictionaries by /t/. The other lingua-alveolar stop is voiced (produced with vibration of the vocal cords); it is represented in both IPA and the dictionaries by /d/. In making these sounds you must be careful to narrow the tongue to a point, to press the tongue firmly against the upper gum ridge, and to make the release a quick one.

Precautions

There are five spellings for /t/:

t as in *time*
tt as in *bottom* or *tattoo*
th as in *thyme* or *Thomas*
ght as in *right*
ed as in *missed**

There are three spellings of /d/:

d as in *did*
dd as in *muddy*
ed as in *planned**

Sometimes the letter *t* appears in the spelling of a word, but is not pronounced. *t*, then, can be a "silent letter."

1. In some words ending in the spelling *tle*, the *t* is silent. Here are some examples:
   bristle, thistle, whistle, epistle, wrestle, castle, hustle
2. In some words ending in the spelling *ten*, the *t* is silent. Note these examples:
   often**, soften, hasten, chasten, listen, glisten, fasten,moisten
3. In some other words also, the *t* is a silent letter:
   Christmas, chestnut, mortgage

In a few words in English, *d* is a silent letter. Note these examples:
Wednesday, handkerchief, handsome

Problems

There are eight common problems associated with the production of the /t/ and /d/. As we look at each of these deviations, check to see if you have that problem with these sounds.

* Review pp. 20-21 for a full explanation of the past tense morpheme in English.

** Pronunciation without /t/ is more common, but pronunciation with /t/ is acceptable.

Problem 1: Incomplete closure

The alveolar sounds occur very often in English speech, so any slackness in their articulation is quite noticeable. Lazy articulation of the alveolar sounds will interfere with your ability to be understood. The /t/ and /d/ are *stop* sounds; the air stream must be stopped completely. If you articulate the stops correctly, for an instant no air at all is coming out; it is *stopped*. To stop the outgoing breath stream completely, you must get good, firm contact of the articulators. For /t/ and /d/, you must press the tongue tip firmly against the gum ridge. If you do not get that firm contact, these sounds will not be clear and crisp, and your speech will have a lazy, careless, slovenly character. Check to be sure whether the air is completely stopped and the tongue tip is firmly pressed against the upper gum ridge for /t/ and /d/ in these examples:

/t/	/d/
writing	riding
betting	bedding
rating	raiding
metal	medal
petal	pedal
center	sender
latter	ladder
He let her go.	He led her away.
I'm not bitter	I'm not a bidder.

Problem 2: Omission

Because /t/ and /d/ are used so often in our words, the tendency to leave out these sounds is a serious problem. One very common fault is to leave these sounds off at the ends of words—especially if another consonant comes just before the /t/ or /d/. Check your pronunciation of these words and phrases to be sure the final /t/ or /d/ is not dropped:

/t/	/d/
East	eased
colt	cold
can't	canned
lacked	lagged
cost	caused
molt	mold
erupt	he rubbed
lift	lived
bent	bend

ant	and
etched	edged
Luft	loved

The /t/ and /d/ are in danger of being omitted in the middle of words, especially after other consonants. Check your pronunciation of these words and phrases to see if you face that problem:

/t/	**/d/**
center	sender
venting	vending
hunter	under
renting	rending
Can't he?	candy
altar man	alderman
filter	filled her
molting	molding
halter	hauled her
Easter	eased her
Buster	buzzed her
master	Mazda

The omission of /t/ and /d/ when they occur between two other consonants (the three consonants together are called a consonant cluster) is very common, but it is a mark of lazy articulation. Check to see if you omit the /t/ and /d/ between two other consonants in the following words:

/ftl/	softly	swiftly	deftly
/fts/	lofts	lifts	crafts
/sts/	costs	casts	lists
/lts/	wilts	melts	colts
/stl/	costly	ghostly	ghastly
/ptl/	aptly	abruptly	ineptly
/ktl/	exactly	correctly	directly
/kts/	attracts	selects	inflicts
/nts/	dents	pints	grunts
/ndz/	hands	spends	blinds
/ldz/	fields	colds	scalds
/ldl/	coldly	wildly	mildly

► *Problem 3:* Dentalization

The customary place to articulate the /t/ and /d/ sounds in American English is the upper gum ridge. If you put your tongue on the teeth instead of the gum ridge (or just at the point where the teeth and gum meet), you have dentalized these alveolar sounds. Since the conventional way of producing /t/ and /d/ in many European languages is on the teeth, speakers of these languages often produce /t/ and /d/ in English in the same place. Dentalization changes the sound of these phonemes.

We have one allophone of /t/ and one of /d/ made on the teeth in English. When these phonemes come before one of the two "th" sounds, they are produced on the teeth to get ready for the coming "th" sound. But dentalization of /t/ and /d/ at any other time distorts the sounds. This change in tongue placement releases extra air on the plosion.

Check to be sure that your tongue tip goes to the gum ridge—about a quarter of an inch behind the teeth—when you make the /t/ and /d/ sounds. Pluck that point on the gum ridge with your tongue tip. Be sure your tongue is pointed to a tip, not flattened into a blade. The /t/ and /d/ should be quick, firm clicks—not prolonged, breathy explosions. Pronounce these words out loud to check for dentalization:

/t/	**/d/**
time	dime
team	deem
toll	dole
ten	den
tout	doubt
tab	dab
tuck	duck
tame	dame

▶ ***Problem 4:*** Overaspiration

Overaspiration means "release of too much air" on the production of a voiceless sound. Overaspiration of /t/ can result if you press the tongue too tightly against the ridge, spread the tongue touching the ridge into a blade rather than a tip, and slide the tongue forward on release rather than drop it down.

This change in tongue placement and release gives a fricative quality to a sound that is supposed to be a stop. Indeed, the resulting /t/ sounds a bit like /ts/, and the distorted /d/ sounds something like /dz/.

Reread the last paragraph under "Dentalization." Those instructions apply to this problem as well. Pronounce the following words out loud to check for overaspiration:

/t/	**/d/**
tear	dear
tip	dip
Ted	dead

too	do
ton	done
tail	dale

Problem 5: Substitution of Glottal Stop for /t/ or /d/

The glottis is the space between the vocal cords. Some languages have a phoneme that is a stop made by the vocal cords. If you close the vocal cords, build up the air pressure, and then release it in an explosion at the vocal cords, you have produced a glottal stop.

We do not have such a phoneme in English, but the sound is sometimes heard as a nonstandard substitute for /t/ or /d/. There are a number of languages that contain a glottal stop phoneme, and speakers of those languages may bring that sound over when they speak English.

The glottal stop is most often substituted for the /t/ and /d/ before /l/ or /n/ when the /l/ or /n/ is syllabic. (That means the /l/ or /n/ provides the carrying power for a syllable without a vowel being present in that syllable.) The glottal stop is sometimes substituted for /t/ and /d/ before other consonants as well. Check your pronunciation of these examples for the glottal stop substitution:

/tl/	**/dl/**
beetle	needle
battle	saddle
bottle	coddle
kettle	meddle
little	riddle
metal	medal
mental	kindle
fundamental	cradle
subtle	fiddle
hospital	poodle

/tn/	**/dn/**
written	ridden
rotten	couldn't
mittens	shouldn't
button	didn't
batten	hadn't
cotton	wouldn't

Read the following phrases aloud, and check for glottal stops:

a little mistake
needle and thread

a rotten tomato
didn't listen

Read these sentences aloud, and check for glottal stops:

The bottle isn't full.
I'm a fiddler—not a violinist.
The mittens were made of cotton.
I couldn't stand it.
The battle made a fundamental change.
I hadn't meddled in your affairs then.
What needless pain we bear!
Let me entertain you a little while.
What's he written? Not much.

When /tl/, /tn/, /dl/, or /dn/ form a syllable (usually a final syllable) without a vowel, the tongue goes up to the gum ridge for the stop and stays there for the /l/ or /n/. The tongue must stay in firm contact with the gum ridge. The plosion then occurs with the tongue tip still in firm contact with the gum ridge: over the sides of the tongue for /l/ and up through the nose for /n/. Say the words and phrases out loud again. Be certain that you hold your tongue tip firmly against the gum ridge continuously on these combinations. The tongue does not drop down (thus releasing a plosion and forming a vowel) between the /t/ or /d/ and the /l/ or /n/.

► ***Problem 6:*** Nonstandard assimilations

Assimilations are changes in sounds caused by neighboring sounds. (See pp. 343-348 for a fuller explanation.) Many assimilations occur in the Standard Dialect. Some assimilations, however, are still nonstandard. If you change a /t/ or /d/ into the following sound, you are substituting the next sound for the /t/ or /d/. Essentially, you anticipate the next consonant, omit the /t/ or /d/, and double the next consonant. Here are some examples. Remember we are telling you about a problem some people have. We are telling you what to avoid, not what to imitate! Read the following phrases aloud. Check to see if they sound like the errors (the nonstandard assimilations) in the second column.

that present	thap present
hot potato	hop potato
it could	ik could
it feels	if feels
could go	coug go
had been	hab been
had seen	has seen

Problem 7: Addition of /t/

Some people add a /t/ to the ends of words where it does not belong. This problem is not very common, but it does occur. Instead of saying *once*, they say *oncet*. Instead of saying *twice*, they say *twicet*.

Problem 8: Unvoicing of /d/

Like the other voiced stops, /d/ may be slightly devoiced before voiceless sounds and as the final sound in a phrase, but even in final position it should not be totally *un*voiced. You should not make the kind of mistake made by one of our students who read aloud to her class about a horse who was to be *shot* when the author had written about a horse who was to be *shod*.

If your first language is one in which some final consonants are regularly unvoiced, you may be tempted to bring this pattern over into English.

The words in the first column end in /d/. They should not sound like the words in the second column, which end in /t/. Check for unvoicing of /d/ as you read the pairs of words aloud:

/d/	**/t/**
feed	feet
bid	bit
laid	late
bed	bet
pad	pat
loud	lout
rude	root
mud	mutt

Pragmatics

Review the instructions on producing the /t/ and /d/. Placement of the tongue tip on the alveolar ridge is essential. Tap the tip of the tongue on the ridge and drop it down.

Readiness Exercises

The sounds /n/, /l/, /d/, and /t/ are all made on the upper gum ridge. Most people place the tongue in the correct position to produce the /n/ in American English, so we start with words beginning with /n/. Here are some exercises to get you ready for more work on /t/ and /d/. Read the words across the line. Be sure to place the tongue tip in the proper place on the initial sounds in the words. The tongue tip should go to the same spot to make all four beginning sounds.

/n/	/l/	/d/	/t/
nigh	lie	die	tie
know	low	dough	toe
nip	lip	dip	tip
not	lot	dot	tot
name	lame	dame	tame
napper	lapper	dapper	tapper
net	let	debt	Tet
knee	Lee	D	tea
numb	Lum	dumb	Tum
nab	lab	dab	tab
noon	loon	dune	tune
nil	Lil	dill	till
near	leer	dear	tear
Nome	loam	dome	tome
nor	lore	door	tore

Between vowels, /t/ often becomes somewhat voiced and therefore sounds a little like a /d/. Many careful speakers want to make a very clear distinction between /t/ and /d/ between vowels. For them, we pass along a trick given us by the late Dr. Claude Wise. The voiceless sound /t/ can have aspiration in contrast with the voiced /d/. Therefore, to insure making the distinction, you can add a tiny puff of breath after the medial /t/ and before the next vowel. That is, put a very tiny /h/ between the /t/ and the following vowel. For *bitter*, think *bit her*; for *better*, think *bet her*; for *butter*, think *but her*. Of course, the /h/ should be tiny—much shorter than a regular /h/. Try these pairs out loud to get the distinct /t/:

bit her	bitter
bet her	better
but her	butter
sit he	city
wit he	witty
pit he	pity
mat her	matter
pat her	patter
fat her	fatter
bet he	Betty
fret hing	fretting
get hing	getting

Reinforcement Exercises

Practice Words for /t/ and /d/

Beginning		Middle		End	
/d/	/t/	/d/	/t/	/d/	/t/
den	ten	medal	metal	Ned	net
dime	time	shudder	shutter	aid	ate
dip	tip	ruder	rooter	rude	root
dare	tear	raiding	rating	raid	rate
doe	toe	boding	boating	owed	oat
dub	tub	bidder	bitter	bud	but
Dan	tan	biding	biting	sad	sat
deem	team	plodding	plotting	Mead	meet
doubt	tout	contended	contented	tied	tight
daunt	taunt	herding	hurting	Swede	sweet

Practice phrases for /t/ and /d/

toast of the town
a dented fender
attempt a duet
a terrible disaster
attend a wedding
lost all the computer data
ten to fifty dollars
a deep subject
didn't study too much
shudder at the thought
a dramatic tag team
a little bitter and disturbed
doing his master's bidding
attempting to delay the inevitable
debating about what to do

Practice sentences for /t/ and /d/

1. Touch the tip of the tongue to the alveolar ridge.
2. Do not explode it; tap it.
3. Do not let the tongue tip slide forward.
4. Do not touch the teeth on the /t/ and /d/ sounds.
5. You must undo an old habit to develop a new one.
6. Try to practice daily—just a few minutes a day.
7. Do not dentalize these sounds.

8. Can you distinguish between correct and incorrect placement?
9. Can we depend on you to do your part?
10. It's best to double your pleasure: work twice as hard.

Practice sentences for /t/ and /d/ (More Challenging)

1. Do you feel it when your tongue goes too far forward?
2. Avoid omitting /t/ and /d/ after another consonant.
3. Develop your auditory acuity; that means train your ears.
4. Do not deceive yourself. It is your duty to be honest.
5. It's a matter of steady progress for lasting results.
6. Do I detect a bit of skepticism about heeding our advice?
7. We are not leading you astray; do what we tell you.
8. Tom used every extra minute to develop new speech patterns.
9. Twenty sessions of five minutes each would doubtless be better than one session of a hundred minutes.
10. Be a model of good articulation; intelligibility impresses everybody.

Practice Sentences for /t/ and /d/ (Most Challenging)

1. I shudder every time I think about it.
   We prefer shutters to drapes at the windows.
2. We are plodding along, but progress should be faster.
   Malcontents are plotting against the authorities.
3. Coding messages is an interesting, but difficult, task.
   That old house needs a protective coating of paint.
4. You ought to be put in a padded cell.
   I hate to be patted on the head.
5. Puritans were particular about what puddings they would eat.
   I'm putting this episode into your permanent record.
6. Adam had marital problems too.
   We live in the shadow of the atom bomb.
7. It was an effort, but we weighed her.
   Waiter, I don't want this dessert.
8. Today you should bet on a mudder—my kind of horse.
   That little disturbance made him mutter constantly.
9. I plan to audit the course discreetly.
   Ought it to be decided in a short amount of time?
10. I'm amazed they are herding so many students into one class.
    Dale has only one sadistic attribute: he enjoys hurting others.

/k/ and /g/

Principles

Production

If you raise the velum to prevent the air from escaping through the nose, block the air stream by pressing the back of the tongue against the soft palate, and then release the compressed air quickly by dropping the tongue from the soft palate, you will produce a lingua-velar (tongue and soft palate) stop. There are two lingua-velar stops in English: one that is voiceless, represented in IPA and in the dictionaries by /k/, and one that is voiced, represented in IPA and in the dictionaries by /g/.

Precautions

There are eleven spellings for /k/:

c as in *cold*
cc as in *accord*
cch as in *Bacchus*
ch as in *chord*
ck as in *pick*
cq as in *acquaint*
cu as in *biscuit*
k as in *kiss*
q as in *quick*
qu as in *liquor*
que as in *antique*

There are five spellings for /g/:

g as in *gun*
gg as in *egg*
gu as in *guess*
gue as in *dialogue*
gh as in *ghost*

Sometimes the letters *k* and g appear in the spelling of a word, but are not pronounced. When *k* or g come before an *n* at the beginning of a written word, the *k* and g are silent. Pronounce the following examples out loud. Remember that all these words begin with the /n/ phoneme:

knack	knit	gnat
knave	knob	gnash
knead	knock	gnarl
knee	knoll	gnaw
kneel	knot	gnome
knell	know	Gnostic
knife	knuckle	gnu

The letter g before *m* or *n* at the end of a word is silent. Pronounce these words out loud, remembering that the /g/ phoneme does not occur at the end of these words:

diaphragm	sign	reign	impugn	ensign
paradigm	align	arraign		
phlegm	assign	deign		
	benign	feign		
	consign	campaign		
	design	champagne		
	malign			
	resign			

In the preceding words, the g remains a silent letter when some suffixes are added to the words, and it is pronounced when other suffixes are added.

In general, there is no /g/ if the suffixes *-ing*, *-ment*, or *-er* are added. In general, there is a /g/ if the suffixes *-al*, *-ance*, *-ant*, *-atic*, *-ation*, *-ia*, *-ify*, or *-ity* are added. Pronounce these examples out loud:

Without /g/	**With /g/**
signer	signal
resigning	resignation
maligning	malignant
alignment	malignance
designer	designation
arraignment	signify
feigning	malignity

As we noted earlier, the letter x represents either *ks* or gz which may be particularly confusing if you learned English after learning another language. Not to worry! There are simple rules to guide you.

If the x comes at the end of the word, pronounce it /ks/. These examples illustrate the rule:

ax	sax
wax	ox
box	fox
fix	mix
ex	tux

If a consonant sound comes right after the *x*, it is pronounced /ks/. Say these examples out loud:

axle	exchange
exclaim	exclude
expand	expatriate
expect	explain
explore	express
exquisite	extension
external	extinct
extort	extraordinary

If an unstressed syllable (with a vowel or silent *h*) comes after the *x*, it is pronounced /ks/. Note these examples:

anxious	axiom
axis	execute
execution	exegesis
exercise	exhale
exhalation	ex officio
exorcism	exultation
Exxon	exhibition

If a vowel or silent *h* follows the *x* and that syllable is stressed, the *x* is pronounced as /gz/. Pronounce these examples out loud:

exact	exaggerate
exalt	examine
example	exert
exhaust	exhort
exist	exuberant
exude	exult

Of course, there have to be a couple of exceptions. *Luxury* can be pronounced either with /ks/ or /gz/. *Anxiety* contains no /g/; the first syllable ends with /ŋ/ (ng), and the second syllable begins with /z/.

Our last word of caution: The spelling *cc* sometimes represents /ks/. The first *c* is /k/, the second *c* is /s/. Pronounce the following examples and be sure to get a good, firm stop on the /k/:

accede	accelerate
accent	accentuate

accept	acceptable
access	accessible
accession	accessory
accident	occident

Problems

There are five common problems associated with the phonemes /k/ and /g/. As we discuss each of these problems, check to be sure you do not have that problem with these sounds.

Problem 1: Incomplete closure

As in the case of the other stops, it is necessary to block the air stream completely on /k/ and /g/. Careless speakers pronounce such words as *accept*, *accede*, and *success* without making a complete stop on the /k/ sound at the end of each first syllable. The same problem occurs when people do not fully close the /g/ in such words as *ignition*, *cognitive*, and *recognize*. The tongue is not pressed firmly enough against the soft palate to completely stop the outgoing air. For these sounds to be stops, the breath stream must be fully stopped. Check to see whether you make clear, complete stops for the /k/ and /g/ in these words and phrases:

uncle	bungle
bicker	bigger
Buckley	ugly
bucking	bugging
vicar	vigor
activate	aggravate
actually	agonize
accept	segment
accident	agreement
acupuncture	agriculture

Problem 2: Omission

There seems to be a great temptation to leave out /k/ and /g/ sounds altogether, especially at the ends of words and in certain other contexts. We will give you some words where there is a danger of omitting these stops. Do not yield to the temptation. Check your pronunciation of these words and phrases out loud:

Final /k/	Final /g/
back	bag
Huck	hug

Rick	rig
plaque	plague

/ks/	**/gz/**
leaks	leagues
racks	rags
bricks	brigs
accede	exact
access	exalt
accent	exert
accelerate	exist
accident	exotic
succeed	exult

/kt/	**/gd/**
decked	begged
joked	jogged
whacked	wagged
lacked	lagged
chucked	chugged
tact	tagged
plucked	plugged
locked	logged

/sk/	**/sks/**	**/skt/**
ask	asks	asked
mask	masks	masked
bask	basks	basked
cask	casks	casked
disc	discs	disked
risk	risks	risked

Here are some words where the /k/ or /g/ come before a variety of consonants and consonant groups. Check to be sure you do not omit the /k/ or /g/:

/k/	**/g/**
arctic	exist
tactic	exile
expect	exam
explain	exact
extent	example
explode	exhaust
express	ignite
export	signify

extra	ignition
extort	recognize
exploit	significance
disc brakes	big boy
blackboard	pig pen
bleak picture	stag party
ask questions	rag doll

Problem 3: Overaspiration

The amount of air released on the /k/ varies, and the amount of force with which /g/ is released also varies. It is possible, however, to overexplode these consonants—attacking them with too much force. This problem could occur on any word with /k/ or /g/.

Problem 4: Addition of /k/

Some speakers add an extra /k/ to a few words. There is no /k/ in the *first* syllable of the following words. Check your own pronunciation to be sure the first syllable is not *eks*.

escape
escaped
escapee
escapade
escalator

Problem 5: Unvoicing of /g/

Like the other voiced stops, /g/ is slightly unvoiced before voiceless sounds and as the final sound in a phrase. But the /g/ should not be completely *un*voiced. Even when it is the last word in a phrase or sentence, *lug* should not sound like *luck* and *stag* should not sound like *stack*.

Speakers who learned another language before learning English may have trouble with unvoicing. Check to be sure you voice final /g/. Note the contrast in the following pairs of words. The first word ends with /k/, the second with /g/:

Final /k/	**Final /g/**
back	bag
pick	pig
buck	bug
sack	sag
Rick	rig

luck	lug
leak	league
Bach	bog
peck	peg
hawk	hog

Pragmatics

Review the instructions for producing the /k/ and /g/. Work for complete closure and work on putting the sounds in wherever they belong.

Reinforcement Exercises

Practice Words for /k/ and /g/

Beginning		**Middle**		**End**	
/k/	**/g/**	**/k/**	**/g/**	**/k/**	**/g/**
cave	gave	anchor	anger	flack	flag
coast	ghost	backing	bagging	lock	log
cause	gauze	meeker	meager	Rick	rig
crime	grime	racket	ragged	leak	league
craze	graze	Becker	beggar	snack	snag
crypt	gripped	ankle	angle	hawk	hog
class	glass	Orkin	organ	tuck	tug
clean	glean	clocking	clogging	peck	peg

Practice Phrases for /k/ and /g/

get a drink
keep a drinking mug
aching again
give a cloth coat
package of gold coins
baking a good chocolate cake
snug as a bug in a rug
coping with greedy beggars
except for a meager bit of guilt
giving the doctor a checkup
escape from the plague of drugs
accept the gratitude of the crowd
exploring a bogus claim
ignorance—the key to failure and grief
recognize the guest in disguise

Practice Sentences for /k/ and /g/

1. Come and get it. Then keep going.
2. Never give a joker an even break.
3. I gather that doctors and chiropractors don't always agree.
4. Can you begin to check your own conversation?
5. His first act as governor was to go out and wave a flag.
6. The book is out of stock, so give us a staggering order.
7. I cannot forget, because she forgave.
8. A big group of people was saved by his quick reaction to the explosion.
9. The anchor punctured the hull. The captain's anger was obvious.
10. I become aggressive when I glimpse a parking place.

Practice Sentences for /k/ and /g/ (More Challenging)

1. A smuggler is not a common crook, but a racketeer and a rogue.
2. I'm very unlucky, actually. Some time ago, all my luggage was taken from my locker.
3. You must be rugged and clever to survive in a struggle like this contest.
4. I liked the work at first, but my interest lagged and I offered my resignation.
5. I cannot guess why he's beginning to "back out" of this deal.
6. I came to inquire about working here as a guide. I play the bagpipe.
7. I am negotiating to get the free gift promised in the contest.
8. With some luck and a little risk, we will get the recognition we deserve.
9. The car thieves only took the disc brakes, the ignition, and the lock on the trunk.
10. I guarantee you will have only good luck from now on. Ten bucks for this consultation.

Practice Sentences for /k/ and /g/ (Most Challenging)

1. The lecher gave a lecture on self-control.
2. The picture was a still life of a pitcher and a glass.
3. I regard the accident as totally fictitious.

4. How can I ignore the regulations on smoking?
5. Rock could be the classical music of the future, I guess.
6. I think you are exaggerating the significance of Rock Music.
7. The house was almost perfect: the back porch sagged, and the roof leaked.
8. I couldn't detect his agony—except for his gasping and groaning.
9. To keep students from haggling over grades, some professors make all questions exceptionally vague.
10. Actually, I cannot accede to your request, because I would be an accessory to your crime.

4

The Lateral

A lateral sound is one on which the air is emitted over the sides of the tongue and comes out the sides of the mouth. There is only one lateral phoneme in English, which we represent in IPA and the dictionaries by /l/.

/l/

Principles

Production

To form the /l/ continuant consonant, you close off the nasal passages by raising the velum, touch the tip of the tongue to the upper gum ridge, and allow the air to pass over the sides of the tongue out of the mouth. The /l/ is a voiced sound (produced with vocal fold vibration). The /l/ is a *voiced lingua-alveolar lateral*. The point of articulation for the /l/ is the same as for /t/ and /d/—tongue tip to gum ridge. However, on /t/ and /d/, the tongue is held against the insides of the back teeth to prevent the air from coming out over the sides of the tongue. The sides of the tongue are dropped down on /l/ to let the air come out over the sides. The tongue tip is held on the gum ridge to divide the air stream in two.

There are two important allophones of /l/ which you must understand and be able to produce. They differ slightly in production and in acoustic quality (how they sound). One is called "light /l/," and the other is called "dark /l/."

The light /l/ is articulated as we indicated earlier, but with this addition: the back of the tongue is low in the mouth. The phonetic symbol for light /l/ is [l̥].

The dark /l/ is articulated as we indicated earlier, but with the back of tongue raised toward the soft palate—about as high in back as for the vowels in the words *took* and *stood* (represented in IPA by /U/ and in the dictionaries by oo. The phonetic symbol for dark /l/ is [ɫ].

This distinction between light /l/ and dark /l/ may be especially confusing if you learned another language before learning English. Here are guidelines on which allophones to use when:

1. The light /l/ occurs at the beginning of a syllable (either alone or after another consonant in a blend) before vowels formed by the tongue in the front of the mouth. Note these examples, and pronounce them out loud:

leap	gleam
lip	clip
late	play
let	sled
lack	black
light	fly
loud	cloud

2. In American English, the dark /l/ occurs at the beginning of a syllable (either alone or after another consonant in a blend) before vowels formed by the tongue in the back of the mouth. Pronounce these words containing dark /l/ before back vowels and diphthongs:

Luke	look	law
lot	loin	glue
claw	blot	ploy

3. The dark /l/ occurs at the ends of all words in all dialects of American English. Pronounce these words containing dark /l/ at the ends of words—either as the final consonant or before the final consonant(s):

feel	field	fields
bill	build	builds
hell	help	helps
hall	halt	halts
coal	cold	colds
ghoul	Gould	Gould's
cull	cult	cults
whirl	world	worlds

4. Generally, Americans use the dark /l/ in the middle of words, although many Southerners use the light /l/ in the middle

of a word if it comes before a front vowel. (See Chapter 10 for a discussion of front vowels.) The easiest way to detect this difference is to listen to where the speaker divides the syllables. The speaker who uses the dark /l/ in the middle of words (between vowels) will put the /l/ at the end of a syllable. The speaker who uses the light /l/ in that position in a word will start the next syllable with the /l/. The dark /l/ speaker will say *yell-ing*, while the light /l/ speaker will say *ye-lling*. The first will call the young lady *Lill-y,* and the second will call her *Li-ly*. If your first language is not English, do not be concerned about this difference. Either is acceptable and standard.

In summary, then, on light and dark /l/: There is a difference in acoustic quality (a difference in sound) caused by a difference in the position of the back of the tongue. The back of the tongue is low on light /l/ and is raised toward the soft palate on dark /l/. The position of the tip of the tongue is the same for both allophones. The sounds that follow the /l/ and the position of an /l/ in a word determine which of the two allophones we will use.

Precautions

There are two spellings for /l/:

l as in *let*

ll as in *tell*

Some words spelled with *l* do not contain the /l/ phoneme. Some speakers, with the best of intentions, are misled by the spelling and put in an /l/. Such mispronunciations are called "spelling pronunciations." We do want you to be precise in your articulation, but pronouncing silent letters is not "being precise." Read the following lists of words out loud. You should discover, as you pronounce them, that the spelled *l* is silent.

balk	caulk	chalk
stalk	talk	walk
alms	balm	calm
palm	psalm	qualm
almond	salmon	salve
half	behalf	calf
could	should	would

Problems

There are seven common problems associated with the articulation of /l/. As we look at each of these problems, check to see if you have that problem with this phoneme.

Problem 1: Slack articulation

You have probably heard a speaker whose /l/ sound, especially in the middle of words, was not distinct. It is quite likely that the speaker was simply not touching the upper gum ridge with the tongue tip to form the sound. Aiming the tongue in the right direction is not enough. The tongue must touch the gum ridge. No matter where the /l/ is in the word (beginning, middle, end) and no matter what sound comes before or after the /l/, the tip of the tongue must firmly press against the gum ridge to articulate the /l/. Read the following words out loud, and check to be sure that your tongue tip presses against the alveolar ridge on the /l/ sounds:

relevant	truly
challenge	million
tranquillity	violent
quality	violate
analysis	silly
William	delicate
silence	swelling
inland	boiler

In addition to the /l/ in the middle of words, there is another place where the /l/ is in danger of being articulated slackly, or halfheartedly. This distortion is especially common in the South. In words where the /l/ comes before the final consonant, some speakers fail to touch the gum ridge with their tongue tips on the /l/. Because the /l/ will be a dark /l/, the back of the tongue will be raised up toward the soft palate. Without firm tongue-tip articulation and with the tongue humped up in the back of the mouth, this distorted /l/ may sound more like the vowel in the word *took* (/ʊ/ in IPA and oo in the dictionaries) or like the first sound in the word *above* (/ə/ in both IPA and the dictionaries) than like an /l/. Distorted in this slovenly way, the word *help* would become *he oop* (/hɛʊp/ in IPA) or /heəp/ ([hɛəp] in IPA). In both cases, the /l/ is distorted and the pronunciation is nonstandard.

Problem 2: Lalling

This problem is slack articulation *plus*. The tongue lies flat and rather relaxed in the mouth. The tongue movements are weak and sluggish. Rather than make the /l/ with the tongue sufficiently tense and the tip lifted up to the gum ridge, the speaker lifts the *back* of the tongue a bit and retracts it (pulls it back). The standard /l/ is made in the front of the mouth—the tongue tip on the upper ridge right behind the front teeth. Lalling produces an /l/ with the entire articulation movement occurring in the back of the mouth. The sound produced is muddy and "swallowed."

If you have this problem, you will emit the air over the sides of the tongue, but the sound produced will not have the liquid quality of a conventional /l/. Instead, it may have a fricative kind of quality.

Some speakers with this problem round the lips a bit so the /l/ they produce has a little /u/ (oo)—the vowel in *moon*—or /w/ overlay to it. Look in a mirror as you pronounce the word list below to see if you tend to round the lips while making the /l/.

low	below
low	yellow
leave	believe
long	along
line	allign
lease	release
let	sublet

Other speakers with this problem produce an /l/ that sounds a little bit like the *y* phoneme (/j/ in IPA). Although this is not too common, you might want to read the following pairs of words out loud to contrast the /j/ (y) and /l/ phonemes:

/j/ (y)	**/l/**
yeast	least
year	leer
yes	less
yet	let
yank	lank
yak	lack
yacht	lot
yard	lard
yearn	learn
young	lung
yawn	lawn
you	lieu

Pronounce these words aloud. Check to see if your tongue tip goes up to the alveolar ridge, as it should, for every /l/. **Or**: Can you feel the tongue lifting up in back? Is the tongue tip lying behind the *lower* front teeth? Is the blade of the tongue relaxed—just lying there—as you make the /l/? Is the air release breathy, slushy? If you are uncertain, ask your instructor to listen to determine if you have this problem.

leaping	lizards	lesson
lime	lung	lend
learn	bell	male
peel	Earl	bill

If you determine you do have this problem, use the special readiness exercises at the beginning of your practice sessions.

Problem 3: Omission

Some speakers omit the /l/ altogether. This omission is most likely to happen when the /l/ (it will be a dark /l/) comes before another consonant. Pronounce the following words and phrases out loud, and check to be sure you include the /l/. Articulate it by touching the tip of your tongue to the alveolar ridge.

all gone	all right	all hands on deck	William
all week	all clear	tall man	million
all kinds	all-round	soldier	billion
all fours	already	civilian	railroad

As a further check, pronounce these pairs of words out loud. Make the distinction clear by articulating a good tongue-tip-to-upper gum ridge /l/.

Without /l/	**With /l/**
odor	older
code	cold
goad	gold
fitter	filter
jade	jailed
sewed	sold
Mick	milk

Problem 4: Confusion of light and dark /l/

We have already discussed the difference between light and dark /l/. (See pp. 84-86.) Some speakers are confused about when to use which allophone. Some native speakers of American English use the dark /l/ in all positions in words. Some speakers for whom English is a second language always use the light /l/ no matter where the sound occurs. If you have either version of this problem, you can correct it by reviewing the material on producing light and dark /l/, by learning to produce both, to feel the difference between them (in terms of back-of-tongue placement), to hear the difference between them, and to put them in the proper place. This will require practice.

Problem 5: Dentalization

When an /l/ phoneme comes before either the voiced or voiceless *th* sounds, the /l/ will be made with the tongue on the teeth. This is a standard allophone of American English. But dentalization of the /l/, except before these sounds, is a distortion. If you discovered that you dentalized /t/ and /d/, you may also dentalize the /l/. Check your pronunciation of the following examples to be certain you do not put your tongue on the upper teeth or between the teeth when you make the /l/.

Let me do it.
Ted tells everything.
All I want is love.
hill and dale
"Hello Dolly"
Leave me alone.

► *Problem 6:* Labialization

The word *labialization* refers to misarticulation in which sounds are made by the lips (*labia*) rather than the customary articulators. You are said to have labialized the sound if lip movement is substituted for tongue movement in the formation of /l/. You labialize the /l/ if you do not lift your tongue tip to the upper gum ridge but instead raise the back of the tongue and pucker your lips as if for /u/ (the vowel in *boot*) or /w/.

This distortion is associated in many people's minds with "baby talk" and you should practice to get your tongue moving to the correct spot to make the phoneme if you have this problem.

Although the labialized distortion can occur on /l/ in any context, the greatest danger is in an initial consonant blend after /p/ or /b/—both bilabial (two lip) sounds. Remember the /l/ is made with tongue movement, not lip movement. *Lead* should not sound like *weed*; *laid* should not resemble *wade*; *plead* and *bleed* should not become *pwead* and *bweed*; and *played* and *blame* should not become *pwayed* and *bwame*.

Read aloud (left to right) the word lists below. Look in the mirror to check to see that you do not pucker your lips for the /l/ in the following words:

lead	bleed	plead
land	bland	planned
lot	blot	plot
light	blight	plight
loom	bloom	plume
lank	blank	plank
lush	blush	plush
lack	black	plaque

Problem 7: Confusion of /l/ and /r/

Speakers of American English who learned an Oriental language before learning English may have some difficulty hearing and making the difference between /l/ and /r/. Although these two sounds are quite separate phonemes in the English language, they are not separate phonemes in Oriental languages. If your first language is Japanese, Chinese, Korean or another Oriental language, you may think of /l/ and /r/ as allophones of the same phoneme—rather than as separate, different phonemes.

There is a difference in the articulation of the /l/ and /r/ phonemes in American English. The /l/ is made with the tip of the tongue *touching* the *upper gum ridge*. It touches firmly. As long as the /l/ is being sounded, the tongue is held against the ridge. Then, the tongue pushes off to go into position for the following sound. The /r/, on the other hand, is made with the tongue tensed up in the middle of the mouth and the tip pointing up to the area just *behind* the alveolar ridge—but not touching it. From this position, the tongue slides to the position for the vowel that follows the /r/. The /l/ tongue tip touches the gum ridge; the /r/ tongue tip points up to the area back of the gum ridge.

If you have this problem, you will have to work to feel where the tongue goes to make these sounds, to feel the difference in tension between the two sounds, and to see the difference both in lip and tongue position between the two sounds. (The difference in tension will affect the jaw and lips.)

Pronounce the following pairs of words and phrases. Check to be sure you make a clear contrast between the /l/ and /r/.

/l/	**/r/**	**/l/**	**/r/**
leap	reap	limb	rim
late	rate	led	red
land	Rand	light	right
lout	rout	lewd	rude
load	road	lot	rot
lug	rug	alive	arrive
jelly	Jerry	belong	be wrong
flee	free	fly	fry
play	pray	plowed	proud
bleed	breed	blessed	breast
cloud	crowd	climb	crime

Pragmatics

Review the instructions on producing the /l/ phoneme. Placement of the tip of the tongue on the alveolar ridge is essential.

Readiness Exercises

We told you earlier our program of speech improvement is cumulative. We build one skill on top of another. We deal with the /l/ right after the stops because it is articulated at the same place as the /t/ and /d/, which you have already mastered.

To prepare for the /l/ reinforcement exercises, go back to the readiness exercise on pp. 71-72. Read those words (across the line) aloud. Be sure there is a good, firm touch of the tongue tip on the gum ridge. Then drop the tongue tip down. The typical movements of the tongue in American English are up and down. That is why these readiness exercises are so important. On the /n/, /l/, /d/, and /t/, we lift the tongue tip up, touch it firmly to the ridge, and drop it down. Up and down, up and down. Exercise, exercise!

Here is a Readiness Exercise to help you develop adequate tension on the /l/ phoneme. If the tongue is too relaxed and its movements sluggish, we may have slack articulation of /l/ or even a lall. To be sure that the tongue tip goes *up* and that there is firm closure, we will move from /n/ to /l/. It is quite likely that you place your tongue in the right place to produce /n/. Therefore, we will say words ending in /n/ just before words beginning with /l/. Do not change the tip of the tongue after the /n/. Push the /l/ from that spot (the /n/ spot). Feel where your tongue goes for the /n/. Close your eyes if that helps you feel it better. That spot on the gum ridge is where all the /l/'s must be. Remember we are working for adequate tongue tension, for accurate placement, and for energetic tongue movements down from the gum ridge—in the front of your mouth. On the /l/, at least, it's what's up front that counts! Remember: Press the tongue tip against the ridge for /n/, hold the tongue there for the /l/, and then release the /l/ by dropping the tip down to form the next vowel.

on line	turn left	ten lines
fine lace	then leave	nine lives
Ben lied	pan lid	gone lame
can leak	spin long	own lamp
sign letters	wine list	gun lobby
one loss	in life	win-loss record

Reinforcement Exercises

Practice Words for /l/

Beginning	**Middle**	**End**
led	teller	dell
lip	pillow	pill
leave	velar	veal
late	tailor	tail

Beginning	Middle	End
loud	aloud	dowel
lap	pallid	pal
leap	peeling	peel
lick	killer	kill
lease	ceiling	seal
lace	sailor	sale
loot	toolbox	tool
lean	kneeling	kneel
load	older	dole
lied	wilder	dial
laid	daily	dale

Practice Words for /w/ and /l/ Contrast

/w/	/l/	/w/	/l/
we	Lee	wick	lick
wait	late	wet	let
wag	lag	watt	lot
womb	loom	woe	low
Wong	long	wowed	loud
wine	line	work	lurk
awake	a lake	a way	allay
be wise	belies	a wife	a life

Practice Words for /l/ and /bl/ Contrast

/l/	/bl/	/l/	/bl/
lead	bleed	link	blink
lame	blame	lend	blend
land	bland	lack	black
lot	blot	Lou	blue
low	blow	light	blight
luster	bluster	lank	blank
lake	Blake	lose	blues
lined	blind	lone	blown
lock	block	leak	bleak

Practice Words for /l/ and /pl/ Contrast

lace	place	luck	pluck
land	planned	lane	plane/plain
loom	plume	lad	plaid
lump	plump	ledge	pledge
lead	plead	lug	plug
lot	plot	loud	plowed
lack	plaque	lied	plied

Lee's	please	late	plate
lacquered	placard	latitude	platitude
laud	applaud	lunge	plunge

Practice Words for /bl/ and /pl/ Contrast

bleed	plead	bleat	pleat
blink	plink	blaze	plays
blank	plank	black	plaque
blot	plot	bland	planned
bloom	plume	blouse (v.)	plows
blush	plush	blunder	plunder
blight	plight	blaster	plaster

Practice Phrases for /l/

light and lively
live and let live
alone in the elevator
silly selections
all too pleasant
fall in love
follow the leader
cleaning the plaster
glad to be in college
an old flame (slang for "a past romance")
look around
ready to leave early
arrive for lunch
correct the blunder
allowance for the collection

Practice Sentences for /l/

1. He led a quiet life until he met Lily.
2. She knelt at the altar rail.
3. Let me call you sweetheart.
4. You call everybody darling.
5. I'll sell it to you for a dollar.
6. Most lovers think jealousy should be a felony.
7. Don't be silly. Of course, I'm willing.
8. Leonard has failed the oral exam again.
9. Are all the lectures in this college dull?
10. We'll sail for London on the first of April.
11. I'm looking forward to a glorious summer at the lake.
12. It is a delicate matter to expose a friend's fallacy.

13. The Long Island Railroad is asking for help from the federal government.
14. I've already violated my sacred pledge.
15. I told her in the hallway, but she didn't believe me.

Practice Sentences for /l/ (More Challenging)

1. Don't let them bluff you. Claim you're a civilian!
2. Everything was all right—till I got the bill.
3. Sally and Bill belong to a mutual admiration society.
4. Thelma will never stop traveling; she'd go to hell if the airline would give her a ticket.
5. His refusal to take the pledge should have given us a clue.
6. I'll tell you no lies, but I'm likely to tell little fibs.
7. I'll be glad to call you in the morning. Have a pleasant sleep.
8. I sleep well on a plane. Flying is the safest form of travel.
9. Where there's a will, there's a relative—or at least, a lawyer.
10. I'd like to believe the Oval Office is made of glass.

Practice Sentences for /l/ (Most Challenging)

1. I'd like to allay your fears, but let's face it—it would all be lies.
2. I know a billion ways to make a million dollars—all of them illegal.
3. William bought a silk shirt in Thailand that almost fits.
4. My elder brother is not the least bit like me. You're welcome to meet him.
5. I had a list of a million memory aids, but I lost it.
6. The place has a fifty-foot pool, but lack of water is a little problem.
7. We climbed to the top of the hill and played there until it got light.
8. I'm relatively sure I have no culpability, but just in case, I carry liability insurance.
9. Relax, slow down and allow yourself some lawful relaxation. Calm evenings are full of delight.
10. All right, we won't inflict more examples on you. Let us hear the dazzling exercises that come out of *your* files!

5

Some Fricatives

If you bring two articulators together (not enough to completely close off the outgoing air stream) and squeeze the breath between the two articulators, you will produce a friction like noise. These frictionlike speech sounds are called fricatives. There are ten fricative consonants in American English. We will deal with six of them in this chapter. The six are the first sounds in the words *wheel* (the *hw* sound), *feel*, *veal*, *thin*, *then*, and *heal*. The first and last of these six phonemes are individual sounds, and the other four are two pairs of cognates.

Principles

Production

Several movements are involved in the production of this fricative sound. You must raise the velum to prevent air from escaping through the nose, pucker the lips as if you were going to make the /u/ vowel (the first sound in the word *ooze*), let the tip of the tongue rest behind the lower front teeth, and raise the back of the tongue toward the velum. Together with these simultaneous movements, you blow the air through the lips in a friction-type noise without the vocal folds vibrating. The sound produced is a voiceless bilabial fricative. The IPA symbol for this sound is /ʍ/, and the dictionary symbol is hw.

Some phoneticians consider this sound the voiceless cognate of /w/. It sounds like an *hw* combination, except that it has no voicing. Like the /ʍ/, the /ʍ/ always occurs at the beginning of syllables—never at the end.

Precautions

There is one spelling for /ʍ/:

wh as in *why*

This voiceless bilabial fricative is the first sound in most words beginning with the spelling *wh*—as pronounced by many speakers of Standard American English. The use of /ʍ/ seems to be declining, however, both in the United States and Great Britain. In parts of the eastern United States, especially in New York City and other urban areas, the /ʍ/ is rarely used and /w/ is regularly used in its place on *wh* words. These writers (one a Southerner and the other a Midwesterner) both live in New York City, but they continue to include the /ʍ/ in their idiolects. We prefer not to use the /w/ on these *wh* words, simply because doing so results in so many homophones (words that sound alike but differ in spelling and meaning).

Pronounce the following pairs of words aloud. Do you use /ʍ/ (hw) to begin the first word of each pair, or do you begin both words in each pair with /w/? In either case, the use of /w/ for all these words is so widespread among speakers of the Status Dialect that its use certainly cannot be labeled nonstandard. Still, check to see if you use the /ʍ/ (hw) to make these words contrast:

/ʍ/ (hw)	/w/
wheel	we'll
whine	wine
where	wear
whale	wail
why	Y
what	Watt
whet	wet
which	witch
whit	wit
whirred	word
whirled	world
while	wile
whether	weather
Whig	wig
whacks	wax

In some words beginning with the spelling *wh*, the initial sound is not /ʍ/ (hw) or /w/. Instead, the initial sound is /h/. The following words and all the words made from them all begin with the /h/ phoneme:

who	whose	whom
whole	whore	whoop

Problems

There are two problems associated with this phoneme. As we examine each of these problems, check to see if you have that problem with this sound.

▶ ***Problem 1:*** Inadequate lip tension and movement

You must round the lips to make the /ʍ/ sound. Earlier, we said to pucker the lips. If you do not tense the lips enough, the articulation will be slack and inexact. To be sure you get sufficient tension and rounding of the lips, look in the mirror as you say the words *ooze*, *you*, and *whim*. The lips should be puckered (or pursed) for the beginning of all three words. The lips should be as tightly rounded for /ʍ/ (or /w/) as for the vowel in *ooze* and *you*. Looking in the mirror, check for adequate lip rounding as you pronounce these words out loud:

whip	whim
whelp	whimper
whimsy	whisper
wheat	whiff
whistle	whisky
whiz	wheel

▶ ***Problem 2:*** Substitution of /v/ for /ʍ/ (hw)

If you learned English after learning another language, or if your English patterns were influenced by someone who learned English after another language, you may substitute /v/ for the /ʍ/ (and for the /w/). The /ʍ/ fricative is made by forcing air between the two lips, which have been tensed into a pucker. The /v/ is made by squeezing the air between the upper teeth and the lower lip.

Look in the mirror as you pronounce the following pairs of words. Check to be sure that the initial sound in the first word of each pair is articulated by the two lips and the initial sound in the second word in each pair is articulated by the upper teeth and lower lip:

/ʍ/ (hw)	**/v/**
whine	vine
while	vile
why	vie
wheel	veal

whale	vale
whet	vet
whim	vim
in white	invite
a whale	avail

Pragmatics

Reinforcement Exercises

Practice Words for /ʍ/ (hw)

Beginning	**Middle**
what	somewhat
where	anywhere
	elsewhere
	nowhere
	somewhere
while	awhile
	meanwhile
whirl	awhirl

Practice Phrases for /ʍ/ (hw)

wheel of fortune
a very loud whisper
without a whimper
whatever you say
whenever you want
whether you will or won't
somewhat evil
a whirling dervish
every which way
wheezing and whining
where or when
the whys and wherefores
Whitman versus Whittier
which is which

Practice Sentences for /ʍ/

1. Why did the bridesmaids wear white dresses?
2. Of course we will, but who knows when or where?
3. Meanwhile, she just kept whispering in his ear.
4. The witch did not know which way to turn.
5. Do you prefer white bread or whole wheat?
6. Why in the world did she whack him with a broom?

7. When I returned, the dervish was still whirling.
8. Whenever you want me, just whistle.
9. It's wicked to whet my appetite when I'm trying to diet.
10. What will Mr. Watts do when he leaves the company?

/f/ and /v/

Principles

Production

If you raise the velum so no air can escape through the nose, bring the edges of the upper teeth and the lower lip together, and force the air out between the upper teeth and lower lip, you will produce a labiodental (lip and teeth) fricative. There are two labiodental fricatives in English: one voiceless and one voiced. The voiceless cognate is represented in IPA and in the dictionaries by /f/. The voiced cognate is represented in IPA and in the dictionaries by /v/.

Precautions

There are four spellings for the phoneme /f/:

f as in *feel*
ff as in *off*
gh as in *rough*
ph as in *phone*

There are four spellings for the phoneme /v/:

v as in *vest*
vv as in *savvy*
f as in *of*
ph as in *Stephen*

Problems

There are five common problems associated with these two fricative phonemes. As we discuss each deviation in turn, check to see if you have that problem.

► *Problem 1:* Slack articulation

To produce these two sounds, you must bring the upper teeth and the lower lip together. They must touch. If you only raise the lower lip a little, you will produce a bilabial (two lip) fricative rather than a labiodental fricative. That is a different kind of sound altogether. If your lips are too lazy to move, you will have to get them used to articulating. Slack articulation of the /f/ and /v/ creates the impression of careless, slovenly speech. As you pronounce these words out loud, check to be certain that the upper teeth and lower lip *touch*:

Initial	**Final**
feel	leaf
fine	knife
fall	off
fool	aloof
vague	gave
vast	starve
veer	Reeve
vile	alive

Problem 2: Omission

Many speakers are tempted to omit /f/ and /v/—especially before other consonants. Of the two sounds, /v/ is more often omitted because the voiced cognate is always the less forceful of the two cognate phonemes. Many speakers who omit these sounds are not aware of doing so. Check carefully, therefore, while pronouncing the following examples, to be sure the /f/ and /v/ are not omitted.

lifetime	slaveship
off-white	evening
afternoon	love story
laugh meter	leave time
graph paper	save something
enough trouble	five goals
It's half time.	Give me some.
Cough syrup, please.	Love me or leave me.
It's a rough time.	I have to go.
There's enough work.	I've heard worse.
What a golf course!	He's saved a lot of money.

Problem 3: Unvoicing of /v/

Like other voiced consonants, /v/ may be slightly devoiced before voiceless sounds and as the final sound in a phrase. But the /v/ should not be completely unvoiced. *Save* should not become *safe*, for example, and *have* should not become *half*. As you pronounce these words out loud, check to be sure the /v/ is clearly a voiced sound and the /f/ is clearly voiceless.

Beginning		Middle		End	
/f/	**/v/**	**/f/**	**/v/**	**/f/**	**/v/**
fan	van	rifle	rival	waif	wave
fine	vine	surfer	server	proof	prove
face	vase	defied	divide	leaf	leave
few	view	surface	service	grief	grieve
fault	vault	define	devine	strife	strive

Problem 4: Substitution of /w/ for /v/

Some speakers who learned English as a second language substitute /w/ for /v/. The /w/ is articulated by puckering the two lips, but the /v/ is articulated by bringing the upper teeth and lower lip together. Check to see if you make a clear distinction between these sets of words:

wail	vale	wane	vain
wary	vary	want	vaunt
wend	vend	went	vent
west	vest	wet	vet
wicker	vicar	wide	vied
wile	vile	wine	vine
wince	Vince	wiper	viper
Weiss	vice	worse	verse

Problem 5: Substitution of /b/ for /v/

Some speakers who learned English as a second language (especially those who first spoke Latin-American Spanish) substitute /b/ for /v/ in English. This confusion is understandable, because of the phonemic system of their first language. Check to be sure you articulate the first sound in the words starting with /v/ with the upper teeth and lower lip touching. Use a mirror to check your articulation of the /v/.

bale	vale	bicker	vicar
bane	vain	bowel	vowel
ban	van	a boat	a vote
bend	vend	Cabot	Cavett
Bender	vendor	Hubbard	hovered
berry	very	saber	savor
beer	veer	labor	laver
banish	vanish	Bieber	beaver
bet	vet	a bale	avail
bile	vile	abide	divide
boat	vote	about	devout

Pragmatics

Reinforcement Exercises

Practice Words for /f/ and /v/

Initial /f/ and /v/ contrast

feel	veal	fine	vine
fairy	very	first	versed
few	view	face	vase
fast	vast	file	vile
fear	veer	fought	Vought
focal	vocal	fender	vendor
fault	vault	fire us	virus

Medial /f/ and /v/ contrast

infest	invest	defied	divide
refile	revile	surface	service
rifle	rival	surfer	server
define	divine	safer	savor
leafing	leaving	refuse (v.)	reviews
infighting	inviting	proof it	prove it

Final /f/ and /v/ contrast

leaf	leave	safe	save
waif	wave	belief	believe
serf	serve	life	live (adj.)
strife	strive	proof	prove
grief	grieve	fife	five
shelf	shelve	half	have
relief	relieve	fife	five

Practice Phrases for /f/ and /v/

a fast food vendor
after the victory
above the fight
love at first sight
winning every volley
proof of purchase
full of flavor
a very rough surface
if you believe me
fully cover the wound
cup of coffee
a confusing event on television

Practice Sentences for /f/ and /v/

1. I may be very foolish, but I do not fear the future.
2. I cannot afford to invite every visitor.
3. My staff couldn't get enough information to develop a brief.
4. My wife has a vast store of facts—all of them trivial.
5. I've made an effort to tell everything I know.
6. Phillip, have you read *Leaves of Grass*?
7. Victor may be a fool, but he would never deceive anybody.
8. They found me subversive because of my friends.
9. I'd love to be invisible for just a few hours.
10. They've started to investigate his involvement in the fraud.

Practice Sentences for /f/ and /v/ (More Challenging)

1. It's obvious to everybody who knows him he's in difficulty.
2. *Twelfth Night* is one of my favorite plays.
3. I feel it is better to have loved and won than never to have loved at all.
4. He views all work as evil; he must have a phobia.
5. Would you think it fine if every revolver in America vanished overnight?
6. Evelyn was frightened of being stuck in the voting booth.
7. I'm not afraid of flying; I thrive on adventure.
8. Live every day as if that day were to be your final one.
9. The Chief informed her that it was vital she testify before the defendant.
10. What proof do you have that he is in favor of revolution?

Practice Sentences for /f/ and /v/ (Most Challenging)

1. What's the advantage of taking vitamins fifty times a day?
2. I marvel that he deceives so many people without being really vicious.
3. This university has audiences of fifty for a lecture and crowds of seventy-five thousand for a football game.
4. I haven't the foggiest idea why he's so vindictive.
5. For the sake of our friendship, please turn down the volume on that stereophonic torture device.
6. Expecting to fail, he refused to study. He received an F—a self-fulfilling prophecy.

7. Even if you grovel, I am resolved to find this defendant guilty of some kind of felony.
8. Being invisible would be very convenient—the perfect way to observe the staff.
9. After receiving the valentine and the expensive gift, she found him less repulsive.
10. I will give five thousand dollars to the ''Victory Drive,'' if you will name the alcove after me.

Practice Sentences for /v/ and /b/ Contrast

1. Everybody on the boat voted to abandon ship.
2. I'm very fond of any kind of berry.
3. He's the bane of my existence—an utterly vain man.
4. We tried to banish him, and then he vanished.
5. I will never abide an effort to divide us.
6. Have you ever been in service? No, but I've been in the Boy Scouts.
7. Don't get involved with little vices. Think big.
8. Above all, be virtuous—whatever that means.
9. The fire fighters believe the blaze started in the oven.
10. Victor invited everyone to the party, but I didn't believe him.

Practice Sentences for /v/ and /w/ Contrast

1. I'm willing to wait. I just hope it is not in vain.
2. Dr. Vest traveled West in his BMW.
3. The vicar prefers to sit on the wicker furniture.
4. I won't ever get involved again! Never again!
5. I've never felt worse; it was stupid behavior.
6. Hoping to make his own wine, Dad has bought some grape vines.
7. I don't want them to vaunt their achievements—just work hard.
8. Our team vied for the honor, but lost by a wide margin.
9. I'm not averse to poetry, but that is the worst I have ever heard.
10. Who would have thought David would grieve so over a dog?

/θ/ and /ð/

Principles

Production

If you raise the velum so no air can escape through the nose, bring the upper teeth and the blade of the tongue together, and let the air ooze out between the upper teeth edges and the tongue blade, you will produce a linguadental (tongue and teeth) fricative. The tongue may be placed either against the inside surfaces of the upper front teeth or beneath the edges of the upper front teeth. There are two linguadental fricatives in English. One is voiceless, represented in IPA by /θ/ and in the dictionaries by th. The other is voiced, represented in IPA by /ð/ and in the dictionaries by *th*.

Precautions

Both /θ/ and /ð/ are represented in regular spelling by the digraph (letter combination) *th*. You cannot tell from the spelling whether a word contains the voiceless or the voiced cognate.

Sometimes *th* does not represent either linguadental phoneme. Note these words:

courthouse
outhouse
Thomas

Problems

There are five common problems associated with these sounds. As we examine each of these deviations, check to see if you have that problem with these phonemes.

► *Problem 1:* Omission

Some speakers omit these sounds at the ends of words. Check your pronunciation of the following phrases to be sure the final /θ/ (th) and /ð/ (*th*) are not omitted:

both of them	tithe our income
birth of the blues	bathe a child
south of Boston	teethe all year
path of least resistance	clothe a family
wrath of God	breathe our pure air

The /θ/ (th) and /ð/ (*th*) are in danger of being omitted if the next sound is a consonant. As you pronounce these examples out loud, check for omission of /θ/ (th) and /ð/ (*th*):

birthday
bathroom
pathway
cloth coat
mouth to mouth
oath taken
with Terry
north wind
moth balls
ninth circle

soothe Tom
bathe daily
breathe freely
clothe children
tithe faithfully
lathe machine
writhe frantically
seethe constantly
smooth sailing
loathe hypocrisy

The /θ/ (th) and /ð/ (*th*) are in danger of being omitted when either begins a syllable after another syllable that ends in a consonant or consonants. Read the following phrases aloud. Check to see if you tend to omit the /θ/ (th) or /ð/ (*th*).

Just think
fix things
fast thinking
miss theater
past thirty
shock therapy
six thrilling episodes

What's that?
miss the point
Pick the winner.
pass the course
gave them up
Who's there?
I can't stand this!

The greatest temptation to omit /θ/ (th) and /ð/ (*th*) occurs when they appear in consonant clusters—that is, groups of consonants that have no vowels between them. It takes extra effort to put these sounds in when they appear in difficult combinations. Pronounce the following groups of words aloud, and check to be sure you do not omit the /θ/ (th) or /ð/ (*th*):

/θ's/ (ths)	**/ðz/ (*thz*)**	**/ðd/ (*th*d)**
breaths	breathes	breathed
bath's	bathes	bathed
deaths	writhes	writhed
Booth's	soothes	soothed
myths	seethes	seethed
wreath's	wreathes (verb)	wreathed
youth's	truths	clothed

	/θm/ (thm)	/ðm/ (*th*m)	
	anthem	rhythm	
/fθ/ (fth)	**/fθs/ (fths)**	**/pθ/ (pth)**	**/pθs/ (pts)**
fifth	fifths	depth	depths
/dθ/ (dth)	**/dθs (dths)**	**/lθ/ (lth)**	**/lθs/ (lths)**
width	widths	wealth	wealth's
breadth	breadths	health	health's
hundredth	hundredths	stealth	stealth's
/nθ/ (nth)	**/nθs/ (nths)**	**/ksθ/ (ksth)**	**/ksθs/ (ksths)**
seventh	sevenths	sixth	sixths
ninth	ninths		
tenth	tenths	**/ŋθ/ (ngth)**	**/ŋθs/ (ngths)**
eleventh	elevenths	length	lengths
month	months	strength	strengths

Problem 2: Unvoicing of /ð/ (*th*)

Although the /ð/ will be slightly devoiced before voiceless sounds and when it is the last sound in a phrase, it should never be completely unvoiced. *Soothe* should never be turned into *sooth*, for example, and *teethe* should never become *teeth*. Read these sentences out loud and check for unvoicing of the /ð/ (*th*):

I can hardly breathe.
I wish he'd bathe.
Watch that wrestler writhe!
Larry is using the lathe.
Lying is one thing I loathe.

Problem 3: Raising*

Raising the tongue behind the teeth on the production of the two "th" phonemes produces a distortion. To the untrained ear, the resulting /θ/ (th) sounds like a /t/, and the resulting /ð/ (*th*) sounds like a /d/. Actually, the people who raise the tongue on these sounds do not articulate a real American English /t/ or /d/, but the distortion is great enough to sound that way. Remember that in American English, /t/ and /d/ are articulated by the tongue tip on the upper gum ridge. The tongue is not raised that high on these distortions. It is raised up behind the

* The phonetic symbol for raising is ˔; it is placed to the right and a little above the symbol for the sound—that is , [θ˔] and [ð˔].

teeth, but it never gets as high as the gum ridge. Still, when raised that high, the sounds do sound more plosive than fricative.

If you raise the tongue up on the inner surfaces of the teeth to make the /θ/ and /ð/, others will think you are saying "*dis, dat, dese*, and *doze*" for *this, that, these, and those*. And "Come with me, I'll go with you," and "nothing doing" will turn into "Come wit me, I'll go witcha," and "nuttin' doin'."

You must place the tongue at the bottom of the upper teeth, or these phonemes will be distorted. The tongue does not have to be under the teeth to produce the sounds, but the blade of the tongue must be at the bottom of the teeth.

Because these phonemes do not occur in many other languages, speakers of other languages often have trouble with them. Problems with these phonemes are not limited to speakers whose first language is not English, however. In fact, such problems are common, and other speakers of English find them quite distracting.

If you have difficulty with this distortion and tend to raise the tongue behind the teeth when producing these phonemes, we suggest you use a mirror to make sure the tongue is under the upper teeth when producing the two "th" sounds. Check your production of /θ/ (th) and /ð/ (*th*) as you read these examples out loud:

/θ/ **(th)**	/ð/ (***th***)
thigh	thy
thin	then
ether	either
mouth (noun)	mouth (verb)
teeth	teethe
cloth	clothe

He's at the school.
Hit the road.
I read the book.
I made that mistake.
I'll take this one.
Who will go with you?
You can't soothe my feelings.
Now it will be smooth sailing.
It's no bother; I'll get another one.
Birth and death are mysteries.
I think those are the right ones.
Other than earth, where are there intelligent beings?
Both of them were thieves—or so I thought!

▶ *Problem 4:* Substitution of /f/ for /θ/ (th) and /v/ for /ð/ (*th*)

In some non-standard (although thoroughly self-consistent) dialects of American English, speakers substitute /f/ for /θ/ and /v/ for /ð/—especially in the middle and at the ends of words. Check your own pronunciation of these words and phrases to see if you make this substitution. If you are not sure, watch in a mirror to be sure the sounds are made with the tongue and teeth rather than with the lower lip and teeth.

/θ/ **(th)**	**/f/**
death	deaf
oath	oaf
wreath	reef
roof	Ruth
miff	myth
hath	half

/ð/**(*th*)**	**/v/**
clothe	clove
smooth	move
wreathe	Reeve
lathe	slave
writhe	arrive
swathe	suave

/θ/ **(th)**	/ð/ **(*th*)**
to the death	*Other Voices, Other Rooms*
on my birthday	either way, neither way
with ease	another shop farther along
Come with me.	whether to go with mother
a new toothbrush	a leather coat
anything you say	although it's rather soothing
pathway to the South	the other gathering
the North Pole	I'd rather not.
from both of us	It's no bother.
within the month	either alone or together

▶ *Problem 5:* Substitution of /s/ for /θ/ (th) and /z/ for /ð/ (*th*)

If you learned English as a second language, you may substitute /s/ for /θ/ and /z/ for /ð/. Your first language probably did not have the /θ/ and /ð/ phonemes, so you substituted a familiar sound for the unfamiliar new phonemes of English. Remember that /θ/ (th) and /ð/ (*th*) are made with the tongue at the bottom of the upper teeth and, although they are friction noises, they are not hissing noises like /s/

and /z/. Read the following words and phrases aloud. Check to see if you make these substitutions.

/s/	**/θ/ (th)**
sank	thank
sinking	thinking
sick	thick
saw	thaw
seems	themes
sought	thought
sin	thin
sigh	thigh

/z/	**/ð/ (*th*)**
Zen	then
Z	thee
Zayre	there
Xanadu	than I do
(Auld Lang) Syne	thine

/s/ and /θ/ (th) contrast

It's a sin to be that thin!
My hopes sank. Thank you.
I think I'll go or sink trying.
A good girl is a myth—not a miss.
I saw the ice beginning to thaw.
The end ran a straight path and caught the pass.
I sought in vain for a brilliant thought.

/z/ and /ð/ (*th*) contrast

I resemble them a little.
The breeze is so strong I can hardly breathe.
The cop seized her; she just seethed.
The bar was named "Z-Bar."
As long as you writhe, you'll never rise.
Don't tease the baby; he's trying to teethe.
Then I studied Zen Buddhism.

Pragmatics

Readiness Exercises

If you have a problem with raising the tongue on /θ/ and /ð/, with substituting /f/ and /v/, or with substituting /s/ and /z/, begin your practice session with some negative practice to contrast the "wrong way" with the "right way" to produce the sounds.

Use a mirror to be sure the tongue can be seen at the bottom of the upper four front teeth on /θ/ and /ð/. Can you *feel* the difference between the "wrong way" and the "right way?" Close your eyes and check where the tongue goes.

Contrast /t/ and /θ/ (th) in these pairs of words. Make sure the tongue tip goes up to the gum ridge for /t/ and the tongue blade goes under the upper teeth for /θ/.

/t/	/θ/ (th)	/t/	/θ/ (th)
tin	thin	tinker	thinker
taught	thought	tick	thick
tie	thigh	team	theme
tank	thank	tree	three
true	through	trust	thrust
tread	thread	trill	thrill
bat	bath	rat	wrath
pit	pith	wit	with
brought	broth	boat	both
set	Seth	bet	Beth
dirt	dearth	fort	forth

Contrast the /d/ and /ð/ (*th*) in these pairs of words.

/d/	/ð/ (*th*)	/d/	/ð/ (*th*)
doze	those	D's	these
day	they	die	thy
dine	thine	den	then
Dan	than	dough	though
dare	there	D	thee
dismiss	this miss	discharge	this charge
disagreement	this agreement	disapproval	this approval
tide	tithe	reed	wreathe
sued	soothe	breed	breathe
laid	lathe	ride	writhe
seed	seethe	load	loathe

Contrast the /f/ and /θ/ (th) in these pairs of words. Remember, the /f/ is made with the upper teeth touching the lower lip, while the /θ/ is made with the upper teeth touching the blade of the tongue.

/f/	/θ/(th)	/f/	/θ/(th)
fin	thin	Fred	thread
fret	threat	free	three
fro	throw	frill	thrill
deaf	death	reef	wreath
roof	Ruth	oaf	oath

Contrast /v/ and /ð/ (*th*) in these pairs of words.

/v/	**/ð/(*th*)**	**/v/**	**/ð/(*th*)**
V	thee	V's	these
van	than	vat	that
vale	they'll	vie	thy
vine	thine	vow	thou
clove	clothe	live	lithe

Contrast /s/ and /θ/(th) in these pairs of words. We will discuss production of /s/ later (See p. 122). Remember, for now, that the tongue tip is behind the teeth and under the ridge for /s/, while the tongue blade is under the upper teeth for /θ/ (th).

/s/	**/θ/ (th)**	**/s/**	**/θ/(th)**
sin	thin	sing	thing
sink	think	sank	thank
sunder	thunder	some	thumb

Contrast the /z/ and /ð/(*th*) in the following pairs of words.

/z/	**/ð/(*th*)**	**/z/**	**/ð/(*th*)**
Z	thee	Zen	then
bays	bathe	close (v.)	clothe
breeze	breathe	tease	teethe
lays	lathe	sues	soothe

Reinforcement Exercises

Practice Words for /θ/(th)

Beginning	**Middle**	**End**
thief	author	teeth
theme	Athens	breath
theist	atheist	both
thesis	breathy	bath
thick	nothing	north
think	earthy	earth
thing	ether	booth
thirty	method	truth
thirsty	mythical	month
theory	pathetic	mouth
thimble	Gothic	moth
theater	Martha	birth
thaw	pathway	path

theology	wealthy	wealth
therapy	ethnic	oath
thicket	anthem	myth
third	healthy	health
thong	youthful	youth
thorn	authority	south
thorough	toothache	worth
thumb	python	length
thunder	something	faith
threat	bathtub	wrath
thrift	athlete	death
thrill	ethics	tooth
throat	plaything	beneath
throb	withhold	wreath
three	birthday	math
thrive	lengthy	tenth
through	anything	warmth

Practice Words for /ð/ (*th*)

Beginning	**Middle**	**End**
the	either	bathe
than	mother	clothe
that	father	breathe
thee	bother	lathe
then	other	lithe
there	another	soothe
therefore	breathing	smooth
these	gather	mouth (verb)
they	rather	teethe
their	soothing	writhe
them	smoother	wreathe
this	smother	scathe
those	leather	tithe
though	further	swathe
thus	bathing	loathe

Practice Phrases for /θ/ (th) and /ð/(*th*)

both of them
thing of beauty
in this theater
the ticket booth
faith of our mothers and fathers
neither one nor the other

a thoughtless untruth
to the north of the river
smooth the ruffled feathers
anything but the school anthem
with all his authority
a pathetic bag of clothing
ethics of the heathen
birth and death
a gathering thunderstorm

Practice Sentences for /θ/ (th) and /ð/ (*th*)

1. They say nothing is certain but death and taxes.
2. The people of earth are threatened by pollution.
3. They are going home for Thanksgiving.
4. I'm healthy. A trip to Athens is therapeutic.
5. Sun bathing turns your skin to leather.
6. Thank you for suggesting a title for my theme.
7. There's a wealth of information on both topics.
8. We know nothing about the authorship of the material in our files.
9. I have faith in the ethics of most other professors.
10. "Is this the face that launched a thousand ships?"
11. I live on the South Side, but I'm going to move on Thursday.
12. I'd rather associate with someone who bathes regularly.
13. We got five thousand answers to the ad; two thousand were threatening.
14. Soothing irate professors is a hard thing to do.
15. Although she is a pathological liar, she has a method to it.

Practice Sentences for /θ/ (th) and /ð/ (*th*) (More Challenging)

1. Although we sat there through the whole lecture, none of us accepted his theories.
2. There are many paths to success—all of them crooked.
3. My mother and father had a smooth marriage for more than thirty years.
4. The Egyptian dancer writhed for an hour, but stayed fully clothed.
5. Thus, an author's pen can be a lethal weapon.
6. Thelma is rather unenthusiastic about birthdays.

7. Another human being is not a plaything; I loathe sexists.
8. The truth is that I lost the thread of the narrative in that Elizabethan novel.
9. Myth is to theology what broth is to the stew.
10. Screaming, "Not another breathy voice," the therapist threw a tantrum.

Practice Sentences for /t/ and /θ/ Contrast

1. I forgot to thank you for the tank top.
2. The room, made entirely of tin, was really quite thin.
3. Don't be a big eater just before taking ether.
4. It took both of them to control the boat.
5. I thought I had taught you better than that!
6. She was enchanted with his charm and wit.
7. Every paragraph in his theme teems with smut.
8. Rodin's "The Thinker" wasn't made by a tinker.
9. There were only three apples on the entire tree.
10. Beth refused to bet on the outcome.

Practice Sentences for /d/ and /ð/ Contrast

1. He wasn't there. How dare he?
2. I fed her a line about liking feathers.
3. One day soon they will understand.
4. He laid a new piece of metal on the lathe.
5. These students will not accept D's and F's.
6. Not until then did I go into the den.
7. The minister said my prosperity is tied to the tithe.
8. The new breed of young people are "yearning to breathe free."
9. This charge will be dropped and the prisoner discharged.
10. Whenever we dine, we say, "Thine is the glory."

Practice Sentences for /f/ and /θ/ Contrast

1. To the day of his death he was deaf as a post.
2. The captain threw a wreath on the reef as we hit it.
3. Ruth sunbathes on the roof every day.
4. He called me an oaf for not taking the oath.
5. Breaking a lath is not something to laugh about.
6. Fly around the earth? Not on your life!
7. I found the leaf underneath our table.

8. Both of them brought us a loaf of bread.
9. There was no roof to the kissing booth.
10. It looked better when she took that cloth off of it.

Principles

Production

If you bring the vocal bands together enough to cause friction, but not vibration, and force the air through while keeping the velum raised to prevent the air from escaping through the nose, you will produce the glottal fricative. This phoneme is called *glottal fricative* because it is articulated at the *glottis*, the space between the vocal folds (also called "vocal cords" and "vocal bands").

This phoneme occurs in English only at the beginning of a syllable, and, while the /h/ is produced, the lips and tongue are in the position of the vowel that follows. Pronounce the words *he*, *had*, and *who* and you will see that the lips and tongue are already in position for the following vowel when the /h/ is uttered. We represent this sound in both IPA and the dictionaries by the symbol /h/.

Precautions

There are two spellings for /h/:

h as in *he*
wh as in *who*

Not every word that is spelled with the letter *h* contains the /h/ phoneme. Some words preserve the silent *h* of their French origin. Pronounce these words out loud, remembering that the *h* letter is silent:

heir	heirloom
hour	hourly
honor	honorable
honest	honesty

There are some words spelled with the letter *h* that some speakers of the Standard Dialect pronounce with /h/, whereas other speakers of the Standard Dialect do not. Either pronunciation, therefore, is "standard." Here are three such words:

herb homage humble

In the middle of words, the spelling *h* is silent if it begins an unstressed syllable, but it is sometimes pronounced /h/ if it begins a stressed syllable. The *h* in *prohibit*, for example, is pronounced because it starts the stressed syllable of the word. The *h* in *prohibition*, however, is not pronounced because it starts an unstressed syllable. In some words, the *h* is silent even though it is the stressed syllable on which the *h* spelling occurs. Note the lack of /h/ in *exhibit*, *exhaust*, *exhaustion*, *exhilarant*, *exhilarate*, and *exhort*.

When the unstressed form of a form word beginning with /h/ occurs in the middle or at the end of a phrase, the /h/ is often omitted. This omission, especially in conversational speech, should not be considered nonstandard. Read the following phrases out loud—as you would say them in conversation. Each time, check to hear if you pronounce the /h/ or not:

I told her.
How could he do it?
I found her weakness.
That's his job.
Where have they gone?
It has not been finished.
We had gone by then.
We forgave him.

The /h/ phoneme never occurs at the end of a syllable. The *h* letter at the end of a written word or syllable is silent. Pronounce these examples out loud:

Ah!	Oh!
Allah	blah
Torah	Shah
hutzpah	Sikh
pariah	matzoh
huzzah	hurrah
hallelujah	Hanukkah

Problems

There are two problems associated with the /h/ phoneme. As we examine each of these problems, check to see if you have that problem with this phoneme.

Problem 1: Omission

In some areas of the United States (especially in metropolitan New York) the /h/ is omitted by most speakers in words beginning with

/hju/ (hyōō), such as *hue* and *human*. Even cultivated speakers make homophones (words that sound alike) of *hue* and *you* and of *human* and *Youman*. In most of the United States, however, the omission of /h/ in such words is considered nonstandard and should be avoided. As you pronounce these words aloud, check to be sure you pronounce them with /h/, not with /j/ (y):

hue	human	Hume
huge	humane	humid
Hugh	humanism	humidity
Hugo	humanity	humiliate
Huguenot	Houston	humility
humor	humorous	humorist

Be careful not to omit the /h/ in the middle of words, and be especially wary of an /h/ after consonants in the middle of words. Pronounce the following examples out loud, and check for omission of /h/:

inhuman	inhumane	unhealthy
exhale	exhalant	exhaling
unholy	unhappy	unhurried
withhold	withheld	bathhouse
mishap	dishearten	disharmony
inhale	inhabit	inhibit
somehow	perhaps	behind

If you come from one of the English-speaking islands of the Caribbean or your first language is French, you may be likely to omit the /h/—especially at the beginning of words. Pronounce these pairs of words aloud, and check for the omission of the /h/:

Without /h/	With /h/	Without /h/	With /h/
add	had	ear	hear
arm	harm	is	his
art	heart	it	hit
at	hat	ill	hill
eat	heat	ohm	home
Ed	head	old	hold
edge	hedge	Ollie	holly
Earl	hurl	earn	Hearn

Problem 2: Overaspiration

This problem is not very common, but we include it for the sake of completeness. If you push too much air through on the /h/ sound, your speech will sound breathy. Move off the /h/ quickly and on to the next vowel. Do not huff and puff too forcefully on the /h/ phoneme.

Pragmatics

Reinforcement Exercises

Practice Words for /h/

Without /h/	**With /h/**	**Without /h/**	**With /h/**
eel	heal	ate	hate
E	he	ale	hail
Ow!	how	and	hand
I	high	airy	Harry
Eld	held	id	hid
I'd	hide	oil	Hoyle
asp	hasp	as	has
ease	he's	errs	hers
Evans	heavens	aced	haste
iced	heist	el	hell
air	hair	act	hacked
ooze	who's	anchor	hanker
us	Huss	Ott	hot
and some	handsome	Ought he?	haughty

Practice Sentences for /h/

1. The halfback was late getting back to the huddle.
2. Henry thinks humility is his greatest virtue.
3. How many wives did Henry the Eighth behead?
4. Behold I show you a great mystery: how he passed the exam.
5. She's inhuman; she wants to get ahead.
6. My huge debts keep me humble.
7. Such habitual behavior must be inherited.
8. The whole audience withheld applause—to humiliate him.
9. The house is totally unheated.
10. Anyhow, he's very unhappy in an unhealthy relationship.
11. Hugh has no sense of humor—just a huge ego.
12. Hospital rates are higher than those of most hotels.
13. The heat and humidity have taken their toll on my heart.
14. Once you get behind, it's hard to catch up.
15. I heard that Henry is back home from the hospital. He's bankrupt.

6

Sibilants

Sibilants are a group of hissing speech sounds. There are six of them in English. Most of the textbooks in voice and diction do not group them together, but there are several reasons for doing so.

Most textbooks group consonants on the basis of their emission, so all fricatives are studied as a group—including four of the sibilant sounds. Then they present affricates as a separate category for study. From a purely theoretical, phonetic point of view, that makes perfectly good sense. From an operational and clinical point of view, however, we believe our approach more practical.

The six sibilant consonant phonemes come from two phonetic categories—fricatives and affricates. Four of these sounds are classified as fricatives, and two are classified as affricates. The four fricative sibilants are single sounds, while each affricate is two inseparable sounds combined into one phoneme. (Phonetically, that is what affricates are—a consonant combination composed of a stop and a fricative.)

We are examining the six sibilants together for two reasons:(1) they are related in production, and (2) they are related in problems. It is easier to teach (and to learn) them together, and it is easier to solve the related problems together.

The six sibilants are the /s/, /z/, /ʃ/ (sh), /ʒ/ (zh), /tʃ/ (ch), and /dʒ/ (j). They are grouped into three pairs of cognates. Let's look at them, pair by pair.

/s/ and /z/

Principles

Production

If you raise the velum so no air comes out through the nose, line up your front upper and lower teeth, lightly touch the tongue tip against the lower or near the upper gum ridge, and shoot the air stream out of the grooved tongue over the tongue tip and between the front teeth, you will produce a lingua-alveolar fricative. We know that is a long sentence, because the number of necessary movements makes a long list; perhaps you had better read it again—a couple of times.

There are two lingua-alveolar (tongue and gum ridge) fricatives in English. One is voiceless and is represented in both IPA and the dictionaries by /s/. The other is voiced and is represented in both IPA and the dictionaries by /z/. These two consonants are our first pair of sibilant cognates. Both are hissing sounds—one without and one with vocal vibration.

If you read that first sentence in this section on production carefully, you noticed that the tongue tip can go to one of two places to make these sounds. Most people articulate these consonants with the tongue tip under the alveolar ridge (and, therefore, somewhat in back of the upper front teeth). When the /s/ is blended with other sounds that are made on the alveolar ridge (the upper gum ridge), the /s/ is made in the upper position—by all speakers.

Precautions

There are seven spellings for /s/:

s as in *so*
sc as in *science*
sch as in *schism*
ss as in *pass*
c as in *cent*
ce as in *lace*
se as in *case*

There are seven spellings for /z/:

z as in *zero*
zz as in *buzzer*

ze as in *prize*
s as in *easy*
se as in *rise*
ss as in *scissors*
x as in *Xerox*

The difference between /s/ and /z/ can sometimes distinguish one word from another and indicate how the word is used in a sentence. In those cases, the word ending with /s/ is a noun (or occasionally an adjective), and the word ending with /z/ is a verb. Here are several pairs of words. The words in the left column are nouns (*close* is the only adjective); the words in the right column are verbs. Pronounce these pairs of words out loud, checking to be sure you make the distinction. (Also note that spelling is no guide. The words in a pair may be spelled differently—or exactly alike.)

Ending in /s/	Ending in /z/
advice	advise
device	devise
use	use
abuse	abuse
misuse	misuse
excuse	excuse
close	close
house	house

Problems

The sounds /s/ and /z/ are high-frequency noises (all the sibilants, you remember, are hissing sounds) and are not too pleasant at best. Distortions of these sounds, known as lisps, are common and quite noticeable. The /s/ should be short and sharp (but not whistled), and the /z/ should be voiced and correctly articulated.

Although there are a number of other distortions of these sounds, there are seven problems that are most common. As we look at each of these these deviations, check to see if you have that problem with these sounds.

▶ *Problem 1:* Lingual protrusion lisp

The name of this distortion tells you exactly what it is. The tongue is thrust out between the teeth so that these sibilants resemble the /θ/ (th) and /ð/ (*th*) sounds. This problem is the one commonly thought of as "the lisp." If you have a lingual protrusion lisp, you will have to work to replace your present habit with conventional placement of the tongue. *Sing* should not sound like *thing*. As you pronounce these pairs of words, check to be sure the tongue tip is up near the alveolar ridge on the /s/ and /z/, while the tongue blade is at the bottom of the upper teeth for the /θ/ (th) and /ð/ (*th*).

/s/	**/θ/ (th)**
sick	thick
sing	thing
sin	thin
sink	think
sank	thank
sought	thought
saw	thaw
some	thumb
seem	theme
sigh	thigh

/z/	**/ð/ (th)**
Z	thee
Zen	then
(Auld Lang) Syne	thine

▶ *Problem 2:* Dental Lisp

The dental lisp results from incorrect placement of the tongue tip on the teeth. If you have discovered that you tend to dentalize the alveolar consonants /t/, /d/, /l/, and /n/, check to see if you also dentalize the /s/ and /z/. If you do place the tongue on the teeth when making these sounds, the /s/ and /z/ will be distorted.

▶ *Problem 3:* Lateral emission lisp

The lateral emission lisp is that deviation of /s/ and /z/ on which the air stream comes over the sides of the tongue rather than through the center over the tongue tip. (You football players—and fans—know what lateral means. The pass goes to the side, rather than forward. The lateral emission is similar. The air comes out of the sides of the mouth, rather than over the top of the tongue and out the front of the mouth.) This problem may result from the tongue lying flat in the mouth—ungrooved and unpointed. This problem can also be the result of pointing the tongue (tip or blade) up toward the alveolar ridge and failing to tense the sides of the tongue against the sides of the hard palate or against the inner surfaces of the side teeth. The air, therefore, escapes over the sides of the tongue, similar to the production of a correct /l/ sound.

To correct this distortion:

(1) tense the tongue as you place it in either position to make the /s/ or /z/ (remember we said you can make these sounds in two places);

(2) line up the front upper and lower teeth to help you in focusing the breath over the top of the tongue tip and out through the center of the mouth; and

(3) seal off the air on each side with the sides of the tongue. (To do this, you must tighten the inside of the mouth. See the ''helpful trick'' on p. 145.)

If you have difficulty getting the proper amount of tension and preventing the air from coming out over the sides of the tongue, try this: Use the ''helpful trick'' to get the air coming out over the top of the tongue and through the center of the mouth on /tʃ/ (ch). Then try to get the air shooting out only through the center on /ts/. *Then* try to get the air coming out the same place on /s/. *Finally* try to get the air coming out the center on /z/.

See if this progression (read across the page) works for you:

/tʃ/ (ch)	**/ts/**	**/s/**
match	mats	mass
hitch	hits	hiss
catch	cats	Cass
peach	Pete's	peace
much	mutts	muss
hutch	huts	Huss
patch	pats	pass
ouch	outs	house
coach	coats	Cos

▶ *Problem 4:* Whistling (or high-frequency) lisp

As we noted earlier, the sibilants are high-frequency sounds, but the /s/ and /z/ should not ''whistle.'' Usually this deviation results from *too much* tension of the tongue. It may be that, as you attempt to position the tongue correctly, you make it too tense. Just relaxing the tongue slightly may correct the whistling distortion.

If you make the sounds on the upper ridge, it may be that you are pulling the tongue too far back in the mouth. If so, pull the tongue up a little closer to the teeth (but not on them) to correct this distortion. If you make the sound on the bottom ridge, your tongue tip may be too high—that is, too near the lower teeth. If so, lower the tongue slightly to correct this deviation.

Problem 5: The overaspirated /s/

The overaspirated /s/ results from pushing too much air through on the sound and from prolonging the sound, if you ssssssee what we mean. Of course, /z/ should be given its proper duration in the final position in a word, but /s/ is never a long sound. Move on to the sound that follows. In a phrase such as "The grass is green," for example, you should practice *the-gra-siz-green*, getting off the /s/ quickly and getting on to the next sound.

Problem 6: Lack of adequate aspiration and friction

Although some speakers push too much air through on these sounds—especially the /s/ and, thus, produce overaspirated sounds, other speakers fail to emit enough air on the sounds. The sounds then not only lack friction, they are almost inaudible. If this is your problem, work for adequate tension of the tongue and adequate air pressure.

Problem 7: Unvoicing of the /z/

Although the /z/ will be slightly devoiced before voiceless sounds and as the last sound in a phrase, it should not be completely *unvoiced*. Even at the end of a sentence, *his* should not sound like *hiss*, *fleas* like *fleece*, *pays* like *pace*, or *cards* like *carts*. Pronounce the following examples out loud to check for unvoicing of the final /z/:

I broke two ribs.	(not *rips!*)
My attention lags.	(not *lacks!*)
There are two beds.	(not *bets!*)
Cheating never pays.	(not *pace!*)
They're my wards.	(not *warts!*)
We may lose.	(not *loose!*)
My cat purrs.	(not *purse!*)
Pass the peas.	(not *peace!*)

Pragmatics

Review the instructions on producing the /s/ and /z/. Proper placement and proper tension is essential.

Readiness Exercises

To get ready for your /s/ and /z/ exercises, practice the /n/, /l/, /d/, /t/ exercises (on pp. 71-72) again. These exercises get you used to pointing the tongue tip and to lifting the tongue to the alveolar ridge.

Since the /s/ and /z/ are made with the tongue just under the alveolar ridge, they should be easier to produce right after a /t/ or /d/ (correctly made). Read these phrases aloud, being sure to touch the tongue tip to the alveolar ridge for /t/ and /d/ and dropping the tongue slightly from that position for /s/ and /z/.

/t/ - /s/	**/d/ - /z/**
Eat some.	sad zebra
hot cereal	dead zombie
not safe	mad czar
neat scene	odd zest
cute seal	red zone
not sick	add zinnias
quite sane	lead zipper
but secret	found zero
fit several	find zinc
right side	old zoo
what city	bad zucchini
bet six	rude zealot

Reinforcement Exercises

Practice Words for /s/ and /z/

Beginning		**Middle**		**End**	
/s/	**/z/**	**/s/**	**/z/**	**/s/**	**/z/**
see	Z	racing	razing	cease	seize
sip	zip	busing	buzzing	price	prize
sink	zinc	looser	loser	lice	lies
seal	zeal	racer	razor	race	raise
sap	zap	lacy	lazy	lace	lays
said	Zed	prices	prizes	loose	lose
sown	zone	re-sort	resort	false	falls
Sue	zoo	devices	devises	mace	maze
sane	Zane	lacer	laser	once	ones

/s/

Beginning	**Middle**	**End**
seal	sealing	lease
safe	safer	face
sap	sapping	pass
sail	assail	lace
sell	lesson	less
sign	nicer	nice
set	Tesser	Tess

Beginning	**Middle**	**End**
sum	mussing	muss
sake	casing	case
seep	piecing	piece
sigh	icing	ice
sub	bussing	bus
sob	bossing	boss
sought	tossing	toss

/z/

End	**Middle**
ease	easy
is	busy
days/daze	daisy
raise/raze	razor
buzz	buzzing
muse	music
freeze	freezer
wise	wiser
cruise	cruiser
noise	noisy
tease	teasing
haze	hazy
rise	rising
use (v.)	using
nose/knows	nosy

Remembering to articulate the alveolar stops with a firm tongue tip on the gum ridge and to give the /s/ no more duration than you give to /t/ and /d/, read the following word sequences aloud:

/d/	**/t/**	**/st/**
deem	team	steam
deal	teal	steal
Dick	tick	stick
dale	tale	stale
dead	Ted	stead
dill	till	still
Dan	tan	Stan
dear	tear	steer
dub	tub	stub
die	tie	sty
dough	toe	stow
dock	tock	stock
doubt	tout	stout

/d/	/t/	/st/
do	to	stew
date	Tate	state
duck	tuck	stuck

We want you to shoot a thin stream of air over the center line of the tongue tip on the /s/. Because the tongue tip is sharply pointed for the /t/, made on the alveolar ridge, and because the /s/ shoots the air out over the tip just under the alveolar ridge, we can work for a tight, forward-focused, brief /s/ in these pairs of words:

/st/	/s/	/st/	/s/
stead	said	store	sore
steed	seed	steep	seep
steal	seal	stag	sag
stick	sick	stuck	suck
stale	sale	stoop	soup
steak	sake	stir	sir
steam	seem	stone	sown
sting	sing	stay	say
stand	sand	stole	soul
stage	sage	still	sill

If you have a problem with lateral emission of the air, practice reading these sequences (reading across). Refer back to p. 125 for a review of suggestions to correct this problem.

/t/	/st/	/s/
team	steam	seem
tear (n.)	steer	seer
tick	stick	sick
Ted	stead	said
take	steak	sake
to	stew	sue
tanned	stand	sand
tow	stow	sow
tie	sty	sigh
tougher	stuffer	suffer
tag	stag	sag
tore	store	sore
top	stop	sop
tone	stone	sown
tock	stock	sock
tinker	stinker	sinker
tack	stack	sack
teal	steal	seal

The /s/ occurs at the beginning of words blended with several other consonants. Here are some pairs of words, contrasting initial /s/ alone with initial /s/ blends. (If you have difficulty with a lateral lisp, do not practice the /sl/ blend words until you have received instructions and assistance from your instructor.

/sn/	**/s/**	**/sn/**	**/s/**
snap	sap	snoop	soup
snake	sake	snow	sew
sneak	seek	sneeze	seize
snail	sail	sneer	sear
snack	sack	snore	sore
snob	sob	snoot	suit
snag	sag	snub	sub
snip	sip	snicker	sicker

/sm/	**/s/**	**/sm/**	**/s/**
smear	seer	smock	sock
smite	site/cite	Smuckers	suckers
smack	sack	smooth	soothe
smell	sell	smoke	soak
smash	sash	smirch	search

/sk/	**/s/**	**/sk/**	**/s/**
ski	see	scale	sail/sale
scheme	seem	skin	sin
skit	sit	skip	sip
scandal	sandal	skeptic	septic
scanned	sand	scope	soap
scold	sold	score	sore
sky	sigh	skunk	sunk
scoop	soup	scoot	suit

/sp/	**/s/**	**/sp/**	**/s/**
speak	seek	spank	sank
speed	seed	spine	sign
spear	sear	spun	sun
spell	sell	spur	sir
sped	said	spite	site/cite
spent	sent/cent	spoke	soak
spend	send	spoon	soon
spin	sin	spill	sill

/sw/	/s/	/sw/	/s/
sweet	seat	swell	sell
Swede	seed/cede	swam	Sam
sweep	seep	swank	sank
swing	sing	swab	sob
swift	sift	swore	sore
sway	say	swung	sung
sweat	set	swerve	serve

/sl/	/s/	/sl/	/s/
sleek	seek	slat	sat
sleet	seat	slack	sack
sleep	seep	slam	Sam
slick	sick	slash	sash
sling	sing	slew	sue
slip	sip	sly	sigh
slay	say	slide	side
slave	save	slum	sum
slain	sane	slow	sew
sled	said	slop	sop

Now try these sequences. Work to get a good /s/, not a /ʃ/ (sh).

/r/	/tr/	/str/
rip	trip	strip
rate	trait	straight
ricked	tricked	strict
ray	tray	stray
rain	train	strain
rap	trap	strap
rue	true	strew
ride	tried	stride
ripe	tripe	stripe
roll	troll	stroll
raid	trade	strayed
ruck	truck	struck

Practice Phrases for /s/ and /z/

easy to say
examine the ceiling
freezing in the blizzard
an unseen guest
sailing to Brazil
a single cause
a second example

Practice Phrases for /s/ and /z/

a crazy circus
accept the results
a success or a disaster
refusing to discuss it
amazing system
using all his senses
some noise at the ceremony
passing Zoology (Be careful! No *zoo* here!)

Practice Sentences for /s/ and /z/

1. Stop, look, and listen!
2. Of course, it's all the same to me.
3. It isn't the same thing.
4. I said I was sorry. Isn't that enough?
5. I refuse to admit I'm clumsy; I just have no sense of balance.
6. Spring is his favorite season.
7. Many of us have strong feelings about civil liberties.
8. Saints are totally unselfish—and not by design!
9. I refuse to concede she is crazy.
10. Star light, star bright; First star I've seen tonight.
11. His sermons are sometimes inspiring.
12. Save me a slice of his prize-winning pie.
13. Who says that crime never pays?
14. He sees his duty and does it.
15. The fanciest blazers were on sale.

Practice Sentences for /s/ and /z/ (More Challenging)

1. Some days he rides a bus to school.
2. Suzie was carried into the hospital on a stretcher.
3. Select ties that express your personality and moods.
4. Why did you disclose that Susan works for the CIA?
5. At the zenith of his career, he's still miserable!
6. If he's working on a Ph.D., he's dying by degrees.
7. Her husband is always present when she performs.
8. It takes me all week to read the Sunday *New York Times*.
9. Please select your purchase. The store is closing.
10. I have chosen to standardize our procedures.

Practice Sentences for /s/ and /z/ (Most Challenging)

1. To tremendous applause, he certainly performed mysterious tricks with those cards.
2. Sonia believes there's no difference between the sacred and the secular.
3. There can be no excuses for the constant wisecracks and outrageous lies.
4. According to the newspaper, the audience liked the last scene best of all.
5. Ozzie is afraid of snakes—and not just poisonous ones.
6. Aside from my zest for life and my zeal for good causes, I have no interest in anything.
7. Unless I am prosecuted for a serious crime, I will not resign.
8. What secrets I could discover if I were invisible for just a few days!
9. There was absolutely no sentiment to pass a strongly worded resolution.
10. He considers the Zodiac watching of the astrologers unscientific.

Principles

Production

If you raise the velum so no air can escape up through the nose, round the lips slightly, line up the front upper and lower teeth, place the front of the tongue blade either near the back of the alveolar ridge or behind the lower gum ridge, press the sides of the tongue against the sides of the hard palate or against the inner surfaces of the side teeth, and shoot the air stream out of the grooved tongue over the center of the front of the tongue blade and between the teeth, you will produce a lingua-post alveolar fricative. Because that sentence is a paragraph long, and because each of those movements is important to the production of these two phonemes, you should read that sentence again—a few times.

There are two lingua-post alveolar fricatives in English. One is voiceless; it is the consonant in the middle of *assure*. It is represented in IPA by /ʃ/ and in the dictionaries by sh. The other lingua-post alveolar fricative is voiced; it is the consonant in the middle of *azure*. It is represented in IPA by /ʒ/ and in the dictionaries by zh.

There are several differences between the production of these two sibilants and the production of /s/ and /z/. Although these sounds are also hissing noises and are in the sibilant family of speech sounds, they do differ from /s/ and /z/ in several respects. Note these differences:

(1) The lips are usually spread for /s/ and /z/; they are slightly rounded (pursed) for /ʃ/ (sh) and /ʒ/ (zh).

(2) The air stream is shot out over the tongue tip on /s/ and /z/ but comes over the front of the tongue on /ʃ/ (sh) and /ʒ/ (zh).

(3) The groove of the tongue is wider on /ʃ/ (sh) and /ʒ/ (zh) than on /s/ and /z/.

(4) The entire tongue is pulled farther back on /ʃ/ (sh) and /ʒ/ (zh) than on /s/ and /z/.

Precautions

There are at least fifteen (count them, fifteen!) spellings for /ʃ/ (sh):

ce as in *ocean*
ch as in *chic*
chsi as in *fuchsia*
ci as in *vicious*
s as in *sure*
sc as in *Fascist*
sch as in *Scheherazade*
sci as in *conscious*
sh as in *shine*
shi as in *fashion*
si as in *pension*
ss as in *tissue*
ssi as in *passion*
ti as in *lotion*
psh as in *pshaw*

There are seven spellings for /ʒ/ (zh):

g as in *protege*
ge as in *corsage*
j as in *bijou*
s as in *pleasure*
si as in *evasion*
z as in *seizure*
zi as in *glazier*

The /ʃ/ (sh) phoneme can occur at the beginning, in the middle, and at the ends of English words.

The /ʒ/ (zh) phoneme generally occurs only in the middle and at the end of English words.

On a few words we have borrowed from the French we have kept the French pronunciation and thus start the word with /ʒ/ (zh).Note these borrowed words with /ʒ/ (zh) preserved at the beginning:

jabot
genre
gendarme

Persons' names that begin with this sound in French are also pronounced with /ʒ/ (zh) in English. Note these examples:

Gide Genet Giraud Jacques Jeanne d'Arc

Problems

Problem 1: Dentalization

If you dentalize the /s/ and /z/ sounds, it is likely you will also make the /ʃ/ (sh) and /ʒ/ (zh) with the tongue touching the front teeth. Placing the front of the tongue on the teeth will distort these sounds. Correct tongue placement (with the front of the tongue in back of the gum ridge—whichever one you use, upper or lower) is essential to production of conventional sounding /ʃ/ (sh) and /ʒ/ (zh). Pronounce the following words and check to be sure the tongue is not on the teeth, not touching the teeth at all as you produce these two sibilants.

/ʃ/ (sh)	/ʒ/ (zh)
shield	leisure
Shah (of Iran?)	Zsa Zsa (Gabor, of course)
ship	genre

Problem 2: Lateral omission

We told you earlier that we are studying the sibilants together because they have related problems. If you have lateral emission on /s/ and /z/, it is very likely that you will also have that problem with the other sibilants.

When there is lateral emission (on English phonemes other than /l/), the air comes out over the sides of the tongue—and it shouldn't. In the case of the sibilants, the air should come out of the center of the mouth—not out of the two sides. Check your pronunciation of the following phrases to see if the air is coming out of the sides of the mouth on the /ʃ/ (sh) and /ʒ/ (zh):

What's the rush?	I am under a barrage!
I'm very cautious.	This job has no prestige.
What is Tom's mission?	I found a treasure.
Success is crucial.	I'm going to Asia.

Problem 3: Unvoicing of the /ʒ/ (zh)

The /ʒ/ (zh) will be slightly devoiced when it comes before voiceless sounds or is the last sound in a phrase. But it should not be totally unvoiced. If you tend to unvoice voiced consonants, you should check to be certain you do not unvoice /ʒ/ (zh). *Vision* should not rhyme with *fission*, and *mirage* should not rhyme with *Dear Osh*.

Pragmatics

Readiness Exercises

First practice the alveolar sounds (/n/, /l/, /d/, /t/). See p. 72.
Then practice the relevant /s/ and /z/ exercises. See pp. 126-131.

Reinforcement Exercises

Practice Words for /ʃ/ (sh) and /ʒ/(zh)

/ʃ/ (sh)

Beginning	Middle	End
she	unleashing	leash
chic	machine	quiche
sheen	polishing	polish
shield	windshield	perish
ship	warship	push
shift	fishing	fish
shin	furnishing	finish
sheer	wishful	wish
shave	unshaven	flesh
shame	ashamed	blush
shape	crochet	mesh
chef	dishes	dish
shelter	refreshing	refresh
shell	bombshell	demolish
shed	bloodshed	foolish
sham	passion	mash
shack	cashier	cash

shall	lashes	lash
shag	gashes	gash
shaft	crankshaft	trash
shadow	foreshadow	dash
shallow	caution	crash
sharp	washing	wash
shine	sunshine	brush
shrimp	ocean	lush
sure	insurance	rush
should	pushcart	push
shellac	brushing	varnish
chandelier	smashing	smash
chauffeur	facial	mustache

/ʒ/ (zh)

Middle	End
regime	prestige
vision	mirage
invasion	sabotage
confusion	camouflage
occasion	corsage
usual	garage
casual	beige
pleasure	massage
leisure	rouge
explosion	barrage

Initial /s/ and /ʃ/ (sh) Contrast

/s/	/ʃ/(sh)	/s/	/ʃ/(sh)
see	she	sell	shell
seek	chic	self	shelf
seat	sheet	sack	shack
seen	sheen	sag	shag
sealed	shield	sank	shank
seep	sheep	sad	shad
sin	shin	Sam	sham
sip	ship	sock	shock
sift	shift	sort	short
single	shingle	sew	show
simmer	shimmer	sown	shown
sake	shake	soul	shoal
same	shame	sue	shoe
save	shave	suit	shoot
said	shed	suck	shuck

/s/	/ʃ/ (sh)	/s/	/ʃ/ (sh)
sun	shun	subtle	shuttle
Sir Locke	Sherlock	sigh	shy

Final /s/ and /ʃ/ (sh) Contrast

/s/	/ʃ/ (sh)	/s/	/ʃ/ (sh)
lease	leash	Swiss	swish
mess	mesh	crass	crash
brass	brash	gas	gash
class	clash	mass	mash
puss	push	Russ	rush
Gus	gush	plus	plush
muss	mush	lass	lash

Final /z/ and /ʒ/ (zh) Contrast

/z/	/ʒ/ (zh)
bays	beige
ruse	rouge

Practice Phrases for /ʃ/ (sh) and /ʒ/ (zh)

national treasure
measure my share
shopping for a corsage
a vanishing illusion
additional leisure
foolish conclusions
a casual introduction
pushing for a decision
shedding their camouflage
an Asian education
a washing machine
a short television commercial
no closure in the discussion
an occupation with prestige
an explosion in the garage

Practice Sentences for /ʃ/ (sh) and /ʒ/(zh)

1. She never seems to agree with my decisions.
2. I'm going to the garage to have the car washed.
3. Will you show us where the treasure is hidden?
4. Harsh punishments are usually reserved for felons.
5. Failure of this operation would damage my prestige.

6. "Minds are like parachutes; they function only when open." —Harry Emerson Fosdick
7. Occasionally he comes with his entire entourage.
8. Are you sure you it's a genuine Persian rug?
9. How do you measure depth of devotion?
10. The dinner was delicious, as usual.
11. There was great confusion at the last session.
12. The anesthesia left the patient in fair condition.
13. The shaky regime could not stand derision.
14. Occasionally we need to go in a fresh direction.
15. I wish I had more leisure time.

Practice Sentences for /ʃ/ (sh) and /ʒ/ (zh) (More Challenging)

1. I was shocked at the shoddy workmanship of the negligee.
2. There are blushes in profusion, but she feels no shame.
3. We should be free from unreasonable search and seizure.
4. Without evasion, I assure you I will not shirk my duty.
5. His version of the event is full of deception.
6. Sharlene may be shy, but she's not ready for seclusion!
7. The corsage complemented the gown, which was beige.
8. Such intrusions usually get a lot of attention.
9. We offered to provide the professor with some new illustrations and allusions.
10. Candidates' evasion of the issues is shameful.

Practice Sentences for /ʃ/ (sh) and /ʒ/ (zh) (Most Challenging)

1. I'm anxious to know the neighbors' reaction to the new massage parlor.
2. Charlotte says her new washing machine makes washing a pleasure.
3. After she claimed to have had a vision, the neighbors made her garage a shrine.
4. She kept her composure and showed no emotion when I told her about my fetish.
5. Sheila took an excursion that included visits to glaciers.
6. Why this conviction he has amnesia? His memory was always atrocious.
7. I did not envision so many confessions in a two-page composition!

8. Because he deducted contributions to controversial social clubs, he was accused of tax evasion.
9. Although everyone suspects sabotage, the commission has issued no official report.
10. He escaped the explosion with minor abrasions, but he appears to be shellshocked.

/tʃ/ and /dʒ/

The last two sibilants in English are not fricatives, but *affricates*. So, before we look at this pair of cognates, we should discuss what affricates are.

An *affricate* is, phonetically, a combination of two consonants—a stop and a fricative. /tʃ/ (ch) and /dʒ/ (j) are affricates phonetically, but phonemically they are single phonemes. In other words, these affricates function in our language as a single unit, and speakers of English do not think of them as two separate sounds.

Separate and distinct phonemes function individually; they cannot be divided into smaller units. Even though these two affricates require us to make two kinds of movements to produce them, they cannot be divided; they are indivisible. They function as a single unit.

The word *hit* is made up of three phonemes: the initial fricative consonant /h/, the vowel (represented in IPA by /ɪ/ and in the dictionaries by i), and the final stop consonant /t/. We can add another sound /s/ to the word to make it *hits*. Now the syllable ends with a stop and a fricative. But this stop and fricative are separate units; we can take them apart and leave one off. They are, therefore, a combination of two consonants, but not an affricate. They are still two phonemes—not one. But look at the word *hitch*. This word also has three phonemes. The first two are the same ones we had in the word *hit*, but the third one is a different phoneme. The last sound in the word *hitch* is an affricate represented in IPA by /tʃ/ and in the dictionaries by *ch*. You cannot divide that last sound in the same way you could divide /t/ and /s/; it is one sound indivisible!

Look at another example. The word *head* also has three sounds in it: the initial consonant /h/, the vowel (which we represent in IPA by /ɛ/ and in the dictionaries by ĕ), and the final stop /d/. Again you can add another sound to make the word plural: /z/. The word is now spelled *heads*, and the syllable ends with a stop (/d/) and a fricative (/z/). But, clearly, the /d/ and /z/ are separate phonemes and can be divided. Compare the word *heads* with its four phonemes with the word hedge, which has three phonemes. *Hedge* has the same first two sounds as the word *head*, but the last sound is a voiced affricate represented in IPA by /dʒ/ and in the dictionaries by j. It is one sound and cannot be pulled apart into other phonemes.

In summary, then, consonant combinations that combine a stop and a fricative, such as /ts/ and /dz/, are not affricates because each individual sound retains its own identity. Affricates, on the other hand, are articulated as half stop-half fricative, but are perceived as single sounds (phonemes). There are two affricates in English. One is voiceless and is the first and last sound in the word *church*. The other is voiced and is the first and last sound in the word *judge*.

Principles

Production

If you raise the velum to prevent air from escaping through the nose, stop the outgoing air stream by firmly touching the tip of the tongue to the alveolar ridge or the blade of the tongue to the area just in back of the ridge, bring the sides of the tongue into contact with the sides of the palate or the inner surfaces of the back teeth (to prevent the air from escaping over the sides of the tongue), and then drop the tongue tip quickly—shooting the air out the center over the grooved blade of the tongue—you will produce an affricate. As we said, there are two affricates in English: one voiceless, which we represent in IPA by /tʃ/ and in the dictionaries by ch; and one voiced, which we represent in IPA by /dʒ/ and in the dictionaries by *j*.

Perhaps it would have been easier to tell you to produce the voiceless affricate by putting your tongue in the position to form a /t/, making a good firm stop, and releasing the air quickly in a /ʃ/ (sh). Does it work? Actually, that is what we told you before—in slightly more detail. It might also have been easier to follow if we had told you to make the voiced affricate by putting your tongue in the position to form a /d/, making a good firm voiced stop, and then releasing the air in a /ʒ/ (zh).

Precautions

There are eight spellings for /tʃ/ (ch):

c as in *cello*
ch as in *child*
che as in *luncheon*
t as in *factual*
tch as in *catch*

te as in *righteous*
ti as in *question*
tu as in *future*

There are nine spellings for /dʒ/ (j):

d as in *gradual*
dg as in *judgment*
dge as in *lodge*
di as in *soldier*
dj as in *adjective*
g as in *gym*
ge as in *surgeon*
gg as in *exaggerate*
j as in *job*

One other warning: the letters *ch* do not always represent /tʃ/ (ch). Note the words *yacht*, *archangel*, and *Chanukhah*. If you are not sure of their pronunciation, look them up in a good dictionary.

Problems

There are five common problems associated with these two phonemes. As we discuss each deviation, check to see if you have that problem.

▶ ***Problem 1:*** Incomplete closure

As we said before, affricates are single phonemes, but they are composed of a stop and a fricative. All stops must stop. Stop completely. That is just as true when they are part of an affricate phoneme as when they stand alone. Failure to block the air stream completely on the affricates not only distorts the phoneme, it may result in a substitution of a different phoneme.

Whether you learned English first or not, this may be a problem for you. *Watching* should not sound like *washing*, and *ledger* should not be pronounced as a variation of *leisure*.

In the following pairs of words, the first begins with an affricate /tʃ/ (ch), and the second begins with a fricative /ʃ/ (sh). Check to be sure you begin the affricate phoneme with a complete stop. (The first word should not sound like the second one.)

/tʃ/(ch)	/ʃ/	**/tʃ/(ch)**	/ʃ/
chain	Shane	chair	share
cheer	sheer	cheap	sheep
chip	ship	chin	shin

/tʃ/(ch)	/ʃ/	/tʃ/(ch)	/ʃ/
chop	shop	chose	shows
choose	shoes	chore	shore

In the following pairs of words, the first ends in the affricate /tʃ/ (ch), and the second ends in the fricative /ʃ/ (sh). Check to be sure you make the distinction by beginning the affricate with a complete stop of the air stream.

/tʃ/(ch)	/ʃ/(sh)	/tʃ/(ch)	/ʃ/(ch)
catch	cash	crutch	crush
ditch	dish	hutch	hush
Keach	quiche	leech	leash
march	marsh	match	mash
much	mush	witch	wish

In the following pairs of words, the first has the affricate /tʃ/(ch) in the middle, and the second has the fricative /ʃ/ (sh). Check to be sure you make the distinction clear by making a clear, firm stop to begin the affricate.

/tʃ/(ch)	/ʃ/(sh)	/tʃ/(ch)	/ʃ/(sh)
catching	cashing	crutches	crushes
ditches	dishes	roaches	Roche's
marches	marshes	matching	mashing
watching	washing	witches	wishes

We cannot offer you pairs of words to contrast the fricative /ʒ/ (zh) and the affricate /dʒ/ (j). Still, you should pronounce the following words out loud to be certain you make a complete closure at the beginning of the /dʒ/ (j) affricate.

Initial /dʒ/ (j)	Final /dʒ/ (j)
genius	siege
gym	ridge
jade	stage
jet	pledge
jab	badge
job	dodge
junk	grudge
June	huge
germ	purge
jibe	oblige

▶ *Problem 2:* Dentalization

The two affricate consonants should begin with the tongue tip firmly on the gum ridge. If you have found that you have a tendency to dentalize the /t/ and /d/, check to see if you also dentalize the /tʃ/ (ch) and /dʒ/ (j). It is likely that you do. If so, you will have to work to pull the tongue tip back to the alveolar ridge where it belongs for these sounds in American English. Use the preceding /tʃ/ (ch) and /dʒ/ (j) word lists to check for dentalization.

▶ *Problem 3:* Lateral emission

As we have noted before, the affricates belong to the family of high-frequency noises called sibilants. We have already checked to see if you have a lateral emission of /s/ and /z/ (see pp. 124-125) and of /ʃ/ (sh) and /ʒ/ (zh) (see pp. 135-136). If you have a problem of emitting the air over the sides of the tongue on the other four sibilants, it is likely—very likely—that you also have a problem with lateral emission of the air on these two sibilant phonemes. Indeed, in our experience, the problem of lateral emission is, in many people, progressive. By that we mean that it is often worse on /ʃ/ (sh) and /ʒ/ (zh) than on /s/ and /z/ *and* even worse on /tʃ/ (ch) and /dʒ/ (j) than on /ʃ/ (sh) and /ʒ/ zh).

Here are a few phrases. As you read them aloud, check to see if the air is coming out of the sides of the mouth on these two sibilant sounds.

enjoy Chinese food
no chance
join the teenage club
no joke
a hung jury
choosing not to cheat
watch the judge
a chariot on the bridge
George, keep in touch.
jealous of the champion
jump for joy
a real challenge

If you do produce these phonemes with lateral emission of the air, what can be done to correct the problem? How do you produce these sounds correctly? Let's take it step by step. To produce a conventional /tʃ/ (ch):

(1) Place the tongue tip or blade firmly on the alveolar ridge for the /t/ component of this combination consonant.

(2) Purse the lips as for the /ʃ/ (sh).

(3) Tense the tip and sides of the tongue.

(4) Emit the exhaled air with *energy* over the top of the grooved tongue and out the front (center) of the mouth, as you blend the /t/ and /ʃ/ (sh) components into one sound.

Of course, you realize these four steps also apply to the voiced affricate /dʒ/ (j). The difference is that you combine voiced sounds—/d/ and /ʒ/ (zh)—instead of voiceless sounds—/t/ and /ʃ/ (sh). However, we recommend you practice on the voiceless affricate first and master that, because its added aspiration (released air) makes it easier to produce.

NOTE: Sometimes students have difficulty acquiring the skills required in steps 3 and 4. We have found this a "helpful trick":

A. Put an ordinary straw between your lips in the center of your mouth.

B. Blow through the straw for three to four seconds. Be aware of how the inside of your mouth tenses as you push the air through the straw. Do this with your eyes open for tactile stimulation and then with your eyes closed for increased kinesthetic awareness (sensing how it feels).

C. Slowly withdraw the straw as you place the tongue tip on the alveolar ridge to produce the /tʃ/ (ch) sound.

D. Add a tense vowel to the /tʃ/ (ch) consonant as you try the correct production. For example, say:

chew
Choate
chaw (colloquial for *chew*)

These vowels will help you keep adequate tension and also help you round your lips—both of which are needed for correct production of this sibilant.

And now a *challenge*! Your instructor will tell you when to try these words. Read across the page, and check to be sure there is no lateral emission on any of these words.

/tʃ/(ch)	**/ʃ/ (sh)**	**/s/**
chew	shoe	sue
Cho	show	so
chose	shows	sews
chaw	Shaw	saw
chore	shore	sore
choose	shoes	sues
cheat	sheet	seat
chip	ship	sip
chain	Shane	sane
China	shine	sign

▶ *Problem 4:* Unvoicing of dʒ/(j)

Like other voiced sounds, /dʒ/ (j) will be slightly devoiced before voiceless sounds and when final in a phrase. It should not, however, be completely unvoiced. *Ridge* should not become *rich*, *besiege* should not become *beseech*, and *edging* should not become *etching*. If English is the first language you learned and you have this problem, it is a matter of speech habits you have fallen into. If you learned English after learning another language, you may be transferring patterns from your first language into English.

Here are a few pairs. The words ending in the voiced cognate are in the left column. Check to be sure you do not *unvoice* the final sound in those words and make them sound like the words in the right column. Pronounce the pairs aloud:

/dʒ/ (j)	/tʃ/ (ch)
besiege	beseech
liege	leech
ridge	rich
edge	etch
age	H
badge	batch
surge	search
lunge	lunch

If English is not your first language, you may substitute /tʃ/ (ch) for /dʒ/ (j) in the beginning, in the middle, or at the end of a word. Here are a few pairs of words. Check to see if you substitute the voiceless cognate for its voiced partner sound. The first word in each pair contains the *voiced* sound.

Beginning		Middle		End	
/dʒ/(j)	/tʃ/(ch)	/dʒ/(j)	/tʃ/(ch)	/dʒ/(j)	/tʃ/(ch)
jeep	cheap	ledger	lecher	badge	batch
gin	chin	ridges	riches	purge	perch
joke	choke	lunging	lunching	surge	search

▶ *Problem 5:* Substitution of /j/(y) for /dʒ/(j)

If English is not your first language, you may have this problem. Especially if you speak some dialects of Spanish, you may confuse /dʒ/ (j) and /j/ (y) in English. The problem results from an allophone of /j/ (y) in your first language. Although we have heard far more instances where /dʒ/ (j) was substituted for /j/ (y) than the reverse, the confusion *can* result in substitution of /j/ (y) for /dʒ/ (j)—usually at the beginning of a word. New Jersey is not "New Yersey!"

Pronounce the following pairs of words aloud. Check to see if you tend to make them sound alike by using the /j/ (y) at the beginning of both words. To correct this problem, you must review the instructions on producing the /dʒ/ (j). That sound begins with your tongue tip *firmly touching* the upper gum ridge.

/dʒ/ (j)	/j/ (y)	/dʒ/ (j)	(j) (y)
jeer	year	jail	Yale
Jess	yes	jet	yet
gel	yell	Jell-o	yellow
jam	yam	jot	yacht
Joe	yo! (slang for "hello")	jewel	you'll
juice	use	journey	yearn

Pragmatics

Readiness Exercises

Review the instructions on producing /tʃ/ **(ch) and /dʒ/** (j). Proper placement and proper tension are especially crucial.

To get ready for your reinforcement exercises, practice the /n/, /l/, /d/, /t/ exercises (on pp. 71-72). If you have a problem with lateral emission, skip the /l/; use the sequence /n/, /d/, /t/ only. These exercises get you used to pointing the tongue tip and to touching the tongue tip firmly to the alveolar ridge.

Remember /tʃ/ (ch) begins with /t/ and /dʒ/ (j) begins with /d/. For that reason, these readiness exercises may help you get these two sibilants started from the correct position. Read these phrases aloud, being sure to touch the tongue tip to the alveolar ridge for /t/ and /d/. The first word ends in /t/ or /d/ and the second word begins with the appropriate affricate.

/t/—/tʃ/ (ch)	/d/—/dʒ/ (j)
eat cheese	red jeans
not chicken	old gypsy
exact change	add gin
lost checkbook	guard James
fat chance!	made jam
meet Charlie	odd job
quite choppy	wide jaw
hot chocolate	bad joke
not chosen	find Junior
quit choosing it	food junk
What chunk?	toward Japan
cute child	sad journey
What choice?	wood joist

Reinforcement Exercises

Practice Words for /tʃ/ and /dʒ/

Beginning		Middle		End	
/tʃ/(ch)	**/dʒ/j)**	**tʃ/(ch)/**	**/dʒ/(j)**	**/tʃ/(ch)**	**/dʒ/(j)**
cheap	jeep	beseeching	besieging	beseech	besiege
chin	gin	riches	ridges	rich	ridge
chain	Jane	nature	major	H	age
chess	Jess	lecher	ledger	etch	edge
Chan	Jan	batches	badges	match	Madge
char	jar	marches	Marge's	march	Marge
churn	germ	searching	surging	perch	purge
chug	jug	lunches	lunges	lunch	lunge

Practice Phrases for /tʃ/ (ch) and /dʒ/ (j)

watch this jump
a cheap gemstone
allergic to chocolate
charming jewelry
journey to an old church
a major question
a cordial exchange
teaching journalism
just chowder for lunch
suggest a change
ketchup on his jeans
actually very gentle
munching on cabbage
catching the practical jokers

Practice Sentences for /tʃ/ (ch) and /dʒ/ (j)

1. Change it. This Jell-o is yellow.
2. It takes no courage to cheat.
3. Hitchhiking is dangerous. Why take a chance?
4. His championship was in the broad jump.
5. I chose the wrong package.
6. I enjoyed watching the agile performer.
7. He "got it off his chest," but still went to jail.
8. Mrs. Graham loved individuals—not people in bunches.
9. Revenge may be sweet, but it is hard to achieve.
10. Knowledge is power; there is no future in ignorance.

Practice Sentences for /tʃ/ (ch) and /dʒ/ (j) (More Challenging)

1. I am enraged over the media coverage of the speeches.
2. The cheering section was slow to catch on. They jumped to conclusions.
3. His advantage is that he is beyond reproach.
4. Why do you question the motives for his generosity?
5. Actually, Joyce is always punctual.
6. The preacher left one church and joined another.
7. The judge lectured about justice and injustice.
8. I'm reading literature about our cultural heritage.
9. Except for one chair, there is no furniture in the cottage.
10. The church has always been a place of sanctuary and refuge.

Practice Sentence for /tʃ/ (ch) and /dʒ/ (j) (Most Challenging)

1. It's all conjecture. Don't encourage him!
2. "What a collection of intellectual midgets!" the sergeant said.
3. Such changeability is totally unjustified at this juncture.
4. The merchants are providing sandwiches for every passenger on the voyage.
5. Riding is more dangerous for the jockey than for the ranchhand.
6. The judicial system must be adjusted to deal with court congestion.
7. My furniture is in storage in New Jersey.
8. My next venture is planting an orchard in the pasture—if the neighbors don't object.
9. Teach children about right and wrong, and you will see tangible results when they are teenagers.
10. I am no stranger to joy, but my search for rapture is ineffectual.

7

Nasals

There are three nasal consonants in English. All the other phonemes of the language are made with the velum raised so the air cannot escape up through the nose. On these three sounds, however, the velum is lowered. The outgoing air, therefore, is emitted through and resonated in the nose.

All three of the nasals are articulated by blocking the air stream at some point in the mouth. They differ in the amount of oral (mouth) resonance they have because all three use all of the nose for resonance. Each of the nasal consonants (unlike French, there are no nasal vowels in English) is articulated at the place of articulation of one of the pairs of stops. The bilabial /m/ is articulated by the two lips, as are /p/ and /b/; the lingua-alveolar /n/ is articulated with the tip of the tongue on the gum ridge, as are /t/ and /d/; and the lingua-velar /ŋ/ (dictionaries use ng to represent this sound) is articulated with the back of the tongue against the soft palate, as are /k/ and /g/.

The nasal sounds have great resonance when articulated properly. For this reason, they have great carrying power (sonority). Indeed, they have so much carrying power that some final syllables have no vowel at all, and the final nasal sound carries the syllable (provides the sonority for the syllable). When this occurs, the nasal sound is called *syllabic m*, *syllabic n*, or *syllabic ng*. The nasals are humming sounds, and they should be given ample nasal resonance. Lightly touch your thumb and first finger to each side of your nose while you make each of the three nasal sounds. You should be able to feel good reverberation on these sounds.

/m/

Principles

Production

By closing the two lips, as you would to make /p/ and /b/, you make /m/, *a voiced bilabial nasal*. But, instead of stopping the air completely as you do to form /p/ and /b/, you lower the velum so the air can pass out through the nasal passages. The vocal folds vibrate, and the vibrated air is resonated in the whole mouth and the nose. You should get good resonance on this humming sound.

Precautions

There are six spellings for /m/:

m as in *me*
mm as in *hammer*
gm as in *phlegm*
lm as in *palm*
mb as in *limb*
mn as in *autumn*

Problems

There are six common problems associated with the production of the /m/ phoneme. As we look at each of these problems, check to see if you have that problem with this sound.

► *Problem 1:* Denasality

If you do not get enough nasal resonance on the nasal sounds, you have the problem of *denasality*. We have only three nasal sounds in English, and they should be hummed through the nose. Denasality (the lack of adequate nasal resonance) is a cold-in-the-head quality. It may result from colds, adenoids, or some other obstruction of the nasal resonator—or from faulty speech habits. The nasals are long, resonant, humming, continuant (sounds that, unlike stops, can be sustained) consonants. Full nasal resonance is necessary for brilliant tone and good projection. If you have a problem with denasality, you should consult a physician and a speech therapist. On your own, you can work to give adequate duration (as explained below, nasals are two-beat sounds) and full resonance in the nose on the /m/. If possible, tape record your pronunciation of the following words. When you play the tape back, listen to be sure the /m/ sounds do not sound like /p/ or /b/.

my	(not pie or buy)
mare	(not pear or bear)
more	(not pore or bore)
may	(not pay or bay)
me	(not P. or be)
mill	(not pill or Bill)
aim	(not ape or Abe)
come	(not cup or cub)
game	(not gape or Gabe)
cam	(not cap or cab)
bomb	(not bop or Bob)
psalm	(not sop or sob)
trim	(not trip or Trib)
gam	(not gap or gab)
some	(not sup or sub)
flam	(not flap or fab)
lamb	(not lap or lab)
rum	(not Rupp or rub)

► *Problem 2:* Inadequate duration

The word "duration" refers to how long something lasts, to how much time we give something. If you have the problem of inadequate duration on the /m/ phoneme, you simply make that sound too short. You do not hold on to it long enough to give it the time it ordinarily gets in American English. The sound may be articulated at the proper place (the two lips), but it is cut off—that is, it is cut short. The /m/ is cheated of its proper duration. This problem usually occurs when the /m/ is at the end of a syllable or word.

Is this problem of any importance? Yes, it is, because it affects both resonance and rhythm. It may even affect intelligibility (whether you can be understood).

All sounds in American English are not the same length. The stop/plosives just stop, explode, and they're gone. The duration is very short. The rest of the consonants are sometimes called *continuants* because they can be sustained, they can be continued.The continuants are not all the same length, and they are longer in some positions in words than others.

The three nasal phonemes are continuants; at the end of syllables and words, you must hold on to these sounds. At the end of syllables and words, /m/ is a "two-beat word." Read the following words and pat your foot. Begin to pat when the /m/ begins, and stop the /m/ on the second pat of your foot (the second beat). If you are not used to holding the /m/ for the second beat, you are giving it inadequate duration (time). Check for good humming through the nose and adequate duration on the /m/.

Final /m/

bomb	come	some
fame	game	seem
team	tomb	groom
germ	term	home
comb	dime	chime
palm	calm	Tom

Medial /m/

somewhere	blameless	slam dunk
formless	sameness	seemly
something	themselves	timetable
timeless	empty	calmly

Medial and Final /m/

sometime	game time	time bomb
flim flam	prime time	same dream
dream team	same time	seem dumb

Problem 3: Severe nasality on neighboring sounds

The velum (soft palate) is lowered only on the production of the three nasal sounds in English. For all the other sounds (including the vowels), the velum is raised to close off the nasal passages. Obviously we do not talk a word at a time or a single sound at a time. Our speech flow is connected in phrases. The movements to make sounds, therefore, are not separate sets of movements, but a continuous set of overlapping movements. While we are making one sound, we are getting ready for the next sound; and we are still finishing the last sound as we produce the present one. Many different movements occur at the same time, and the movements for the sounds overlap.

It is inevitable that there will be a little nasal resonance on vowel sounds that come before or after nasal consonants. If you say the word *him*, for example, you will begin to drop the velum (getting ready for the nasal consonant /m/) while you are still uttering the vowel (represented in IPA by /ɪ/ and in dictionaries by i). On the other hand, if you say the word *me*, you will not be able to get the velum completely raised and the nasal passages completely closed off before you start to utter the vowel (represented in IPA by /i/ and in dictionaries by ē.

While some nasalization of vowels next to nasal consonants is inevitable, *excessive* nasalization of those vowels is a distortion and a problem. How much is excessive? If most or all of a vowel before or after a nasal consonant is uttered with the velum lowered so that the air stream escapes in part through the nose, the sound becomes quite unpleasant. Try to reduce the nasal resonance on the vowels before and after nasal consonants as much as you possibly can. If most or all of a vowel has nasal resonance (is nasalized), it has excessive nasalization. Vowels, in English, are oral rather than nasal sounds.

Some vowels seem to offer more temptation toward nasalization than others. These are the vowels and diphthongs (diphthongs are vowel combinations that sound like one sound) that present the most tempting opportunities for excessive nasalization:

Key Word	IPA Symbol	Dictionary Symbol
bet	/ɛ/	e
bat	/æ/	a
bait	/eɪ/	a
bite	/ɑɪ/	ī
bout	/ɑʊ/	ou

Pronounce these pairs of words out loud. Compare the way you say the *vowel* in the two words of each pair. There should not be a great difference. Make the vowels as much alike as you can.

hem	head
ham	had
aim	aid
I'm	I'd
Baum	bowed

You must train yourself to direct the air consciously through the mouth or through the nose. The word *how*, for example, because it has no nasal sounds in it, should have no nasal resonance, and no air should come through the nose while it is being pronounced. You could hold your nose, then, and the pronunciation of the word *how* would not be affected. As a further check, pronounce the word *how* out loud with no nasal resonance. If you are not sure, hold your nose while you say the word, and then say the word without holding your nose. There should be absolutely no difference in the way the word sounds. (If you feel air trying to come through the nose while you say the word *how*, you have a real nasality problem!) Now you have pronounced the word *how* aloud with no nasal emission of air at all; next, pronounce the sounds /nd/ aloud with full nasal resonance on the /n/. Finally, try the word *hound* all together—with as little nasality on the /ɑu/ (ou) diphthong as you can achieve. Work to make the diphthong in *hound* as much like it was in *how* as you can. **Also** work to get as much good nasal resonance on the /n/ in *hound* as you can muster. The secret of solving this problem of excessive nasality on neighboring vowels is this: Work for good resonance in the nasal cavity on the nasal sounds—/m/, /n/, and /ŋ/ (ng), and work for as little nasality on the vowels and diphthongs as possible.

Problem 4: Substitution of a nasalized vowel for oral vowel + /m/

When a vowel or diphthong is followed by a nasal consonant, some speakers drop the nasal consonant altogether and simply nasalize the vowel or diphthong. If a word ends in /m/, for example, you may not articulate the /m/ by lightly, but firmly, bringing the two lips together; instead, you may let the air come out through the nose while saying the vowel or diphthong. Many of our students whose first language is Spanish have this problem.

The French and Portuguese languages contain nasalized vowel phonemes, but English has three nasal consonants and *no* nasal vowels. When people whose first language is English have this problem, others regard it as very careless speech. If your first language is not English and you substitute nasalized vowels for an English oral vowel + /m/, others may have difficulty understanding the words.

Check your own pronunciation of each of the following words and phrases to be certain that you get good oral vowels plus a good, firm closure of the lips and two-beat humming on the /m/.

seem	seem nice
time	time off
bomb	bomb scare
calm	Calm down.
some	somewhere
home	homework
same	same time
team	teamwork
rum	rum drink
term	term paper

Refer to the material on hypernasality in the voice section on pp. 461-465.

Problem 5: Substitution of /n/ for /m/

Assimilation is the adapting of sounds to be more like their neighboring sounds, and there are many standard assimilations in English. To change /m/ to /n/ in order to make it easier to say before another sound is not standard, however. There are several contexts that offer the greatest temptation to make this substitution. You may be tempted to substitute /n/ for /m/ before abutting alveolar consonants. (Abutting consonants are those that come right after another consonant but are in a separate syllable.) The sounds /t/, /d/, /l/, and /n/ are made on the gum ridge, and careless speakers are likely to turn /m/ to /n/ (which is on the gum ridge, remember) before these sounds. Pronounce the following material out loud. Check to be certain you make a real /m/ and not an /n/. The lips must close completely and you must hum up through the nose to make the /m/ sound.

/m/ before abutting /t/

sometime
dumb test
came today
calm teacher
a timetable
my hometown
a claim ticket
You seem tired.
I hear him talking.
I'm turning it in.

/m/ before abutting /d/

the same day
some dogs
the dumb dog
room decor
Sam didn't.
The flame died.
Does it seem tasteless?
I'm dead tired.

/m/ before abutting /l/

slim lead
extreme lack
some lady
a grim lesson
so prim looking
a dream location
the same logic
You seem lifeless.
I'm leaving.
See if fame lingers.

/m/ before abutting /n/

some nights
some note
grim necessity
a sham nevertheless
hymn number three
cream nougats
to seem natural
a tame neighborhood

You may be tempted to substitute /n/ for /m/ before several other abutting consonants. Check your pronunciation of these words and phrases to be sure the /m/ is a real /m/.

/m/ before abutting /θ/ (th)

something
the same thought
Some think so.
the same thrill
a dumb theory
a crime thriller
The groom threatened.
calm through it all

/m/ before abutting /s/

theme song
themselves
to blame somebody
another bomb scare
a prime suspect
I'm single.
Not another drum solo!
The alarm sounded.

/m/ before abutting /ʃ/ (sh)

Yes, I'm sure.
Give me some sugar.
Slam shut the door.
The lamb shivers.
some shallow thinking
You don't seem shocked.

/m/ before abutting /z/

Who's clumsy?
You seem zealous.
another time zone
It was all sham zest.

/m/ before abutting /w/

teamwork
some weariness
the same waterproof watch
the dumbwaiter
The climb wore me out.
The chasm widened.
Come with us.
timeworn relics

/m/ before abutting /j/ (y)

I'm your assistant.
a dream yacht
Don't slam your door.
I'm used to that.
That's some youngster!
the same youth

/m/ before abutting /ʍ/ (hw)

somewhere
same whitewash
some wherewithal
I'm whipped.

/m/ in final /md/ combination

I screamed.
It's doomed.
She was framed.
We roomed at the dorm.
She claimed the reward.
They chimed in.
It wasn't aimed at you.
She damned everyone.

Problem 6: Substitution of [ɱ] for /m/ before abutting /f/ or /v/

If an /m/ comes before an /f/ or /v/, some speakers are tempted to articulate the /m/ with the upper teeth and lower lip. Some assimilations, as we have already observed, are accepted as standard. This one is not. In English, it is considered a distortion of the /m/. This variation of /m/ is represented in IPA by [ɱ]. (This symbol is in brackets, [ ], because it is a phone, a sound; it is not in diagonals, / /, because it is not a phoneme.)

As you read the following words and phrases aloud, check to see whether you make this substitution for /m/.

comfort
comfortable
farm for sale
Come fast!
climb fifty steps
You come first.
the same voice

a team vehicle
the same voting district
Some victory!
Get home very fast.
Have some fun.
dream vacation
room vacancies

Pragmatics

Readiness Exercises

Being sure to completely close the two lips and to press them firmly together to prevent the air from coming out the mouth on the /m/, humming the /m/ phoneme up through the nose, and giving the /m/ adequate ti*mmmm*e, read aloud the words and phrases for checking inadequate duration (on pp. 152-153).

Reinforcement Exercises

Practice Words for /m/

Beginning	**Middle**	**End**
Meese	seemly	seem
meet	teeming	team
mill	limber	limb
mit	timber	Tim
mid	dimmer	dim
mate	tamer	tame
male	lame duck	lame
make	Cambridge	came
main/mane	naming	name
mass	Sammy	Sam
mob	bomb shelter	bomb
moot	tomblike	tomb
mud	dumber	dumb
merge	German	germ
might	timing	time

Practice Phrases for /m/

moon over Miami
home-cooked meal
number of memories
meaning of dreams
making the most of it
human comedy
many complaints
numb feeling in my arm
remember the time
climb a mountain
seem very firm
empty rooms
home number
same term paper

Practice Sentences for /m/

1. He didn't mean to alarm you.
2. The room was full of memories.
3. I manage to survive from term to term.
4. Jenny plays on two teams in the summer time.
5. Remind me to rest sometime.
6. We're meeting the same time next month.
7. There must always be time to dream.
8. He's comfortable on the second team.
9. How many homeless people are living in the terminal?
10. It's a mistake to permit her to take the blame.

Practice Sentences for /m/ (More Challenging)

1. My Mary's asleep by the murmuring stream.
2. The big game is the main event of the autumn season.
3. From womb to tomb, men and women dream of the impossible.
4. I'm grumbling because I lost another umbrella.
5. The man is not clumsy; he just stumbles and tumbles a lot.
6. The mechanic moaned. The motor was simply covered with grime.
7. There are a number of new employees, but no time to train them.
8. Pam climbed from the very bottom to the top of the company.
9. She is a prime example of someone determined to succeed.
10. I must be dumb. That math problem is impossible!

Practice Sentences for /m/ (Most Challenging)

1. Sometimes, complex things seem simple and simple things seem complex.
2. I'm going to the museum to see some masterpieces and some mediocre pieces.
3. I'm determined to have lamb chops, prime rib of beef, and some venison—all at the same meal!
4. Mary has little sympathy for those who make mistakes and cost the company money.
5. She maintains I made a fool of myself by claiming to be famous.
6. Do you really maintain common courtesy is uncommon and compassion is rare?

7. Mary has a sense of humor, but she's embarrassed by compliments.
8. The groom's best man seemed to be somebody important.
9. It's summer time, and my aim is to stay home and relax in comfort.
10. My roommate and I are not completely compatible. Do you know of a room vacancy?

Principles

Production

/n/ is a *voiced lingua-alveolar nasal*. It is made by pressing the tongue tip against the gum ridge—the same articulation you would use to make /t/ and /d/. But, instead of stopping the air completely as you would to form /t/ and /d/, you lower the velum so the air can pass out through the nasal passages. The vocal folds vibrate, and the vibrated air is resonated in the area of the mouth behind the upraised tongue and in the nose. You should get good resonance on this humming sound.

Because of the differences in their places of articulation, the /m/ and /n/ sound different; they have different amounts of oral resonance. The /m/ uses the whole mouth for resonance, but the /n/ uses only part of the mouth for resonance. Both, of course, use the nose for amplifying the sound.

Precautions

There are six spellings for /n/:

n as in *not*
nn as in *tunnel*
gn as in *gnaw*
kn as in *knot*
pn as in *pneumonia*
mn as in *mnemonics*

Problems

There are eight common problems associated with the production of the /n/ phoneme. As we look at each of these deviations, check to see if you have that problem with this phoneme.

▶ *Problem 1:* Denasality

Denasality is the lack of adequate nasal resonance on the nasal sounds. If you tended to denasalize the /m/ (see pg. 152) it is likely you will also denasalize the /n/. Check your pronunciation of the following list of words; if possible, tape record them. When you play them back, listen to be sure that the /n/ sounds do not sound like /t/ or /d/.

know	(not toe or dough)
knee	(not tea or D.)
name	(not tame or dame)
nick	(not tick or Dick)
nigh	(not tie or die)
ten	(not Tet or Ted)
men	(not met or med)
moon	(not moot or mood)
June	(not jute or Jude)
can	(not cat or cad)
ban	(not bat or bad)
con	(not cot or cod)
refrain	(not re-freight or refrayed)
pain	(not pate or paid)
brine	(not bright or bride)
bone	(not boat or bowed)
bun	(not but or bud)
Ann	(not at or add)
Ben	(not bet or bed)
crown	(not kraut or crowd)
down	(not doubt or Dowd)
fan	(not fat or fad)

As you read these words beginning and ending with /n/, did you sound as if you had a head cold? If so, you have a problem with denasality. Refer to the material on denasality in the Voice Section.

You must work for full nasal resonance on all the nasals, including /n/. Put your tongue tip up on the gum ridge and hum up through the nose. Put your thumb on one side of your nose and your forefinger on the other as you continue to hum the /n/. Do you feel the vibration? You should. The more humming the better.

▶ *Problem 2:* Inadequate duration

We discussed this same problem related to /m/ on pp. 152-153. Look back at what we said there about duration of nasals. The nasal phonemes are long sounds. Poets use them in poetry for their musical quality.

They give good resonance to the voice—brilliant tone and carrying power. Take advantage of them. Don't cheat them of the time (duration) they are due!

What we said about /m/ and its two beats at the end of syllables and words also applies to /n/. Let's try the same "helpful trick" on /n/ we used on /m/. Read the following words aloud and pat your foot. Begin to pat when the /n/ begins, and stop the /n/ on the second pat of your foot (the second beat). If you are not used to holding the /n/ that long (two beats), then you are giving it inadequate duration. Check for good humming through the nose and adequate duration on the /n/.

Final /n/

mean	scene/seen	bin
sin	gin	sane
rain	Ben	then
hen	tan	fan
ban	lawn	dawn
phone	bone	moon
soon	sun	gun
learn	burn	sign
line	down	gown

Medial /n/

teen years	Finland	painful
pencil	pensive	banter
Band-Aid	bonfire	contact
laundry	phone bill	Sunday
bone dry	lonely	noontime
town meeting	minefield	signpost

Medial and Final /n/

lineman	"con man"	brain drain
downtown	sunshine	unseen
concern	undone	phone line

▶ ***Problem 3:*** Severe nasality on neighboring vowels

We discussed this problem of assimilation nasality when dealing with distortions of the /m/. (See pp. 153-155.) We remind you here that some nasalization of vowels before and after consonants is inevitable, but excessive nasalization of these vowels is a distortion—and it is an unpleasant distortion to hear. Such nasalization gives a harsh quality to the sound, and completely untrained ears can hear it. If most or all of a vowel before or after /n/ is nasalized, the nasalization is excessive.

Because this problem affects the voice, we discuss assimilation nasality at some length in the Voice Section.

Pronounce these pairs of words out loud. Compare the way you say the *vowel* in the two words of each pair. There should be little difference between them. Make the vowels in the two words as much alike as possible.

hen	head	hand	had
gain	gait/gate	fine	fight
town	tout	bin	bid
Ben	bed	ban	bad
crane	crate	sign	sighed/side
gown	gout	pin	pit
pen	pet	pan	pad
brain	braid	line	lied
down	doubt	sin	sit

If you discover that you nasalize the vowels next to /n/ excessively, review the suggestions we gave for a similar problem (/m/) on pp. 154-155.

▶ ***Problem 4:*** Substitution of a nasalized vowel for an oral vowel + /n/

Some speakers do not stop at just nasalizing the vowel before the /n/; they proceed to drop the /n/ consonant altogether and let the nasalized vowel stand in for the original oral vowel and the nasal consonant /n/. The poor distorted vowel has to do double duty! In French and in some other languages, nasal vowels are part of the phonemic structure. In English they are not. This substitution of a nasalized vowel for both an oral vowel (or diphthong) and a nasal consonant is a mark of careless speech in English. The /n/ must be articulated. The tongue tip must touch the gum ridge, and the voiced consonant must be resonated in the nose. Check your pronunciation of all the following material to be sure you are getting a good nasal consonant for /n/ and that you are not using a nasalized vowel substitute.

uncounted	uncanny
unchangeable	unwilling
unconcerned	unconditional
unconscious	uncontrolled
insane	incompetent
onion	canyon
conscience	understand
I can't go.	I won't do it.
It's no fun any more.	Confidence is gone.

▶ *Problem 5:* Dentalization

If you tend to dentalize /t/, /d/, and /l/ in all positions in words, you will likely dentalize the /n/ as well. Like /t/, /d/, and /l/, the /n/ will be made with the tongue on the teeth when it occurs before one of the two *th* phonemes. In all other positions, however, the /n/ should be made on the upper gum ridge.

Check to see if you put your tongue on your teeth to make the /n/ sound in the following words and phrases:

neat	noon
knit	nut
Nate	nerve
net	nine
gnat	green
knob	stun
gnaw	intend
know	unknown

▶ *Problem 6:* Substitution of /m/ for /n/ before abutting /p/ or /b/

If one syllable ends with an /n/ and the next syllable begins with either /p/ or /b/, some speakers change the /n/ to /m/. This assimilation is understandable (/m/ is articulated with the two lips as /p/ and /b/ are), but it is nonstandard. Check to see if you are tempted to make this substitution in the following words and phrases:

unpleasant	unbending
unpolished	unbiased
unprofitable	unbounded
unprovoked	It can be said.
unprotected	It can prove useful.
unproven	He's unpopular
unbalanced	He's unbelievable.
unbearable	When buying groceries . . . .
unbecoming	When people meet . . . .

The /n/ before /p/ and /b/ should be articulated with the tongue tip pressed against the gum ridge. No substitutes, please.

▶ *Problem 7:* Substitution of [ɱ] for /n/ before abutting /f/ or /v/

This variation of /m/ (made by the upper teeth and lower lip) is not generally considered a standard allophone of /m/. It certainly is not accepted as an allophone of /n/. This assimilation, of course, can easily be explained: the /f/ and /v/ are made by bringing the upper teeth and lower lip together; [ɱ] is produced, getting ready for /f/ or /v/. However easy it is to explain (or make!), [ɱ] substituted for /n/ is nonstandard. Check to see if you make this substitution on this material:

unfair	inflate
inviolate	invent
confide	confused
convince	unverified
confess	He can fix anything.
convey	She can visit the children.
unfriendly	In fact, she visits often.
involved	Is lying in fashion?

► *Problem 8:* Substitution of /ŋ/(ng) for /n/

Before certain other consonants, you may be tempted to replace /n/ with /ŋ/—the third nasal consonant (represented in the dictionaries by ng). Of course, this substitution is more likely before /k/ and /g/, which are articulated at the same place as the /ŋ/ (ng), but it may occur before other consonants as well. As you read the following words and phrases aloud, check to determine whether you make this substitution.

/n/ before abutting /k/

incomplete
concave
unkind
unconscious

/n/ before abutting /g/

engrave
ungrateful
ingrained
I can get it.

/n/ before abutting /s/

concerned
construction
insipid
in spite of it

/n/ before abutting /ʃ/ (sh)

conscious
insure
influential
Let the sunshine in.

/n/ before abutting /r/

unreliable
unruly
unreported
Fire when ready.

/n/ before abutting /j/ (y)

union
onion
in your car
Can you wait?

Pragmatics

Reinforcement Exercises

Practice Words for /n/

Beginning	**Middle**	**End**
need	deny	dean
nick	kinfolk	kin

Beginning	**Middle**	**End**
nips	spinning	spin
name	mainly	main/mane
net	tennis	ten
nap	panning	pan
knack	canning	can
gnat	tanner	tan
gnaw	awning	on
nose	zoning	zone
note	toner	tone
no/know	owner	own
nut	tunnel	ton
numb	money	Munn
nice	signer	sign

Practice Phrases for /n/

no human contact
grant me a dance
fun in the sun
in an instant
plans for downtown
onions on the ground
unreported confession
a new understanding
not an unfriendly act
on my conscience
nine ventures at once
an increase in income
not lonely any more
an unprofitable invention

Practice Sentences for /n/

1. I found all the nonsense stunning.
2. I need some human contact.
3. I can go if I want to.
4. My brother went to the barn dance.
5. Nobody is consistently mean.
6. Mr. Jones telephoned to inquire about you.
7. In fact, the union representative mentioned a new plan.
8. I can cook two main dishes—in case I have to.
9. I won't confess; the accusation is unproven.
10. Athletes are not all brawn and no brain.

Practice Sentences for /n/ (More Challenging)

1. Nancy works downtown for a venerable institution.
2. The candidates have begun to invent nonsense issues.
3. Mr. Brown has found out his invitation was counterfeit.
4. In case he was involved, I gave them all unconditional pardons.
5. I don't spurn any reasonable offer—no matter how strange.
6. Seven times my plane has been cancelled. Enough!
7. Ann belongs to the "Lunch Bunch." They meet at noon.
8. I consider your accusation an unfriendly act, and I intend to get even.
9. Fantasy is fine in fiction, but spinning lies in court is unacceptable.
10. Again, I must remind you to give full nasal resonance on the emission of the three nasal consonants.

Principles

Production

The sound /ŋ/ (ng) is a *voiced linguavelar nasal*. It is made by lowering the velum so air can pass out through the nose, arching the back of the tongue against the soft palate (the articulation you would use to make a /k/ or /g/), vibrating the vocal folds, and resonating the vibrated air in the nasopharynx and nose. You articulate this nasal sound with the tongue in the position for /k/ and /g/, but you do not stop the air completely (as you do on /k/ and /g/); you use the raised tongue to redirect the air up and out through the nose. This sound has less oral resonance than the other two nasal sounds in English. Where /m/ used all the mouth as a resonator and /n/ used about two thirds of the mouth as resonator, this nasal sound has only a little oral resonance because of the place where the tongue is raised. You should, however, get good nasal resonance on this sound.

Precautions

There are three spellings for /ŋ/ (ng):

n as in *sink, anchor, or anxious*
ng as in *sing*
ngue as in *tongue*

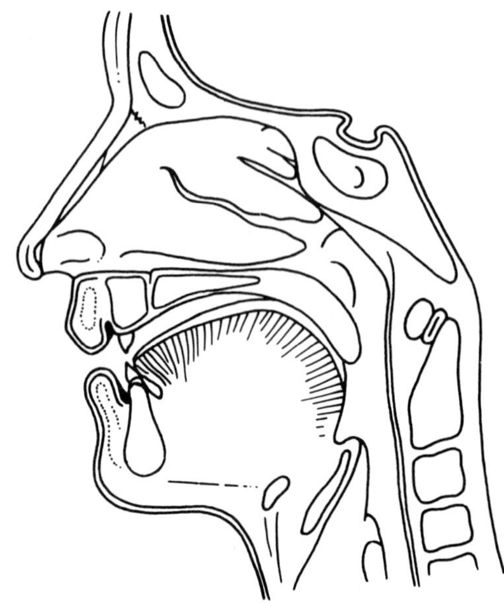

Figure 7.1: Articulatory adjustments for /ŋ/. Note relaxed (lowered) soft palate.

The most common spelling is **ng**, as in *thing*.

The spelling *ng* does not always represent the /ŋ/ (ng) phoneme, however. Here are seven lists of words—all spelled with *ng* and none pronounced with /ŋ/ (ng):

/n/ + /dʒ/ (j)

ingenious	ingenue	ingest

/n/ + /g/

inglorious	ingraft	ingrain
ingrate	ingratiate	ingratitude
ingredient	ingress	ingulf

/n/ + /dʒ/ (j)

engender	engine	engineer

/n/ + /dʒ/ (j)

congenital	congenital	congestive

/n/ + /g/

engage	engorge	engraft
engrain	engrave	engross

/n/ + /dʒ/ (j)

range	grange	strange
lunge	plunge	hinge
singe	impinge	longevity

/n/ + /g/

conglomerate	conglomeration	congratulate

The spelling *ng* sometimes represents only the phoneme /ŋ/ (ng)—a single nasal sound. But sometimes, in the middle of words, it represents that nasal phoneme + /g/. Compare the words *singer* and *finger*. The *ng* in the first word stands for /ŋ/ (ng) alone; the *ng* in the second word stands for /ŋg/ (ng + g). On pp. 173-174, we will explain the pattern for this contrast.

The phoneme /ŋ/ (ng) occurs, in English, only in the middle and at the ends of words—never at the beginning.

Problems

There are six common problems associated with this phoneme. As we discuss each of these deviations in turn, check to see if you have that problem with /ŋ/ (ng).

▶ *Problem 1:* Denasality

We defined denasality as the lack of adequate nasal resonance on the nasal consonant phonemes. If you discovered that you tend to denasalize /m/ and /n/ (see pp. 151 and 161), it is likely that you will also denasalize the /ŋ/ (ng). Pronounce the following words and phrases aloud, and check to see whether you denasalize the /ŋ/ (ng). The /ŋ/ (ng) should not sound like /k/ or /g/. *Sang* should not resemble *sag*, and *ring* should not sound like *rig*. Listen to hear if your /ŋ/ (ng) really hums in the nose.

ring	king
sang	bang
wrong	song
young	hung
mingle	strangle
hunger	elongate
bungalow	angular
singular	longing to go
completely hung up	"The Star-Spangled Banner"
flinging out a challenge	hanging around

If you sound like you have a "cold in the head" on these words and phrases, you probably have a problem of denasality. Refer to suggestions for coping with this problem on pp. 151 and 161.

▶ *Problem 2:* Inadequate duration

Like the /m/ and /n/, the /ŋ/ (ng) needs proper nasal resonance. These nasal consonants are continuants and give good carrying power to the voice. They provide a musical element to the sound of your speech. Don't cheat the /ŋ/ (ng) sound. It is a long sound. Give it its full amount of time. (Remember our two-beat "helpful trick.")

▶ *Problem 3:* Severe nasality on neighboring sounds

We have already discussed the problem of assimilation nasality with regard to /m/ (see pp. 153-155) and /n/ (see pp. 162-163). Just as with the other two nasal consonants, some nasalization of a vowel occurring before or after /ŋ/ (ng) is inevitable. You should be careful, however, to keep this amount of nasalization to a minimum. You want to work for good *nasal* resonance on the nasal consonants and good *oral* resonance on the vowels.

Pronounce these pairs of words out loud. Compare the way you say the *vowel* in the two words of each pair. There should be little difference in the vowel sound of the two words. Work to make the *vowels* in these word pairs as much alike as possible.

swing	swig	long	log
ring	rig	tongs	togs
wing	wig	tongue	tug
brink	brick	hung	hug
rang	rag	dunk	duck
sang	sag	rung	rug
bang	bag	slung	slug
slang	slag	lung	lug
gang	gag	among	a mug
blank	black	slink	slick

▶ *Problem 4:* Substitution of a nasalized vowel for an oral vowel + /ŋ/ (ng)

This problem was also a danger associated with the other two nasal consonants. It involves leaving out the nasal consonant completely and simply nasalizing the preceding vowel to make up the difference. It is not an acceptable substitute in English. The /n/ (ng) must be articulated; the movements involved in making the "ng" sound must be made. That means all the movements—not just dropping the velum down! Check your pronunciation of the following sentences to see if you use a nasalized vowel in place of an oral vowel and the /ŋ/ (ng).

We need strong leaders.
It's the wrong thing to do.
The pianist was banging away.
I need a drink.
We have an elected king.
She flung the ring at him.
The gang hid the loot.
The throng ganged up on him.
She's not too young.

Problem 5: Substitution of /n/ for final /ŋ/ (ng)

In informal speech situation, especially in southern areas of the United States, many educated, cultivated speakers use *in* in place of *ing* in such words as *coming* and *going*. The use of *in* is widespread, but generally, educated speakers are expected to use *ing*—especially in more formal situations. We would encourage you not to be hasty in judging speakers who do use *in* for *ing*, but we would also encourage you to use *ing* yourself.

Check to see if substitute /n/ for /ŋ/ (ng) on these *ing* words:

seeing	giving
taking	getting
wrapping	hopping
hanging	joking
talking	losing
earning	reading
going	doing
being	dying
bowing	learning

Problem 6: /ŋ/(ng) click or /ŋ/(ng) confusion

Sometimes, in English, the /ŋ/ (ng) phoneme is followed by a /k/ or /g/ sound. Sometimes it is not followed by either of these sounds. Some people who have learned English as a second language and many speakers in the metropolitan New York area demonstrate confusion about when a /k/ or /g/ should follow /ŋ/ (ng) and when it should not.

There seem to be two sources of confusion with regard to this sound. One is the influence of a language that does not include the pronunciation of both /ŋ/ and /ŋg/. The other is spelling, which contributes to the confusion. Although /ŋ/ is a single sound, it is usually represented in our spelling by the two letters *n* and g. It is also sometimes spelled *ngue* (in words such as *meringue* and *tongue*) and in other words is represented by the single letter *n* (as in words such as *blink* and *bank*).

Do you know whether you have this problem? Are you sure you know when to include /k/ or /g/ and when not to? You can check yourself right now. Pronounce the following material out loud. Listen each time to see if a /k/ or /g/ was pronounced after the /ŋ/ (ng) in the word or phrase.

Hang it up.	among us
Bring it here.	long ago
Sing a new song.	wing on the plane
on Long Island	wrong or right
boring us all	the ringing phone
strongly	swinging along
bang a drum	longing to return

Did you pronounce a /k/ or /g/ in any of the examples? If you did, you have added the sound where it does not belong. And you have, therefore, an "NG Click."

Let us check once more to see if we understand the patterns for the /ŋ/ (ng) in English. Read the following list of words and phrases aloud. Check again to see if any example contains a /k/ or /g/ sound as you pronounce it.

stronger than ever	a difficult language
the youngest member	very angry
every single time	a broken finger
every angle	hungry for success

What did you discover this time? Did all the examples have a /g/ after the /ŋ/ (ng)? They did? No, that is not an "NG Click." The words, correctly pronounced, contain both an /ŋ/ (ng) and /g/. If you did not include /g/ after the /ŋ/ (ng) in these words, then you are confused about when to include /g/ and when not to.

Let us try one more experiment. Pronounce the following list of words out loud. Again, listen to determine whether you include a /k/ or /g/ after the /ŋ/ (ng) sound.

bank	banker
banking	drunk
drunkard	wrinkle
tanks	think
Lincoln	anchor
ankle	cranky

Did you hear something different this time? We hope so. This time every word contained a /k/ after the /ŋ/ (ng).

Can you see any pattern here at all? There is one. The following four generalizations will make the pattern clear to you.

A. When a word ends in the spelling *ng* or *ngue*, the word ends in the single nasal consonant sound /ŋ/ (ng). No /g/ or /k/ is ever sounded at the end of those words, even if the next word begins with a vowel. Adding the extra sound is nonstandard.

   Check to be sure you do not add /k/ or /g/ after the nasal consonant in the following phrases:

sing it	sang a song
hang on	among us
king and his crown	meringue on the pie
strong or weak	stung on the hand

B. When you add a word-forming suffix to a word that ends in *ng* or *ngue*, there is usually no /g/. In other words, when the *ng* spelling is in the middle of a word and you can divide that word into a root word ending in /ŋ/ (ng) and a suffix, the spelling *ng* represents the one sound /ŋ/ (ng).

   Let's take an example. *Singer* can be divided into the root *sing* and a suffix *er*. There is, therefore, no /g/.The word *finger*, on the other hand, cannot be divided into a root and suffix, so there *is* a /g/ after the medial /ŋ/ (ng).

   Another example: Compare the words *singer* and *single*. *Singer* still can be divided into root ending in /ŋ/ (ng) and suffix, so it has no /g/. *Single* is not made out of the word *sing*; it has nothing whatsoever to do with singing. It does have a /g/ after the /ŋ/ (ng).

   There are two sets of exceptions to this rule:

   1. If you add *er* or *est* (the comparative and superlative suffixes) to *long*, *strong*, or *young*, there is a /g/. Note:

longer	longest
stronger	strongest
younger	youngest

   2. If you add *ate*, *ation*, or *al* to form a word, there is a /g/. Note:

      elongate
      prolongation
      diphthongal

C. When *ng* occurs in the middle of a word and is followed by sounds that do not constitute a word-forming suffix, that word will be pronounced with /ŋg/ (ng + g). These words are examples:

linger	finger
anger	angry

language	English
singular	single
distinguish	angular

D. When the spelling *nc*, *nk*, or *nx* ends a syllable, the syllable contains /ŋk/ (ng + k). Pronounce these examples out loud:

nc	**nk**	**nx**
anchor	bank	lynx
Lincoln	link	minx
zinc	bunk	Manx
uncle	shrink	sphinx
distinct	cranky	larynx
succinct	ankle	pharynx
instinct	twinkle	Bronx
tincture	thinker	anxious

Just for review purposes, here are the generalizations in summary:

1. Word ending in *ng* or *ngue:* /ŋ/ (/ng/) only; no /k/ or /g/
2. Root ending in *ng* + suffix: /ŋ/ (/ng/) only; two exceptions
3. Root (indivisible) word with *ng* in middle: /ŋg/ (ng + k); two exceptions
4. Syllable ending in *nc, nk, or nx:* /ŋk/ (ng + k)

Pragmatics

Work for good nasal resonance and sufficient duration on /ŋ/ (ng) in the reinforcement exercises.

Reinforcement Exercises

Practice Words for /ŋ/ (ng)

Final: /ŋ/ (ng) only—no /k/ or /g/)

sing	swing	sang	hang
sung	rung	long	song
young	stung	joking	laughing
strong	prolong	slang	rang
king	ring	tongue	meringue

Medial: /ŋ/ (ng) only—no /k/ or /g/

singer	kingly	strongly	banged
wingless	hangar	hanger	hangman
thronged	gangster	youngster	length
strength	lengthen	wrongly	swinger

Medial: /ŋ/ (ng) + /k/

anchor	banker	tanker	sinker
thinker	rancor	donkey	blanket
sprinkle	anxious	sunken	bunker
wrinkle	inkpen	ankle	uncle

Medial: /ŋ/ (ng) + /g/

mingle	tingle	jingle	jungle
jangle	tangle	wrangle	mangle
spangle	languish	language	dungarees
distinguish	longer	youngest	elongation
congregate	Congo	wrangler	anguish
finger	hungry	linger	fungus
Angus	angular	single	singular

Medial and Final: /ŋ/ (ng) only—no /k/ or /g/

ringing	singing	banging	longing
hanging	clinging	thronging	belonging
springing	prolonging	bringing	Ping-Pong
singsong	clanging	swinging	stinging

Final /n/ and /ŋ/ (ng) Contrast

thin	thing	ran	rang
kin	king	sun	sung
win	wing	ban	bang
run	rung	sin	sing
gone	gong	fan	fang
done	dung	pan	pang

Final /ŋ/ (ng) and /ŋk/ (ngk) Contrast

ring	rink	bang	bank
thing	think	clang	clank
sung	sunk	wing	wink
rang	rank	hung	hunk
tang	tank	sting	stink
hang	Hank	sling	slink
dung	dunk	Hong	honk
pink	ping	ling	link

Practice Phrases for /ŋ/ (ng)

trying new things
watching a long movie
waiting for spring
a singular sensation
writing a hit song

a distinguished singer
a stronger argument
staying single
drinking nothing but water
speaking four languages
extinguishing a string of fires
mingling with the throng
finding a hanger
anxious to belong

Practice Sentences for /ŋ/ (ng)

1. Sing a song of six pence.
2. To be thin requires staying in training.
3. He's been working on all the angles.
4. I'm trying to keep looking without blinking.
5. As long as you are coming anyway, bring it with you.
6. Her use of strong language caused him anguish.
7. I think she's stringing him along.
8. I have the distinct feeling you're pointing a finger at me!
9. Hank cannot distinguish right from wrong.
10. I haven't the strength to swim the length of the pool.

Practice Sentences for /ŋ/ (ng) (More Challenging)

1. Practicing every day is necessary for improving your language skills.
2. The ship dropped anchor and lingered two more days.
3. "Amazing Grace" is among my favorite songs.
4. My backyard is a jungle, but I can't bring myself to do anything about it.
5. Drinking and driving is asking for trouble.
6. Don't extinguish the fire. You're doing something right.
7. There's more to life than coming and going, getting and spending.
8. The wrangler was wearing dungarees and riding a donkey.
9. Seeing Joann isn't so easy since she moved from the Bronx to Long Island.
10. We have prolonged these exercises long enough. Now we're leaving it to you to think of better ones.

8

Glides

In Chapter 2, we noted that consonants and vowels differ in the way they are produced and in the way they are used. In general, this statement is true. There are differences between consonants and vowels in terms of production and function. Now, however, we have to qualify those statements a bit.

We have a group of sounds that clearly function in the language as consonants. They act like consonants. They do the things consonants do: they begin syllables rather than serve as the peak of sonority (carrying power) of the syllables. *However*, in terms of their production, they are not formed the same way as the other consonants.

Consonants in this group are not nearly so obstructed as the rest of the consonants. (Remember, we said vowels are relatively open sounds, and consonants are either partially or completely obstructed.) In terms of the way these sounds are made, these consonants don't quite match the definition we gave you.

The glides differ from the other consonants in two major regards: (1) the articulators move from one position to another in the formation of these sounds, and (2) there is less obstruction of the air stream on glide sounds than on most of the other consonants. In connection with the first difference, you should remember that glides always glide into a vowel. They never appear in final position in a syllable or before a consonant. Because of the second difference, glides are sometimes called semivowels. In fact, each of the glides moves from the position of one of the vowels and is, therefore, no more obstructed than its related vowel.

There are three glides (or semi-vowels) in American English.They are /w/, which begins from the position of the vowel that begins the word *ooze*; /j/ (y), which begins from the position of the vowel that begins the word *each*; and /r/, which begins from the position of the vowel that begins the word *earth*.

Let us examine each of these three glide phonemes.

Principles

Production

If you put your lips and tongue in position for the vowel in the word *boo*, let the vocal folds vibrate, and glide from this position into the next vowel, you will produce the *voiced bilabial* (two-lip) *glide*. In both IPA and the dictionary, this sound is represented by /w/. Let us be a little more specific about how the sound is formed. Pucker the lips. Letting the tongue tip rest behind the lower front teeth, raise the back of the tongue toward the soft palate. Close the velum so no air will escape up through the nose, and let the vocal folds vibrate.

This sound is the voiced partner (cognate) of the /ʍ/ (hw) sound, but it lacks the fricative nature of its voiceless cognate.

Precautions

There are three spellings for /w/:

w as in *win*
o as in *choir*
u as in *quiz*

The letter *w* is silent in words beginning with the spelling *wr*. All the following words begin with the /r/ phoneme:

wrack	wrangle	wrap
wrath	wreak	wreath
wreathe	wreck	wren
wrench	wrest	wrestle
wretch	wretched	wriggle
Wright	wring	wrinkle
wrist	writ	write
writhe	written	wrong
wroth	wrought	wry

The letter *w* is silent in the middle of certain words. Note these examples and how they are pronounced:

Word	in IPA	in Dictionaries	
answer	/ˈæn sɚ/	(an-sər)	
toward	/toʊɚd/	(tōrd)	or
	[tɔɚd]	(tôrd)	

sword	/souɚd/	(sōrd)	or
	[sɔɚd]	(sôrd)	
two	/tu/	(to͞o)	

Like the other two glides, the /w/ phoneme occurs only at the beginning of syllables—never, never at the end of a syllable. The *w* spelling, however, *can* occur at the end of syllables. When it does, the *w*, of course, is silent. Here are four lists of words spelled with silent *w*. The words are listed in columns according to the vowel (or diphthong) in the syllable with the silent *w*.

/o/ (o)	**/aʊ/ (ou)**	**/u/ (o͞o) or /ju/ (yo͞o)**	**/ɔ/ (ô)**
row (a line)	row (a fight)	dew	saw
low	cow	few	draw
blow	how	flew	flaw
grow	now	brew	claw
flow	plow	crew	craw
bow (a knot)	bow (v.)	pew	jaw
sow (v.)	sow (n.)	mew	gnaw
tow	Dow	grew	law
sew	pow!	Jew	paw
show	vow	new	maw
shew	wow	threw	raw
window	fowl	lewd	straw
yellow	jowl	stew	yawl
bellow	owl		awl
pillow			shawl
minnow			awful
tallow			lawman
			a*w*kward

Problems

There are four common problems associated with the /w/ phoneme. As we discuss each deviation, check to see if you have that problem with this phoneme.

► *Problem 1:* Slack articulation

If you do not round your lips enough and have sufficient tension of the lips when you produce this phoneme, the articulation will be careless and slack, and the sound will be weakened almost beyond recognition.

Did you find that you had slack or lazy articulation on /p/, /b/, and /m/—three other consonants formed by the two lips? Have you worked sufficiently on lip movement to produce a firm, clear /p/, /b/, and /m/? Unless you get sufficient lip movement and lip tension (the lips must be puckered to make this phoneme), you will not produce a clear /w/.

Let's try some words beginning with /p/, /b/, /m/, and then /w/. We are working for lip movement. To produce /p/, /b/, and /m/, the lips have to close completely. The lips do not close completely on /w/, but they must close down to a tight, round circle. Read these sequences across the page, and check your lips:

/p/	**/b/**	**/m/**	**/w/**
peak	beak	meek	weak
pie	buy	my	Y
pay	bay	may	weigh
peal	Beale	meal	weal
pate	bait	mate	wait
pail	bail	mail	wail
pet	bet	met	wet
P	be	me	we
pit	bit	mit	wit
pear	bare	mare	wear
Poe	bow	mow	woe
pill	bill	mill	will
penned	bend	mend	wend
purr	burr	myrrh	were

If English is not your first language (especially if your first language is Spanish), you may have this problem producing /w/ in English. To check, round your lips for the /u/ (oo) vowel. (This vowel is the first sound in the English words *oops*, *oodles*, and *ooze*.) The lips are tightly puckered for /u/ (oo). Just say the vowel /u/. (If you speak Spanish, you can use the /u/ from Spanish for this exercise.) Do you feel how tight, how tense your lips are for this sound? That is how tight the lips must be at the beginning of /w/!

Here are some exercises to help you get the right amount of tension on /w/. We will combine the vowel /u/ with some words. Do not stop and pause between the /u/ and the next word. See what happens!

The first time you say the combination, hold the /u/ for three beats and then slide into the next word. The next time, hold the /u/ for two beats and then slide into the next word. The third time, hold the /u/ for one beat and then slide into the next word. Now you should almost be up to tempo and ready to move from /u/ to the next vowel quickly enough to turn the /u/ into a /w/!

/u/ ($\overline{\text{oo}}$) - - - eke	/u/ ($\overline{\text{oo}}$) - - eke	/u/ ($\overline{\text{oo}}$) - eke	weak
/u/ ($\overline{\text{oo}}$) - - - it	/u/ ($\overline{\text{oo}}$) - - it	/u/ ($\overline{\text{oo}}$) - it	wit
/u/ ($\overline{\text{oo}}$) - - - ale	/u/ ($\overline{\text{oo}}$) - - ale	/u/ ($\overline{\text{oo}}$) - ale	wail

/u/ (o͞o) - - - Ed	/u/ (o͞o) - - Ed	/u/ (o͞o) - Ed	wed
/u/ (o͞o) - - - odd	/u/ (o͞o) - - odd	/u/ (o͞o) - odd	wad
/u/ (o͞o) - - - all	/u/ (o͞o) - - all	/u/ (o͞o) - all	wall
/u/ (o͞o) - - - owe	/u/ (o͞o) - - owe	/u/ (o͞o) - owe	woe
/u/ (o͞o) - - - I'll	/u/ (o͞o) - - I'll	/u/ (o͞o) - I'll	wile
/u/ (o͞o) - - - ow	/u/ (o͞o) - - ow	/u/ (o͞o) - ow	wow

You can follow the same pattern, using the words *air, edge, eyes, aid, itch, ill*, and *end*. This list will produce *wear, wedge, wise, wade, witch, will*, and *wend*.

Try to develop the sensitivity to feel the proper lip tension for /w/. If necessary, get a mirror and look to see where the lips are for the vowel /u/, and (if that is pursed enough) get the same lip position for the beginning of /w/.

The greatest temptation to slack articulation of the /w/ occurs in consonant blends at the beginning of words—when /w/ follows /k/, /s/, /t/, or /d/. Check your pronunciation of these pairs of words. Be careful to get good lip rounding for the initial /w/, and then listen, look, and feel to check to see if you get equally good articulation of the second word (where the /w/ follows another consonant).

/w/ and /kw/ contrast

wad	quad	wit	quit
wake	quake	wail	quail
waver	quaver	wilt	quilt
work	quirk	wire	choir
ween	queen	wick	quick
west	quest	Wyatt	quiet
will	quill	well	quell
wench	quench	wash	quash
wary	quarry	wart	quart

/w/ and /sw/ Contrast

weep	sweep	well	swell
wig	swig	will	swill
wing	swing	wag	swag
warm	swarm	watt	swat
way	sway	wish	swish
wan	swan	witch	switch
wallow	swallow	wear	swear
wet	sweat	wane	swain
wetter	sweater	we'd	Swede
welling	swelling	welter	swelter
wine	swine	wipe	swipe

/w/ and /tw/ Contrast

weak	tweak	weed	tweed
wig	twig	will	twill
win	twin	wit	twit
wane	twain	wine	twine
Winkle	twinkle	witch	twitch

/w/ and /dw/ Contrast

well	dwell	welling	dwelling

Problem 2: Omission

Some speakers go beyond loosely articulating the /w/ and omit it from some words completely. The /w/ most in danger of omission is the one after an abutting consonant. Pronounce these words, and listen to be sure the /w/ is not left out:

awk*w*ard	team*w*ork	home*w*ork
un*w*orthy	stal*w*art	on*w*ard
up*w*ard	un*w*ise	mid*w*eek
sub*w*ay	up*w*ind	down*w*ind

The /w/ in the middle of a word is in some danger of omission—even if it is preceded by a vowel or diphthong. Pronounce these words out loud, and check for omission of /w/:

for*w*ard	way*w*ard	sea*w*orthy
any*o*ne	every*o*ne	any*w*ay

Problem 3: Substitution of /v/ for /w/

/w/ and /v/ are separate phonemes in English. One is not an allophone of the other. If you use one in place of the other, you will probably change the meaning completely. It is important to make a clear distinction between the two sounds in English.

There are languages with different patterns, however. If English is not your first language (or your parents' first language), you may confuse /w/ and /v/, substituting one for the other.

These two phonemes are formed in very different ways. The /v/ is articulated by the upper teeth and the lower lip. The /w/ is articulated by tensely rounding the two lips and suddenly opening them as you utter the next vowel.

Here are some pairs of words that contrast the /w/ and /v/. Check to see if you are tempted to make the words with /w/ in the same way you make the words with /v/.

/w/ and /v/ Contrast

wail	vale/veil	wet	vet
wicker	vicar	we	V
wane	vane/vain	Walt	vault
Y	vie	wow!	vow
wiser	visor	wine	vine
wiper	viper	worse	verse
Willa	villa	wile	vile
Weiss	vice	west	vest
weal/we'll	veal	waltz	vaults

If you have difficulty making this distinction, work on articulation of the /w/ being sure your tongue and lips are in the position for the vowel in the word *do*. Look in the mirror to see the position of the lips as you utter *do*. The lips should be slightly protruded and tensed into a little circle. That is exactly the position from which the /w/ starts. Therefore, we will try a word beginning with /w/ right after that vowel in *do* (the vowel is represented in IPA by /u/ and in the dictionaries by o͞o). Be sure to hold your lips in the position of the last sound in the word *do* as you begin the /w/ of the next word. The /w/, being a glide, does not keep the lips in that position but slides into the next vowel position.

Remembering these instructions, try saying "Do well" out loud. Could you feel that the /w/ started out right where the /u/ (o͞o) was? If so, then try these other phrases—all of which have an /u/ (o͞o) followed immediately by a /w/. The /u/ (o͞o) should give you the proper jumping off place for the /w/.

you want	new one
who would	flew once
too wise	do one
new wing	too wet
to wed	to win
Sue will	two wives (a tough one!)

Problem 4: Addition

Some speakers insert a /w/ sound if a syllable ends with /o/ (the vowel at the beginning of the word *own*) or /u/ (the vowel at the beginning of the word *ooze*) and the next syllable begins with a vowel. Because the lips are rounded for the vowels /o/ and /u/, it is easy to voice the glide /w/ as the lips and tongue move to the position for the next vowel.

Understandable as this insertion may be, it is nonstandard and should be avoided. Check your own pronunciation of these words and phrases. If you insert a /w/, the words in the left-hand column will sound like the ones in the right-hand column:

you are	you war	you ate	you wait
doing	do wing	knew it	new wit
sewing	so wing	know it	no wit
no air	no wear/ware	go in	go win

Pragmatics

Readiness Exercises

We have already offered you some readiness exercises—as we discussed the problems related to this phoneme. Excellent exercises for warming up and getting ready for /w/ reinforcement exercises are:

/p/ - /b/ - /m/ - /w/	page 180
/u/ ($\overline{oo}$) + word	pages 180-181
/u/ ($\overline{oo}$) + /w/	page 183

Reinforcement Exercises

Practice Words for /w/

Beginning	**Middle**		
wake	awake		
ward	award	reward	
wait	await	Kuwait	dumbwaiter
walk	sidewalk	crosswalk	boardwalk
west	request	conquest	inquest
wise	otherwise	unwise	clockwise
way	byway	highway	thruway
wired	acquired	inquired	required
wear	beware	aware	hardware
word	forward	backward	afterward
worthy	unworthy	seaworthy	trustworthy
one	anyone	everyone	someone

Practice Phrases for /w/

a wonderful welcome
willing to work
twelve quick baskets
wiser than anyone else
a wishing well
wearing a tweed coat
a reward every week
just once, quickly
windows on the world

the worst highway
waiting and watching
washing the windows
upward and onward
wet weather

Practice Sentences for /w/

1. Winning would be wonderful!
2. Waltz with me anyway.
3. Watch out! It's getting worse.
4. Wise voters check on the views a candidate is quiet about.
5. I look forward to working with you.
6. Water is the only liquid that can quench my thirst.
7. The Queen's face began twitching. How awkward!
8. The choir sang well enough to suit me. I didn't awaken.
9. You warned me, but it was worse than I expected.
10. Dr. Vest went to the West Coast without reservations.

Practice Sentences for /w/ (More Challenging)

1. Thanks to the well-informed voters, the reformers made a clean sweep.
2. The witch had a twinkle in her eye as she swore I'd become rich.
3. You're not unwelcome or unwanted, but you are one hour early.
4. Dailey and Nancy are wise. They're planning a quiet wedding and a quick escape.
5. By midweek, supplies were dwindling, and resistance was weakening.
6. Studying is frequently required on difficult quizzes.
7. This is the worst weather we have ever had: wet and windy.
8. What wine goes with veal? Everyone will have a glass.
9. Their mother swears she can't tell the twins apart.
10. I am unwilling to walk out without a backward glance, a witty remark, and a farewell wave.

/j/

Principles

Production

If you put your tongue in the position for the vowel in the word *eat*, let your vocal folds vibrate, and glide from this position into the next vowel, you will produce the *voiced lingua-palatal glide*. This phoneme is represented in IPA by /j/ and in the dictionaries by *y*.

The sound is made by letting the tongue tip rest behind the lower front teeth, raising the front of the tongue nearly to the hard palate, raising the velum, and vibrating the vocal folds. The lips will be in the position for whatever vowel follows.

This phoneme, like the other glides, *always* precedes a vowel and is *never* at the end of a syllable.

Precautions

There are two *common* spellings for /j/ (y):

y as in *yes*
i as in *onion*

There are two uncommon spellings for /j/ (y):

j as in *hallelujah*
g as in *monsignor* [NOTE: this *gn* is /n/ + /j/ (y)]

At the beginning of words, there are three spellings for /j/ (y) + /u/ ($\overline{oo}$):

u as in *unite*
eu as in *Europe*
ew as in *Ewing*

REMINDER: like the other two glides, /w/ and /r/, /j/ (y) only occurs at the beginning of syllables—never at the end. The *y* spelling at the ends of syllables and words (such as *say* and *saying*) does *not* stand for this consonant phoneme.

Problems

There are four common problems associated with this phoneme. As we discuss each deviation in turn, check to see if you have that problem with this phoneme.

▶ *Problem 1:* Omission

You may be tempted to omit the /j/ in the middle of words after /l/ and /n/. Do not yield to that temptation! It is an *image-breaker*—thought by others to be a sign of careless speech.

Check your own pronunciation of the following words and phrases to be sure you do not omit the /j/ (y) phoneme after the /l/ or /n/.

/j/ (y) After Abutting /l/

million	hellion
billion	rebellion
trillion	Collier
civilian	stallion
pavilion	battalion
billiards	halyard
William	galleon
familiar	scallion
Will you try?	I'll tell you.
Did it fill you up?	sell your car
Did it thrill you?	a swell year

/j/ (y) After Abutting /n/

onion	union
grunion	communion
Bunyan	canyon
minion	companion
pinion	lanyard
opinion	banyan
dominion	lorgnette
filet mignon	*Agnus Dei*
monsignor	junior
in your car	Can you go?
a fine year	ran you over

As we explained earlier, /j/ (y) slides from the position where the vowel in *eat* is made. That is, the tongue is in the position used for the vowel in *eat* or *each* (represented in IPA by /i/ and in the dictionaries by ē) as the /j/ (y) glide begins. Ordinarily, the tongue then slides into the position for the vowel that follows the /j/ (y).

But what happens if the vowel after the /j/ (y) is an /i/ (ē) vowel? Your tongue is already in that position. What do you slide *to*? To get both the consonant /j/ (y) and the vowel /i/ (ē), you must push the front of the tongue forward toward the hard palate for the /j/ (y). If you make the /j/ (y) alone, you should feel tongue movement and hear that voiced /j/ (y) sound. You must get that same movement and hear that same sound *before* the /i/ (ē) vowel.

Check your own pronunciation of the following pairs of words to be sure you do not omit the /j/ (y) on the second word. Do you hear the difference between the words? Can you feel the tongue movement on the /j/ (y)?

Without /j/ (y)	**With /j/ (y)**
E	ye
ear	year
east	yeast

Now, what happens if the sound just before the /j/ (y) is the /i/ (ē) vowel? Well, of course, some people take the easy way out and omit the gliding consonant /j/ (y)! Granted, it does take extra effort and energy to get the /j/ (y) in. There has to be that tongue movement. But you *are* already in position for /j/ (y)—having just produced the /i/ (ē) vowel.

Compare your pronunciation of the following pairs of phrases. Do you include the /j/ (y) in the second phrase of each pair, or do you omit it?

Without /j/ (y)	**With /j/ (y)**
he earns	he yearns
the ear	the year
the "el"	the yell
the awning	the yawning

► *Problem 2:* Confusion of /u/ (o͞o) and /ju/ (yo͞o)

Many people are confused about when to use the vowel /u/ (o͞o) (the opening vowel in the word *ooze*) and when to use that vowel with /j/ (y) in front of it. Here are three general principles to guide you:

A. At the beginning of a word, the spellings *u*, *eu*, *ue*, and *ew* are pronounced /ju/ (yo͞o).

Note these examples:

uniform	unit	unity	unify
use	usage	usable	usual
useful	usury	union	utopia
uranium	utilize	Eucharist	eulogy
euphemism	euphoria	Europe	euthanasia
eureka	ewe	Ewell	Ewing

B. Generally, after /p/, /b/, /k/ /m/, /f/, /v/, and /h/, the spellings *u*, *eu*, *ue*, *ew*, and *iew* are pronounced /ju/ (yo͞o).

/p/ + /ju/ (yo͞o)

pure	puerile	pew

/b/ + /ju/ (yo͞o)

bugle Beulah

/k/ + /ju/ (yo͞o)

cute

/m/ + /ju/ (yo͞o)

mute	Meuse	muezzin	mew

/f/ + /ju/ (yo͞o)

fusion	feud	fuel	few

v/ + /ju/ (yo͞o)

revue view

/h/ + /ju/ (yo͞o)

huge	hue	human	hew	humanity

C. After /t/, /d/, and /n/, the spellings *u*, *eu*, *ue*, and *ew* are pronounced either /u/ (o͞o), /ju/ (yo͞o), or /ɪu/. (See p. 243 for a discussion of the vowel /ɪ/.)

Although the use of /u/ (o͞o) predominates nationally, the most careful speakers use either /ju/ (yo͞o) or /Iu/. We prefer the use of /ju/ on such words as those in the following list. Read the words aloud; check to see whether you use /u/ (o͞o) or /ju/ (yo͞o) in such words:

Tuesday	tuna	tune	fortitude
due	dew	duplex	duty
news	nuclear	nutrition	nucleus

D. Generally, the spelling *oo* represents the simple vowel /u/ (o͞o). Note these examples:

food	soon	loon	cool
moon	mood	too	noose
goose	poor	tool	spoon

▶ *Problem 3:* Substitution of /dʒ/ (j) for /j/ (y)

Some speakers substitute /dʒ/ (j)—the first sound in the word *jet*—for the voiced linguapalatal glide /j/ (y)—the first sound in the word *yet*.

If English is not your first language (especially if your first language is some dialects of Spanish), you may make this substitution. We have already discussed /j/ (y) - /dʒ/ (j) confusion from the other point of view. (See pp. 146-147.) At that point, we mentioned that substitution of /dʒ/ (j) for /j/ (y) is much more common than the other way around. Now we examine the more common of the two substitutions.

If /dʒ/ (j) is an allophone of /j/ (y) in your first language, you can see how easy it would be to confuse the two phonemes in English. And it is important to remember that they are two completely separate, unrelated phonemes in English. You cannot substitute one for the other without changing meaning and confusing listeners.

The two phonemes are articulated in very different ways. The /j/ (y) is made with the tongue tip behind the lower front teeth and the front of the tongue lifted up tensely almost to the hard palate (although it does not touch the palate). The /dʒ/ (j) is made with the tongue tip and blade firmly pressed against the upper gum ridge and the back of the upper gum ridge—from which point it pushes away, dropping down.

Check your own pronunciation of the following pairs of words. The first word in each pair begins with /j/ (y), and the second begins with /dʒ/ (j).

/j/ (y)	**/dʒ/ (j)**
ye (old form of "you")	gee
yip	gyp
yea	Jay
yak	Jack
yet	jet
yard	jarred
yoke	joke
a yearning	adjourning
you know	Juno

▶ *Problem 4:* Addition

Some speakers add the /j/ (y) sound if a syllable ends in the vowel /i/ (ē)—the first sound in the word *eat*—or in the three diphthongs ending in the vowel /ɪ/ (i)—the first sound in the word *it*. These three diphthongs are the last sounds in the words *buy*, *boy*, and *bay*. Because the tongue is already in the position for the /i/ (ē) or /ɪ/ (i) vowel, it is easy to glide with voicing to the position of the next vowel. In that way, /j/ has been articulated. If the next syllable is a stressed syllable, it is especially easy to fall into this problem. However easy it may be, it is not considered standard. In the old Popeye cartoons, you remember, Popeye often said, "I yam!" Popeye was noted for his brawn—not his brains or his speech patterns! In the left-hand column, there are a few phrases that contain the temptation to add a /j/ (y). If you add the /j/ (y), the phrase will sound like the phrase in the right-hand column.

see it	see yit
be over	be yover
I am	I yam
my arm	my yarm

joy in	joy yin
toy is	toy yiz
may eat	may yeat
Say "S."	Say yes.

Pragmatics

Reinforcement Exercises

Practice Words for /j/ (y)

Beginning	**Middle**
unity	disunity
union	communion
yards	billiards
yon	scallion
use	misuse
yell	Daniel
you	review

/u/ ($\overline{oo}$) - /ju/ (y$\overline{oo}$) Contrast

coo	cue
poor	pure
do	due/dew
booty	beauty
who	hue
moo	mew
food	feud
coot	cute
ooze	use

	Beginning	**Middle**
/pj/ (py)	pure	impute
	pew	impugn
	pupil	compute
/bj/ (by)	butane	imbue
	beauty	abuse
	beautiful	abusive
/tj/ (ty)	tune	platitude
	tuba	constitute
	tutor	gratuity
/dj/ (dy)	dew	induce
	duty	endure
	duly	unduly

/kj/ (ky)	cue	accuse
	cute	acute
	cure	incurable
/fj/ (fy)	few	confuse
	fuse	infuse
	future	refute
/mj/ (my)	muse	amused
	mute	commute
	music	immune
/nj/ (ny)	new	anew
	nuisance	renew
	nuance	annuity

Practice Phrases for /j/ (y)

a young senior
a huge onion
a few decent human beings
a familiar yen
a united labor union
a popular kind of music
a million flights to Europe
the year of royalty
eulogy for a computer
humility and humor
a triangular unit
an amusing tune
a curious feud

Practice Sentences for /j/

1. Sometimes, duty is a nuisance. I'm confused!
2. Yesterday he yawned in my class again!
3. The yield of yellow corn has doubled in the last year.
4. The eulogy was delivered by a young priest from the Humane Society.
5. In my opinion, her beauty will endure.
6. The student's paper is due on Tuesday.
7. He yelled his abuse until it was almost humorous.
8. We use millions of them every year.
9. You look good in your uniform. Your companions do not.
10. Illegal gambling takes in more than nine billion dollars a year.

Practice Sentences for /j/ (y) (More Challenging)

1. How can you refuse to recognize his genius?
2. The youth decided to renew his annuity.
3. During all the verbal abuse, he stood mute.
4. I am not yet ready to believe Cupid has died.
5. This university has millions of regulations. Yes, millions!
6. I am not really stupid; I am only confused.
7. Juniors and seniors at the institute gave a huge donation.
8. The community refused to allow the billiards parlor to renew its license.
9. Are you accusing me of being a Yankee fan? I'm familiar with your attitude.
10. I am looking for a city with low altitude and no humidity. How's Houston?

/r/

Principles

Production

Because the /r/ sound is made by different people in different ways, especially people from various regions of the country, it is difficult to describe this consonant with exactness. In addition, because the /r/ is a glide, which implies continuous movement of the tongue from the sound that precedes it to the sound that follows it, the surrounding sounds cause variation in the production of /r/.

If you put your tongue in the position for the vowel in the word *burr* (see pp. 306-315 for a discussion of the vowels /ɝ/ and /ɚ/), let the vocal folds vibrate, and glide immediately into the vowel that follows, you will produce a *lingua-postalveolar glide*. We represent this sound by /r/. More specifically, the sound is formed by pointing the tensed tip of the tongue upward to a position just in back of the alveolar ridge or by slightly curling the raised tongue tip back toward the palate, closing the velum, and vibrating the vocal folds. From this position, the tongue slides toward the position of the vowel that follows. If the following vowel is made in the back of the mouth, the tongue tip will usually be slightly retroflexed on the /r/. If the vowel following is made in the front of the mouth, the tongue tip will be slightly turned toward the alveolar ridge. You should remember in forming this sound that there is a minimum of lip movement. The sound is articulated chiefly by the movement of the tongue.

Precautions

There are four spellings for /r/:

r as in *red*
rr as in *berry*
rh as in *rhyme*
wr as in *wreck*

Like the other two glides, /r/ occurs only before vowels and never at the end of syllables. The r spelling however can occur at the end of syllables. When it does, it represents a vowel—either a long vowel (represented in IPA by /ɝ/) or a short vowel (represented in IPA by /ɚ/).

Problems

There are six common problems associated with the /r/ phoneme. As we discuss each of these deviations, check to see if you have that problem with this phoneme.

Problem 1: Trilled or flapped /r/

In certain other English-speaking countries, the /r/ is either trilled or flapped against the upper gum ridge or palate. In the United States, however, trilling or flapping the /r/ is uncommon and is considered an affectation.

If English is not your first language, you may be inclined to flap or trill the /r/ because of the phonemic patterns in your first language. In Spanish, for example, there are two phonemes where we have only one in English. Both differ in production from the /r/ in American English. The r in Spanish touches the upper gum ridge with a tap or flap, but the tongue does *not* touch the upper gum ridge on /r/ in American English. The rr in Spanish is trilled (rapid, repeated tapping of the tongue) on the upper gum ridge, but we have no comparable phoneme in English. If you use one of these Spanish sounds for the American English /r/, we will probably understand you, but we will definitely notice the difference in sound!

Whether English is your first language or not, we advise against flapping or trilling the /r/.

As you read the following words aloud, check to see whether you tend to flap or trill the /r/:

read	rip	rain	red
wrap	rock	wrong	rude

story	sorry	scary	berry
ferry	around	arrange	arrive

Problem 2: Excessive friction

If you push the air stream with considerable force through the opening between the tongue tip and the palate when making the /r/, the sound will possess a fricative quality. In the speech of most Americans, fricative /r/ is unusual except in the consonant combinations /tr/ and /dr/. Even in those combinations you should be careful not to attack the /r/ sound with too much force. The slight devoicing of the /r/ that occurs after the voiceless sounds in the combinations /pr/, /tr/, /kr/, /fr/, /θr/, and /ʃr/ seems to increase the danger of excessive friction. If you have discovered that you tend to overaspirate some consonants, check to be certain that you do not push too much air through on the /r/, especially in these combinations.

Read the following words aloud. Check to see if you produce the /r/ with too much friction, too much force, too much air:

rye	try	dry	prize
cries	fries	thread	shred

Problem 3: Excessive retraction

In many parts of the United States, especially in the Midwest, the /r/ is often produced with the tongue tip turned backward toward the palate. If this retroflexion is excessive, the vowels that surround the /r/ will be distorted. You may have read a story in which an author spelled *very* as ''vurry'' and *American* as ''Amurrucan'' to represent this kind of pronunciation. If you produce the /r/ with the tongue tip curled back toward the palate, check to be certain you do not pull the tongue back so far that the vowels are noticeably distorted.

Some speakers use another form of retracted /r/ that sounds a great deal like the retroflex deviation we have just discussed. In this variation, the tongue tip remains low in the front of the mouth and the back of the tongue is raised toward the soft palate. This retraction (pulling back) of the tongue, like excessive retroflexion, markedly changes the quality of the adjacent vowels and should be avoided.

Read the following words aloud. Check to see if you tend to retract the tongue (either tip or back of the tongue) on the /r/:

very	berry	scary	Larry
hurry	America	herring	orange
tomorrow	arrest	arrange	carry

▶ *Problem 4:* Labialization

The labialized /r/ results from excessive lip movement in forming the sound. It produces a distorted consonant that sounds something like /w/. If you discovered that you tended to labialize the /l/, you may also discover that you substitute lip movement for tongue movement on the /r/.

Pronounce the word *red* and listen to determine if it sounds like *wed*. Next, check with a mirror to see if you are moving your lips as you pronounce the /r/. When /r/ is the first sound in a word, the lips will be in the position for the vowel that follows while the /r/ is being uttered. In the word *reed*, then, the lips should be spread for the vowel in the word and should not move while the /r/ is being emitted.

Most people who have difficulty with the labialized deviation of /r/ do not lift the tongue tip up near the alveolar ridge or the palate but instead let the tongue tip lie low in the front of the mouth and raise the back of the tongue up toward the soft palate (in the position of /u/ (oo) and /w/).

To correct this distortion, you must raise your tensed tongue tip toward the proper spot and prevent the lips from moving. Make the tongue—not the lips—do the work. It is the tongue that must move to produce a satisfactory /r/. No lip movement. And remember: tongue tension is essential!

Warning: If you use the lips to produce /r/, you will have particular trouble on consonant blends (with /r/) that require the lips for the other sound in the combination, such as /pr/ and /br/. Another warning: Since many people with this articulation problem let the tongue tip lie low in the mouth and raise the back of the tongue near the position for the vowel /u/ (o͞o), /r/ before back vowels—such as /u/ (o͞o) and /ʊ/ (oo)—may be especially troublesome.

Read the following words aloud. Listen to the sounds, and look in the mirror as you speak. Check to see if you substitute lip movement for tongue movement on the /r/.

reach	preach	breach
rim	prim	brim
raid	prayed	braid
rest	pressed	breast
ride	pride	bride
rude (Don't lift back of tongue on /r/)	prude (Difficult! Same warning)	brood (Same warning)

▶ *Problem 5:* Addition

This problem is also called "intrusive r" because the /r/ intrudes where it does not belong.

When one syllable ends in a vowel, and the next syllable begins in a vowel, we separate the syllables with a little space or break. That space is called *hiatus*. A *hiatus* is a little pause that keeps the two vowels apart and indicates they are in different syllables.

Granted, it is easier to separate syllables by having them start with consonants. But it is possible to have syllables *end* with a vowel or diphthong rather than with a consonant, and it is also possible to have a syllable *start* with a vowel or diphthong rather than with a consonant. It is when you have both such syllables together that some people run into trouble. They want to add an /r/ to help them keep the syllables separated. This is the added, or intrusive, /r/.

Let us look at an example to help make this problem clearer. The word *going* has two syllables (or rhythmic beats). The first syllable ends with the /o/ phoneme (actually, here it will be the diphthongal allophone, but that is not relevant to this problem), and the second syllable starts with the /ɪ/ (i) vowel phoneme—the vowel in the word *it*. Between these two syllables (between the two vowels), some people are tempted to insert an /r/—transforming the word from *going* into *goring*.

This problem does not just pop up inside words. The two syllables that present the problem can be in successive words. If a word ends in a vowel, and the next word starts with a vowel, you may also be tempted to insert an /r/. The words *idea of it* become *idear of it* with the addition of the intrusive *r*.

Pronounce the phrases that follow. Check to see if you add an /r/ at the hiatus.

the *idea* of it
a *law* office
I *saw* it.
He ate a *raw* egg.
It will *thaw* out.
Can you *draw* a face?
Cuba is a neighbor.
Atlanta is lovely.
the *cawing* of the crows
Drawing is not difficult.
a *flaw* in the plan
the *Shah* of Persia
Utah is unique.
Emma and Mary
law of the land
The *comma* is out of place.
Medea is a witch.

We recognize that there are educated, cultivated speakers who add the /r/ to words and syllables. President Kennedy talked to the nation about "Cuber." This pronunciation was a source of amusement to many and an annoyance to some. The vast majority of Americans certainly noticed it and found it strange. We think it best to become aware of this habit if you have it and to omit the added /r/.

Problem 6: Confusion of /r/ and /l/

We have already discussed this problem in relation to the /l/ phoneme. See p. 91 for an explanation of and suggestions for this problem.

If your first language is one of the languages of the Orient, it is quite possible you will face this problem in English. You must learn to distinguish between the phonemic structure of your first language and that of American English.

Read the following pairs of words aloud. Check to see if there is a clear distinction between the words with /l/ and those with /r/.

/l/	**/r/**	**/l/**	**/r/**
leak	reek	lid	rid
lip	rip	laid	raid
lead	reed	ledge	Reg
/l/	**/r/**	**/l/**	**/r/**
lag	rag	belly	berry
lend	rend	collect	correct
lack	rack	collection	correction
lock	rock	allay	array
light	right	alive	arrive
lute	route	unless	unrest
/kl/	**/kr/**	**/kl/**	**/kr/**
clipped	crypt	clam	cram
clown	crown	class	crass
/gl/	**/gr/**	**/gl/**	**/gr/**
glaze	graze	glean	green
glow	grow	glass	grass
/fl/	**/fr/**	**/fl/**	**/fr/**
flat	frat	flows	froze
flight	fright	flute	fruit
/pl/	**/pr/**	**/pl/**	**/pr/**
plow	prow	plied	pride
plays	praise	pleasant	present

/bl/	/br/	/bl/	/br/
blue	brew	bled	bread
blade	braid	blink	brink

Pragmatics

Readiness Exercises

The /r/ consonant phoneme drops down into position for the next vowel from the position of the vowel /ɝ/. If your /ɝ/ vowel is produced correctly, we can start from that position to help get the feel for /r/.

Here are some phrases in which the first word ends with the vowel /ɝ/, and the second word begins with the glide /r/. The first word puts us in position for the correct articulation of /r/.

Read each phrase aloud, and then read the /r/ word alone.

her reach	reach
her ring	ring
her reign	reign
her rent	rent
her rank	rank
her rock	rock
her robe	robe
her room	room
her rice	rice
her round	round

Reinforcement Exercises

Practice Words for /r/

Beginning	Middle	Beginning	Middle
Reeve	bereave	ravel	unravel
real	unreal	rode	erode
rich	enrich	Rome	aroma
rage	enrage	root	uproot
rate	berate	rise	arise
wrecked	direct	ride	deride
rest	arrest	round	around

Beginning /r/ and /tr/ Contrast

rain	train	rim	trim
rend	trend	rash	trash

Beginning /r/ and /tr/ Contrast

rip	trip	raid	trade
rue	true	Rio	trio
right	trite	rye	try
rack	track	ripple	triple
rigger	trigger	rust	trust

Beginning /r/ and /dr/ Contrast

ream	dream	Rama	drama
rear	drear	raw	draw
rink	drink	Ross	dross
rip	drip	roll	droll
rill	drill	rue	drew
rain	drain	rule	drool
red	dread	rug	drug
rest	dressed	rum	drum
wrench	drench	round	drowned
rag	drag	rye	dry

Beginning /r/ and /kr/ Contrast

reek	creek	rock	crock
ripped	crypt	Ross	cross
rave	crave	row	crow
rate	crate	rude	crude
read it	credit	ruse	cruise
ram	cram	rook	crook
rash	crash	rust	crust

Beginning /r/ and /gr/ Contrast

reed	greed	Rand	grand
Reeve	grieve	ratify	gratify
rid	grid	row	grow
rip	grip	rope	grope
rave	grave	room	groom
rain	grain	runt	grunt
raid	grade	ripe	gripe
raft	graft	round	ground
rant	grant	rate	great

Beginning /r/ and /fr/ Contrast

reed	freed	rigid	frigid
risky	frisky	ray	fray
rill	frill	rail	frail

Beginning /r/ and /fr/ Contrast

rate	freight	red	Fred
ank	Frank	wrench	French
rend	friend	rock	frock
wrought	fraught	root	fruit
runt	front	right	fright
ride	fried	round	frowned

Beginning /r/ and /θr/ (thr) Contrast

rift	thrift	rue	through
rash	thrash	rill	thrill
Rhett	threat	row	throw
rob	throb	red	thread
wrong	throng	Retin	threaten

Beginning /r/ and /br/ Contrast

reef	brief	rat	brat
reach	breach	racket	bracket
reed	breed	rag	brag
rig	brig	ranch	branch
ridge	bridge	Rand	brand
ring	bring	rash	brash
risk	brisk	roach	broach
rain	brain	rook	brook
raid	braid	rude	brood
race	brace	rue	brew
rake	break	ruse	bruise
rave	brave	root	brute
raisin	brazen	rush	brush
red	bread	ride	bride
rest	breast	round	browned

Beginning /r/ and /pr/ Contrast

reach	preach	rank	prank
recede	precede	robbable	probable
repair	prepare	robe	probe
rinse	prince	roof	proof
ray	pray	rhyme	prime
rep	prep	rice	price
ram	pram	rise	prize

Beginning /r/ and /ʃr/ (shr) Contrast

reek	shriek	rug	shrug
rink	shrink	rub	shrub
rude	shrewd	rill	shrill

Beginning /r/ and /spr/ Contrast

ray	spray	rout	sprout
ring	spring	right	sprite
rye	spry	right	sprightly
rocket	sprocket	wrinkle	sprinkle

Beginning /r/ and /skr/ Contrast

reach	screech	rue	screw
ream	scream	rub	scrub
wrap	scrap	roll	scroll
ramble	scramble	ripped	script

Beginning /r/ and /str/ Contrast

Warning: Be careful not only to get a good /r/ in these words, but a good /s/ as well. Don't turn /s/ into /ʃ/ (sh).

raid	strayed	reek	streak
wrangle	strangle	wretch	stretch
Ruggles	struggles	ray	stray
rip	strip	ripe	stripe
rate	straight	roll	stroll
wrong	strong	rut	strut
rest	stressed	rider	strider
rain	strain	rum	strum
raw	straw	rife	strife
range	strange	ream	stream
ride	stride	wrapping	strapping
rap	strap	Rand	strand
ring	string	ray	stray

Practice Phrases for /r/

the old red rooster
around the perimeter
hurry to Rome
arrange a marriage
correct the writing
trying to improve
the roll of the drum
a broken record
renting a room
a brief romance
ready to run
dreaming of royalty
appreciate a good restaurant

express surprise
celebrate patriotism
a narrow victory
freedom and democracy
rules of the freeway
driving to the entrance
a uranium mine in rural Colorado

Practice Sentences for /r/

1. If I broke it, I'm very sorry.
2. The new director will present his first play on Friday.
3. I arrived recently—during a riot.
4. He eats french fries three times a day.
5. They sent me a crate of Florida oranges.
6. The train leaves at three o'clock and will arrive around six.
7. Not very happy? He's miserable!
8. Try to make other arrangements for the irate passenger.
9. Her requirements were rather unrealistic.
10. The wrestler groaned a lot to prove the match was real.
11. Bring your rich uncle. I want to drive his Rolls-Royce.
12. Don't be afraid. He'll approve anything.
13. Rain, rain, rain—a horrible day for the Macy's parade.
14. I hear you all right, but I don't grasp the meaning of your remarks.
15. I'm sorry I don't have a very good reason for it.

Practice Sentences for /r/ (More Challenging)

1. Straight-laced and prudish, she brands everything obscene.
2. He retreated to Arizona or Colorado. I can't remember which.
3. I'm not worried about the alarm. Really, I'm terrified!
4. Ralph threatened suicide to trick the professor into a better grade.
5. There's no glory in being arrested, but I really wouldn't resist.
6. The florist provided all the floral arrangements for the restaurant. Very impressive!
7. It was wrong of the crowd to disrupt the meeting of the Rapid Transit Authority.

8. Returning from the arena, I realized I had enraged all my friends.
9. Larry says all operas are boring and ridiculous.
10. You can't borrow the car. Your driving record is terrible.

Practice Sentences for /r/ (Most Challenging)

1. He thinks he's patriotic because he carries a flag and cries on hearing the ''Star-Bangled Banner.''
2. All I require is a little respect, a lot of consideration, and a reasonable salary.
3. He's reverent around priests and preachers, but a rascal all other times.
4. The idea of a raw onion sandwich makes me cringe.
5. The rainstorm will not destroy my reliable waterproof watch.
6. In what area of the country do you reside?
7. Randy saw Karen across the crowded room, and a new romance began.
8. Ray is his own favorite charity. He has trouble sharing his wealth.
9. I have travelled a great deal in Asia and Africa, and I'm ready to return right now.
10. I'm reading *Pride and Prejudice*, but it's too heavy to carry around.

9

Consonant Combinations

Thus far in studying articulation, we have discussed individual phonemes. But it is not just lone sounds that give us difficulty in articulation. Some combinations of sounds offer special difficulties for many speakers. Because sounds put together in groups are different from sounds uttered alone, we must look at some of the particular problems presented by difficult sound combinations.

We will certainly not give attention to all the possible consonant combinations in this chapter. We will concentrate on those consonant combinations that present special stumbling blocks to many speakers of American English. Because these combinations pose problems for many speakers, you should check all of them to see if you need to work on your production of these common consonant groupings.

We are dividing these consonant combinations into *abutting consonants* (two consonants in a row, but in separate syllables) and *compound consonants* (consonants in a row in the same syllable). Compound consonants with two consonants together are called *blends*; compound consonants with more than two consonants are called *clusters*.

Abutting Consonants

Abutting consonants are two successive consonants (two consonants in a row) that belong to separate syllables. That would mean, then, that one consonant ends a syllable and the next consonant begins the following syllable. There are two instances of abutting consonants that offer particular difficulty to many speakers: consecutive stops (two different stops in succession) and "doubled" stops (the same stop in abutting position—one ending and the other beginning a syllable). Let us look at each of these types of problem consonant combinations.

Two Different Stops in Succession

You will remember that we defined stops as consonants on which the air stream was stopped completely by the articulators. Sometimes the air pressure is built up at the point of blockage and then released in a little explosion.

We noted that stops always stop the outgoing breath stream, but they do not always explode. When two stop consonants come together one after another, there is only one explosion, although there are two stops. You stop the first stop consonant with a good firm closure, but do not release it in a plosion. Then you stop the second stop consonant with a complete closure and *do* release it in a plosion.

Check what you do when you say the word *act*, for example. The /k/ closes off the air stream for an instant, but you do not explode the /k/ as you would in the word *keep*. Instead, you move on to the closure for the /t/ and explode only the second plosive (/t/).

The same thing occurs if the two stop/plosives are in successive syllables—even in different words. Read these words aloud, and note what happens on the two abutting stop consonants:

back*b*one
sub*t*ract
foot*b*all
rub*d*own
rock-*b*ottom

If you pronounced these words correctly, in *backbone* the /k/ stopped but did not explode and the /b/ both fully stopped *and* exploded. In *subtract*, the /b/ stopped but did not explode and the /t/ stopped and exploded. In *football*, the /t/ stopped but did not explode and the /b/ both stopped and exploded. Well, we hope you have the idea! Just in case: on *rubdown*, the /b/ stopped but did not explode and the /d/ stopped and exploded, while on *rock-bottom*, the /k/ stopped without exploding and the /b/ stopped and exploded.

Now read these words and phrases aloud, and note the same pattern for abutting stops:

hot dog	rib cage
back door	hot drink
hop down	sick time
sad case	big time
rag content	ripe tomato

Now re-read those words and phrases, checking to be sure you fully obstruct the air stream for an instant on the first stop consonant and voice it if it should have vocal vibration.

If English is not your first language, this pattern is very important to learn, because it will affect both your intelligibility (whether other people can understand you) and the rhythm of your speech.

Here are some practice sentences for abutting stops. Each of the following sentences contains two different stops in succession.

1. He was in a ba**d** **p**osition.
2. He began to dro**p** **b**ehind rather quickly.
3. They mus**t** **b**egin at once.
4. Tom carried the pac**k** **d**ownstairs.
5. They said it couldn'**t** **b**e done.
6. The performance was qui**te** **g**ood.
7. Ho**p** **d**own from the bar, toad.
8. Be sure to pic**k** **g**ood examples.
9. Pupils are not allowe**d** **t**o do homework.
10. It's a waste**d** **t**wo points.
11. It was har**d** **t**o get him to do that.
12. I can'**t** **b**elieve that they have turne**d** **t**o alcohol!
13. They ma**de** **t**wo touchdowns in the las**t** **q**uarter of the game.
14. Don'**t** **b**e satisfied with slack articulation of the plosives.
15. He lived in the high ren**t** **d**istrict.
16. The hi**p** **b**one's connecte**d** **t**o the thigh bone.
17. Grea**t** **d**ay in the morning!
18. I ha**d** **t**rouble with the assignment.
19. That act is har**d** **t**o follow.
20. He sagged and reele**d** **t**oo much in the firs**t** **p**erformance.
21. We ha**d** **t**o write a term paper.
22. Everyone ha**d** **t**o wor**k** **t**o complete it.
23. I've hear**d** **t**errible things about that chea**p** **t**rinket.
24. Actually, tha**t** **p**roduct is qui**te** **g**ood.
25. With his bac**kg**round, he's lucky the judge didn'**t** **c**onvict him.
26. Why di**d** **C**al deci**de** **t**o ta**ke** **p**art in that affair?
27. I came bac**k** **t**o work, but I'm no**t** **g**oing to work hard.
28. She really doesn't want Davi**d** **t**o kee**p** **b**elieving her lies.
29. **It** **c**ould be called a chea**p** **t**rick, but **it** **c**ost **D**ave plenty.
30. I trie**d** **t**o tell him, but he jus**t** **p**refers his present activities.

"Doubled" Stops

If you have one syllable ending with a stop consonant, and the next syllable begins with the same stop, you do not have two stops but one—with the difference between a single consonant and a "doubled" consonant indicated by a lengthening of the time of the closure before the release of the plosion. That means that, if you have two abutting stops (and the two are the same phoneme), you make only one stop (you block the air only once), but you block off the air stream longer than you would for the same stop if it were a single consonant.

In the word *bookcase*, for example, you do not stop and release the first /k/ and then stop and release the second /k/. You obstruct the air stream with the back of the tongue as you would on a single /k/, but you hold the air stream closed off for a longer time before you release it.

The same principle holds true even if the two stops are in successive words. Note that *last time* is not pronounced the same as *lass time*, *right time* is not pronounced the same as *rye time*, and *keep punching* differs from *key punching*.

There are two distortions associated with "doubled" stops against which you should guard:

(1) Careless speakers tend to treat "doubled" stops as if they were single ones, and

(2) Pedantic (*overly* precise) speakers tend to stop and explode each stop in the pair.

Pronounce these words and phrases aloud. On each phrase, check to be sure you get a good, firm stop and hold it closed the extra time to indicate the "doubling."

keep pace	stop pouting
Club Bizarre	lab book
night time	meet Tom
bad dream	sad day
trick case	drink Coke
big game	vague guess

Here are some practice sentences for "doubled" stops. Each of the following sentences contains at least one example of "doubled" stops.

1. You ough**t t**o vote in this election.
2. Hi**t t**o center field.
3. I ha**te t**o attend that class.
4. The coach will pic**k K**im for the award.
5. We ha**d d**ozens of offers of help.
6. We all hope to win the bi**g g**ame next week.

7. He dyed the ro**be** **b**rown.
8. What is a "hi**p** **p**erson"?
9. We had to be**d** **d**own in the backyard.
10. The children begged to go along, but they were turne**d** **d**own.
11. No one go**t** **t**o look at it.
12. Can't you ta**k**e **K**evin with you?
13. I am looking for a ri**d**e **d**owntown.
14. No honest player would ri**g** **g**ames for profit.
15. I forgo**t** **t**o pac**k** **c**lean shirts for the trip.
16. I pass**ed** **t**en cars before the crash.
17. He told me he could ty**p**e **p**erfectly.
18. Who would ro**b** **B**en of his last dollar?
19. All he had to do was qui**t** **t**o prove his point.
20. Ma**d** **d**ogs and Englishmen go out in the noonday sun.
21. Tak**e** **c**are of yourself, and don't forge**t** **t**o write.
22. I fough**t** **t**o get into the show, but they insisted that I loo**k** **c**losely at the sign: "For Trade Only."
23. I trie**d** **d**riving to work, but I found taking a ca**b** **b**etter.
24. The Exhibition Center won'**t** **t**ake fa**k**e **c**redentials.
25. Don't dra**g** **g**randmother's name into tha**t** **t**errible argument.
26. Tha**t** **t**estimony is no**t** **t**rue.
27. I've go**t** **t**o get a jo**b** **b**efore I can pay those bi**g** **g**ambling debts.
28. How can I rea**p** **p**rofits? I lac**k** **c**apital.
29. Wha**t** **t**ouching loyalty! She hi**d** **d**ozens of his letters.
30. Kee**p** **p**racticing. Gra**b** **b**locks of time. Wor**k** **c**onsistently. Ge**t** **t**ogether with your instructor. Rea**d** **d**aily and hee**d** **d**irections. Then you can bra**g** **g**reatly.

Compound Consonants

We defined abutting consonants as two successive consonants that belong to separate syllables; one ends the first syllable and the other begins the following syllable. *Compound consonants*, on the other hand, are consonant combinations that occur *within* one syllable, either beginning the syllable or ending it.

Although books on phonetics are not consistent in their terminology, we are going to use the term *consonant blend* to refer to a compound consonant combination of two consonants and the term *consonant cluster* to refer to a compound consonant combination of three or more consonants.

We will not give instructions and practice materials for all the possible consonant blends or consonant clusters that occur in English. We will limit our attention to those combinations that give speakers the most trouble. (We have already given you some exercises for the initial consonant blends /bl/, /pl/, /br/, and /pr/, among others. See pp. 90, 93-94 and 201.) Now we turn our attention to those consonant blends and consonant clusters that, especially because of their final position in words, may give you the most problems.

Blends

Stop Plus Nasal

These are blends in which a nasal sound follows one of the stops. They are articulated in a special way—as a combination. When a nasal consonant follows a stop, the air stream is obstructed by the articulators for the stop in the usual way, the closure is held for a moment while the velum drops down to open the passage to the nose, and the air is then popped up through the nasal passages. Some writers call this release a nasal plosion. However, be certain you do not insert the vowel /ə/ between the stop consonant and the nasal. The nasal sound itself will "carry" the syllable; the nasal, which is providing the sonority for the syllable, is called a syllabic nasal. Also be careful not to turn /pn/ into /pm/ or /kn/ into /kŋ/ (kng).

Here are some practice materials for consonant blends made of a stop plus a nasal.

/pn/

1. Open the door, please.
2. How did it happen?
3. The entire torso of the sculpture seemed misshapen to me.
4. We had a wreck on the Tappan Zee Bridge.
5. We cleaned the canvas with turpentine.
6. It seemed a curious happenstance to me.
7. Does his firm have any openings I would be interested in?
8. The little fellow couldn't wait for the watermelon to ripen.
9. What's happening?
10. The bottle was a terrible weapon.

/bn/

1. She cut the ribbon.
2. Who was Ibn Saud?

3. Abba Eban is world-famous.
4. Durban is in South Africa.
5. Mr. Rubin is a gentleman.
6. Don Fabun wrote an excellent book.
7. Why is she wearing a turban?
8. The march was led by Tobin himself.
9. Seventy per cent of Americans live in urban areas.
10. Laban is a Biblical name.

/tn/

1. They threw rotten tomatoes at the speaker.
2. She was wearing a simple cotton dress.
3. Seton Hall hasn't lost a game this season.
4. The mailman was bitten three times last week.
5. Ill-gotten gains will do you no good.
6. Why haven't you written the report?
7. He appears to be smitten by her charms.
8. Farmers fatten up the hogs before slaughtering time.
9. Have you ever eaten rattlesnake? Certainly not!
10. Batten down the hatches!
11. Put on your hat and coat.
12. Who wants to buy a Siamese kitten?
13. Button up your overcoat.
14. The Titans are at the bottom of the league.
15. He wants to straighten this mess out.
16. The president has asked us to tighten our belts.
17. The theater could use new curtains.
18. Are you certain he hasn't written in a year?
19. Mutton can taste rotten unless seasoned properly.
20. Doesn't anybody wear mittens any more? I've gotten used to them.

/dn/

1. He burst into the room suddenly.
2. This product was made in France.
3. Who let the snake into the Garden of Eden?
4. I have joined the Rod and Gun Club.
5. Auden is one of my favorite modern poets.

6. Why have you hardened your heart against me?
7. The dentist could not deaden the pain.
8. The entire university was saddened by the news.
9. It was the ship's maiden voyage.
10. Is that a symphony by Haydn?
11. It's too heavy a burden for you to bear.
12. Personally I think it's good riddance.
13. He had an answer for everything.
14. The judge refused to pardon him.
15. The suspense was maddening.
16. I saw no wooden shoes in Holland.
17. This card is laden with good wishes.
18. According to the teachers, Mr. McFadden is the principal problem.
19. The news gladdened our hearts.
20. I'm good and tired of these exercises.

/dnt/*

1. You shouldn't have done that.
2. I couldn't care less.
3. He said he wouldn't go, but he did.
4. These shoes are wooden ones. Wouldn't you like to see them?
5. Are you sure they didn't like the play?
6. It's true I hadn't eaten frog legs before.
7. The doctor said we shouldn't eat mutton.
8. All the students insisted they couldn't understand the assignment.
9. The instructor didn't believe them.
10. I could tell he hadn't practiced. Couldn't you?
11. I didn't hear the phone ring.
12. The adviser insisted that pledges shouldn't be beaten.
13. Wouldn't it be better to decide for yourself?
14. Aren't you afraid of rodents?
15. I hadn't thought much about it.

* Yes, this is a cluster rather than a blend. But the logical time to practice it is after mastering the *dn* blend.

/kn/

1. My faith in human beings has been shaken.
2. The phonograph is broken and should be repaired.
3. I think her resistance is weakening.
4. Stephen has become a deacon now.
5. Have you eaten Canadian bacon?
6. The thought of eating snails is sickening.
7. The day of reckoning has come.
8. The cook couldn't get the gravy to thicken.
9. Chicken is a meal most foul.
10. You've been my friend through thick and thin!

/gn/

1. No, I'm not Henry Higgins.
2. Who's left but Mrs. Dugan?
3. Is the Coogan family moving next door?
4. Have you ever been in Copenhagen?
5. I bought her a little red wagon.
6. Megin has started to school.
7. He only speaks in jargon.
8. I love "Puff, the Magic Dragon."
9. Is Sheboygan in Michigan?
10. Do you know Hulk Hogan's real name?

Stop Plus Lateral

We have called this section "stop plus lateral" rather than "stop followed by lateral," because we do not produce one and then the other. They are truly blended together. On all six of these blends—/pl/, /bl/, /tl/, /dl/, /kl/, and /gl/—we must be careful not to insert a vowel (usually schwa) between the stop and the lateral.

On /pl/ and /bl/, we articulate the bilabial plosive by firmly, completely closing the two lips; we build up the air pressure behind the two lips; we raise the tongue tip to the upper gum ridge and hold it there (for /l/) while we release the built-up air, which continues to come out over the sides of the tongue as the /l/ is sustained.

/tl/ and /dl/ are unusual consonant combinations. When the lateral consonant (/l/) "follows" a homorganic stop (a stop articulated in the same place as the /l/—on the alveolar ridge), the air is released in an interesting way. The air is exploded over the sides of the tongue. There are two stops, you remember, that are articulated by pressing the tip of the tongue against the upper gum ridge: /t/ and /d/. They are usually released by dropping the tongue tip down from the gum ridge. When /t/ and /d/ occur as a blend with /l/, however, they are not released (ploded) in the center. The tongue does not drop down from the center of the gum ridge. Instead, it stays firmly touching that ridge and the air pops out over the two sides of the tongue.

To repeat: To make the /tl/, you place the tongue tip firmly on the upper gum ridge, hold the tongue tip firmly against the ridge, and pop the air over the sides of the tongue. The difference between /tl/ and /dl/ is this: The /tl/ *begins* voiceless and is a bit more aspirated; the /dl/ is fully voiced from the beginning and is less aspirated. Do not let the tongue drop between the /t/ or /d/ and /l/, because that will insert a vowel between the two consonants. The /tl/ and /dl/ are consonant combinations—lateral plosions—and you should not conceive of the consonants as being formed separately, but together.

On /kl/ and /gl/, the back of the tongue is raised toward the soft palate to stop the air stream while the tongue tip is raised to the gum ridge. The back of the tongue pops the air, which comes out over the sides of the tongue, because the tongue tip stays firmly touching the gum ridge to sustain the /l/.

There are three common distortions of these consonant combinations:

(1) Incomplete closure,
(2) Insertion of a vowel, and
(3) Substitution of the glottal stop for the /t/ in the /tl/ blend.

Important reminders:

(1) These combinations begin with a stop, and all stops must stop. Always. Alone or in combination.
(2) *Mantle* should not sound like *man tull*, and *candle* should not sound like *can dull*.
(3) A glottal stop is a stop made at the glottis—the space between the vocal folds. If you bring the vocal cords together, build up the air pressure there, and then release the air in a little plosion, you produce a glottal stop. Although the sound is sometimes heard in the greater New York City area, it is not an English phoneme or an allophone of a phoneme. (See pp. 69-70.) As you pronounce the following words aloud, check to be certain that you do not substitute this down-in-the-throat sound for one made with the tongue tip on the upper gum ridge:

battle	rattle	bottle	futile
fundamental	beetle	myrtle	gentle
mantle	subtle	antlers	cattle

Here are some practice words for all the stop + lateral combinations:

/pl/	**/bl/**
apple	dabble
staple	able
steeple	feeble
cripple	nibble
Koppel	cobble
purple	rubble
/tl/	**/dl/**
title	tidal
petal	pedal
mental	Mendel
cattle	paddle
total	modal
brutal	poodle
/kl/	**/gl/**
ankle	angle
pickle	giggle
tackle	tangle
fickle	haggle
sparkle	gurgle
twinkle	wiggle

Practice sentences for /tl/

1. I'm hoping to settle the case out of court.
2. I have a mutilated copy of my own.
3. We are studying the fundamentals of speech.
4. They used bottles for weapons in the street battle.
5. The subtleties of the story escaped him.
6. The children called the informer a tattletale.
7. The teacher did not think I was entitled to an A.
8. In Westerns, cattle rustlers are never gentlemen.
9. She threw a bottle of ink at me in a futile attempt to stop me.
10. They looked up the vital statistics in the atlas.
11. Do not use a glottal stop in these exercises.
12. Every time I met Tom, he was hatless.
13. Myrtle is doing volunteer work at a mental hospital.
14. He always puts a little something in the Salvation Army's kettles.

15. I wasn't startled by the influence of the Beatles.
16. It'll be a long time before I learn this.
17. Her tongue is a cutlass; she's not very subtle.
18. I prefer a metal one to plastic.
19. My wife tried to whittle down the price.
20. Enough of this prattle! It's a total waste.

Practice sentences for /dl/

1. Handle it with care.
2. How can you choose between Tweedledum and Tweedledee?
3. Paddle your own canoe!
4. The warden was accused of coddling the prisoners.
5. Is yodeling good for your voice?
6. The little toddler fell constantly.
7. We ate by candlelight.
8. I read a story about a headless horseman.
9. Oddly enough, he hit the wrong pedal on the organ.
10. Stop meddling in my affairs.
11. Our senator straddles every issue. He's a Mugwump!
12. I'm in the middle of something important.
13. She loved her poodle a lot more than she loved me.
14. They still paddle children at that school.
15. Sandals let in the air—and the dirt.
16. A little scandal can sell a lot of newspapers.
17. I don't want to saddle you with my worries.
18. I'm entering the country fiddle contest at the fair.
19. George IV was too fat even to waddle around the palace.
20. Don't bother to ladle out any turtle soup for me!

Stop Followed by a Fricative

When a fricative follows a stop, a firm closure is made for the stop, the air pressure is built up at the point of closure, and the air is then released through the opening of the fricative.

Here are some words ending with a stop plus a fricative. Read the words aloud, and check to be certain you get a good firm closure on the stop and a quick accurate release on the fricative. Also be certain you get good vocal vibration on the voiced consonants.

Voiceless Stop + /s/	Voiced Stop + /z/
rips	ribs
rates	raids
rock	rugs

/ps/ and /bz/ Contrast

rips	ribs	ropes	robes
apes	Abe's	lopes	lobes
Epps	ebbs	Rupp's	rubs
sops	sobs	cops	Cobb's
mops	mobs	cups	cubs
caps	cabs	sups	subs
laps	labs	hops	Hobbs
tripe's	tribes	gaps	gabs

Practice Sentences for /ps/ and /bz/

1. She hopes to become a star in Mr. Webb's movie.
2. The tops of the drapes are on fire.
3. Be sure to buy enough tubes of paint to finish the jobs.
4. He often rubs the lamps, but nobody appears.
5. Mr. Cobb's a friend to all the cops in the neighborhood.
6. If anyone robs him, he hopes they'll catch the thief.
7. Now in the U.S. Navy, he hopes to get into subs.
8. After the mobs mess up the kitchen, she mops the floor.
9. There were gaps in his story, but Hobbs spotted them all.
10. She sobs and weeps when her fibs are found out.

/ts/ and /dz/ Contrast

beets	beads	bets	beds
pats	pads	knots	nods
fates	fades	bites	bides
newts	nudes	hurts	herds
carts	cards	rots	rods
rites	rides	cats	cads
rates	raids	boats	bodes
mates	maids	bits	bids
huts	Hud's	Gert's	girds
nets	Ned's	greets	greed's
Kurt's	curds	notes	nodes
sweets	Swedes	waits	wades
totes	toads	sits	Sid's
sights	sides	Burt's	birds

Practice Sentences for /ts/ and /dz/

1. It's not a waste of time.
2. The boats are docked in the harbor.
3. That store sells many brands of paint.
4. Birds of a feather flock together.
5. It's what's up front that counts.
6. God's in His heaven, all's right with the world.
7. The administration followed a "hands-off" policy.
8. The tax will finance new roads.
9. His doubts are well founded.
10. We want deeds, not words.
11. He lifts weights once a week at the gym.
12. She bites her nails; he bides his time.
13. Hope fades. My fate's in his hands.
14. The boat's sinking. That bodes ill for all of us.
15. There are more than two sides in a controversy.
16. That's what so many fights are about.
17. She just waits while he wades in over his head.
18. Greed's a powerful force; it greets you everywhere.
19. That's all. The period's over.
20. Check on the hotel rates, and bring credit cards.

/ks/ and /gz/ Contrast

lax	lags	leaks	leagues
picks	pigs	jocks	jogs
tucks	tugs	tacks	tags
racks	rags	wicks	wigs
hawks	hogs	fox	fogs
box	bogs	hacks	hags
sacks	sags	chucks	chugs
bucks	bugs	pecks	pegs
Beck's	begs	Burke's	burg's
Lux	lugs	Volks	*Vogue's*

Practice Sentences for /ks/ and /gz/

1. The little boy was throwing rocks at the pigs.
2. He brags about the books he reads.
3. He picks fresh figs from the tree.
4. He jokes about "rags to riches."
5. He works on those dialogues in acting class.

6. Mr. Burke's election bogs down every time.
7. The dogs are waiting at the docks.
8. Rick's denying he rigs the outcome.
9. The fraternity lacks scholars; it lags in scholarship.
10. The ship's logs indicated all locks were broken.
11. They forgot to charge tax on the tags I bought.
12. Terry never nags at him to fix the car.
13. Bobby begs for mercy as the thirty clocks start to chime midnight.
14. Jerry always leaks the results of the league's tournament.
15. Only a fool picks pit bulldogs for pets.

Two Fricatives

When two fricatives occur together, you must be sure to articulate both consonants and permit the air stream to come through the first obstruction before permitting it to come through the second.

There are three dangers related to blends of two fricatives:

(1) Omission of one of the consonants,
(2) Addition of a vowel between the two consonants, and
(3) Unvoicing of voiced sounds.

Some examples as reminders:

(1) *Leaf's* should not become *lease* or *leaf*.
Leaves should not become *Lee's* or *leave*.
Youth's should not become *use* or *youth*.
Breathes should not become *breeze* or *breathe*.

(2) *Safe's* should not sound like *safe us*.
Saves should not sound like *save us*.
Wreath's should not sound like *wreath us*.
Wreathes should not sound like *wreathe us*.

(3) *Waves* should not become *waif's*.
Oaths should not become *oath's*.

/fs/ and /vz/ Contrast

leaf's	leaves	thief's	thieves
knife's	knives	waif's	waves
proof's	proves	half's	halves
shelf's	shelves	scarf's	scarves
strife's	strives	safe's	saves
loaf's	loaves	wife's	wives
Duff's	doves	serfs	serves

Practice sentences for /fs/ and /vz/

1. Your beliefs are your own business.
2. Life's a vapor that quickly vanishes.
3. The safes were supposed to be burglarproof.
4. The roof's on fire!
5. Jerry loafs around the house all day.
6. He often reads from *Leaves of Grass*.
7. A good politician, she loves a difficult campaign.
8. He lives in an adjoining county.
9. Mark believes in miracles, but never performs any.
10. The "haves" must help the "have-nots."

Practice Sentences for /fs/ and /vz/ (More Challenging)

1. He thinks he deceives us, but his life's an open book.
2. His wife's motto is "Don't make waves!"
3. His story? He laughs, he loves, he leaves.
4. The proof's missing. That proves the lawyer's incompetent.
5. He thrives on controversy. Strife's a medicine to him.
6. The more he delves into philosophy, the more his beliefs change.
7. I like your new shelves, but this shelf's warped.
8. We must buy a new set of knives. This knife's really dull.
9. My wife's getting uneasy. My first four wives have been talking to her.
10. The little waifs are playing in the waves. They may hurt themselves.

/θs/(ths)	**/ðz/(*thz*)**
youth's	youths
breath's	breathes
wreath's	wreaths/wreathes
bath's	bathes
tooth's	teethes
oath's	oaths
path's	paths
cloth's	cloths

Practice Sentences for /θs/ (ths) and /ðz/ (*ths*)

1. We were unable to reach the youth's parents.
2. For your health's sake, you should stop drinking.

3. Myths are stories that teach moral lessons.
4. With his last breaths, he was still arguing.
5. The moth's attracted to the flame.
6. Listening to Bach soothes my nerves.
7. Paths that are "untrod" are not paths at all.
8. She bathes in goat's milk.
9. The dancer writhes six hours a night at the club.
10. When the discussion gets heated, she smooths things over.

Practice Sentences for /θs/ (ths) and /ðz/ (*th*z) (More Challenging)

1. He says his wealth's a curse. But he lives and breathes money.
2. How can he believe an oath's worthless? He takes oaths often.
3. He mouths the right words when his wrath's not kindled.
4. Youth's worshipped in America. I wish truths were too.
5. There are many paths to success. Which path's the easiest?

Sibilant Followed by a Stop

When a stop consonant follows a sibilant at the end of a word, the sibilant is articulated in the usual way, and the stop must be fully closed. Unless the final stop is followed immediately by a word beginning in a vowel, the stop will not be released with aspiration (an explosive puff of breath) in American English.

Compare the /k/ in these two sentences to understand this difference in aspiration—the way the final stop is released:

> Don't ask.
> Don't ask a favor.

The /k/ in the first sentence did not explode. It stopped, but did not explode. But the /k/ in the second sentence both stopped *and* exploded, because of the vowel following.

There are two common dangers, or problems, associated with this consonant combination (sibilant + stop):

(1) Omission of the stop consonant, and
(2) Overaspiration of the release of the stop.

Important reminders:

(1) Again, although the stop does not always explode in this combination, it does always *stop*. The air stream is completely obstructed for a moment. During the time the stop is being articulated, no air at all is emitted, and the time taken by the

closure is necessary to indicate the presence of the stop consonant. You must be sure, in these combinations, that the articulators completely block off the air for the stop.

(2) The second danger is almost the opposite of the first. Some speakers, in an effort to be precise, overarticulate the stop sound in the combination, releasing the stop in a *great* puff of air. To most listeners, this sounds pedantic and affected. We do not recommend it.

(3) The word *ask* poses a special problem. You may be tempted to reverse the sibilant and the stop—putting the /k/ before the /s/ rather than after it. This turns the word *ask* into *axe*. Many listeners find this deviation particularly annoying. Pronounce these phrases aloud and check to be sure the /s/ comes before the /k/:

Don't ask a favor.
ask a question
Let me ask you . . . .
Ask me no questions . . . .

Here are some practice sentences for sibilant + stop:

/sk/

1. I only ask for what is just.
2. The risk is too great for so small a reward.
3. He said it was carved from an elephant's tusk.
4. Mr. Fiske wore his uniform to the party.
5. Everyone had his own task to perform.
6. A brisk walk is good for what ails you.
7. Nothing is more beautiful than Big Sur at dusk.
8. My desk is a dreadful mess.
9. He had a flask in his pocket, but I didn't ask what was in it.
10. He must have bathed in musk oil.
11. She shouldn't have taken the mask off.
12. I want to whisk you away to some deserted island!
13. I would risk everything to bask in your smiles.
14. The farmer taught me how to husk the corn.
15. Mr. Rusk's car has disc brakes.

/sp/

1. The cookies were not crisp.
2. Have you detected a lisp in my speech?

3. No one told her that the clasp was not fastened.
4. A wasp sting can be very painful.
5. You could have heard the gasp ten miles away!
6. I told you not to grasp my hand that way!
7. Your lisp doesn't bother me.
8. There was a tiny wisp of smoke on the horizon.
9. The hasp on the trunk is broken.
10. You can grasp my meaning, if you try.

/st/

1. She is the least beautiful of the sisters.
2. Roast pork is on the menu tonight.
3. The note is past due.
4. What is your worst problem in speech?
5. I want your best quality of merchandise.
6. I missed Carolyn in the crowd.
7. The horse is now at the post position.
8. What is your next question?
9. The enemy was forced back by the advancing troops.
10. I disagreed with the last proposition.
11. I trust you will rest better tonight.
12. The famous journalist was almost blind.
13. His taste buds must be dead.
14. They lost money on that investment.
15. You must go to the game next week.

/ʃt/ (sht)

1. He was lashed to the mast.
2. Mashed potatoes are somewhat fattening.
3. She secretly wished for more, but said nothing.
4. He pushed his way through the crowd.
5. Several were crushed by the stampeding mob.
6. We meshed immediately.
7. She looked crushed when I said we had rushed into it.
8. What fury was unleashed on me!
9. I looked away when the car crashed.
10. She flashed a big smile, and I hushed instantly.
11. When the stocks went up, I cashed in.

12. Eleanor laughed at the joke—but she blushed.
13. He has been punished enough.
14. She furnished the entire house in Early Tacky.
15. He brandished a knife, took what he wished, and vanished.

Clusters

Stop Between Two Continuants

When a stop consonant occurs between two continuants (consonants that, unlike stops, can be sustained), you must take care to make a firm and complete closure for the stop phoneme. The stop will not be released in an explosion, but will be released instead through the opening for the fricative that follows.

The danger, of course, is that you will omit the stop consonant altogether and combine the two continuant consonants that remain. Listen to these clusters. There should be an instant between the two continuant sounds when no air is coming out at all, because the articulators have completely stopped the breath stream to form the stop consonant in the middle of the cluster.

Grafts should not sound like *graphs*.
Pelts should not sound like *else* with /p/ in front.
Dents should not sound like *dense*.
Masts should not sound like *mass*.
Holds should not sound like *holes*.
Bands should not sound like *bans*.
Tasks should not sound like *Tass*.
Grasps should not sound like *grass*.

Here are some practice materials for these consonant clusters.

/fts/

1. Dick is studying arts and crafts at the college.
2. The posse is searching all the hay lofts in the county.
3. She lifts our spirits when she enters the room.
4. The Crofts plan to spend their honeymoon in the Virgin Islands.
5. The lawn mower left tufts of grass here and there.
6. They all ran to the left side of the ship.
7. I cross my fingers when he shifts gears.
8. He never lifts a hand to help around the house.
9. I never laughed so much in all my life.
10. She records the gifts as they come in.

/lts/

1. He tilts the machine every time he plays.
2. The coat was made from dozens of pelts.
3. The gold is stored in underground vaults.
4. Every sweet saying melts in her mouth.
5. Fearful of burglars, she always bolts the door.
6. I like the way she belts out a song.
7. He paid a fortune for those colts.
8. He wilts if she so much as looks at him.
9. Her remedy for every ailment was "a dose of salts."
10. How those clowns walk on stilts is a mystery to me.

/nts/

1. She put several new dents in the fenders today.
2. We bought six pints of sherbet for the punch.
3. One of the mints is in Denver.
4. At the party she performed unusual stunts.
5. The Senate consents more than it advises.
6. He recants every other day.
7. Larry is worse; he rants and raves every day.
8. Rents in New York City are outrageous.
9. Other than that, I have no major complaints.
10. He faints at the sight of blood; she faints at the sight of flesh.

/sts/

Distinguish between the following pairs of words by making a firm closure between the two /s/ sounds in the second word with the tongue tip on the gum ridge:

mass	masts
guess	guests
lass	lasts
Joyce	joists
Tess	tests
miss	mists
pass	past's
Bess	bests

Practice Phrases for /sts/

East Side, West Side
last season, next season

first semester, last semester
most certain, least certain
best sort, worst sort
last summer, next summer

Practice Sentences for /sts/

1. I want to take the test some other day.
2. The host spoke with all the guests.
3. Last season, I played on the varsity.
4. Next summer, I'm going to Europe.
5. We lost several games last season.
6. We must see them tonight.
7. Of all the employees, he is least secure.
8. She passed seven courses in basket weaving.
9. Mine will be the last speech of the evening.
10. There are seven tests scheduled for tomorrow.
11. They have wasted vast sums. The costs are unbelievable.
12. I hope it lasts a long time.
13. He produced lists of names.
14. Our host's maid took the night off. The roast's ruined.
15. The guests hardly noticed.
16. She trusts anyone—even the worst sort of people.
17. Bob resists believing in ghosts and goblins.
18. The hotel's breakfasts are incredible feasts.
19. Aunt Boots wastes a lot of time on those contests.
20. Jimmy blasts everyone when he has one of his outbursts.

/ldz/

1. That sorority holds a meeting only once a month.
2. Ruthlessly he wields his power.
3. Our contractor builds each house to the owner's specifications.
4. The child's every whim is indulged.
5. A good leader welds a group into a cohesive unit.
6. I don't understand how he holds on to his power.
7. A walk in the fields is therapy for me.
8. She shields her children from the realities of life.
9. The guild's power has been broken by the strike.
10. He fields questions like a professional politician.

/ndz/

1. He lends his name to every liberal cause that comes along.
2. The bands are massed for the big parade.
3. Wally is effective at predicting economic trends.
4. Blest be the tie that blinds!
5. She had no grounds for that action.
6. I hope he finds out in time.
7. Friends are a necessity—not a luxury.
8. The boss made unreasonable demands on me.
9. The ends do not justify the means. Well, that depends.
10. I think he stepped out of bounds on that play.

/sks/

1. She asks every teacher the same question.
2. Who carves those symbols on the desks?
3. He refuses to take any risks at all.
4. Joyce never shirks her tasks.
5. The Rusks are an old, respected family in this community.
6. The flasks are all empty.
7. What makes this desk so rough?
8. I think the elephant tusks are fake.
9. He has several slipped discs in his back.
10. Now Shelley basks in the Florida sun.
11. Do the police have the right to frisk suspects that way?
12. What makes musk so pungent?
13. You have to risk something to get something.
14. These tasks are not menial.
15. It's illegal to wear the masks out on the street.

/sps/

1. My sister is afraid of wasps.
2. Wisps of smoke were visible on the horizon.
3. She grasps everything very quickly.
4. Cleopatra and the asps were bosom pals.
5. She said that malocclusion was the reason she lisps.
6. The hasps are always broken on these doors.
7. I wish I could grasp some of your ideas.
8. The dentist mentioned defective cusps—whatever they are.
9. He told me to make a clear, crisp sound.
10. She tightly clasps every new psychological fad to her tortured psyche.

Two Stops Followed by a Sibilant

To master these consonant clusters, you should remember two principles we have told you earlier:

(1) when two stop sounds come together, the first is stopped, but not exploded, and then the second is stopped and exploded, and

(2) when a stop is followed by a fricative, a firm closure is made for the stop, but the release is made through the opening for the fricative.

If you combine these two principles, you will have no difficulty with these clusters. Be sure that you completely obstruct the outgoing breath stream to form the first stop; stop the air completely for the second stop; and, finally, release the second stop at the place of articulation of the sibilant.

Important reminder:

The /ts/ is a consonant *combination*, and there is only one release of air on that combination. The /t/ is released through the /s/ position. That still holds true when you put /k/ or /p/ in front of that combination to form a cluster.

Read the following pairs of words aloud. Check to be certain you distinguish the first word from the second by getting a good firm closure for both stop consonants.

/ks/	**/kts/**
axe	acts
packs	pacts
tracks	tracts
Fax	facts
sex	sects
ducks	ducts

/kts/

1. He tried to get all the facts.
2. My partner deducts his gambling losses on his tax return.
3. I didn't say "What sex do you know about?"; I said "What sects do you know about?"
4. This course inflicts a lot of pain on the students.
5. She certainly expects a lot from us.
6. That statement conflicts with your earlier position.
7. The ducts are clogged, and the ducks are dying.
8. I've got to reject some of these demands.
9. She attracts a lot of admirers.
10. After those willful acts, the ax fell.

/pts/

1. That fiend corrupts everyone with whom he has contact.
2. The orchestra performed excerpts from a number of longer works.
3. The crypts are beneath the church.
4. That clique disrupts every meeting of the fraternity.
5. I'm told that she accepts any invitation she receives.
6. I don't want to be around when she erupts again.
7. He interrupts every sentence his wife starts.
8. Everybody's coming except Sam.
9. He's a very inept soldier.
10. They kept searching until they found it.

Sibilant Plus Two Stops

This cluster formation should offer you no difficulty if you have mastered the principle related to two consecutive stop consonants. Remember: both stops stop, but only the second one explodes. On this cluster, it is important to keep in mind that we must get both stops in. Both must stop, even if both do not explode.

The usual simplification of these clusters results from leaving out the first of the two stops and then combining the two remaining sounds. We end up with one stop and a sibilant rather than two stops and a sibilant.

This omission is a mark of careless speech. You certainly don't want careless speech, do you? Is that the image you want to project?

Reminders:

(1) *Masked* should not become *massed*.
Masked should not become *mask*, either.
Clasped should not become *classed*.
Clasped should not become *clasp*, either.

(2) The /skt/ in the word *asked* seems to pose special problems for many people. Be careful. Pronounce the word *asked* out loud. Do you get all three sounds in the cluster? Do you get them in the right order?
Asked should not become *ast*.
Asked should not become *ask*.
Asked certainly should not become ***axed***!!!

Practice sentences for /skt/

1. She risked her reputation to come tonight.
2. I asked her a dozen times and always got the same reply.

3. All day at the beach we basked in the sun.
4. We attended every masked ball during Carnival.
5. That tremendous tusked animal came charging at us.
6. He frisked us but found nothing.
7. The performers were whisked away quickly.
8. She said I asked a lot of senseless questions.
9. The farmer disked the field.
10. The masked actor could not see; he risked injury every performance.

Practice Sentences for /spt/

1. I gasped in wonder at the sight.
2. She thrust her tongue between her teeth when she lisped.
3. He grasped my hand and welcomed me to the United States.
4. In her clenched hand she clasped the dollar bill.
5. His voice rasped out its angry message.

Three Consecutive Continuants

We grant that you must have flexibility and control to produce a cluster made up of three continuant consonants in a row. As we always do, we will try to build on the skills you have already mastered. We have already learned to produce two consecutive fricatives. Now, we are just putting one more continuant (a consonant that's not a stop) in front of such a blend to make it a three-consonant cluster. (Don't panic, but it's possible to have a *four*-consonant cluster such as the /lfθs/ in the word *twelfths*.)

The most common distortion of this cluster formation is the omission of the second continuant—the middle consonant in the cluster. For example, *wealth's* then rhymes with *else*, and *fifths* rhymes with *ifs*.

As you read the following sentences aloud (each one contains a three-continuant cluster), check to be sure you articulate all three consonants in the cluster.

1. The mo**nths** of Spring are the best in the year.
2. I need three le**ngths** of material.
3. Hea**lth's** a blessing; wea**lth's** a curse.
4. He said those strange chords were ni**nths** and thirtee**nths**.
5. Three fi**fths** of the class is passing.
6. He could not add three-fourths and nine-sixtee**nths**.
7. Not prelaw, but prewea**lth's** his major.

8. Her stre**ngth's** returning slowly.
9. I am in the top nine-te**nths** of the class.
10. The fable was about e**lves** and ny**mphs**.
11. The Se**lf's** a mystery to all of us.
12. He will go to any le**ngths** to win.
13. Move West for your hea**lth's** sake.
14. Bill received two-fi**fths** for his birthday.
15. Stea**lth's** a virtue—if you're planning a sneak attack!

10

Vowels

We have already defined vowels as speech sounds that are emitted with relatively little obstruction of the air stream. Vowels, then, are not articulated in the same way as consonants. They are distinguished one from another by slight changes in resonance in the oral cavity (mouth). By shifting the tongue around in the mouth, by changing the shape of the opening formed by the lips, and by varying the amount of muscular tension and the time we hold onto the sounds, we produce the different vowels of American English.

We cannot be nearly so exact in describing the formation of vowels as we were for consonants, because we cannot be precise in describing the height to which the tongue is raised on any given sound, in pinpointing the exact area of the mouth to which the tongue is pulled forward or back, or in depicting the exact degree to which the lips are rounded. Vowels are influenced by the consonants that precede and follow them, and different people produce the same vowels differently. We will have to discuss the production of each vowel in rather general terms, and you will have to train your ears to recognize the slight differences that will distinguish one vowel from another.

Distinctive Features: Classification of Vowels

Every sound in the language can be identified (set off from all other sounds in the language) on the basis of a group of distinctive characteristics. These distinctive features, or components, are the means of classifying and describing sounds. Consonants, you remember, are distinguished from each other on the basis of three classes of features. Two of those classes are irrelevant in distinguishing vowels. All vowels are voiced; they are made out of tones produced by the vocal folds. Too, all vowels are emitted through a rather open passage out of the mouth. Unlike consonants, vowels cannot be classified by whether or not they have voicing (they all do) or how they are emitted (they are all emitted in relatively the same way). On all the vowels, the velum is raised to prevent air from escaping through the nose; we have no nasal vowels in English. (In languages such as French and Portuguese, whether vowels are emitted orally or nasally is a distinguishing feature.)

Each vowel in American English can be described (or classified) in terms of five classes of basic characteristics:

(1) lip position,
(2) tongue position,
(3) tongue elevation,
(4) duration, and
(5) tension.

Although it may not take all five characteristics to distinguish a given vowel from all the other vowel phonemes of the language, it does take all five characteristics to describe the vowel fully.

For example, to identify or classify the vowel at the end of the word *boo*, you would note its characteristics: /u/ (o͞o) is a tense, long, tightly lip-rounded, high (the back of the tongue raised high—nearly to the soft palate), back (the tongue raised in the back of the mouth) vowel. These five descriptive features pinpoint, or classify, this vowel. There is no other vowel phoneme in American English with all five of these distinctive features.

Let us look at each of these five classes of characteristics separately.

Lip Position

If you look in a mirror at the position of your lips as you pronounce the vowels in the words moo, me, and ma, you will notice that the lips are tightly rounded for the first, unrounded and spread for the second, and unrounded and quite open for the third. Vowels may be classified as to whether or not they are uttered with the lips rounded. In general, the lips are more or less spread for the vowels formed by raising the tongue in the front of the mouth, and they are more or less rounded for the vowels formed by raising the tongue in the back of the mouth. Furthermore, there is a parallel between the amount of lip rounding and the degree to which the tongue is raised in the back of the mouth: the higher the tongue to form the vowel, the more tightly the lips are rounded.

The way you shape the opening of the mouth with your lips affects the resonance of the vowels. It is theoretically possible to produce recognizable back vowels without the usual lip rounding, but the resonance of the vowels is clearly affected. The sound is different and distorted, if recognizable, and we certainly do not advise it.

Tongue Position

When you form all the vowels, your tongue tip remains behind your lower front teeth. It is the rest of the tongue that moves around in the mouth to produce the different vowels. If you raise the front of the tongue high in the mouth up near the hard palate and, while the vocal folds are vibrating, slowly lower the front of the tongue until the tongue lies flat in the mouth, you will produce a number of vowel sounds that are called *front vowels*. Similarly, if you round the lips tightly and raise the back of the tongue high up in the back of the mouth near the soft palate and, while the vocal folds are vibrating, slowly lower the tongue and gradually relax the rounding of the lips, you will produce a number of vowel sounds that are called *back vowels*. In addition to the front and back vowels, there is a group of vowels made with the center of the tongue raised up in the center of the mouth; these vowels are called, logically enough, *central vowels*. *Front, back*, and *central vowels*, then, refer to the area of the oral cavity (mouth) in which the tongue is raised to produce the vowel.

Tongue Elevation

Each vowel in each of the three groups of vowels (back, front, and central) can be further described in terms of the relative height to which the highest part of the tongue is raised to make the sound. For example, the vowel in the word be is made with the front of the tongue raised very high in the mouth. The vowel /i/ (ē) is therefore called a *high* front vowel. The vowel at the beginning of the word *ooze*, on the other hand, is made with the back of the tongue raised very high in the mouth. The vowel /u/ (o͞o) is a *high* back vowel. Another example is the vowel at the beginning of the word *up*, which is made with the center of the tongue raised up to the middle of the mouth; this vowel /ʌ/ (u) is a *mid* central vowel. For a clearer understanding of the relative positions and heights of the vowels, see the vowel diagram.

Duration

The duration of a vowel, of course, is how long you hold or sustain it. A vowel is a speech sound that can be sustained or prolonged. How long you prolong a vowel depends on three factors:

(1) the nature of the vowel itself (some vowels are inherently longer—in English, at least—than other vowels);

(2) whether the vowel occurs in a stressed syllable (and, if so, the degree of stress); and

(3) the vowel's position in a syllable and its neighboring sounds.

We said that some vowels are naturally longer (in English) than other vowels. Some might dispute that statement, because theoretically you could hold any vowel for a long time. In connected speech, however, some vowels are given longer duration than others. True, there are other factors involved here, but /u/ (o͞o) is ordinarily held longer than /ʊ/(oo). Poets know the value of using long and short vowels (we are not talking about diacritics in the dictionaries, but about the length of time a vowel lasts!) to suit their purposes in poems. Edgar Allen Poe wrote an essay about the use of sounds and the choice of sounds to create certain moods. You must give vowels their proper length to catch the music and rhythm built into our speech patterns.

Another factor determining the length of time a vowel gets is syllabic stress. We make some syllables stand out by giving them more stress (prominence) than other syllables. We accomplish this stressing of the syllable by increasing loudness, raising pitch, *and* increasing the duration of the vowel. We stretch out syllables we want to stand out. Stressed syllables are longer, because the vowels are held longer. You can check this for yourself. Say the words *no* and *piano* out loud. Is the *o* in each of equal lengths? No, because in the first word the syllable is stressed and in the second it is unstressed.

Finally, how long a vowel will be sustained depends also on what position it has in a syllable and in a word and on what sound follows. Try the words *row* and *romance* out loud. The /o/ phoneme of the first word is longer than the /o/ of the second word. This is partly so because the first is in a stressed syllable and the second in an unstressed syllable. However, another explanation is that the /o/ is final in the first word and it is not final in the second. Maybe we should have had you use the word *robot* as the second (contrast) word. There the difference is not in stress, but in position, and still *row* contains a longer vowel.

Let's check on the effect of the sound that follows the vowel. Pronounce the words *rope* and *robe* aloud. Which one has the longer /o/? You are right. The /o/ in *robe* is the longer one. If a voiced consonant comes after the vowel at the end of a syllable, the vowel will be longer than when the vowel is followed by a voiceless consonant. Compare *right* and *ride*, *lace* and *lays*, and *half* and *have*. In each case, the syllable ended by a voiced consonant contains a longer vowel.

Tension

Vowels differ in the amount of tension there is in the oral cavity when they are formed. The tongue, of course, has muscles, and these muscles—like others—can be tensed or relaxed. To form some vowels, you tense the side-to-side muscles of the tongue, but to form other vowels you do not tense them.

Say the words *eat* and *it* aloud. Can you feel the tongue tension on the vowel in the first word? Can you feel the tongue relax to make the vowel in the second word? Try the two words out loud again, but this time as you say them, put your thumb and forefinger on your neck under your jawbone. Hold the fingers there lightly as you pronounce the two words. *Now* can you feel the tension on the first word (because of the tense vowel)? Do you feel the tightening for /i/ (ē) and the relaxing for /ɪ/ (i)? If you are pronouncing these words in the customary way—producing the vowels properly, you should be able to detect the marked difference in tension.

We could have given you other words to show the contrast in tension also. The vowel in *fool* is tense; the vowel in *full* is relaxed. The vowel in *age* is tense; the vowel in *edge* is relaxed.

Without the proper amount of tension, a vowel may be distorted and resemble another vowel of American English.

The Fourteen Vowel Phonemes

There are fourteen vowel phonemes in American English. As we have noted, each language has its own phonemic system. If English is not your first language, you probably cannot transfer intact the vowels from your first language into English. Your first language may have some vowels we do not have in English. On the other hand, English may have some vowels your first language does not use.

It may be true, as some have said, that consonant production is the key to intelligibility (being understood). But, vowel production is a key to the sonority (resonances) and character (quality) of your speech. Teachers of singing concentrate heavily on the formation of vowels for that reason.

We will divide the vowels into three groups, using tongue position as the basis for the grouping. There will be a chapter each on Front Vowels, Back Vowels, and Central Vowels. Then we will discuss the three Phonemic Diphthongs and finally consider some Non-Phonemic Diphthongs and Triphthongs.

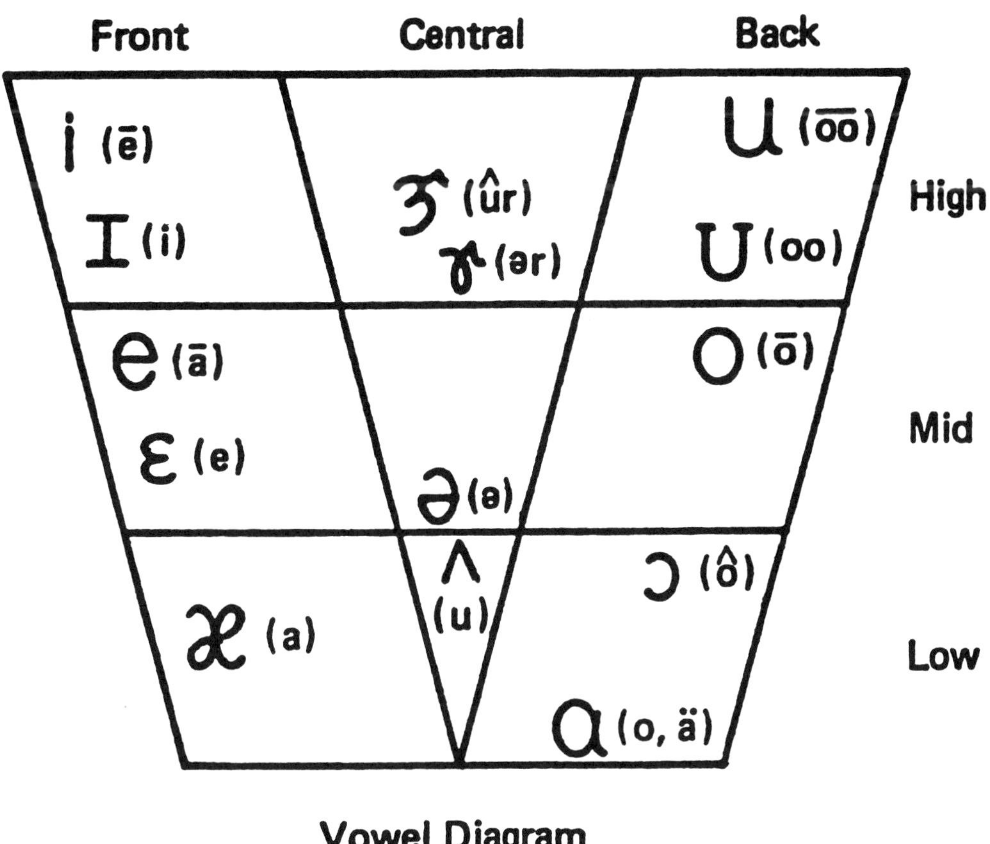

Vowel Diagram

11

Front Vowels

Almost all vowels are formed with the tongue tip resting behind the lower front teeth. It is the rest of the tongue that moves around to make the distinctions among vowel sounds.

Front vowels are the five vowel phonemes of American English that are produced by raising the front of the tongue in the front area of the mouth. Now, isn't that logical?

We will discuss each vowel phoneme in turn. We will give you the important principles related to each one, including how it is produced and some precautions you must know. Then we will identify common problems and provide exercises designed to help you overcome any deficits you may have. Finally we will integrate the correct sound into connected speech.

Remember, as we start working on vowel phonemes, we are focusing on *sounds*—not *letters of the alphabet*. Our Latin alphabet has only five vowel letters (A, E, I, O, U), and our language has fourteen vowel phonemes. Think **sounds**—not letters written down!

/i/ (ē)

Principles

Production

If you lift the front of the tongue nearly to the hard palate while the tip of the tongue rests behind the lower front teeth, tense the tongue, spread the slightly tensed lips into a smile, and emit the breath stream through the mouth with the vocal folds vibrating, you will produce the

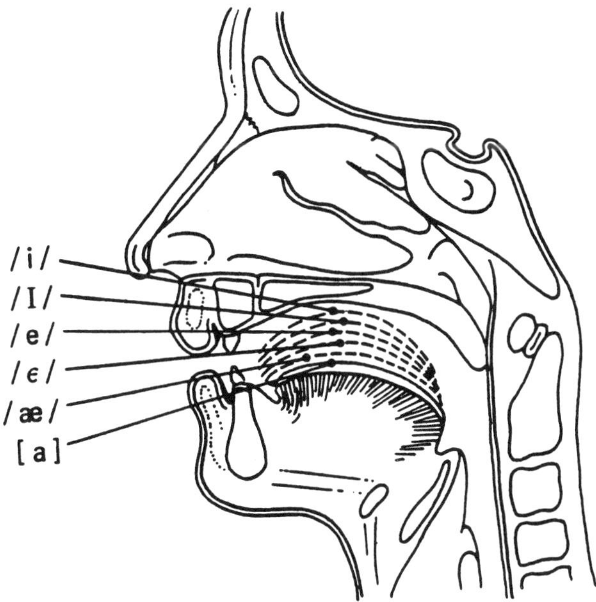

Figure 11.1. *Representative tongue positions for front vowels. [Phonemes in slashes; allophones in brackets.]*

highest front vowel. It is the vowel phoneme in the word *beat*, which is represented in IPA by /i/ and in the dictionaries by ē. The sound /i/ (ē) is classified as a *long, lip-spread, tense, high front vowel.*

Precautions

There are twelve ways of spelling /i/ (ē):

e as in *be*
ee as in *see*
ea as in *seat*
ae as in *Caesar*
i as in *marine*
ie as in *piece*
ei as in *receive*
eo as in *people*
oe as in *amoeba*
ey as in *monkey*
y as in *ready*
uay as in *quay*

Problems

There are two common problems associated with this phoneme. As we discuss each problem, check to see if you distort the /i/ (ē) in that way.

▶ ***Problem 1:*** Diphthongation or triphthongation

In the South and Southwest of the United States, there is a tendency for some speakers to "drawl." That means that they elongate their vowels into diphthongs and triphthongs. Diphthongs, you remember, are blends of two vowels, and triphthongs are blends of three vowels.

You may be most tempted to add an extra vowel (or two) after the /i/ (ē) when the consonant /l/ follows in the same syllable. Then /i/ (ē) may turn into /iə/ (remember that /ə/ is the little vowel at the beginning of the word *above*) or even /ijə/ (eyə).

Check your pronunciation of the following words. Is there an extra sound or two after the /i/ (ē) and before the /l/?

feel	kneel	wheel
meal	keel	deal
seal	peel	heal

Let's check again. You probably will not elongate the vowel before a /t/ phoneme. The /t/ stop tends to check the vowel. That will give us a good basis for comparison. Here are a few pairs of words. Pronounce the pairs, and check to hear if the vowels are alike in both words.

feet	feel
neat	kneel
wheat	wheel
meat	meal
seat	seal
peat	peel
heat	heal
beat	Beale

▶ ***Problem 2:*** Lack of adequate tension

Unless the /i/ (ē) phoneme is adequately tensed, it will lack its distinctive character and sound like the more relaxed vowel /ɪ/ (i). If your first language is not English, you may have difficulty getting enough tension in the production of this vowel. Many people do. The tongue must be very tense and the front of the tongue must be raised very high in the front of the mouth. You should be able to feel the tension in the muscles.

One lovely lady came to us for help on this problem a few years ago because she had provoked gales of laughter in a New York department store when she tried to buy a sheet for her bed. She could not make the difference between /i/ (ē) and /ɪ/ (i) at that time, and she could not hear the difference either. In her first language (Spanish), she did not need to be able to hear or produce this distinction. The Spanish language has one vowel phoneme where we have two, and she used that one Spanish sound for both phonemes in English. To people who knew only English, it always sounded backwards—whichever it was supposed to be!

The Romance languages, such as Spanish, have only one high front vowel phoneme, and that sound is about half way between our /i/ (ē) and /ɪ/ (i). As we said, native speakers of English will recognize that sound as "different" and probably identify it as the other one of our two. If the word was supposed to be *each*, it will be heard as *itch*, and if it was supposed to be *itch*, it will probably be heard as *each*! There are three differences between /i/ (ē) and /ɪ/ (i) in English:

(1) height of the tongue,
(2) tension, and
(3) duration.

/i/ (ē) is higher, more tense, and longer than /ɪ/ (i).

Most people who confuse /i/ (ē) and /ɪ/ (i) have most trouble with *tension*. Tightening up the mouth and tongue muscles enough seems to be the major obstacle to good /i/ (ē) production.

Here are a few words to check for a clear distinction between /i/ (ē) and /ɪ/ (i). Be sure to lift the tongue high enough, make the tongue tense enough, and hold the vowel long enough (double length) to make a good, clear /i/ (ē).

Beginning /i/ (ē) and /ɪ/ (i) Contrast

eat	it
each	itch
eel	ill
ease	is
easy	Izzy

Middle /i/ (ē) and /ɪ/ (i) Contrast

leave	live
reach	rich
seen	sin
feel	fill
tease	'tis

Pragmatics

Reinforcement Exercises

Practice Words for /i/ (ē)

Beginning	Middle	End
eat	beach	be
each	deal	D.
Eve	feed	fee
eager	agreed	agree
eagle	he'd/heed	he
Egypt	jeep	gee (slang)
easy	keen	key
ego	lied (a song)	Lee
equal	meat	me
even	neat	knee
evil	peer	pea
ether	scene	see
Easter	teach	tea
Eden	veal	V.
ear	wield	we
east	priest	E.

Practice Phrases for /i/ (ē)

to Greece and Egypt
eager to see
a deep feeling
each evening
green beans
sweet peas
sleet on the tree
a new fee each week
an increase of three dollars
please believe me
either agree or leave
fleeing at great speed

Practice Sentences for /i/ (ē)

1. Each of them attended the Easter service.
2. He's a "big wheel" in the city machine.
3. Please leave me out of your plans.
4. The speech was about peace and freedom.

5. How did Eve feel—after leaving Eden?
6. Our team has never been defeated.
7. They greeted the new teacher with eerie sounds.
8. She's not conceited—just pleased with herself.
9. Even in his sleep, he's dreaming up new schemes.
10. I agree with what the preacher said this week.

Practice Sentences for /i/ (ē) (More Challenging)

1. The team needs a victory to increase their confidence.
2. The marines cannot conceive of defeat.
3. Send those cheese pizzas to the fieldhouse for the team.
4. They seem eager to please, but no one believes it's real.
5. The people of Egypt received me with great hospitality.
6. Hear no evil; see no evil; speak no evil.
7. All the teenagers were squealing with glee.
8. Keep the heat even as you cook the meatloaf.
9. We could not see how he could make evil appealing.
10. We feel the need of healing. Don't you agree?

Principles

Production

If you allow the front of the tongue to relax into a position slightly lower and farther back than the height it assumed for /i/ (ē), relax the lips slightly but continue to leave them spread, and emit the air stream through the mouth with the vocal folds vibrating, you will produce the vowel in the word *bit*. We represent this vowel phoneme in IPA by /ɪ/ and in the dictionaries by i.

The /ɪ/ (i) is classified as a *short, lip-spread, lax, high front vowel.*

Precautions

There are nine spellings for /ɪ/ (i):

e as in *English*
ee as in *been*
ei as in *forfeit*
i as in *fit*

ie as in *sieve*
o as in *women*
u as in *busy*
ui as in *guild*
y as in *lyric*

Problems

There are three common problems or distortions associated with this phoneme. As we discuss each deviation, check to see whether you have that problem with this phoneme.

► *Problem 1:* Diphthongation and triphthongation

We have already discussed this problem in relation to the /i/ (ē). It is probably even more of a temptation on the /ɪ/ (i) phoneme. Speakers who tend to elongate their vowels and turn one sound into two or three can have a field day with the /ɪ/ (i). *Hit*, which has three sounds—the middle of which is the vowel /ɪ/ (i)—can be turned into [hɪət] (hiət) or even [hijət] (hiyət). This last version has a good /j/ (y) sound in the middle of it.

Our advice, if you have this problem, is: get off the sound quickly; don't hold on to the sound long enough to let it turn into two or three sounds. Move on, and tack on the consonant.

► *Problem 2:* Substitution of /i/ (ē) for /ɪ/ (i)

The /ɪ/ vowel phoneme is very difficult for many whose first language is not English. Many languages do not contain this phoneme, and speakers of those languages are not used to hearing or making this vowel.

You have probably heard a student from another country say *eat* for *it*, *seat* for *sit*, and *team* for *Tim*. Actually, they may be using a sound from their first language that is not quite our /i/ (ē), but it sounds like /i/ (ē) to us.

As we noted earlier, there are three differences between /i/(ē) and /ɪ/ (i): the height to which the tongue is raised, the tension of the tongue, and the length of the sound. /ɪ/ (i) is not quite as high in the mouth as the /i/ (ē). You must not only drop the tongue a little bit from the /i/ (ē) position to make the /ɪ/ (i), you must also relax the tongue muscles to produce a good /ɪ/ (i). And remember that /ɪ/ (i) is a much shorter sound than /i/ (ē) in English.

Again, here are a few words to contrast the two high front vowels of English. Listen, feel and see the difference between the two vowels as you read the word pairs aloud.

Beginning /i/ (e) and /ɪ/ (i) Contrast

eel	ill	e'en (poetry)	in
eat	it	ease	is
each	itch	easy	Izzy

Middle /i/ (e) and /ɪ/ (i) Contrast

leak	lick	bead	bid
peak	pick	reed	rid
peach	pitch	heed	hid
heap	hip	team	Tim
deep	dip	Jean	gin
seep	sip	reek	Rick
leap	lip	sheen	shin
meal	mill	heat	hit
seal	sill	beat	bit
peal	pill	feet	fit
cheap	chip	meet	mitt
sleep	slip	neat	knit
sheep	ship	bean	bin/been
steal	still	leafed	lift

▶ *Problem 3:* Substitution of /ε (e) for /ɪ/ (i)

In the problem we just discussed, a higher, more tense vowel was substituted for the /ɪ/ (i) vowel. In the substitution we are facing now, a lower vowel is being used in place of the /ɪ/ (i). The tongue is lowered from the position for /ɪ/ (i) and relaxed down to (or almost down to) the position for /ε/ (e)—the vowel in the word *Ed*.

Have you heard someone say "Set down" for "Sit down"? Or perhaps "It's on the sell" for "It's on the sill"? This substitution, although not very common, does occur. Check your pronunciation of the following pairs of words to be sure you do not make this substitution.

Beginning /ɪ/ (i) and /ε/ (e) Contrast

ill	el
itch	etch
Id	Ed

Middle /ɪ/ (i) and /ε/ (e) Contrast

will	well	sill	sell
hill	hell	bill	bell
dilly	deli	bid	bed
fill	fell	hid	head
nil	knell	lid	led

Middle /ɪ/ (i) and /ɛ/ (e) Contrast

till	tell	slid	sled
sit	set	miss	mess
bit	bet	wrist	rest
mitt	met	list	lest
wit	wet	hiss	Hess

Pragmatics

Readiness Exercises

Use the /i/ (ē) - /ɪ/ (i) contrasting pairs on pp. 241 and 245 for your warm-up. Check particularly for the difference in height, tension, and length of the two vowel phonemes.

Now read these phrases out loud. Each phrase contains both the /i/ (ē) and /ɪ/ (i) phonemes.

filthy streets
resist evil
keep pitching
leaving the city
keep fifty
a big secret
a quick meeting
quit cheating

an Easter visit
keeping a list
a quick meal
pick a peach
see a picture
agree to fix it
trick or treat
quick and easy

Reinforcement Exercises

Practice Phrases for /ɪ/ (i)

"filthy rich"
live and let live
the city's children
a big hit
fit for a king
dripping liquid
fix it quickly
picking everything
tricky business
visit Egypt
swimming in the chilly water
written in Old English script

Practice Sentences for /ɪ/ (i)

1. The inn is still in business.
2. Jim referred me to his physician.

3. Is there any city without a "skid row?"
4. I believe he is on the list.
5. This is a sickening dinner—a big disappointment.
6. The committee report had no impact.
7. Did you bring the chicken?
8. Little things mean a bit.
9. There's many a slip between the cup and the lip.
10. I did not imply he is without wit.

Practice Sentences for /ɪ/ (i) (More Challenging)

1. Ignorance is not bliss. That is ridiculous.
2. I admit I resent his inheritance.
3. I refuse to indicate it will end in disaster.
4. He was hit repeatedly, but still kept grinning.
5. Rick is interested in becoming rich.
6. I had a ticket but was refused admittance.
7. One instant he is timid; the next minute, he is brash.
8. If the work is so simple, why did his sister quit?
9. That building is still a symbol of Big Business.
10. If I win this free trip, I can visit Disney World.

/e/ (ā)

Principles

Production

If you open the lips a bit more and spread them a bit less than for producing the /ɪ/ (i), lift the front of the tongue to a position slightly below the height it assumed to produce /ɪ/ (i), and emit the air stream through the mouth with the vocal folds vibrating, you will produce the first vowel in the words *chaotic* and *detente.* We represent this phoneme by the IPA symbol /e/ and by the dictionary symbol ā. The tongue is tense, and this phoneme is of very long duration in stressed syllables. Indeed, it is so long (as we will see in a moment) that it is actually a diphthong in stressed syllables in American English, rather than a pure vowel.

Because the phoneme /e/ (ā) is made with the tensed front of the tongue raised midway up in the front of the mouth, it is classified as a *long, tense, lip-spread, mid front vowel.*

Precautions

There are nine spellings for /e/ (ā) in American English plus another for British English:

a as in *ate*
ai as in *aid*
au as in *gauge*
ay as in *say*
ea as in *break*
ee as in *fiancee*
ei as in *neighbor*
et as in *cachet*
ey as in *obey*
\+ **ao** as in *gaol* (It's *jail* in American English.)

In this handbook, we have not been discussing the allophones of each phoneme. In this instance, however, we think it wise to do so. If American English is your first language, you will probably have no difficulty with the two allophones of the phoneme /e/ (ā). You may not even have noticed that you use different variations of /e/ (ā) for stressed and unstressed syllables. But you almost certainly do. If English is not your first language, you should read this material on the two allophones of /e/ (ā) carefully.

There are two allophones of this phoneme in American English. The pure vowel [e] occurs only in unstressed syllables and is, therefore, the less common allophone. It is heard in the word *peyote* as the vowel in the first syllable. Contrast that vowel with the /e/ (ā) phoneme that occurs in the word *pay*, where the diphthongal allophone occurs. Another contrast would be between the pure vowel allophone used in the words *birthday* and *holiday* with the diphthongal allophone used in the word *day* alone. The names of the days of the week that include the unstressed syllable *day* in their names are pronounced with the pure vowel, as opposed to the diphthong form of the phoneme. (They can also be pronounced with /di/ (dē) or /dɪ/ (dĭ). *Monday* is not Mon-day, however, with the second syllable containing the stressed dipthongal allophone.

The more common allophone of the /e/ (ā) phoneme is the diphthong represented in IPA by [eɪ]. In this variation of the phoneme, the sound is a vowel blend made of two vowels (even though they are perceived by native listeners as one sound). The first of the two vowels is the longer and stronger one, but the second is clearly heard. We start with the /e/ (ā) vowel, but raise the tongue in a continuous movement toward the high front vowel /i/ (ē). We do not get the tongue as high as /i/ (ē), nor do we hold the second vowel of the diphthong as long as /i/ (ē) is usually held. For that reason, the diphthong is represented with [ɪ] (ĭ) as the second vowel. If you have difficulty hearing or producing this diphthong, it might be wise to think of the second element in the diphthong as an /i/ (ē).

Pronounce the word *aim* in slow motion to check on what your tongue does as it makes the word. The word has two phonemes in it: /e/ and /m/. The first phoneme, however, is not a pure vowel sound in American English; phonetically, it is a diphthong. You should be able to tell that the front of your tongue moves on the "*a* sound" upward toward the position of /i/ (ē). This tongue movement while the /e/ (ā) is being made produces the diphthongal allophone of the sound. Remember that this is the variation of the phoneme that will occur most often in American English, because native speakers use this diphthongal allophone for the "long *a*" in any stressed syllable.

Problems

There are four problems commonly associated with this phoneme. As we discuss each deviation in turn, check to see if you have that problem with /e/ (ā).

▶ *Problem 1:* diphthongation and triphthongation

Turning single sounds into two or even three sounds is clearly a distortion. And this vowel suffers as much from drawlers as any. The temptation is greatest before the /l/ in the same syllable. Get off the /e/ (ā) before you turn it into [eə] (āə) or [ejə] (āyə)! In stressed syllables the /e/ (ā) will be a diphthong [eɪ] anyway. No need to add another sound or two!

Here are some sequences. Read them across the line. Use them to check for the problem and also for practice. Try to keep the /e/ (ā) phoneme (it will be the standard diphthongal allophone in each word) consistent across the sequence. Be especially careful not to add [ə] or [jə] (yə) before /l/ in the last word of each sequence.

Kaye	Kate	kale
pay	pate	pale
hay	hate	hale
Faye	fate	fail
way	wait	wail
tray	trait	trail
bay	bait	bail
stay	state	stale
day	date	dale
gray	great	grail

fray	freight	frail
may	mate	male
gay	gate	gale
ray	rate	rail
nay	Nate	nail

Problem 2: Lowering

If you lower the tongue slightly from the position required for /e/ (a), relax the tongue muscles, and shorten the duration somewhat, you will produce a sound very close to the vowel phoneme in *egg* rather than the vowel phoneme in *age*.

Indeed, you may actually be substituting the /ɛ/ (e) vowel for the /e/ (ā). The phoneme /e/ (ā) is a tense sound, and relaxing the tongue will distort it, changing it into (or almost into) /ɛ/ (e).

Read the following pairs of words aloud, and check to be sure you clearly differentiate /e/ (ā) from the more lax and slightly lower vowel /ɛ/ (e).

/ɛ/ (e)	/e/ (ā)	/ɛ/ (e)	/e/ (ā)
yell	Yale	bell	bale
sell	sale	well	wail
shell	shale	tell	tale
Vel	vale	dell	dale
fell	fail	hell	hail
jell	jail	Nell	nail

For some unknown reason (or maybe known only to Freud), some speakers substitute the /ɛ/ (e) for /e/ (ā) in the word *naked*. Maybe *nekkid* sounds worse to them. It certainly does to us. It is nonstandard.

Problem 3: Substitution of /æ/ (a) for /e/ (ā)

Some speakers, particularly in the East, substitute /æ/ (a) for /e/ (ā). Again, the place of greatest temptation seems to be before /l/ in the same syllable. Check your own pronunciation of *pale* and *pal*. Is there a clear distinction between them? Is the full diphthong [eɪ] present for the /e/ (ā) phoneme?

Here are a few pairs of words for you to check this contrast. Read them aloud and be sure the /e/ (ā) is [eɪ].

/æ/ (a)	/e/ (ā)
Al	ale
pal	pale/pail
Cal	kale

/æ/ (a)	/e/ (ā)
Hal	hail
mal-	male
Sal	sail
Val	vale

Problem 4: Substitution of a pure vowel for [eɪ]

We have already discussed the two allophones of /e/ (ā) and noted that they may pose a problem if English is not your first language.

Many other languages do not have the /e/ (ā) phoneme. Speakers of those languages might easily transfer into English the phoneme from their first language that was closest to our "long *a*." Or they might hear (and produce) a pure vowel and leave off the second part (the tail) of the allophone of /e/ (ā) used in stressed syllables.

Remember that on this diphthong [eɪ], the tongue moves from the position of one vowel to another. The two vowels are blended together. The first vowel is stronger, but the second vowel must be there. Think in terms of /i/ (ē) as the second vowel, because the tongue moves in that direction, and it will help you produce the right sound.

If you have this problem, you should work on ear training, so you can perceive the difference between the two allophones of this phoneme. Then you should work to elongate the sound for the diphthongal allophone. When working to stretch (elongate) the diphthong variation, remember that the tongue moves from the position of the first vowel to the second in one continuous movement.

Pronounce these words out loud and listen for the second part of this phoneme.

say	play	stay	may
weigh	tray	bay	day
grey	away	pray	ray
obey	today	convey	inveigh

Pragmatics

Reinforcement Exercises

Practice Words for /e/ (ā)

Beginning	**Middle**	**End**
ape	grape	grey
ate	date	day
aim	lame	lay
ale	sale	say

Practice Words for /e/ (ā)

Beginning	Middle	End
eight	weight	weigh/way
age	cage	Kaye
ache	fake	Faye
aid	staid	stay
ace	trace	tray
A	praise	pray

Practice Phrases for /e/ (ā)

a player's agent
my claim to fame
for the same pay
a delayed plane
break the chain
a matinee today
came late
a great vacation
a place on the lake
May Day in Asia
age of the neighbor
waiting for a train
able to vacate in eight days

Practice Sentences for /e/ (ā)

1. We were sailing along on Moonlight Bay.
2. He has gained a lot of weight.
3. I may be sent to a new station.
4. Ray lies about his age.
5. No raisins? Take it away!
6. He took the blame for David's mistake.
7. I don't take Jane's tale at face value.
8. James explained the plan in great detail.
9. I'm afraid she's naked as a jaybird!
10. Play their game? Not at this late date.
11. I am just not able to obey.
12. The neighbors are away on vacation.
13. Steak and potatoes are basic food.
14. I would pay a great deal for a good piece of cake.
15. I waited in vain for a change in his ways.

Practice Sentences for /e/ (ā) (More Challenging)

1. Macy's is having a "Whale of a Sale."
2. He wasn't a failure, though he wasted his talents.
3. Daisy always ate on paper plates. Larry fainted.
4. Because she was famous, Diane retained her maiden name.
5. My head aches. My back aches. The pain is driving me insane!
6. The Empire State Building, a skyscraper, points straight at the sky.
7. He stayed a safe distance from the raging fire. Amazing.
8. I'm not lazy—just saving my energy for some outrageous effort.
9. If I've invaded your space, forgive me. I just strayed into this place.
10. All right, Ace, use your brain and create some great exercises.

Principles

Production

If you open the lips just a bit more than you did for forming /e/ (ā), allow the front of the tongue to relax into a position slightly lower and farther back than the height it assumed for /e/ (ā), and emit the air stream through the mouth with the vocal folds vibrating, you will produce the vowel phoneme in the word *bet*. This vowel is represented in IPA by /ɛ/ and in the dictionaries by e.

Both /e/ (ā) and /ɛ/ (e) are mid front vowels, but /ɛ/ (e) is more lax in its tongue tension, lower in tongue position, and usually shorter in duration than /a/ (ā).

/ɛ/ (e) is classified as a short, lip-spread, lax, mid front vowel.

Precautions

There are eleven spellings for /ɛ/ (e):

a as in *any*
ae as in *aesthetic*
ai as in *said*

ay as in *says*
e as in *red*
ea as in *read* (past tense of verb *read*)
ei as in *heifer*
eo as in *leopard*
ie as in *friend*
oe as in *Oedipus*
u as in *bury*

Problems

There are five common problems or distortions associated with this phoneme. As we discuss each deviation, check to determine if you have that problem with /ɛ/ (e).

▶ *Problem 1:* Diphthongizing and triphthongizing

We have discussed this kind of problem in relation to other phonemes. If you have a tendency to "drawl" your vowels and diphthongs—stretching them into two or three extra sounds, you may have this problem with the /ɛ/ (e) phoneme.

Pronounce the word *yes* out loud. Do you hold on to the vowel and get a little *uh* sound (/ə/) before the /s/? Now pronounce the word *well*. Is there a little *uh* (/ə/) or even a little *yuh* (/jə/) after the /ɛ/ (e) and before the /l/? If so, you are diphthongizing or triphthongizing the simple vowel.

Solution: Make it short. /ɛ/ (e) is a short vowel. Do not stretch it out. Move on to the following consonant quickly.

Pronounce the following words aloud. Check to see if you add a vowel (or so) to the /ɛ/ (e).

yes	less	stress	get
bet	set	fed	said
head	shell	fell	well
tell	ten	when	then
men	hem	them	Thames (Check the pronunciation!)

▶ *Problem 2:* Substitution of /e/ (ā) for /ɛ/ (e)

Before the consonant /r/ and the vowel /ɚ/ (ər), the /ɛ/ (e) varies a great deal in the United States. The sound varies both by dialect and idiolect. In that context, /ɛ/ (e) may be /ɛ/ (e), /æ/ (a), or /e/ (ā). These variations are acceptable. The name *Mary* offers an interesting example. You may hear any one of the three vowels used in that name. We cannot point to any consistent pattern, although you are more likely to hear /æ/ (a) and /e/ (ā) in the South than in other regions.

These substitutions are acceptable variants *only* on the words where the vowel is followed by /r/ or /ɚ/ (ɚr). If you substitute /e/ (ā) for /ɛ/ (e) in other words, it is a distortion and is nonstandard. This distortion is more common in the South than in the rest of the country.

If you make this substitution, you use the higher, more tense mid front vowel for the lower, more lax one. If someone says *haid* for *head* and *laig* for *leg*, they are making this distortion of the /ɛ/ (e) vowel.

Read these words aloud, and check to be sure you do not substitute /e/ (ā) for /ɛ/ (e).

leg	keg	egg
bed	head	red
measure	pleasure	treasure
says	said	segment

If you have this problem, you will probably find it easier to produce the conventional sound before /t/ and /d/ than before consonants articulated further back in the mouth. Try to get the correct short, lax vowel on the first word of the following pairs. Then try to match that vowel in the second (greater temptation) word.

Ed	egg	bet	beg
pet	peg	met	Meg
let	leg	kettle	keg
Ed	edge	led	ledge
pled	pledge	red	regular
pled	pleasure	med	measure
tread	treasure	set	segment

Now try these pairs aloud. They contrast /ɛ/(e) and /e/ (ā). The first word should not sound like the second one.

/ɛ/ (e) and /e/ (ā) Contrast

let	late	get	gate
met	mate	fret	freight
led	laid	bread	braid
stead	stayed/staid	pled	played
fed	fade	tread	trade
fleck	flake	wreck	rake
mess	mace	less	lace
west	waist	rest	raced
meld	mailed	held	hailed
fell	fail	tell	tale
heaven	haven	men	main

/ɛ/ (e) and /e/ (ā) Contrast

den	Dane	pen	pain
pent	paint	scent	saint
ebb	Abe	Ed	aid/aide
edge	age	S.	ace

Problem 3: Substitution of /ɪ/ (i) for /ɛ/ (e)

This distortion, although common in the South, Midwest, and Southwest, is nonstandard. If you substitute the high front lax vowel for the mid front lax vowel, you get this distortion. This substitution of /ɪ/ (i) for /ɛ/ (e) often occurs before consonants made on the upper gum ridge. Anticipating the coming consonant, the speakers lift the tongue to the higher /ɪ/ (i) position and thus replace the lower /ɛ/ (e) vowel with the higher vowel sound.

This distortion is *most* likely to occur, however, just before nasal consonants—especially /n/ and /m/. *Ten soldiers* thus become *tin soldiers* and a *hem* becomes a *him* or a *hymn*.

Pronounce the following contrasting pairs aloud to hear whether you make a distinction between /ɪ/ (i) and /ɛ/ (e)—or if you are tempted to substitute /ɪ/ (i) for /ɛ/ (e) in some (or all) of the words with /ɛ/ (e).

/ɪ/ (i) and /ɛ/ (e) Contrast

lit	let	lid	led
hid	head	rid	red
bit	bet	mitt	met
sit	set	litter	letter
kit	kettle	lift	left
Min	men	Minnie	many
been	Ben	tin	ten
pin	pen	din	den
him	hem	lint	lent
mint	meant	tint	tent
rinse	rents	since	cents
wind	wend	sinned	send
pinned	penned	timber	member

If you have found that you tend to substitute /ɪ/ (i) for /ɛ/ (e), especially before /n/ and /m/, try these sequences. You will probably get a good /ɛ/ (e) before the stop consonants. Therefore, pronounce the first word with the /ɛ/ (e) before a stop and then try, as you pronounce the second word, to make the vowel the same.

bed	Ben	dead	den
head	hen	med	men

Ted	ten	Tet	tenth
whet	when	Jed	gem
head	hem	led	Lem
stead	stem	educate	emulate
Edna	Emma	said	send

Problem 4: Substitution of /æ/ (a) for /ɛ/ (e)

Another distortion of the /ɛ/ (e), sometimes heard, is the substitution of the vowel in *add* and *had* for the /ɛ/ (e). In this case, the speaker is dropping the tongue down and back from the usual position for /ɛ/ (e). The result is that *yes* may sound something like *yass* and *guess* something like *gas*.

To produce a good /ɛ/ (e) vowel, your tongue must be lower and more relaxed than on /e/ (ā), but not so far down to be /æ/ (a).

Pronounce the following pairs of words aloud. Listen to be sure there is a clear distinction between the words.

/æ/ (a) and /ɛ/ (e) Contrast

mat	met	bat	bet
pat	pet	gnat	net
gas	guess	Yassir	yes sir
bass (fish)	Bess	mass	mess
blast	blessed	last	lest
massed/mast	messed	past	pest
vast	vest	faster	fester
pastor	pester	cattle	kettle
bad	bed	add	Ed
and	end	lag	leg
Cagney	keg	knack	neck
pack	peck	rack	wreck
ham	hem	pan	pen
than	then	sand	send
fanned	fend	Manny	many

Problem 5: Substitution of /ɝ/ (ur) for /ɛ/ (e) before /r/ or /ɚ/ (ər)

This problem is related to excessive retraction of the /r/ phoneme, which we have already discussed. (See p. 195.) If the tongue tip is turned too far backward toward the palate, the vowel before it may be distorted. Getting ready for that retroflex articulation, you may pull the tongue back on the vowel and produce the central vowel /ɝ/ (ur) instead of the front vowel /ɛ/ (e). This is another example of assimilation, but generally unaccepted assimilation.

If you make this substitution, *ferry* will sound like *furry*, and *very* will sound like "vurry." Read the following pairs of words. Check to see if you make a clear distinction between the two words. Listen to be sure the vowel in the words with /ɛ/ (e) is not /ɝ/ (ur).

With /ɛ/ (e)	With /ɝ/ (ûr)
hairy	hurry
merry	Murray
scary	scurry
berry/bury	burry
wary	worry
ferry/fairy	furry
Carey	curry
staring	stirring
air	err
mare	myrrh
care	cur
stare	stir
fair/fare	fur/fir

Pragmatics

Readiness Exercises

Depending on what problem you are working to overcome, review the discussion of that problem and the materials provided for checking and improving that specific problem. Then go on to the Reinforcement Exercises to help transfer the corrected sound into connected speech.

Reinforcement Exercises

Practice Words for /ɛ/ (e)

Beginning	Middle
edge	ledge
ebb	deb
end	mend
egg	leg
ere	there
etch	wretch
ever	sever
ember	member
enter	center
Evan	heaven
airy	merry
any	many
elder	held her

Several names begin with the vowel /ɛ/ (e). For example:

Edward	Edwin
Edgar	Edna
Elwin	Emma
Esther	Evelyn

Practice Phrases for /ɛ/ (e)

many exercises
best friend
forgetting the pledge
empty pleasure
a questionable ledger
extra energy
fled the wreck
King Edward's bed
a dreadful mess
healthy, wealthy, and wise
September weather
fender bender
never better
edit that special text
better than I guessed

Practice Sentences for /ɛ/ (e)

1. Make an extra effort to be ready on time.
2. I meant every word I said.
3. Ed has moved into a penthouse.
4. The President pays no rent.
5. For excellent opportunities, you must be educated.
6. We kept a separate set of books just for debts.
7. Emma broke both legs in the wreck.
8. I guess I will lend him a few dollars when I get the check.
9. Ten and ten and two are twenty-two.
10. That present is my most precious possession.
11. The boss blessed me as I tendered my resignation.
12. She says eating eggs will raise my cholesterol level.
13. I begged them to repair the elevator.
14. There was a measure of success, but a lot of stress as well.
15. We left the wrecked car on the edge of the cliff.

Practice Sentences for /ɛ/ (e) (More Challenging)

1. I never dreamt you would empty the entire account!
2. Anyone who says they don't care about money is extremely dishonest.
3. She said she didn't feel well. It was the anesthetic.
4. Yes, there is an echo in the lecture hall. Quit yelling.
5. Buried treasure is very difficult to find. A useless exercise.
6. All the men got a pen and pencil set. I wanted a watch instead.
7. Eddie, the new chef, is very depressed. He left the keg open.
8. I begged and pled for an end to the contest.
9. Many Americans intend to exercise, but don't.
10. Make every effort to attend. The show will be the best one yet.

/æ/ (a)

Principles

Production

If you raise the front of the tongue to a position slightly below and behind the height it assumed for producing the /ɛ/ (e) phoneme, open the lips without much tension, and emit the air stream through the mouth with the vocal folds vibrating, you will produce the *lax low front vowel* that occurs in the words *add* and *mad*. We represent this phoneme by /æ/ in IPA and by a in the dictionaries.

When you make this sound, the tongue is raised low in the front of the mouth (remember the tongue tip is behind the lower front teeth on almost all the vowels). That is why the vowel is classified as a *lax low front vowel*. The lips are neither spread nor rounded, but quite open. The jaw is dropped and relaxed.

The phoneme /æ/ (a) has a variant form, or allophone, that is heard mostly in New England. This second vowel, which can be used interchangeably with the [æ] (a), is a lower front vowel than the [æ] (a). It is about halfway between the vowel sound in *at* ([æ] in IPA) and the vowel sound in *alms* (/ɑ/ in IPA and ä in the dictionaries). This allophone is represented in IPA by the symbol [a].

Some people use the [æ] allophone in some words and the [a]

allophone in others. You might check your own idiolect. Do you use the same form of this phoneme in the words *at* and *ask*? Or *cad* and *Cathy*? Or *hat* and *half*? Or *lad* and *laugh*?

The lower variation [a] is used by some speakers of American English as the first sound in the phonemic diphthongs heard in the words *buy* and *bough*, *I* and *ouch*, *eyes* and *out*.

Precautions

There are three spellings for /æ/ (a):

> **a** as in *glad*
> **ai** as in *plaid*
> **au** as in *laugh*

Problems

There are four common distortions or problems associated with the /æ/ (a). As we discuss each deviation, check to see if you have that problem with this phoneme.

▶ *Problem 1:* Raising

Not long ago one of our students told us that nothing was inevitable but death and Texas. The pronunciation of *Texas* for *taxes* is an extreme example of raising the vowel, because the speaker actually substituted /ɛ/ (e) for the /æ/ (a). Most speakers who distort the vowel by tensing and raising the tongue do not go that far. You can check in the mirror to see if you raise the tongue on this sound. Watch to see where the tongue is when you pronounce the /ɛ/ (e); then watch to see if it drops considerably to form the /æ/ (a). It should drop so that the tongue is *almost* flat in the mouth on the low front vowel.

As you pronounce the following pairs of words and phrases, check to be sure you get a good distinction between /ɛ/ (e) and /æ/ (a). Listen and look for any raising of the /æ/ (a) vowel toward the position of /ɛ/ (e).

/ɛ/ (e) and /æ/ (a) Contrast

Ed	add	led	lad
left	laughed	mess	mass
deft	daft	pest	past
bet	bat	Beth	bath
less	lass	hell	Hal
men	man	neck	knack
fleck	flack	leg	lag
bed	bad	said	sad

/ɛ/ (e) and /æ/ (a) Contrast

peck	pack	wreck	rack
beggar	bagger	Becker	backer
wreck it	racket	pen	pan
ten	tan	den	Dan
Ben	ban	fend	fanned
mesh	mash	creche	crash

A word that gives some Southern speakers trouble is *can't*. If these speakers tend to use a raised form of /æ/ (a) anyway, the /æ/ (a) before /n/ *really* gets lifted up. The common word *can't* gets the most extreme treatment of all. It becomes *cain't* [keɪnt]. Perhaps the extra lifting and tension of the tongue give it extra emphasis. In any case, it is considered nonstandard.

Some pairs of words follow in which the sounds /æ/ (a) and /e/ (a) are contrasted. Be sure that the /æ/ (a) is relaxed and low, that the tongue is *almost* flat in the mouth—lifted *very* slightly in the front.

/æ/ (a) and /e/ (ā) Contrast

am	aim	dam	Dame
lamb	lame	tam	tame
Sam	same	can	cane
ran	rain	man	main/mane
van	vain	ban	bane
plan	plane/plain	Dan	Dane
Jan	Jane	fan	feign
pan	pain	bran	brain
Strand	strained	planned	planed
Rand	rained	canned	caned
pant	paint	sand	seined

▶ *Problem 2:* Nasalizing

Many speakers who raise and front the /æ/ (a) also nasalize the vowel, producing a particularly unpleasant sound. Be especially careful when the vowel precedes a nasal consonant. Listen to your own pronunciation of such words as *can*, *Sam*, and *bang* to see if you detect excessive nasalization of the vowel.

Next, pronounce the word *cad*, being certain not to raise and nasalize the vowel. Then pronounce the word *can*, trying to get the same open, oral vowel you produced in *cad*—if, indeed, you produced an "open, oral vowel" in *cad*.

If you are not sure whether you are producing the /æ/ (a) in *cad* without any nasality, try this trick: There are no nasal consonants in the word *cad*, so you do not need the nose for resonance. Indeed, no air should come out of the nose at all on that word. So: Pronounce the word *cad* in the regular way. Then pronounce the same word while holding both nostrils closed with your fingers. Is the pronunciation the same? It should be. Did you feel any air trying to come out of the nose? If you did, then you are nasalizing the vowel in *cad*. Work to get the two *cads* exactly alike. Then try the same procedure (regular way first, held nose second) on the following words:

bad	had	glad
sad	Sal	pal

Now that you have mastered words without nasal consonants containing /æ/ (a), we can turn again to the problem of excessive nasalization of the vowel before a nasal consonant. Here are some pairs of words. If you get a good, relatively low, relaxed vowel in the first word, try to match that vowel (without adding nasality) in the second word.

sad	Sam	mad	ma'am
rad	ram	jab	jam
cab	cam	lab	lamb
tab	tam	dab	dam
crab	cram	stab	stamp
cad	can	add	Ann
mad	man	dad	Dan
bad	ban	fad	fan
plaid	plan	rat	ran
fat	fan	begat	began
rag	rang	bag	bang
tag	tang	sag	sang
gag	gang	wag	Wang
pack	pang	hack	hang

Problem 3: Diphthongizing

If you tend to drawl, you probably elongate the vowel /æ/ (a). Some speakers stretch the simple vowel not just into a diphthong but into a triphthong. Have you ever heard someone say /mæjən/ (mayən) for *man*? The substitution of the diphthong /æə/ (aə) is probably more common, but it is no more acceptable. Remember to move on to the next consonant. Do not try to hang on to the vowel.

If you have a doubt about whether you stretch this vowel out by adding a sound or two, re-read aloud the words in the second column we just gave you in Problem 2. Listen. Do you get off the vowel promptly, or do you *hayung* on and *ayuhd* on to the vowel?

Problem 4: Substitution of /ɑ/ (ä) for /æ/ (a)

If you learned English as a second language, you may have difficulty with this phoneme of the English language. Your first language may not have had this phoneme in its sound system, and you may therefore substitute a vowel from that language for the unfamiliar sound. The /ɑ/ sound (represented in the dictionaries by ä) is a vowel sound made with the tongue lying relatively flat (unraised) in the mouth. It is a separate phoneme in English from the /æ/ (a) sound, because the two cannot often be substituted for each other without changing the meaning. That is why it is important for you to be able to distinguish between the two sounds, to make them both, and to use them at the right times.

Remember that the tongue is in a different position on the two sounds. The tongue tip will be behind the lower front teeth on both sounds, but the front of the tongue will be raised slightly in the front of the mouth to produce the /æ/ (a). The tongue will *not* be raised noticeably to produce the /ɑ/ (ä). If you are in doubt about what you are doing with your tongue on these sounds, check by using a mirror.

The following pairs of words contain a contrast between these two vowels. The first word of each pair will have an /ɑ/ (ä), and the second word will have an /æ/ (a).

/ɑ/ (ä) and /æ/ (a) Contrast

bond	band	clock	claque
cot	cat	con	can
Dodd	Dad	Don	Dan
dolly	dally	fond	fanned
hot	hat	job	jab
cop	cap	lots	lats
mop	map	mock	Mack
knob	nab	pond	panned
pot	pat	Ron	ran
sock	sack	sop	sap
psalm	Sam	togs	tags
top	tap	von	van

Pragmatics

Readiness Exercises

If you have discovered you have one (or more) of the problems with /æ/ (a) we have discussed, review the discussion and the exercises related to that problem. Then, having worked through the problem, begin the Reinforcement Exercises to transfer the corrected sound into everyday speech.

Reinforcement Exercises

Practice Words for /æ/ (a)

Beginning		**Middle**		
actual	factual			
as	has	jazz		
apple	dapple	grapple	snapple	
act	fact	lacked	packed	cracked
add	bad	had	sad	glad
at	bat	cat	mat	pat
after	laughter	rafter	drafter	crafter
ask	mask	task	flask	cask
aster	faster	master	pastor	caster
am	ham	jam	lamb	gram
an	can	tan	ran	ban
ant	can't	pant	rant	slant
and	band	gland	planned	hand
amp	camp	damp	lamp	tramp
anchor	banker	rancor	tanker	hanker

Practice Phrases for /æ/ (a)

an active class
the last laugh
an apple in the package
a bad habit
have a new task
batting average
a fast answer
passing the exam
after the standing ovation
no chance to thank you
a fancy stamp
planned the afternoon

I can't stand him
grab the candy
''The Star-Spangled Banner''

Practice Sentences for /æ/ (a)

1. I will catch the last bus back home.
2. There will be a mass meeting of the faculty this afternoon.
3. The attic is filled with trash.
4. Actually, it doesn't matter.
5. He came back after the crash.
6. As usual, Ann had the last laugh.
7. I'm glad you had a grand time.
8. Dad thinks my present income is adequate.
9. We have had a very happy time in Paris.
10. Ask me no questions and I'll not have to lie.

Practice Sentences for /æ/ (a) (More Challenging)

1. His constant use of slang added to his handicaps.
2. Tad was the champion but refused the plaque.
3. We're not planning to drop anchor until we get back.
4. There were ample chances to pass the exam.
5. The cab driver ignored the traffic as we began the trip.
6. A good sun tan is not worth the chance of skin cancer.
7. A few inaccurate answers kept me from passing the course.
8. After the excursion, there was sand on the blanket.
9. Andy did not ask for his money back. He planned to return.
10. I'm not angry. I love being stranded in Gravel Switch!

Practice Sentences for /æ/ (a) (Most Challenging)

1. I laughed as I left the amateurish dance.
2. It seems odd to add an extra lock, but I can't afford to lack one.
3. For ten days I tried to get a tan, but then I just ran through the rain.
4. Some top executives tapped the funds and ruined the company's finances.
5. The cop put on his cap before he began his tour of the campus.

6. Shall I stand when the band plays Mrs. Bond's song?
7. Ask as many questions as you want in class, but don't expect an answer.
8. Tom said he was sad to have to leave, but he planned to catch the plane anyway.
9. Shall I give you a last chance to visit Alaska? No, I'm going to gather shells in Florida.
10. What was in the bag Mr. Bassey threw into the bog? I can't imagine.

12

Back Vowels

There are five vowel phonemes in American English produced by raising the back of the tongue in the back of the mouth. Logically enough, these phonemes are called *back vowels*. We will discuss each of these phonemes one by one.

/ɑ/ (ä)

Principles

Production

If you let the tongue lie low in the mouth, open the unrounded lips rather wide, and emit the air stream through the mouth with the vocal folds vibrating, you will produce the long, lax, low back vowel in the words *arm* and *odd*. We represent this sound in IPA by /ɑ/ and in the dictionaries by ä.

When physicians want to look down a throat, they usually ask the patient to say *ah*. The reason: when you produce /ɑ/ (ä), you open the mouth wider and drop your tongue lower than when making any other vowel in English.

There is an allophone of /ɑ/ (ä) used by some speakers in "short *o*" words such as *odd*, *hot*, and *stop*. This variation of the /ɑ/ (ä) phoneme is formed by raising the tongue slightly in back and rounding and tensing the lips slightly. This allophone, represented in IPA by [ɒ], is shorter than the long, wide open allophone [ɑ].

There is another allophone of /ɑ/ (ä). If this phoneme comes after /w/ (the sound; not just the spelling) and before /r/ or /ɚ/ (ər)—the unstressed

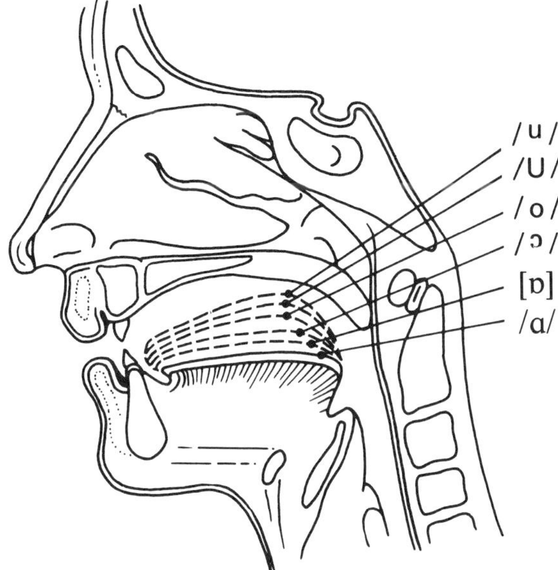

Figure 12.1. *Representative tongue positions for back vowels.*

er vowel in the second syllable of *other*, it may change to [ɔ] (ô), the vowel in the word *ought*. Before the vowel /ɚ/ (ər), it always changes; before the consonant /r/, it sometimes changes.

Check your pronunciation of the word *car*. The /ɑ/ (ä) comes before /ɚ/ (ər)—always represented by the r letter when it occurs after another vowel, but there is no /w/ in front. The /ɑ/ (ä) is unchanged. Now pronounce the word *war*. This time there is a change to [ɔ] (ô), a vowel made by rounding and tensing the lips more and raising the tongue higher in back.

Now pronounce the word *Warren*. Here you have a choice. There is a /w/ in front, but the next sound is the consonant /r/ used to begin the next syllable. The vowel may be either [ɑ] (ä) or [ɔ] (ô). Which do you say?

Note these contrasts:

/ɑɚ/ (äər)	**[wɔ] (wô) Before /ɚ/ (ər)**
car	war
farm	warm
dart	wart
cart	quart
barter	quarter
barn	warn
arm	swarm
hearth	swarth
starship	warship
hard hearted	warmhearted

/wɑ/ (wä) Before /r/ (Choose your allophone!)

Warren	warrant
warrantee	warranty
Warrick	warrior

Precautions

There are six spellings for /ɑ/ (ä):

a as in *arm*
aa as in *salaam*
e as in *sergeant*
ea as in *heart*
o as in *odd*
ow as in *knowledge*

Problems

There are two common problems associated with the production of this phoneme. As we discuss each of them, check to see if you have that problem with /ɑ/ (ä).

▶ *Problem 1:* Raising and Fronting

The most common distortion of /ɑ/ (ä) is that of raising and fronting the vowel by pulling the tongue up and forward toward the position used in forming the vowel /æ/ (a) and its allophone [a]. If this vowel is made with too much tension, with the lips slightly spread, and with the tongue slightly lifted toward the front of the mouth, the sound will be distorted. The /ɑ/ (ä) should be open, free, and relaxed. Drop the tongue and open the mouth to form it. *Pop* should not sound like *Papp*, and the first syllable of *father* should not sound like the first syllable of *fathom*.

▶ *Problem 2:* Substitution of /ɔ/ (ô) for /ɑ/ (ä)

We have noted that in one context, /ɑ/ (ä) does become [ɔ] (ô): after /w/, before /ɚ/ (ɚr) and sometimes before /r/. In other contexts, however, substituting the /ɔ/ (ô) (the vowel phoneme in the word *awe*) for the /ɑ/ (ä) is nonstandard.

Check your pronunciation of the following pairs of words. The first word should not sound like the second.

With /ɑ/ (ä)	With /ɔ/ (ô)
are	or
odd	awed

cot	caught
car	core/corps
not	naught
rot	wrought
chock	chalk
far	for
lard	lord
barn	born
farm	form
stark	stork
ardor	order

Pragmatics

Readiness Exercises

Pretend you are at the doctor's office. Open your mouth, drop and relax your jaw, keep your tongue flat on the bottom of your mouth, and say *Ah* several times.

Reinforcement Exercises

Practice Words for /ɑ/ (ä)

Beginning	**Middle**
odd	modern
ox	box
occupy	lock
otter	bother
obvious	robin
octave	cottage
olive	Dolly
honest	dishonest
opposite	response
arm	alarm
art	heart
arch	march
arc/ark	park
arbor	harbor
alms	palms

A few words end in /ɑ/ (ä). Here are a few examples:

Ah	Bah!	Hah!
Aha!	Allah	hurrah

Practice Phrases for /ɑ/ (ä)

cops and robbers
stock market
a shot in the dark
solving problems
an obvious option
a solid contribution
father of the star
beyond the bazaar
a calm sergeant
stop the argument
not so honest
watch the pot
from top to bottom
carbon dioxide
forgotten knowledge

Practice Sentences for /ɑ/ (ä)

1. Robert's not calm. He's preoccupied.
2. No, my father was not a locksmith.
3. I've been warned I can't expect a pardon.
4. I got to shop at Harrod's. A charming spot!
5. What was your response to the article?
6. I had no knowledge of that shocking operation.
7. You've got to watch the honest ones too.
8. I have my stocks and bonds stored in my locker.
9. Fort Knox would be a golden opportunity.
10. Give alms. Coffins are not equipped with pockets.

Practice Sentences for /ɑ/ (ä) (More Challenging)

1. My father had a problem getting a ticket for the opera.
2. I want a top lock for the door. It's not optional.
3. The doctor wanted to operate on my heart.
4. The congressman helped Molly get the contract. No harm in that.
5. The contractor has his yacht docked in the harbor.
6. My reputation was tarnished by a few heartless remarks.
7. His partner's visit has him alarmed. He has a lot to hide.
8. The market advertised bargains, but I could not find them.

9. It's not smart to argue with cops. They're armed.
10. Charlie's smart remarks marred the reunion.

Practice Sentences for /ɑ/ (ä) (Most Challenging)

1. Tom promised to go shopping, but he forgot.
2. Mrs. Stark's news was ominous, but Bob remained calm.
3. It's hard to believe that used car belonged to a warmhearted sergeant.
4. The octet tried to sing in harmony, but were an octave off.
5. Our democracy is based on the Constitution and on the knowledge and cooperation of our citizens.

Principles

Production

If you raise the back of the tongue up slightly toward the soft palate, round the lips a bit more than you did in forming the [ɒ] allophone of /ɑ/ (ä), and emit the air stream through the mouth with the vocal folds vibrating, you will produce the tense, lip-rounded,low back vowel phoneme in the words *all* and *ought*. We represent this vowel phoneme in IPA by /ɔ/—not quite an *o*, you see—and in the dictionaries by ô.

The ''short *o*'' allophone of /ɑ/ (ä), which we discussed earlier, is a *lax* low back vowel. The vowel phoneme we are examining now is a *tense* low back vowel. To form this vowel, you raise the tongue a little bit higher in back, round and tense the lips a little bit more, and tense the tongue a little more than you did to produce [ɒ]. On /ɔ/ (ô), your lips will be a vertical ellipse.

The [ɒ] is used as an allophone, or variant form, of this vowel in some regions. An author trying to represent these dialectal differences with regular spelling might spell the word *forest* as *fawrest* or *fahrest* to indicate the difference in pronunciation. To see which of these allophones you use, read the following list of words aloud. Either allophone is acceptable, but most speakers of American English use the [ɔ] (ô), and in many parts of the United States the [ɒ] would be thought an affectation.

caught	coffee	forest	foreign
talk	walk	cause	lawn

Precautions

There are nine spellings for /ɔ/ (ô):

a as in *call*
ah as in *Utah*
au as in *launder*
augh as in *fraught*
aw as in *law*
o as in *off*
oa as in *broad*
ou as in *cough*
ough as in *bought*

Problems

There are three common distortions of the vowel /ɔ/ (ô). As we discuss each of these deviations, check to see if you have that problem with this vowel.

▶ *Problem 1:* Substitution of /o/ for /ɔ/ (ô)

If English is not your first language, you may have difficulty with /ɔ/ (ô). Many languages do not include this phoneme, and you may substitute the vowel /o/ in its place when you speak English. /o/ and /ɔ/ (ô) are separate phonemes in English. Many word pairs depend on these vowels to distinguish between them. If you substitute /o/ for /ɔ/ (ô), *I saw it* would sound like *I sew it*, and *I was called* would sound like *I was cold*.

Read the following pairs of words aloud. Check to be sure you use /ɔ/ (ô) in the words in the left column.

/ɔ/ (ô) and /o/ (ō) Contrast

bought	boat	caught	coat
wrought	wrote	naught	note
awning	owning	awed	owed
Saul	soul	saw	so/sew
flaw	flow	flawed	flowed
law	low	call	coal
ball	bowl	chalk	choke
walk	woke	vault	volt
fawn	phone	lawn	loan
fall	foal	called	cold
tall	toll	mall	mole
gnaw	know/no	off	oaf

laud	load	claws	clothes
hall	whole/hole	raw	row

The distinction between the following words is not maintained in all dialects of American English. A Southern speaker is more likely to preserve the difference in these word pairs. Others may pronounce both with /ɔ/ (ô).

or	oar
horse	hoarse
Mawr	more
for	four/fore
war	wore
morn	mourn
warn	worn
border	boarder

Problem 2: Retraction

The distortion that we label retraction of the /ɔ/ (ô) is produced by doing two things: first, by puckering the lips excessively so they are noticeably protruded, and second, by pulling the tongue back in the mouth. You may have heard someone imitating the stereotyped impression of "New Yorkese" by asking for *cawfee* and for a *chawklet maulted* or complaining that something was *awwful*.

The retracted /ɔ/ (ô) is a tense, grating sound and should be avoided. If you tend to retract the vowel, you should relax the lips slightly and open the mouth a bit wider, being certain that the lips are not protruded (stuck out) and do not move. You should lift the back of the tongue to a position about halfway between /ɑ/ (ä) and /o/ (ō).

Problem 3: Diphthongizing

Another deviation results from replacing the pure vowel /ɔ/ (ô) with a diphthong. If you add /ə/, the first vowel in the word *above*, to the /ɔ/ (ô), you have the diphthong [ɔə] (ôə). This elongation is common in the greater New York area. Combined with retraction of the /ɔ/ (ô), it is a particularly unpleasant distortion to most American ears.

Pronounce the following words aloud. Check to see if *coffee* becomes *caw-uh-fee* or *caw-wuh-fee*. To correct this problem, do not hold on to the /ɔ/ (ô). Move on to the next consonant.

ought	bought	caught	fought
naught	sought	taught	wrought
cause	claws/clause	laws	all
call	fall	hall	tall
talk	walk	dog	log
coffee	awful	chocolate	malted

Pragmatics

Reinforcement Exercises

Practice Words for /ɔ/ (ô)

Beginning	Middle	End
all	tall	taw
often	soften	saw
Ong	wrong	raw
awes	flaws	flaw
ought	naught	gnaw
off	cough	caw
orgy	Georgie	jaw
awed	laud	law
awe	maul	maw
awning	yawning	yaw
on	pawn	paw

More Practice Words for /ɔ/ (ô)

Beginning	Middle
always	forever
awkward	recall
awesome	storm
auditorium	perform
autumn	Fall
order	assault
organ	applause
orchestra	coughing
ordeal	horrible
oracle	authority
ornament	fortune
orator	thought
ornate	formal
organized	morning
ordinary	faulty

Practice Phrases for /ɔ/ (o)

a warning call
walk the horse
wrong form
an awful ordeal
a tall order

corn and slaw
strong coffee
warm and frothy
toss a ball
born in Florida
call them often
moth balls
morning is dawning

Practice Sentences for /ɔ/ (ô)

1. I bought a dog at the auction.
2. I always thought I'd take the offer.
3. I caught a cold and have a cough.
4. It's because I want to go abroad.
5. I was drawn into the fight. It's not my fault.
6. The wrestler lost points for stalling.
7. Paul is going to Orlando in August.
8. We ought to talk in flawless English.
9. I bought an auto from the wrong person.
10. It was an awful mistake to call so late.

Practice Sentences for /ɔ/ (ô) (More Challenging)

1. The lawyer has cost so much I've become a pauper.
2. I want a chocolate malted and a raw hamburger.
3. I'm going to cross the border and go North.
4. There was an awkward pause after he talked.
5. The Civic Auditorium is a difficult place to perform.
6. The audience was in awe as soon as the orchestra began to play.
7. Because of the flaw, I sawed the thing in two.
8. Is it all right to fawn over an author?
9. Doris lives down the hall from me in the dorm.
10. This Fall, I will exercise often. I've already started.

Practice Sentences for /ɔ/ (ô) (Most Challenging)

1. I ought to call a taxi. I don't want to dawdle or walk.
2. I drank orange juice, coffee, and a chocolate malted for breakfast.
3. Caught in the act, the audience mortified him. He is haunted by the event.

4. All of our efforts came to naught. I am no authority on success.
5. I have already caused a problem. That taught me to obey the law.
6. They set all of their priorities by default. They should withdraw from that awful method.
7. The freedom fighters fought for their cause and clawed their way across the border.
8. The lawyer defrauded his client, but the victim saw through the tricky clauses.
9. The lawyer is being sought in three states by the authorities.
10. The inauguration was a raucous, inauspicious affair, filled with maudlin speeches.

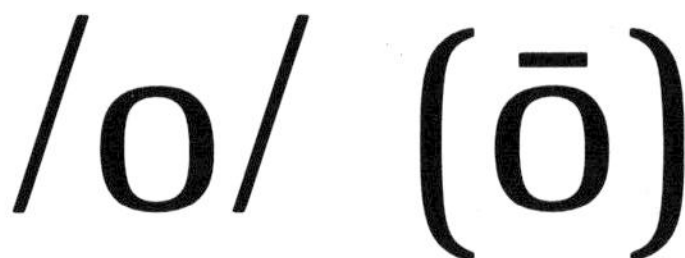

Principles

Production

If you raise the back of the tongue up about midway in the back of the mouth toward the soft palate, round the lips more than you did to form /ɔ/ (ô), and emit the air stream through the mouth with the vocal folds vibrating, you will produce the *tense mid back vowel* represented by /o/ in IPA and by ō in the dictionaries.

The vowel phoneme /o/ occurs in stressed syllables in words such as *no* and *below* and in unstressed syllables in words such as *obey* and *tomato*.

When the /o/ occurs in a stressed syllable in American English, we use a diphthongal allophone [oʊ]. The "long *o*" is not a pure vowel, then, but a diphthong. Two vowels are blended together—the pure vowel [o] and a second weaker, shorter vowel that is almost the *oo* in *ooze*. The lips and tongue both move to produce this diphthong, uttered in one continuous movement. If you substitute the pure vowel [o], you will not change the meaning, but it will be noticed. The dictionaries represent the "long *o*" by ō. We will explain this further when discussing Problem 3.

Here are only a few words in which the diphthongal allophone [oʊ] (ō) is heard:

know	grow	blow	show
boat	soul	beau	load

own	bone	both	broke
host	most	slope	phone
home	rogue	loaf	cold

When /o/ occurs in unstressed syllables in American English, we use the pure vowel allophone [o]. The dictionaries represent this allophone by o. This allophone would be heard in such words as the following:

obey	obedient	omit	omission
obese	Odessa	opine	hotel
hallow	hollow	fellow	follow
yellow	mellow	window	marshmallow
echo	piano	tomato	potato

The words *oboe, cocoa,* and *pogo* (as in "pogo stick") contain both allophones of /o/ (ō). The /o/ in the first syllable is [oʊ] (ō), and the /o/ in the second syllable is [o] (ȯ). Can you think of any other words containing both allophones? We have already alluded to an interesting dialectal variation of /o/ (ō). In New York City and other portions of the Northeast, /o/ (ō) becomes /ɔ/ (ô) before the r-vowel [/ɚ/ (ər)]. In other portions of the country, the use of /ɔ/ (ô) instead of /o/ (ō) before /ɚ/ (ər) seems to be increasing. As we have said, a Southern speaker is more likely to preserve the "long *o*" in this context.

As a reminder, we give a few of these contrasting pairs.

/ɔɚ/ (ôər) and /oɚ/ (ōər) Contrast

or	oar	for	four/fore
horse	hoarse	border	boarder
morn	mourn	morning	mourning
Tor	tore	war	wore
warn	worn	lord	lowered

Precautions

There are twelve spellings for /o/:

o as in *obey* and *rode*
oa as in *road*
oe as in *doe*
oh as in *Oh!*
oo as in *brooch*
ou as in *soul*
ough as in *dough*
ow as in *grow*
au as in *haute*
eau as in *beau*
eo as in *yeoman*
ew as in *sew*

Problems

There are five problems associated with this phoneme. As we discuss each deviation, check to see if you have that problem with /o/ (ō).

Problem 1: Substitution of /ə/ for [o] (ȯ̇)

Substituting the schwa, /ə/—the little vowel in the first syllable of *above*—for the pure vowel allophone [o] is nonstandard in many words. You will have to listen to speakers of the Standard Dialect to learn whether to use /ə/ or [o] in unstressed syllables.

In the verb *opine*, for example, the first, unstressed syllable is [o]. In the noun *opinion*, the first, unstressed syllable is /ə/.

The following words all contain [o]:

obey	obedient	obedience	omit
omission	obese	obesity	obeisance
omega	opaque	oblation	domain
otology	ovarian	ovation	overt
cooperate	cooperation	cooperative	coopt
coexist	cocaine	coordinate	coordination
Copernicus	pillow	fellow	bureau
piano	cello	shadow	window

In these two words, the [o] (ȯ̇) allophone occurs in both first and last syllables:

tomato potato

Many family names begin with [o] (ȯ̇). Here are a few examples:

O'Neal	O'Shea	O'Reilly
O'Shanihan	O'Shaughnessy	O'Toole

Read all the above examples related to this problem aloud. Check to be sure you do not substitute /ə/ for [o] (ȯ̇).

Problem 2: Substitution of /ɚ/ (ər) for [o] (ȯ̇)

Some speakers substitute the unstressed *-er* vowel heard in the word *mother* for the [o] in unstressed syllables. Read the lists we gave in discussing the first problem associated with this phoneme. Check to see if you are tempted to make this substitution. It is nonstandard. Use the [o] instead.

Problem 3: Substitution of [o] (ȯ̇) for [oʊ] (ō)

Many languages use the pure vowel [o] consistently and never use the diphthong variation heard in English in stressed syllables. If English is not your first language, you may substitute the pure vowel allophone for the diphthongal allophone [oʊ] in stressed syllables.

If you do not add the second vowel in this vowel blend, the off-glide vowel, you will not give the phoneme its customary duration (length). That will affect the rhythm of your words and sentences as well as the sound.

Pronounce the word *no*. Now pronounce the word in very slow motion as you watch your lips in a mirror. (You probably cannot see the tongue movement, but it should move also.) You should see the lips closing down considerably during the production of the /o/. The first part of the diphthong—the [o]—will be wider open than the second part of the diphthong—the [ʊ]. You lips will close down like the lens of a camera can close down. During the diphthong, the lips and tongue (yes, the tongue moves too) move from one position to another in a continuous movement, as the two vowels are blended together.

The second half of the diphthong we represent in IPA with [ʊ], because the second vowel is shorter than the [o], but it may be helpful for you to think of moving your tongue in the direction of /u/ (o͞o)—the vowel at the end of the word *shoe*. (If your first language is Spanish, that English vowel is the same as at the beginning of the Spanish word *uno*.) The /o/ in stressed syllables in English must have an /u/ tail on it, or it is not a real English /o/.

Pronounce these few words out loud. Check to be sure you are using a diphthong and not a pure vowel on these words with /o/ in a stressed syllable.

know	so	low	go
old	oak	road	toe
over	o.k.	open	drove
soul	home	grow	phone

▶ ***Problem 4:*** Centralizing

Some speakers pull the entire diphthong allophone [oʊ] forward in the mouth by lifting the tongue in the center of the mouth rather than in the back of the mouth. This centering of the phoneme (in its diphthongal form) results in a distortion that causes *home* to sound something like *hum*, *most* like *must*, and *soak* like *suck*. We consider this substitution nonstandard and suggest you avoid it.

Here are a few pairs of words that contrast /o/ (ō) with /ʌ/ (u)—the vowel in the word *up*. Pronounce them aloud, and check to see if the first one sounds like the second. There should be a clear contrast between the two words in each pair.

/o/ (ō) and /ʌ/ (u) Contrast

home	hum	most	must
soak	suck	mode	mud

/o/ (ō) and /ʌ/ (u) Contrast

goat	gut	roam	rum
tomes	Tums	choke	chuck
rowed	Rudd	goal	gull
roan	run	phone	fun
sown	sun	bone	bun
Nome	numb	dome	dumb
known	none	boat	but

Problem 5: Triphthongizing

/o/ is usually a diphthong, as we have observed. Adding another vowel to the diphthong would turn it into a triphthong (three vowels blended together).

Especially before /n/ and /l/, some speakers are tempted to add the little vowel /ə/ to the [oʊ]. This addition could turn a one syllable word into a two syllable word. *Joan* would become *Jo-uhn* and *coal* would become *coa-uhl*.

If you have a tendency to drag the /o/ phoneme out in stressed syllables, you may be tempted to put in *two* sounds between the /o/ and the /n/ or /l/. Before the extra /ə/, you may also add a /w/. That adds insult to injury—or, more accurately, compounds the distortion. Now, *foam* would become *foa-wuhm*, and *gold* would become *go-wuhld*.

Check your pronunciation of the following words.

/o/ (ō) Before /n/

bone	cone	Doan	phone
hone	Joan	moan	pone
roan	sown	shown	known
tone	stone	won't	don't

/o/ (ō) Before /l/

bowl	coal	dole	foal
goal	hole/whole	soul	mole
knoll	pole/poll	cold	shoal
toll	stole	volt	old

Because you are most likely to add the /ə/ (or the /wə/) before a consonant in the same syllable—especially the /n/ or /l/—you can check the vowel /o/ (ō) you use when no consonant follows and then try to match that vowel in words where /n/ or /l/ follows the /o/ (ō). Try these pairs of words with that in mind. Remember to try to match the vowel in the first word when pronouncing the second word:

/o/ (ō) and /on/ (ōn) Contrast

bow	bone	blow	blown
Coe	cone	dough	Doan
foe	phone	grow	grown
ho	hone	Joe	Joan
low	loan	Moe	moan
know	known	Poe	pone

/o/ (ō) and /ol/ (ōl) Contrast

bow	bowl	Coe	coal
dough	dole	foe	foal
go	goal	ho	hole
stow	stole	Moe	mole
know	knoll	Poe	poll/pole
roe/row	roll/role	sew/so	soul
show	shoal	toe	toll

Pragmatics

Reinforcement Exercises

Practice Words for /o/ (ō)

Beginning	Middle	End
oh	float	flow
	note	no/know
owed	rowed/rode	roe
	node	know/no
	goad	go
oaf	loaf	low
oak	soak	so/sew
own	blown	blow
	grown	grow
oat	boat	beau/bow
	dote	doe
	tote	toe
oar	door	dough

Practice Phrases for /o/ (ō)

going home
only obey
no cooperation
yellow gold

hello, Joe
an old hotel
a lonely soul
omit the piano
slow motion
toll road
hope to atone
no windows
oats and toast
home-grown tomatoes
the whole zone

Practice Sentences for /o/ (ō)

1. Joe is exploring possibilities in Ohio.
2. I don't suppose the place is open.
3. Nobody knows how old she is.
4. I took an oath never to eat another potato.
5. How long have you known this fellow?
6. Both learned to obey a long time ago.
7. The owner's promises were quite hollow.
8. I spoke to Mr. O'Shea to ask for a loan.
9. I drove through the business zone and found the right road.
10. I told her to learn the oboe, but she did not obey me.

Practice Sentences for /o/ (ō) (More Challenging)

1. I eat a bowl of oats every day to lower my cholesterol.
2. I'm told the new location will be on the West Coast.
3. I've grown more and more weary of this empty show.
4. We chose to forget the whole episode that drove us apart.
5. His home is in Oklahoma, but he works in Ohio.
6. She insisted I row the boat toward the shore.
7. Fort Knox, where the gold is stored, is closed to the public.
8. I don't believe in ghosts, but don't leave me alone in the shadows.
9. There was a small omission in Tony's story, but he's trying to atone.
10. He spoke in opaque terms, and I couldn't follow him.

Practice Sentences for /o/ (ō) (Most Challenging)

1. Too many potatoes and marshmallows can lead to obesity.
2. The snow on the old oak tree and the slopes below was

a sight to behold.
3. Both of them refused to cooperate with the bureau chief. They wanted no-show jobs.
4. Jo-Ann, driving so slow on the open road is dangerous. Go faster.
5. In this domain, throwing stones is no reason to kill some poor soul.
6. While patrolling the area near my abode, I choked on the smoke and car fumes.
7. All alone on the telephone—stuck on hold. How droll!
8. Though we were friends, he tried to goad me into trying a useless approach. That was a long time ago.
9. I don't use Idaho potatoes. I prefer home grown.
10. He's notorious—an egotistical rogue with a cold heart.

Principles

Production

If you lift the back of the tongue up in back toward the soft palate farther than you did in forming the /o/ (ō), round the lips even more than you did on the /o/ (ō), and emit the air stream through the mouth with the vocal folds vibrating, you will produce the *short, lip-rounded, lax high back vowel* heard in the word *look*. We represent this phoneme by /ʊ/ in IPA and by oo in the dictionaries.

This vowel has much the same relation to the vowel sound in the word *Luke* (represented in IPA by /u/ and in the dictionaries by o͞o) as the /ɪ/ (i) vowel has to /i/ (ē). Just as /ɪ/ (i) is formed with the tongue slightly lower and more relaxed than when forming /i/ (ē), so /ʊ/ (oo) is made with the tongue slightly lower and more relaxed (less tense) than when forming /u/ (o͞o). Another parallel is that /ʊ/ (oo) and /ɪ/ (i) are usually short sounds, whereas /u/ (o͞o) and /i/ (ē) are usually long sounds.

Precautions

There are four spellings for /ʊ/ (oo):

o as in *wolf*
oo as in *wood*
ou as in *would*
u as in *put*

Problems

There are four problems associated with this vowel. As we discuss each deviation, check to see if you have that problem with this phoneme.

Problem 1: Centering

Some speakers make this vowel with the tongue too low and too far forward. Usually, speakers who center the /ʊ/ (oo) not only raise the tongue in the center of the mouth rather than in the back, but also relax the lips somewhat.

Carried to an extreme, centering may result in the actual substitution of the central vowel /ʌ/ (u)—heard in the words *mud* and *hut*—for the /ʊ/ (oo). This would turn *look* into *luck*, *took* into *tuck*, and *shook* into *shuck*.

As you pronounce the following pairs of words aloud, check to see if the first word sounds much like the second. There should be a clear contrast.

/ʊ/ (oo) and /ʌ/ (u) Contrast

book	buck	hook	Huck
hood	Hud	look	luck
puss	pus	put	putt
shook	shuck	stood	stud
took	tuck	crooks	crux

Problem 2: Diphthongizing

Like other vowels, /ʊ/ (oo) can be stretched into a diphthong by adding /ə/. Be careful not to drawl this vowel. It is a relatively short sound. Move on to the next consonant, and keep the vowel pure.

Problem 3: Substitution of /u/ (o͞o) for /ʊ/ (oo)

Many languages do not have this vowel phoneme. If your first language is not English, you may not be used to hearing the distinction between the vowels in the words *foot* and *food*. Your first language probably contains /u/ (o͞o), and you may use this vowel sound for both vowel phonemes in English. Although a few words can be pronounced with either vowel, many English words depend on these two vowels to distinguish their meaning.

Pronounce these word pairs. Be sure that there is a clear contrast between the vowel in the first word and the vowel in the second word. The words in the left-hand column contain /ʊ/ (oo)—on which the tongue is lower and more relaxed and the lips slightly less tightly rounded than for /u/ (o͞o), the vowel in the words in the right-hand column.

/ʊ/ (oo) and /u/ (o͞o) Contrast

full	fool	wood	wooed
soot	suit	hood	who'd
should	shooed	could	cooed
look	Luke	pull	pool

Problem 4: Substitution of /o/ (ō) for /ʊ/ (oo)

When the r-vowel follows, some speakers substitute /o/ (ō) for /ʊ/ (oo). This substitution is nonstandard. The /o/ (ō) is made with the tongue raised lower in the back of the mouth than it is raised for /ʊ/ (oo), and the lips are not as rounded on /o/ (ō) as on /ʊ/ (oo).

Remember the /ʊ/ (oo) is almost /u/ (o͞o)—the vowel in *ooze*. If you are in doubt, just remember that the /ʊ/ (oo) before /ɚ/ will sound much more like /u/ (o͞o) than like /o/ (ō).

Pronounce these pairs of words. Check to be sure the first one does not turn into the second one.

/ʊɚ/ (ooər) and /oɚ/ (ōər) Contrast

poor	pour/pore	boor	bore/boar
tour	tore	dour	door
Coors	cores	moor	more
sure	shore	lure	lore
your	yore	gourmet	Gore may

Pragmatics

Reinforcement Exercises

Practice Words for /ʊ/ (oo)

book	brook	bush	bushel
sure	sugar	could	cushion
bull	bullet	foot	full
good	crooked	would	wooden
stood	tourist	put	pudding
wolf	woman	pull	butcher

Practice Phrases for /ʊ/ (oo)

sugar cookies
push and pull
good looking
could not look
pulling the wool
a good cookbook
withstood the crook
hook a wool rug
a rookie courier
unendurable boor

Practice Sentences for /ʊ/ (oo)

1. I understood every word in the bulletin.
2. Some tourists go to Brooklyn.
3. I took the book from the shelves.
4. I'm not exactly a gourmet cook.
5. He shook with fear as the horse raised its foot.
6. I endured the rural life as long as I could.
7. For goodness sake, put an end to this!
8. Put the hook inside the door.
9. Mr. Cooke takes a little coffee in his sugar.
10. The poor rookie was totally confused.
11. That bully should be punished.
12. I was ambushed on the boulevard.
13. The stray bullet was found in the cushion.
14. "Pull the wool over their eyes" means "to deceive."
15. "Put a foot in your mouth" means "to make a mistake."

Practice Sentences for /ʊ/ (oo) (More Challenging)

1. This is a good neighborhood—except for little nooks and corners.
2. Mrs. Cushing shook with laughter at the look on my face.
3. The hood of the car would have hit her, if I had not pushed the woman back.
4. I am looking for an apartment with bookcases and a wood-burning fireplace.
5. That wood-burning fireplace will fill your house with soot.
6. He's a good butcher, but not a good cook.
7. You could have some cookies or some pudding for dessert.

8. The wolf in the woods stood still. Should I have shot?
9. Tom mistook the visitor for a crook and pushed him out the door.
10. There are too many bushes in the woods. I wouldn't call it a moor!

Principles

Production

If you raise the back of the tongue nearly to the soft palate, round the lips tightly (pucker them), and emit the air stream through the mouth with the vocal folds vibrating, you will produce the highest back vowel, heard in the words *ooze* and *Sue*.We represent this vowel phoneme in IPA by /u/ and in the dictionaries by o͞o. Produced with the lips and back of the tongue tense, /u/ (o͞o) is usually a long vowel in duration. The vowel /u/ (o͞o) is classified as a *long, lip-rounded, tense high back vowel.*

Precautions

There are twelve spellings for /u/ (o͞o):

eau as in *beautiful*
eu as in *leukemia*
ew as in *grew*
ieu as in *lieutenant*
o as in *move*
oe as in *canoe*
oo as in *food*
ou as in *group*
ough as in *through*
u as in *rude*
ue as in *blue*
ui as in *fruit*

There are a few words in American English that can be pronounced with either /u/ (o͞o) or /ᴜ/ (oo). Whether you use one vowel or the other depends on your dialect or idiolect. Either vowel is acceptable in these words. Note the following examples:

coop	hoop	hoof	whoop
roof	room	root	

Problems

There are four common distortions associated with this phoneme. As we discuss each deviation, check to see if you have that problem with /u/ (o͞o).

▶ *Problem 1:* Substitution of /ᴜ/ (oo) for /u/ (o͞o)

If you fail to purse (pucker) your lips tightly enough and to get enough tension of the tongue, you may lower the vowel /u/ (o͞o) to the position and relaxation of the lax high back vowel /ᴜ/ (oo).

There are, as we just mentioned, a few words on which this change is acceptable, but the substitution generally is non standard. *She wooed* should not sound like *She would*, and *suit* should not sound like *soot*. Read aloud the word contrasts on p. 287, and check to be sure you make a clear distinction between /u/ (o͞o) and /ᴜ/ (oo).

▶ *Problem 2:* Substitution of /ju/ (yo͞o) for /u/ (o͞o)

When we discussed the /j/ (y) phoneme, we mentioned that some speakers are confused about when to use /u/ (o͞o) and when to use /ju/ (yo͞o). See pp. 188-189 for the principles we gave you to help you decide which times to use which sounds.

Some speakers, intending to be precise (or perhaps elegant) use /ju/ (yo͞o) in place of /u/ (o͞o)—at the wrong times! We noted earlier that /t/, /d/, and /n/ are often followed by /ju/ (yo͞o). We also noted that /p/, /b/, /k/, /m/, /f/, /v/, and /h/ *are* followed by /ju/ (yo͞o)—if the word is spelled with *u*, eu, ew, iew, or *eu*. If a speaker uses /ju/ (yo͞o) after /s/, /z/, /l/, or /θ/ (th), however, it is considered an affectation—and nonstandard.

Check your pronunciation of the following words. There should be no /j/ (y).

sue	suit	resume	Zulu
absolute	delude	enthusiasm	enthusiastic

Here are a few pairs of words that depend on the contrast between /u/ (o͞o) and /ju/ (yo͞o). Pronounce these words aloud.

With /u/ (o͞o)	With /ju/ (yo͞o)
booty	beauty
do	due/dew
food	feud
who	hew/hue/Hugh
moo	mew

▶ ***Problem 3:*** Centralizing

Some speakers distort the /u/ ($\overline{\text{oo}}$) by attempting to make it with the tongue too far forward in the mouth and the lips too relaxed. In this case, they raise the tongue in the center of the mouth rather than at the back. The effect is to distort and "flatten" the vowel.

As with the same distortion of /ʊ/ (oo), this problem carried to its extreme results in a substitution of a central vowel for this back vowel. It could turn *roost* almost (or completely) into *rust*, *boon* into *bun*, and *crude* into *crud*. Work for adequate lip rounding and correct (high, back) tongue placement.

▶ ***Problem 4:*** Diphthongizing

As we said earlier, /u/ ($\overline{\text{oo}}$) is a long sound. Unless you are careful, it can easily be turned into a noticeable diphthong. If you start with the tongue in a position too low and too relaxed to produce a good /u/ ($\overline{\text{oo}}$) and slide slowly up to the customary spot, you will, of course, produce a diphthong. Turning /u/ ($\overline{\text{oo}}$) into a diphthong may also result from starting in the customary tense high position and relaxing the tongue into a lower spot.

Yet another diphthongal distortion results from adding the little neutral vowel /ə/ (the first sound in the word *above*) to the vowel /u/ ($\overline{\text{oo}}$). This last substitution—/uə/ ($\overline{\text{oo}}$ ə) for /u/ ($\overline{\text{oo}}$)—is most likely to occur before /l/ and /n/ in the same syllable. *Cool*, then, becomes *coo-uhl*, and *soon* becomes *soo-uhn*. As we have seen with some other vowels, a /w/ can also be added to turn *soon* into *soo-wuhn* and *cool* into *coo-wuhl*.

Pronounce each of the following words aloud. Check to be sure you do not add a sound (or two) to the vowel.

/ul/ ($\overline{\text{oo}}$l)	**/un/ ($\overline{\text{oo}}$n)**
cool	croon
fool	buffoon
ghoul	goon
drool	dune
spool	spoon
Jules	June
pool	lampoon
school	soon
tool	loon
rule	moon

To avoid drawling, move definitely (not slowly and deliberately) to the right place to form the vowel, and hold the tongue in that place until you move on to the next consonant.

Because you are less likely to make the vowel into a diphthong when it occurs alone at the end of a word, read the following pairs of words aloud. Try to match the vowel from the first word in the second word when the /u/ (oo) is followed by /l/ or /n/.

/u/ ($\overline{\text{oo}}$) and /ul/ ($\overline{\text{oo}}$l) Contrast

coo	cool	Drew	drool
foo	fool	goo	ghoul
who	who'll	poo	pool
too	tool		

/u/ ($\overline{\text{oo}}$) and /un/ ($\overline{\text{oo}}$n) Contrast

boo	boon	coo	'coon
do	dune	goo	goon
Lou	loon	Sue	soon

Pragmatics

Reinforcement Exercises

Practice Words for /u/ ($\overline{\text{oo}}$)

Beginning	Middle	End
ooze	choose	chew
oolong	too long	too
oompah	zoom	zoo
	tomb	to/two
	tool	
	rule	rue
	rude	
	dude	do
	choose	chew
	whose	who
	glued	glue
	suit	sue
	cruise	crew
	group	grew
	groom	
	lieutenant	lieu
	booty	boo
	broom	brew
	truth	true

Practice Phrases for /u/ (o͞o)

an oozing wound
cooling the brew
choosing a route
a gloomy room
suing the school
a shoe in the pool
soup and fruit
an unruly group
foolish rules
moving by canoe
gluing the coupons
throughout the cruise
a new moon
union dues

Practice Sentences for /u/ (o͞o)

1. Louise, a pessimist, spreads gloom and doom.
2. We did not know the truth—only rumors.
3. Truth should not be the exception, but the rule.
4. I'll soon be involved in another crusade.
5. His case will be reviewed in June.
6. Junior may be ignorant, but he's no fool.
7. I could do it, if I had the right tools.
8. You can't be neutral. You must choose sides.
9. Chew your food well—for good nutrition.
10. The tulips will soon be blooming.
11. What will you do with all those coupons?
12. The troops refused to go through another battle.
13. Reviewing for the test is cruel and unusual punishment.
14. The eulogy was both moving and amusing. He has a unique sense of humor.
15. The suit must be settled soon, or I will be ruined. No fooling!

Practice Sentences for /u/ (o͞o) and /ᴜ/ (oo) Contrast

1. Look for St. Luke's Hospital.
2. I hate to pull trash out of the pool.
3. The soot of New York does not suit me well.

4. That foolish book is full of errors.
5. The baby ''gooed'' as the Mother said, ''Good baby.''
6. I would have wooed her, had she been willing.
7. I stood on the stool; it was my undoing.
8. We should have shooed the flies away.
9. It was a ''kooky'' way to sell cookies.
10. Look at that food. They should be sued.

13

Central Vowels

There are four vowel phonemes in American English produced by raising the center of the tongue in the center of the mouth. These phonemes are logically called *central vowels*. We will discuss each of these vowel phonemes one by one.

/ʌ/ (u)

Principles

Production

If you lift the center of the tongue slightly toward the palate, keep the lips unrounded, and emit the air stream through the mouth with the vocal folds vibrating, you will produce the stressed low central vowel heard in the words *up* and *come*. We represent this phoneme by /ʌ/ in IPA and by u in the dictionaries. It is ordinarily a short sound. We note that it is *stressed*, because we have an *un*stressed central vowel that is very similar to this vowel, but shorter. This vowel is used in stressed syllables.

The /ʌ/ (u) is classified as a *stressed, lax, lip-unrounded*, low central vowel.

Precautions

There are five spellings for /ʌ/ (u):

o as in *done*
oe as in *does*
oo as in *flood*
ou as in *double*
u as in *cut*

Problems

There are five common problems associated with /ʌ/ (u). As we discuss each of these deviations, check to see if you have that problem with this phoneme.

► *Problem 1:* Fronting and Raising

A common distortion of the /ʌ/ (u) made by those who learned American English as a first language is fronting and raising the sound before consonants made in the front of the mouth. Pulling the tongue up and forward in the mouth on the formation of this vowel results in its sounding like /ɪ/ (i) or /ɛ/ (e). The word *just*, then, would sound a great deal like *gist* or *jest*. Perhaps you have heard someone say, "Gist a minute," or "Jest a minute." They were fronting and raising the /ʌ/ (u) vowel.

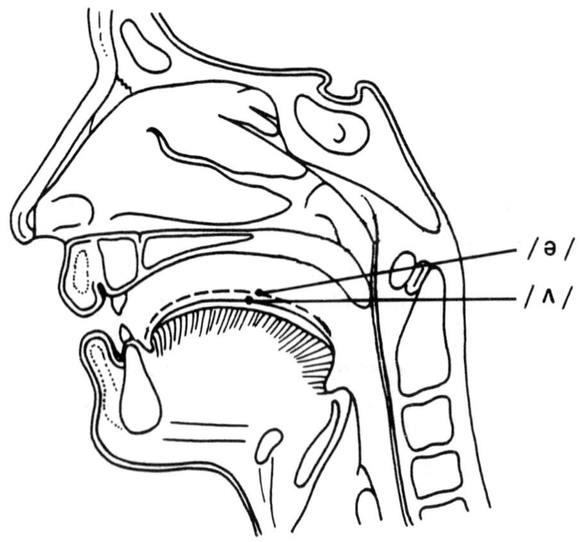

Figure 13.1. *Representative tongue positions for two central vowels: /ə/ and /ʌ/.*

Pronounce the following list of words. Check to be sure you do not distort the vowel in this way.

touch	such	much	hush
mush	shut	brush	lush
hut	hutch	budge	fudge
clutch	judge	smudge	rush
cover	smother	just	justice

▶ *Problem 2:* Raising

Some speakers distort the /ʌ/ (u) vowel by raising the tongue further up in the center of the mouth than is customary. They do not turn this central vowel into a front vowel (as in the first problem we discussed). It is still a central vowel, but it is not the *same* central vowel.

If you distort this phoneme in this way, you substitute an uncommon allophone of the stressed *er* vowel (the vowel in the words *stir* and *blur*). This allophone has no r-coloring, but is a tense high central vowel. (See p. 309.) When the tongue is raised up relatively high in the center of the mouth and tensed a bit, this allophone of /ɝ/ (ûr) is produced. If you substitute this sound for /ʌ/ (u), the /ʌ/ is distorted.

▶ *Problem 3:* Retracting and Raising

Some speakers pull the tongue up and back in the mouth on the formation of this vowel. If you raise the tongue up rather high in back, leaving the tongue somewhat lax, you will produce some variation of the /ʊ/ (oo) vowel. Indeed, this distortion sounds like a substitution of /ʊ/ (oo) for /ʌ/ (u).

Pronounce the following word pairs aloud. Check to be sure you make a clear distinction between the two words. The first should not sound like the second.

/ʌ/ (u) and /ʊ/ (oo) Contrast

luck	look
stud	stood
tuck	took
buck	book
Hud	hood
Huck	hook
crux	crooks
ruck	rook

▶ *Problem 4:* Substitution of /ɑ/ (ä) for /ʌ/ (u)

There are many languages that do not contain the /ʌ/ (u) vowel phoneme at all. If English is not your first language, it is possible—

even likely—that the language you learned first does not include this sound in its phonemic structure. If so, you may have difficulty hearing and making this vowel. It is quite understandable that you might substitute a familiar sound [such as /ɑ/ (ä)] for this unfamiliar sound. In fact, the most common distortion of this vowel for speakers who learned English after learning another language is this substitution—/ɑ/ (ä) for /ʌ/ (u).

To contrast these two vowels, you will have to train your ear and your tongue. Remember, the /ɑ/ (ä) is made with the tongue almost flat in the mouth. There is a slight raising of the tongue in the center of the mouth to form the /ʌ/ (u). That little bit of raising in the center of the mouth makes the difference. But the difference, small as it is, is important in English. These are two separate phonemes in English. They cannot be substituted for each other without changing the meaning of the word. The vowel in the English word *much* is not the same as the vowel in the Spanish word *macho*.

The following pairs of words show the contrast between the two vowels /ɑ/ (ä) and /ʌ/ (u). Pronounce these pairs aloud. Listen and feel the difference. If you have this problem, you will have to work to make the correct difference.

/ɑ/ (ä) and /ʌ/ (u) Contrast

mod	mud	dock	duck
rob	rub	not/knot	nut
rot	rut	sock	suck
bomb	bum	cot	cut
clock	cluck	Don	done
fond	fund	got	gut
hot	hut	jog	jug
lock	luck	mock	muck
knob	nub	pot	putt
rod	Rudd	Ron	run
sob	sub	shock	shuck
chock	chuck	stock	stuck
shot	shut	doll	dull
calm	come	wan	won/one
Tom's	Tums	psalm	sum/some
blonder	blunder	body	buddy
collar	color	robber	rubber

▶ *Problem 5:* Substitution of /u/ (o͞o) for /ʌ/ (u)

If English is not your first language, you may substitute another familiar vowel—/u/ (o͞o)—for the unfamiliar /ʌ/ (u) English vowel. This would be most likely to occur if the English word is spelled with *u*.

Luck should not sound like *Luke*. *Punish* should not sound like *poonish*. *Sup* should not sound like *soup*. The vowel in the English word *much* should not be the same vowel as in the Spanish word *mucho*.

Pronounce the following words aloud. Check to be sure you use the central vowel /ʌ/ (u) instead of the high back vowel /u/ (o͞o) in these words. (We will put the tempting vowel in italics.)

suction	production	induction	instruct
instruction	construct	construction	destruction
umpire	assumption	discussion	concussion

Here are a few pairs of English words to show the contrast. The first word should not sound like the second.

/ʌ/ (u) and /u/ (o͞o) Contrast

sup	soup	mud	mood
luck	Luke	duck	duke
pup	poop	shut	shoot
dumb	doom	done	dune
rub	Rube	smother	smoother

Pragmatics

Reinforcement Exercises

Practice Words for /ʌ/ (u)

Beginning

up	us	other	upward
under	ugly	uncle	umbrella
onion	ultimate	usher	utter
oven	ulcer	ulterior	umpire

Middle

cup	rust	mother	rough
sum/some	club	dunking	done
plunder	wonder	thunder	humble
cucumber	gullible	honey	crusher
instruct	construct	month	brother
discuss	enough	trust	thrust
double	trouble	mumble	tumble
mutton	glutton	hustle	bustle
blood	bubble	hungry	supper
justice	judgment	adjust	unjust

Practice Phrases for /ʌ/ (u)

a lucky couple
a wonderful mother
an usher in trouble
my other cousin
nothing for supper
come on Monday
crush the walnuts
hungry for fudge
my brother's money
a month in the sun
under discussion
enough instructors
a duck in the oven
a cup of diced onions
tough and ugly

Practice Sentences for /ʌ/ (u)

1. None of them is under orders to come.
2. I wonder if he will fund the project.
3. If I am lucky, I will make some money.
4. Uncle Bill is my mother's brother.
5. The rug did not cover the dust on the floor.
6. My son has not done his homework.
7. Nothing is too tough for our company.
8. I'm having lunch with Chuck on Monday.
9. The umpire used some colorful language.
10. Do not touch the upper portion with that brush.

Practice Sentences for /ʌ/ (u) (More Challenging)

1. My young son loves bubble gum, peanut butter, and honey.
2. The punch has just a touch of rum in it. Have a cup.
3. The hut was covered with mud. The door was not shut.
4. The instructor asked us to discuss the story.
5. The love of money is not the root of *all* evil; the lack of money is one of the roots too.
6. I love fudge—with or without nuts. I'll have another one.
7. I am very gullible. I still trust in the justice system.
8. He is a glutton for punishment. He's in trouble again.

9. Too many thunderstorms resulted in a flood.
10. The duck is in the oven. I wonder when it will be done.

Practice Sentences for /ʌ/ (u) (Most Challenging)

1. The curtains shut out the light; the vandals shot out the light.
2. Pronounce that word with this pronunciation.
3. The collar should be the same color as the shirt.
4. I am not fond of trying to raise funds.
5. I think I'm stuck with this worthless stock.
6. With a lot of luck, I may not need a lock on the door.
7. Don has done nothing to deserve this punishment.
8. Do not come unless you are going to be calm.
9. He consumed the cup of soup—a sup at a time.
10. What have you done to this dune buggy?
11. I misconstrued the construction chief's remarks.
12. The producer is responsible for the whole production.
13. The Duke did not duck his unbearable duties.
14. Luke had better luck than the rest of us—but not much.
15. I'm smothering in this rough scarf. I wish it were smoother.

/ə/

Principles

Production

The unstressed equivalent of /ʌ/ (u) is the short neutral central vowel heard in the first syllable of the word *above* and in the second syllable of the word *sofa*. In both IPA and the dictionaries, this sound is represented by /ə/.

The vowel is a lax vowel—formed with the lips and tongue relaxed, the lips unrounded, and the tongue raised up slightly toward the middle in the center of the mouth. The tongue is raised *very* slightly higher for this little vowel than for /ʌ/ (u). That is why we classify /ʌ/ (u) a low central vowel and /ə/ a mid central vowel.

This vowel is classified as a *short, lax, unrounded, mid central vowel*. The /ə/ is the most frequently used vowel in our language. The sound is so short in duration it cannot be uttered alone. It is an unstressed vowel and exists only in unstressed syllables. There must be another syllable pronounced in addition to the syllable in which /ə/ occurs or it is not /ə/.

This vowel has a name: *schwa*. To identify the phonetic symbol and the sound (which could not be uttered alone), phoneticians gave the sound a name. The word *schwa* (according to Claude Wise, the late great Louisiana State University phonetician) is a German modification of the Hebrew word *sheva*, meaning "little" or "weak." The Hebrew language also includes this vowel in its phonemic system; the vowel pointing (representation in Hebrew) is : .

The schwa is the vowel in most unstressed syllables in American English. No matter which vowel occurs in a syllable or word in its stressed form, the vowel usually is reduced to this neutral little central vowel when the syllable is not stressed.

Compare the word *land* with the second syllable of the word *England*. Is the vowel the same when you pronounce the words aloud? No. The vowel in the word *land* is /æ/ (a). The vowel in the second syllable of *England*—if the second syllable has a vowel at all—is /ə/. The difference is that *land*, a one-syllable word, is stressed, while in the word *England*, the primary stress is on the first syllable, and the second is unstressed.

Precautions

There are, by our count, nineteen spellings of /ə/:

a as in *above*
aa as in *Canaan*
ae as in *Michael*
ai as in *captain*
au as in *authority*
e as in *listen*
ea as in *sergeant*
eo as in *dungeon*
eou as in *gorgeous*
i as in *beautiful*
ia as in *parliament*
ie as in *conscience*
io as in *region*
iou as in *vicious*
o as in *bishop*
oi as in *porpoise*
ou as in *furious*
u as in *cranium*
y as in *analysis*

Problems

There are three major problems associated with the /ə/. As we discuss each of these deviations, check to see if you have that problem with this phoneme.

► *Problem 1:* Substitution of a strong (or stressed) vowel for /ə/

It is nonstandard to use the strong vowel /i/ (ē) in the unstressed second syllable in such words as *beauti*ful, *plenti*ful, and *bounti*ful. In such words, you can use /ə/, /ɪ/, or /ɨ/ (a vowel between /ɪ/ and /ə/). All three are unstressed vowels.

It is nonstandard to substitute /ʌ/ (u) for /ə/ in either the stressed or unstressed forms of such words as *of*, *was*, and *from*.

It is nonstandard to substitute /u/ (o͞o) for /ə/ or /ʊ/ (oo) in such words as *regular* and *regulate*. Also please note that there is neither an /u/ (o͞o) or an /ʊ/ (oo) in the middle of the words *simile* and *similar*.

It is nonstandard to substitute the [o] (ō) for /ə/ in such words as *opinion*, *official*, *violent*, and *violate*.

It is nonstandard to substitute /e/ (ā) for /ə/ in such words as *around*, *about*, *arise*, and *account*.

If English is not your first language, and vowel gradation (see pp. 349-354) is not a pattern in your first language, you should check to be certain you do not use strong vowels in all syllables in English. Get used to reducing the stress in unstressed syllables by using schwa (and its variations).

► *Problem 2:* Omission

Some careless speakers omit /ə/. That usually happens when schwa occurs

(1) between consonants in the middle of a word, or

(2) at the beginning of a syllable which follows a syllable ending in a vowel or diphthong.

The following words offer the temptation to omit the schwa between consonants. Pronounce the words aloud, and check to be sure the schwa is present.

bakery	cabinet	corridor	delicate
family	federal	terrible	mercury
parade	police	similar	suppose
support	traveler	unity	naturally

The following words offer a temptation to omit the unstressed vowel after a syllable ending in a vowel or diphthong. Pronounce these words aloud, and check for omission of the endangered vowel.

poem	poetry	lion	li*a*ble
scion	Zion	riot	Ry*a*n
jewel	cruel	society	vari*e*ty
d*i*et	quiet	pious	delirious
medium	sodium	period	stow*a*way

Problem 3: Addition

Just as some speakers are tempted to leave out /ə/, so others are tempted to put in an extra /ə/ occasionally. Have you ever heard anyone turn the two-syllable word *athlete* into a three syllable word by adding a schwa between the /θ/ (th) and the /l/? Or have you heard someone add an /ə/ after the /θ/ (th) in *athletics*? These additions, of course, are nonstandard.

Read the following words aloud. Check to be sure you do not put a schwa in the middle.

athlete	athletics	burglar	business
bracelet	ably	evening	

Pragmatics

Reinforcement Exercises

Practice Words for /ə/

Beginning	Middle	End
around	buffalo	sofa
about	relative	soda
agree	permanent	boa
along	possible	visa
affair	prominent	comma
amaze	photograph	coma
upon	elephant	toga
avoid	baritone	opera
oppose	holiday	cola
offend	delegate	zebra
obtain	camera	panda
arrange	president	data

In the First Syllable	In the Last Syllable
balloon	circus
surprise	delicious
support	nation
parade	famous
confess	patient
control	cruel
garage	riot

In the First *and* Last Syllables

agenda arena banana

Practice Phrases for /ə/

the best of times
a little panda
a cruel charade
adjourn the meeting
debate the method
a legal dependent
of the people
delay the decision

Practice Sentences for /ə/

1. Canada and America have a lot in common.
2. The captain was the one in command.
3. Stella's cooperative, dependable, and consistent.
4. I'm suspicious of one who announces his piety.
5. The professor read the poem with vitality and variety.
6. The soprano needed a good baritone to complement her voice.
7. The president is the hospital's most famous patient.
8. Upon obtaining the approval, I left.
9. A long time ago, I arranged the operation.
10. I love a circus parade—especially the elephants.

Practice Sentences for /ə/ (More Challenging)

1. The police said the crime occurred in the area of the stadium.
2. Of course, there are some honorable politicians and public officials.

3. Yes, I'm consistent. I'm violently opposed to violence and completely intolerant of all intolerance.
4. It's cruel to remind him he's been awfully quiet about his diet of late.
5. I suppose we should use the same criteria to judge all of them.
6. The editor has said all along it is dangerous to express an opinion.
7. The federal treasury is facing another terrible deficit.
8. A syllable is similar to a musical beat and affects the rhythm.
9. It was a beautiful analysis—logical and clear.
10. The officials had no comment on the campus violence. Naturally.

/ɝ/ (ûr)

Principles

Production

If you lift your tongue tip upward to a position just in back of the alveolar ridge, curl the raised tongue tip slightly toward the hard palate, lift the center of the tongue up near the hard palate, leave the lips unrounded, and emit the air stream through the mouth with the vocal folds vibrating, you will produce the stressed, tense high central vowel heard in the words *sir* and *her*. In IPA, this phoneme is represented by /ɝ/. In the dictionaries, it is represented by ûr.

This stressed vowel is tense and long. The amount of retroflexion (curling back) of the tongue (which gives the vowel its "r-coloring") varies greatly from person to person and region to region. We classify this phoneme as a *long, tense, lip-unrounded, high central vowel.*

Precautions

There are nine spellings for /ɝ/:

ear as in *heard*
er as in *herd*
ir as in *fir*
olo as in *colonel*
or as in *word*

our as in *courage*
ur as in *fur*
yr as in *Myrtle*
yrrh as in *myrrh*

Problems

There are three common problems associated with the production of this vowel. As we discuss each deviation, check to see if you have that problem with this phoneme.

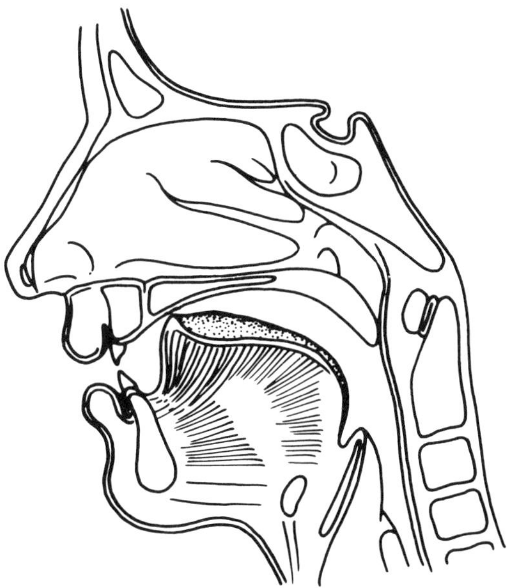

Figure 13.2. *Representative tongue position for two central vowels: /ɝ/ and /ɚ/.*

► ***Problem 1:*** Excessive Retraction

If you pull the tongue tip too far back toward the palate or the center of the tongue too far back in the mouth, you will distort the vowel. This distortion is more common in the Midwest and Southwest than in the rest of the United States. Some authors, to indicate this vowel distortion, have noted that people said *vurry, purrrty*, or *Amurrica*.

► ***Problem 2:*** Substitution of /ɔɪ/ (ôi)

This distortion is not heard as frequently as in the past, but it is still heard occasionally. Substituting this diphthong for the vowel when it occurs before a consonant creates a number of homophones (sound alike words). It is nonstandard.

If you tend to labialize the /r/ phoneme (see p. 90), you may also use the lips to make the related vowel /ɝ/ (ûr). The /ɔɪ/ (oi) substitution results, in part, from using the lips instead of forming the vowel with the correct tongue placement. The /ɝ/ (ûr) vowel is made with the tongue lifted higher in the center of the mouth than it is on the central vowel /ʌ/ (u). If you substitute /ɔɪ/ (oi), you will lift the back of the tongue up in back as you purse the lips. Both of these movements (tongue and lips) distort the /ɝ/ (ûr) vowel.

To get the "feel" of the central position of this vowel, first say a word containing the /ʌ/ (u); then check to see where the tongue and lips are to form that sound. Then, by lifting the tongue up in the *center* toward the palate from the place where you made /ʌ/ (u), and by keeping the lips from rounding and tensing, you can make a good /ɝ/ (ûr) in the same context. Then move on to /ɝ/ (ûr) alone. We will use alveolar sounds before these vowels, because they get your tongue moving in the right neighborhood. Review these instructions, and then try these sequences out loud:

/ʌ/ (u) and /ɝ/ (ûr) Contrast

ton	turn	earn
done	durn	earn
Lund	learned	earned
dud	dirge	urge
luck	lurk	irk
stub	disturb	herb
duck	Dirk	irk
Tum	term	Irma
tuck	Turk	irk
Lux	lurks	irks
stun	stern	earn
tub	turban	urban

Read aloud the following pairs of words. Check to be sure you make a clear distinction between them. Do not turn the word in the left hand column into the word on the right.

/ɝ/ (ûr) and /ɔɪ/ (oi) Contrast

learn	loin	verse	voice
curl	coil	purrs	poise
hurt	Hoyt	bird	Boyd
Kern	coin	Earl	oil
Berle	boil	Serle	soil
furled	foiled	early	oily

Problem 3: Omission of r- coloring Before a Vowel

There are some dialects of American English that omit the r-coloring of this vowel at the end of a syllable before a consonant. The r-less allophone used is represented in phonetics by [ɜ]. Even in those dialects, however, the r-coloring is restored if the next sound is a vowel. This reappearing r-coloring is called ''linking R.''

A speaker of one of those dialects (Southern or Northeastern) would say ''She bought a fur coat'' using [ɜ] in the word *fur*. When saying ''the fur on the couch,'' the r-coloring would be present. To omit it in that context is nonstandard.

Read each of the following sentences aloud. There is a ''linking R'' possibility in each sentence. Do you include or omit the r-coloring?

I told her about it.
Wearing fur is immoral
That ''curr'' is my best friend.
They were even at the turn.
I prefer a new one.
Will it occur again?
It did not deter anyone.
What can I confer on you?
I will defer any more examples.

Pragmatics

Reinforcement Exercises

Practice Words for /ɝ/ (ûr)

Beginning	**Middle**	**End**
err	dirty	deter
early	curly	cur
earn	burn	burr
urn	fervent	fur
erred	heard/herd	her
urgent	servant	sir
earth	nervous	confer
urban	courage	occur
Earl	whirl	whir
irk	work	were
Irwin	mercy	myrrh

Practice Phrases for /ɝ/ (ûr)

search the earth
a dirty curtain

early on Thursday
prefer a curve ball
the nervous urchin
my turn to splurge
a certain verse
learn the worst
a perfect nurse
heard the rehearsal
church service
confer hurriedly
a virtuous person
urge the reversal
germs get on my nerves
a hermit in an urban setting
lurch toward the hurdle

Practice Sentences for /ɝ/ (ûr)

1. The early bird can have the worm.
2. I urge you to come to the rehearsal.
3. The driver averted an accident by swerving to the right.
4. He serves without pay, but never shirks a burden.
5. You don't deserve a third chance.
6. My grades this term are getting worse.
7. So-called "dirty words" do not disturb me.
8. I serve on the merger committee.
9. Urchins followed us through the urban areas.
10. I prefer to watch a circus in person—not on TV.

Practice Sentences for /ɝ/ (ûr) (More Challenging)

1. I'm stunned the teacher is so stern.
2. Her remarks are so curt they cut you dead.
3. A pert little golfer, she putts well.
4. The vehicle weighed ten tons, but turned easily.
5. My cat Anathema has great poise and purrs all the time.
6. I'm not averse to music, but she has no voice.
7. Can't you learn to like pork loin?
8. I bought Mr. Kern's coin collection.
9. I learned early to avoid oily foods.
10. The committees meeting in adjoining rooms were adjourning.

Practice Sentences for /ɝ/ (ûr) (Most Challenging)

1. I heard the colonel give a perfect explanation.
2. Return to earth? Could we confer, Captain Kirk?
3. You have some nerve! That is a worse version than the first!
4. Every person at the service reserved judgment on the sermon.
5. I'm worried. What purpose does that big purse serve?
6. I do not earn enough to be perfectly virtuous.
7. It took courage for the surgeon to tell Shirley the truth.
8. He's being observed by the Internal Revenue Service.
9. I deserve a raise. My work is worth more than the firm pays.
10. He turned purple when the judge confirmed the verdict.

Principles

Production

The unstressed equivalent of the stressed vowel /ɚ/ (ur) is the short neutral vowel with an *r*-coloring heard in unstressed syllables. It is heard, for example, in the first syllable of the word *perhaps* and the second syllable of the word *other*. The IPA symbol for this phoneme is /ɚ/, and the dictionary represents the vowel by ər. The IPA symbol is a schwa with a little r hook on it.

Like the schwa, this vowel phoneme is used in unstressed syllables. Like the /ɝ/ (ûr), it is *r*-colored—made with the tongue tip lifted upward just in back of the alveolar ridge, the tongue tip curled back slightly toward the hard palate, the center of the tongue raised up near the hard palate, and the lips unrounded. The amount of retroflexion (curling back) of the tongue varies greatly. The air is emitted through the mouth with the vocal folds vibrating. The major difference between this vowel phoneme and /ɝ/ (ûr) is that this vowel is shorter and more lax than the /ɝ/ (ûr).

Precautions

There are eleven spellings in American English plus one in British English for /ɚ/ (ər):

ar as in *liar*
er as in *other*
ir as in *nadir*
or as in *actor*
oar as in *cupboard*
r as in *car* and *card*
uo as in *languor*
ur as in *femur*
ure as in *failure*
re as in *theatre* and *are*
yr as in *martyr*
our as in *favour* (British)

/ɚ/ (ər) can occur alone at the end of a syllable. Note these examples:

perhaps
survey (verb)
sug*ar*
bak*er*
flav*or*
pleas*ure*

The unstressed vowel /ɚ/ (ər) also occurs at the end of syllables after vowels and diphthongs. Pronounce the following examples aloud:

ear	air	are
our	ire	oar

Most Americans use the /ɚ/ (ər) vowel when the letter *r* comes before a consonant (or silent *e* plus consonant). Pronounce these examples aloud.

hard	heart	farm
sharp	pardon	Charles
cord	bored	beard
assured	tired	years

Problems

There are three common problems associated with this sound. As we discuss each deviation, check to see if you have that problem.

▶ *Problem 1:* Excessive Retraction

If you pull the tongue too far back toward the back of the mouth and curl the tongue tip too far back toward the palate, you will distort this sound. This vowel is a neutral central vowel—not a back vowel.

Problem 2: Substitution of /ɔɚ/ (ôr)

Some people who think in terms of pronouncing written letters rather than vocal sounds are led into "spelling mispronunciations." You may have heard someone say *educatawr* (ɛdʒʊkeɪtɔɚ) for *educator*. Or *actawr* (/ɚktɔɚ) for *actor*.

This substitution results from a misunderstanding of the way language works. The written letters represent (as best they can) the spoken sounds. The spoken words come first. We don't pronounce letters; we pronounce words made out of *speech sounds*. Don't let the spelling *or* mislead you. This substitution is pedantic, affected, and nonstandard.

Remember that /ɚ/ (ər) can be spelled in *many* different ways. But it is the same little neutral r-colored vowel.

Problem 3: Omission or r-coloring before a Vowel

We have discussed the "linking R" before. (See p. 309.) If you omit the "linking R" before a syllable or word beginning with a vowel, the omission is nonstandard—even in an "r-less dialect."

Read these few sentences aloud. Each sentence affords you an opportunity to use the "linking R." Check to hear whether you omit it.

Mother is at home.
The paper is full of gossip.
A surfer ought to be careful.
Figure it out.
It was a factor in my decision.
I want either a yes or a no. (Two chances here!)
Here is a picture of me. (Another two chances!)

Pragmatics

Reinforcement Exercises

Practice Words for /ɚ/ (ər) at the End

mother	brother	bother	father
further	surfer	weather	whether
clever	sever	water	hotter
enter	center	murder	murmur
teacher	preacher	actor	factor
humor	mirror	labor	tumor
favor	flavor	razor	doctor
anchor	languor	collar	dollar
pillar	sugar	grammar	regular

nadir	similar	pleasure	treasure
pressure	measure	nature	failure
feature	creature	picture	lecture

Practice Words for /ɚ/ (ər) in the Middle

forbid	forbade	forgive	forget
survey (verb)	surmount	surmise	survival
perform	perfume	persuade	perhaps
dullard	collard	eastern	western
wonderful	afternoon	liberty	government
understand	butterfly	advertise	summertime

Practice Phrases for /ɚ/ (ər)

summer and winter
forever and ever
a junior partner
a better performance
our modern age
tired of the farm
Hard-hearted Hannah
our family doctor
sooner or later
ponder the answer
bored with the weather
understood the teacher
a fair neighbor
hard to find treasure

Practice Sentences for /ɚ/ (ər)

1. Are you a performer?
2. Maintain your humor to survive.
3. I would rather not search for the treasure.
4. The speaker needed a lesson in grammar.
5. So little pleasure for a dollar!
6. My brother made his sacrifice at the altar.
7. I hear you work as a baker.
8. He would not consider our offer.
9. The doctor cured my heartburn.
10. The governor should pardon the prisoner.

Practice Sentences for /ɚ/ (ər) (More Challenging)

1. Yes, I care, but I will never be able to forgive her.
2. They fired the reporter before he could tender his resignation.
3. Perhaps she can't be bothered with answering the phone.
4. We persuaded him to walk under a ladder and break the mirror.
5. Surmount your negative ideas if you want power to survive.
6. The wonderful picture I saw this afternoon had great performances.
7. Perhaps nothing is more important than liberty.
8. The baker carefully measured the sugar and butter, and it was still a failure.
9. Do me a favor. Water the flowers for me Saturday.
10. I went berserk. The government said my hundred dollar bill was counterfeit.

Practice Sentences for /ɚ/ (ər) (Most Challenging)

1. I spilled sulfur water on the corner of the sofa.
2. The tailor agreed to measure me this morning and deliver the suit this afternoon.
3. The soldiers performed their colorful ceremony in terrible weather.
4. Should I advertise in the afternoon paper? I'm under pressure to sell.
5. My driver favored leaving the interstate. The other roads were easier for him.

14

Three Phonemic Diphthongs

A *diphthong*, as we said earlier, is a blend of two vowels. Diphthongs function as vowels in the language, but they differ from pure vowels in that the lips and tongue move during the production of the sound. This continuous movement changes the quality of the sound during its production. There are two elements in a diphthong (two simple vowels) that are melded together by continuous movement from the position of one element to the position of the other.

We have discussed two standard diphthongal allophones: [oʊ], an allophone of /o/ (ō), and [eɪ], an allophone of /e/ (ā). These diphthongs are variations of their respective phonemes, rather than separate phonemes. If you replace [o] (ō̵) with [oʊ] (ō) (or vice versa), the meaning is not affected; hence, they are merely variations of the same phoneme. The difference between [o] (ō̵) and [oʊ] (ō) or between [e] (ā̵) and [eɪ] (ā) does not distinguish one word from another. If they were separate phonemes, it would.

We have also looked at the problem of diphthongizing—turning pure vowels into diphthongs and, thus, distorting them. Even though the vowels are distorted by this elongation (and the addition of an extra vowel element), we still recognize them as the same phonemes (even if slightly out of whack).

We have three diphthongs in the language that *are* phonemic diphthongs. These do change meaning when we substitute them for other vowels, and each of them (although made up of two elements) is really a single phoneme unit in the language. These three *phonemic diphthongs* are heard in the words *bough, buy*, and *boy*. The first is represented in IPA by /ɑʊ/ and in the dictionaries by ou; the second is represented in IPA by /ɑɪ/ and in the dictionaries by ī; and the third is represented in IPA by /ɔɪ/ and in the dictionaries by oi.

Let us look at these three sounds a little more to be clear about why they are *phonemic* diphthongs.

The vowel sound in the word *high* is represented in IPA by two symbols because it is made up of two elements. The lips and tongue begin to make the sound at about the position for the vowel in *alms* (the tongue may be a little higher and farther front) and move toward the position for the vowel in the word *eat*. Because the tongue does not get quite as high and tense as in the production of the vowel in *eat*, phoneticians have used the symbol for the vowel in *it* to represent the second element of this diphthong. In IPA, then, the diphthong is represented as /ɑɪ/ (or [aɪ]). We have seen each of those vowels before. /ɑ/ (ä) and /ɪ/ (i) are themselves phonemes in English. Can a sound made by blending the two of them become a third phoneme—different and separate from either of them? Well, let's check. Go back to the word *high* (/haɪ/). Is that word the same or completely different in meaning from the word *ha* (/hɑ/)? And is the word *high* the same or completely different in meaning from the word *he* (/hi/)? (Remember, we move toward the /i/ (ē) vowel when making the /ɑɪ/ phoneme.) The answer is obvious. You cannot substitute /ɑɪ/ (ī) for either /ɑ/ (ä) or /i/ (ē). You cannot substitute it for /ɪ/ (i) either. *Hide* and *hid* are different words in English; the change of /ɑɪ/ (ī) to /ɪ/ (i) changes the meaning, so they are separate and distinct phonemes in English.

You can check on the other two phonemic diphthongs in the same way. Note that *wowed* (/ɑʊ/ or ou), *wad* (/ɑ/ or ä), *wooed* (/u/ or o͞o), and *wood* (/ʊ/ or oo) are all different words in English. Hence, they each contain a distinct vowel phoneme. Now look at the fact that *foil* (/ɔɪ/ or oi), *fall* (/ɔ/ or ô), *feel* (/i/ or ē), and *fill* (/ɪ/ or i) are all different words in English. They, too, each contain a separate and distinct vowel phoneme.

The three phonemic diphthongs definitely function as single sounds—indivisible sounds—in the language; they are vowel phonemes too.

/ɑʊ/ (ou)

Principles

Production

If you start with your lips and tongue in position for forming the /ɑ/ (ä)—the vowel in the word *alms*—and then glide from that vowel smoothly toward the position of the lips and tongue used to form /u/ (o͞o)—the vowel in the word *ooze*—you will produce the phonemic diphthong heard in the words *bough* and *now*. We told you to move *toward* the position for /u/, because it is easier to explain the sound that way. The first element of the diphthong is longer than the second element. The IPA symbol for this diphthong is /aʊ/; it is represented in the dictionaries by ou.

You will notice that at the start of this diphthong, the mouth is open wide and the lips are relaxed; the tongue is almost flat in the mouth. At the end of this diphthong, the lips are closed down into a pucker, the lips are more tense, and the back of the tongue has been raised high in the back of the mouth. The diphthong starts from approximately the position for /ɑ/ (ä) and moves almost to the position for /u/ (o͞o).

There are two allophones, or variations, of this diphthong. We have already explained one variation of the sound and have given you the phonetic symbols for this allophone: [ɑu]. Although we gave you this allophone first, and we have used the symbol /ɑu/ to represent the phoneme itself, this allophone is probably less common than the second variation of the phoneme. We chose to present the sound in this way because it is much less confusing for those of you who speak English as a second language and because it uses phonemic symbols rather than symbols of allophones.

If you have learned English as a second language, you may have some difficulty with this phoneme. You should have little trouble making a perfectly acceptable, standard variation of this phoneme if you combine the /ɑ/ (ä) and /u/ (o͞o)—sounds you probably already use in your first language.

The second variation of this phoneme is made by starting with the lips and tongue in position to form the [a] allophone of /æ/ (a) and gliding from that position up toward the position of /u/ (o͞o). In this allophone, the sound begins with the front of the tongue raised *very* slightly; the tongue is still *almost* flat in the mouth. This variation ([aʊ]) is the more common of the two variants, but both are standard.

Precautions

There are three spellings for /ɑʊ/ (ou):

ou as in *bout*
ough as in *bough*
ow as in *town*

Problems

Of all the diphthongs, this one is the most frequently distorted in all sections of the United States. When distorted, it is also the most unpleasant in sound.

There are five common problems associated with this phoneme. As we discuss each deviation, check to see if you have that problem.

▶ *Problem 1:* Raising and Fronting

If you begin the diphthong with the tongue raised too high in the front of the mouth, you will produce a flat and very unpleasant speech sound. If you tend to raise the /æ/ (a) vowel, you should be especially careful in producing this diphthong. You may find that you not only substitute [æʊ] for [ɑʊ] but that you begin that diphthong with a *raised* form of the /æ/ (a)!

The /ɑʊ/ (ou) should begin with the mouth open and the tongue relatively flat in the mouth. If you are not certain that you are producing the sound correctly, check with a mirror.

Pronounce these words, and check the placement of your tongue at the beginning of the /ɑʊ/ (ou) diphthong.

out	our	owl	outline
bout	pout	crouch	proud
South	doubt	ounce	pounce
town	gown	trounce	outfit

▶ *Problem 2:* Raising and Centering

This distortion is caused, again, by raising your tongue too high in your mouth as you begin the /ɑʊ/ (ou) diphthong. If you raise your tongue in the center of your mouth, you will produce the diphthong [ɜʊ], which (like the raised and fronted distortion) is nonstandard.

▶ *Problem 3:* Nasalization

Many speakers who raise and front the diphthong also nasalize it. The result is that the sound is not only "flattened" but is also "pinched" through the nose. This nasalized form is more likely to occur before the nasal consonants, but it can occur even when there is no nasal consonant before or after it.

You must work to be sure that the velum fully closes off the passage to the nose, that the mouth is open, and that the air stream is emitted only through the mouth.

Pronounce the word *how*. Now hold your nose, closing off both nostrils, and pronounce the word again. It should sound exactly the same, and you should not feel any air trying to come out of the nose while you say the word (which has no nasal consonants in it). If there is air trying to come out of the nose, then you are nasalizing the diphthong and you need practice to make that diphthong oral rather than nasal.

You must be especially careful about nasalizing this diphthong when it comes before a nasal consonant. There the temptation will be severe. Resist it! Work for a good *oral* diphthong and good nasal resonance on the nasal consonant that follows.

Use the nose-holding trick we just used on the word *how* on the first word of the following pairs. Then, when you have a good oral diphthong on the first word (containing no nasal consonant), try for good oral resonance on the *diphthong* of the second word, but be sure to get good nasal humming on the *nasal consonant* of the second word.

Dow	down
brow	brown
sow	sound
cow	count
how	hound
loud	lounge

Try the following words aloud, and check for nasalization of the diphthong:

/ɑʊ/ (ou) Before /n/

found	founder	flounder	fountain
gown	ground	hound	count
mound	mount	pound	pounce
round	town	astounding	bound

Problem 4: Substitution of /ɑ/ (ä), [a], or /æ/ (a)

This distortion is more common in the South than in the rest of the United States. It results from omission of the second element in the diphthong. If the diphthong is shortened by omitting the second vowel ([ʊ]), then /ɑʊ/ (ou) becomes simply /ɑ/ (ä) or [a]—or even /æ/ (a) if that is the vowel they use to begin the "diphthong." This distortion is non-standard. Check to hear if you tend to omit the second element in the diphthong. Say the sentence "How are you?" as you would normally say it. Listen to your pronunciation of the word *how*. Does it sound like the word *ha* or perhaps the word *half* with the /f/ left off? If so, you are not moving to the second element of the diphthong.

If you have this problem, pronounce the word *ha* followed by the word *ooze* without taking a breath or a break between them. Do it in slow motion to see and feel how the lips and tongue move from the end of *ha* to the beginning of *ooze*. Then speed up the pronunciation a little each time until the words are blended into *how*'s. If you preserved the /ɑ/ (ä) from *ha* and the /u/ (o͞o) from *ooze*, you should have a complete diphthong—and not just half an /ɑʊ/ (ou).

Problem 5: Substitution of /ɑə/ (äə) or [aə] (aə)

Some speakers do not omit the second element of the diphthong entirely, but they use a substitute vowel for the second element. They replace [ʊ] with [ə]. Again, this distortion is more common in the South than in the rest of the United States, but it does occur in other parts of the country as well. This distortion is more likely to occur before /l/ or /ɚ/ (ər).

Try the following pairs of words out loud. The first word should not sound like the second one. The first word contains this diphthong /ɑʊ/ (ou); the second contains a vowel before the /l/ or /ɚ/ (ər).

/ɑʊl/ (oul) and /æl/ (al) Contrast

owl	Al	Cowley	Calley
howl	Hal	Powell	pal
vowel	Val	cowl	Cal

/ɑʊɚ/ (ouə) and /ɑɚ/ (äər) Contrast

our/hour	are	cower	car
bower	bar	power	par
showered	shard	tower	tar

Pragmatics

Reinforcement Exercises

Practice Words for /ɑʊ/ (ou)

/æ/ (a) and /ɑʊ/ (ou) Contrast

tan	town	flat	flout
mass	mouse	had	how'd
rat	rout	scat	scout
spat	spout	pat	pout
bad	bowed	lad	loud
cad	cowed	clad	cloud
math	mouth	lot	lout
trance	trounce	catch	couch
sand	sound	grand	ground
band	bound	hand	hound
fanned	found	Rand	round
manned	mound	brand	browned
Flanders	flounders	panned	pound

/ɑ/ (ä) and /ɑʊ/ (ou) Contrast

ha	how	ah	ow!
ma	Mao	holly	Howley
collie	Cowley	lot	lout
clot	clout	pot	pout
prod	proud	Roddy	rowdy

rot	rout	tot	tout
dot	doubt	shot	shout
Koch	couch	clod	cloud
bra	brow	Ott	out
got	gout	bond	bound
fond	found	pond	pound

Beginning	**Middle**	**End**
owl	howl	how
out	rout	row
ounce	bounce	bough/bow
hour	sour	sow
ouch	couch	cow

Practice Phrases for /ɑʊ/ (ou)

proud of the flowers
thousands of towels
out loud
an ounce of power
around the tower
prowl through downtown
shout to the clown
our favorite noun
scowl at the crowd
long drought; dry ground
a brown house
down and out

Practice Sentences for /ɑʊ/ (ou)

1. How can the college increase its endowment?
2. I doubt that I'll be able to meet you at the lounge.
3. The announcer took a bow with the rest of the cast.
4. The coach frowned when the center missed the rebound.
5. The queen was crowned at the witching hour.
6. When he gets angry, he hangs around the house and pouts.
7. He thinks eating flowers will increase his prowess.
8. Why is that clown scowling at me?
9. She paraded as a Boy Scout—until she was found out.
10. I'm proud to say I've lost twenty pounds.

Practice Sentences for /ɑʊ/ (ou) (More Challenging)

1. I would impound every hound in New York—if I had the power.

2. According to the announcement, the crowd numbered over a hundred thousand.
3. Without an ounce of remorse, he pounded his fist on the counter.
4. Anyhow, the drought has kept me from drowning.
5. The county will not allow crowds to gather in the downtown area.
6. How can I live on this allowance, when my bills are mounting?
7. There are plenty of grounds for ousting that outlaw from the board.
8. It's an outrage. The sound of the pounding got louder.
9. Powell raised eyebrows by crouching behind the couch.
10. The hound keeps growling outside the house.

Practice Sentences for /aʊ/ (ou) (Most Challenging)

1. A thief and a scoundrel! He steals a towel from any hotel he encounters.
2. How could such astounding words come out of his mouth?
3. His remarks were out of bounds, but he confounded the crowd.
4. The college does not allow its students to carouse during school hours.
5. The cloud hovered over the mountain, but somehow bounced over the town.

Principles

Production

If you start with your lips and tongue in position for forming the /a/ (ä)—the vowel in the word *alms*—and then glide from that vowel smoothly toward the position of the lips and tongue used to form /i/ (ē)—the vowel in the word *eat*—you will produce the phonemic diphthong heard in the words *lie* and *buy*. Again, we have told you to move *toward* the lip and tongue position for /i/ (ē) rather than to the position for /ɪ/ (i). We believe it is easier to explain the production of the sound in that way, although the phonetic representation of this diphthong is /ɑɪ/,'' rather than /ɑi/. The positions we give you are approximate anyway, and if you are unfamiliar with this phoneme, you will be more likely to make it correctly following these instructions.

There are two elements in this diphthong. A diphthong, you remember, is one sound made by blending two vowels together. The first element is longer and louder than the second. At the start of this diphthong, the mouth is open wide and the lips are relaxed; the tongue is almost flat in the mouth. You will move the lips and tongue in a smooth, continuous movement from this position to the final position—*during* the production of the sound. At the end of the diphthong, the lips will be slightly spread and a little tensed and the front of the tongue will be raised high in the front of the mouth. The diphthong starts from approximately the position for /ɑ/ (ä) and moves almost to the position for /i/ (ē). This phoneme is represented in IPA by /ɑɪ/; it is represented in the dictionaries by (ī).

As with the phonemic diphthong /ɑʊ/ (ou), there are two allophones, or variations, of this phoneme. We have already described the first variety of the sound. The phonetic symbol for that allophone is [ɑɪ]. We have also used /ɑɪ/ to represent the phoneme itself, using the symbol for the lowest back vowel /ɑ/ (ä) to represent the first element and the symbol for the lax high front vowel /ɪ/ (i) to represent the second element of the diphthong. Both of those symbols are symbols of phonemes of the language.

Of the two allophones of this sound, the [ɑɪ] is probably used less frequently than the second allophone, but both are heard throughout the United States and both are standard.

If you learned English as a second language, you may have some difficulty with this phoneme. Your first language may not have included this sound. If you relate this sound to the two vowels with which it can be blended (/ɑ/ (ä) and /i/ (ē), you should be able to make a perfectly acceptable, standard variation of this phoneme.

The second allophone is made by starting with the lips and tongue in position to form the [a] allophone of /æ/ and gliding smoothly from that position up toward the position of /i/ (ē). In this allophone, the sound begins with the front of the tongue raised *very* slightly in the front of the mouth. The tongue is still almost flat in the mouth. This variation, represented in IPA by [aɪ], is the more commonly heard of the two allophones.

Precautions

There are eleven spellings for /ɑɪ/ (ī):

ais as in *aisle*
ay as in *bayou*
eigh as in *sleight*

eye as in *eye*
i as in *ice*
ie as in *pie*
igh as in *right*
ui as in *guile*
uy as in *buy*
y as in *sky*
ye as in *dye*

Problems

There are three common problems associated with this phoneme. As we discuss each deviation, check to see if you have that problem with this diphthong.

► *Problem 1:* Substitution of [a], [aə], /ɑ/ (ä), or /ɑə/ (äə)

You may have read stories in which the author spelled the word *I'm* as *Ah'm* in dialogue to represent the substitution of the vowel /ɑ/(ä) or the combination of the vowel /ɑ/ (ä) plus the off-glide vowel /ə/ for the diphthong /ɑɪ/. This distortion is not uncommon in the South and is characteristic of the speech of the less educated, although you may hear some educated speakers use it as well. Instead of the /ɑ/(ä), some speakers substitute the [a] allophone of the low front vowel /æ/ (a) or that vowel plus the off-glide /ə/. This "flattened sound" is also heard in the South, particularly in the mountain regions. We have heard huge, cheering crowds in sports arenas urging their teams to [faət, faət, faət]! Actually, you will note, these speakers are having trouble with the second vowel of the diphthong. Either they omit the second vowel altogether and leave only the first pure vowel to substitute for the diphthong, or they substitute the schwa for the second vowel /ɪ/ (i). Check your own pronunciation of the personal pronoun *I* to be certain that when the tongue moves from the /a/ or /ɑ/ the front of your tongue moves up to the position of /ɪ/ (i) in the front of your mouth rather than to the position of /ə/ in the center of your mouth. Use a mirror to check the tongue movement.

As you said the word *I* aloud, could you hear, see, and feel the second element of the diphthong? Is the second element (vowel) present? If, in slow motion, the word *I* does not end with a sound very much like /i/ (ē), then you are cutting off the second part of the phoneme.

If you have this problem, pronounce the word *ha* (/hɑ/) followed by the word *eat* without taking a breath or a break between them. Do it in slow motion to see and feel the lips and tongue move from the end of the word *ha* to the beginning of the word *eat*. Then speed up the pronunciation a little each time until the words are blended into the word *height*. The word *height* has three phonemes in it: /h/, /ɑɪ/ (ī), and /t/. The middle phoneme, the peak or nucleus of the syllable, is the phonemic diphthong /ɑɪ/ (ī). Without the second element of the diphthong, however, the word *height* is going to sound like *hot* or *hat*, or some variation of the two words.

Pronounce the following words, reading across the page. The first two words contain simple vowels. The third word contains this /ɑɪ/ (ī) phonemic diphthong. Remember to move the tongue in the direction of /i/ (ē) for the second vowel of the diphthong.

/æ/ (ä) /ɑ/ (ä) and /ɑɪ/ (ī) Contrast

hat	hot	height
rat	rot	right
lat	lot	light
sat	sot	sight
sad	sod	sighed
panned	pond	pined
fanned	fond	fined
gnat	not	night/knight
slat	slot	sleight
canned	conned	kind

▶ *Problem 2:* Retraction

In the metropolitan New York area, many speakers pull the tongue back to the back of the mouth on the opening vowel of the diphthong. Actually, it would be more accurate to say that they raise the back of the tongue up in the back of the mouth to form the opening vowel of this diphthong. This retraction markedly distorts the vowel and therefore the phonemic diphthong. A few speakers actually substitute the /ɔ/ (ô) for the [ɑ] or [a] when they initiate the diphthong, so that the word *buy* sounds like *boy*. Most who retract the sound, however, instead substitute the sound halfway between /ɑ/ (ä) and /ɔ/ (ô)—the allophone of both represented by [ɒ] (o)—for the first vowel in the diphthong.

You must be certain not to round the lips on this sound. Remember that the /ɔ (ô) and [ɒ] (o) are lip-rounded sounds, whereas /ɑ/ (ä) and [a] are not. Do not pull the tongue back or raise the tongue up in back as you begin this diphthong. The words *odd* (or *add*) and *I'd* should both start with the tongue and lips in about the same position. The tongue and lips should not be tensed as the /ɑɪ/ (ī) begins.

▶ *Problem 3:* Raising

If you raise the tongue from the usual position for beginning this diphthong, you will distort the sound. The diphthong begins with the mouth open wide, the jaw relaxed and dropped, and the tongue almost flat in the bottom of the mouth. If, instead, you do not open the mouth sufficiently and raise the tongue, you may produce [æɪ] or [ɛɪ] or [ʌɪ]—depending on whether you raise the tongue in the center or the front of the mouth. The greatest temptation to distort the diphthong in this way occurs after sounds articulated with the tongue tip on the alveolar ridge or the tongue blade on or near the back of the alveolar ridge.

Pronounce these words aloud, and check to be certain that your mouth is wide open, your jaw is lowered and relaxed, and your tongue is almost flat in the bottom of your mouth as you begin the /ɑɪ/ (ī):

I'd	rye	child
tide	sigh	gyro
died	shy	night
lied	xylophone	tight
chide	try	right
strive	dry	strike
retire	rely	deny

If you tend to distort this diphthong by raising the beginning vowel, try these sequences. Try to match the vowel from the first word when you *begin* the diphthong in the other words:

odd	I'd	tide	tried	denied
Oz	eyes	lies	cries	ties
of	I've	chive	drive	strive
ah	I	shy	nigh	gyrate
are	ire	dire	lyre	desire

Pragmatics

Reinforcement Exercises

Practice Words for /ɑɪ/ (ī)

Beginning	**Middle**	**End**
I	height	high
aisle	style	sty
Ives	dives	die
icy	spicy	spy
iris	virus	vie
eyed	dried	dry
Isis	crisis	cry
icing	slicing	sly
idling	sideling	sigh
isle	while	why

Practice Words for /ɑɪ/ (ī)

Beginning	Middle	End
I'd	fried	fry
ice	lice	lie
I'll	Nile	nigh
I'm	time	tie
eyes	buys	buy

/ɑ/ (ä) and /ɑɪ/ (ī) Contrast

rah!	rye	bah!	buy
shah	shy	ha!	high
of	I've	odd	I'd
alm	I'm	are	ire
olive	I live	odyssey	Ida see
hot	height	Tom	time
job	jibe	rod	ride
slot	sleight	Ron	rind
tot	tight	God	guide
conned	kind	plod	plied
fond	find	plot	plight

/ɔɪ/ (oi) and /ɑɪ/ (ī) Contrast

oil	aisle/isle/I'll	devoid	divide
boy	buy	poise	pies
coy	Chi	voice	vice
poi	pie	Hoyle	heil
coined	kind	hoist	heist
ploy	ply	foil	file
Roy	rye	boil	bile
toy	tie	Doyle	dial
loin	line	coil	Kyle

Practice Phrases for /ɑɪ/ (ī)

time and tide
right on the aisle
fried pies
wild with delight
driver's license
"a sight for sore eyes"
fight, team, fight!
fly to the island
time for a smile

a new kind of device
trying to decide
white wine
the spice of life
won't buy ivory
out of sight, out of mind

Practice Sentences for /ɑɪ/ (i)

1. I had no idea you would try to bribe me!
2. I'm tired of bigots who "have no bias."
3. The high jumper is trying for a record height.
4. Time and tide are a temptation for surfers.
5. We can drive it in about five hours.
6. Forgive my prying, but what are your designs?
7. Why are you buying a hundred pounds of ice?
8. I will not retire until the time is right.
9. I didn't mind the citation, but I was required to pay a fine.
10. I've decided striving to be happy is no crime.

Practice Sentences for /ɑɪ/ (i) (More Challenging)

1. Larry's nearly blind, but he would rather drive at night.
2. Don't chime in. You might be even more unkind.
3. Next time, file a little earlier and avoid the fine.
4. The psychiatrist kept reminding me of my identity crisis.
5. They applied calamine lotion to my poison ivy.
6. I'm just beside myself! What item should I buy the bride?
7. There's no time, but I'm still trying to come up with a reply.
8. She was my ideal, but I was too shy to speak that night.
9. Driving home, I was delighted to see the city skyline.
10. Buying a home is quite a frightening experience.

Practice Sentences for /ɑɪ/ (i) (Most Challenging)

1. While I was climbing, Sam was uttering dire predictions about landslides.
2. Control your desires, maximize your effort, and you might reach the top.
3. There's sunshine, but it's not bright enough for me to acquire the tan I'm striving for.
4. The general eyed the pine trees lined up like soldiers and felt right at home.

5. Why are you whining? I take pride in the type of wines I serve!

/ɔɪ/ (oi)

Principles

Production

If you put your lips and tongue in the position for producing /ɔ/ (ô) and move smoothly into the position for producing /ɪ/ (i), you will produce the phonemic diphthong heard in the words *boy* and *joy*. This sound is represented in IPA by /ɔɪ/ and in the dictionaries by oi.

The diphthong begins with the vowel [ɔ] (ô) and ends in the vowel [ɪ] (i). Indeed, if you have trouble getting in the second element of the diphthong, we should tell you (as we did in discussing the phonemic diphthong /ɑɪ/ (ī) to move toward the /i/ (ē) vowel. That advice gives you a target to aim for and should help you get the [ɪ] (i) into the diphthong.

As the diphthong begins, the lips are rounded with some tension and the back of the tongue is raised in the back of the mouth. It is important that you begin the movements required to make this sound in the customary position. Otherwise, the sound will be distorted.

Precautions

There are two spellings for /ɔɪ/ (oi):

oi as in *toil*
oy as in *joy*

Problems

There are five common problems associated with this phonemic diphthong. As we discuss each deviation, check to see if you have that problem with this diphthong.

▶ *Problem 1:* Substitution of /ɝ/ (ûr) for /ɔɪ/ (oi)

Occasionally in metropolitan New York or in the South you may hear someone say *Berle* for *boil*, *Earl* for *oil*, or *furl* for *foil*. It is considered nonstandard.

Problem 2: Substitution of /ɜɪ/ for /ɔɪ/ (oi)

If you raise the center of the tongue high in the center of the mouth rather than the back of the tongue in the back of the mouth at the beginning of this diphthong, you will produce this distortion. This diphthong must begin with lip rounding. Relaxing the lips and starting with the tongue forward in the mouth changes the sound.

Pronounce the following words. Check in a mirror to be sure you begin with a good lip-rounded /ɔ/ (ô).

oil	oyster	ointment
hoist	moist	joist
boil	coil	foil
join	joint	point
spoil	poison	goiter

Problem 3: Substitution of /ɔ/ (ô) or [ɔə] (ôə) for /ɔɪ/ (oi)

In the South, some speakers substitute the vowel /ɔ/ (ô) or the nonstandard diphthong [ɔə] (ôə) for the phonemic diphthong /ɔɪ/ (oi).

If you substitute the pure vowel, you are simply leaving out the second vowel (the "off-glide") of the phonemic diphthong. The result is that you substitute one phoneme [/ɔ/ (ô)] for another [/ɔɪ/ (oi)]. *Oil*, for example, becomes *all*.

If you substitute a schwa for the second element of the phonemic diphthong, you also change the sound greatly. In this case, you still have a diphthong—but a *different* diphthong! The little central neutral vowel /ə/ replaces the high front vowel /ɪ/ (i). Think of moving from the low back vowel /ɔ/ toward the high front vowel /i/ (ē) to produce this phonemic diphthong correctly.

If you make either of these distortions of the /ɔɪ/ (oi), the word *boil* will sound like a drawled version of *ball*. Be certain that the front of your tongue moves to the high front /ɪ/ (i) at the end of this diphthong. The tongue moves front, not center.

Read the following pairs of words aloud. The first word will be pronounced with /ɔ/ (ô), and the second word with /ɔɪ/ (oi). We have chosen words where /l/ follows the two phonemes, because that context offers the greatest temptation to make these substitutions.

/ɔl/ (ôl) and /ɔɪl/ (oil) Contrast

all	oil	ball	boil
bald	boiled	brawled	broiled
call	coil	called	coiled
fall	foil	hall	Hoyle
Saul	soil	tall	toil

Problem 4: Substitution of /ɑɪ/ (ī) for /ɔɪ/ (oi)

Another distortion of /ɔɪ/ (oi) is heard from time to time, particularly in the South. A few speakers say *bile* for *boil*, *tile* for *toil*, and *pint* for *point*. This substitution is nonstandard. It replaces one phonemic diphthong with another one.

Read the following pairs of words aloud. They will help you contrast these two phonemic diphthongs.

/ɔɪ/ (oi) and /ɑɪ/'(ī) Contrast

oil	I'll/isle	boil	bile
foil	file	coil	Kyle
toil	tile	loin	line
coined	kind	point	pint

Problem 5: Triphthongation

When /l/ follows /ɔɪ/ (oi), some speakers turn the diphthong into a triphthong. That means they stretch two elements into three. Either of two distortions creates a triphthong. You can add a schwa to the phonemic diphthong and turn *oil* into *oy-ul*. Or you can both add a schwa plus change the /ɪ/ into /j/ (y). That turns *oil* into *oy-yul*. It might be clearer in phonetics: [ɔɪl] becomes either [ɔɪəl] or [ɔjəl].

Check your own pronunciation of these few words to see if you tend to make the diphthong into a triphthong.

oil	boil	coil	foil
Hoyle	soil	toil	Doyle

Frankly, this distortion makes us *recoyal* (recoil)!

Pragmatics

Reinforcement Exercises

Practice Words for /ɔɪ/ (oi)

Beginning	**Middle**	**End**
oil	boil	boy
	coil	coy
	toil	toy
	soil	soy
ointment	joint	joy
	coin	decoy
	loin	alloy
	point	poi

Beginning	Middle	End
oyster	joist	joy
	Reuters	Roy
	rejoice	enjoy
	noise	annoy
	poison	ploy

Practice Phrases for /ɔɪ/ (oi)

an oily ointment
noisy boys
both spoiled and soiled
avoid the poison
a joyful noise
toiling in the soil
broiled sirloin
an annoying choice
employed in the boiler room
appoint a decoy
enjoy the toys
destroy a voice
boycott the soybeans

Practice Sentences for /ɔɪ/ (oi)

1. The royal family seemed to enjoy the performance.
2. He was anointed with oil and water.
3. The noise seemed to be coming from an adjoining room.
4. Don't join an organization in turmoil.
5. You can't plant if the soil is too moist.
6. You can destroy your voice by screaming.
7. Troy got the internship. He rejoiced.
8. Tom refuses to eat oysters—unless they are boiled.
9. What these boys need is gainful employment.
10. I try to avoid poison ivy.

Practice Sentences for /ɔɪ/ (oi) (More Challenging)

1. The ointment came wrapped in a special foil.
2. Though I recoil from controversy, I am embroiled in a fight.
3. What enjoyment is there in eating oysters—broiled, boiled, or grilled?
4. The ointment soiled the boys' clothes and annoyed their mother.

5. I have an appointment with Mrs. Doyle in Employment.
6. She pointed to the sailors hoisting the sail and destroying the mast.
7. Loitering in the halls was only one of his foibles.
8. He got quite boisterous when he bragged of his exploits.
9. Although I feel exploited, I have been loyal to the company from the moment I joined.
10. I enjoy listening to the joyful music of the cloistered brothers at Gethsemane.

Practice Sentences for /ɔɪ/ (oi) (Most Challenging)

1. You recoiled the last time too, as I recall.
2. I will not be foiled in my attempts this fall.
3. They toiled all day trying to lay the bathroom tile.
4. Mr. Berle has a low boiling point.
5. This is the first time you have been embroiled in a brawl.
6. All of the people slipped on the slick oil.
7. The bald man boiled his toupee by mistake.
8. She just pointed to the empty pint bottle in the cloister.
9. It was too early in the season for the water to be that oily.
10. We coined another name for the new kind of coil.

15

Nonphonemic Diphthongs and Triphthongs

Earlier, we defined a diphthong as a blend of two vowels. We also distinguished between phonemic and nonphonemic diphthongs. The difference, you remember, is that phonemes cannot be broken apart; they are the lowest separate sound unit in a language. If a diphthong functions as a phoneme, its two components cannot be broken apart. They are perceived as a single unit—not as two separate units temporarily pasted together. In a sense, the diphthong's two vowel components have lost their individual identity. The phonemic diphthong is a phoneme—an indivisible sound unit of the language.

Phonemic diphthongs have something in common with affricates. Affricates are two consonants blended into a single phoneme. Phonemic diphthongs are two vowels blended into a single phoneme.

Nonphonemic diphthongs, on the other hand, are diphthongs (blends of two vowels), but each vowel retains its own identity. Each vowel of the blend is functioning as a separate sound unit of the language. The two vowels *can* be pulled apart. This is a significant difference from the three phonemic diphthongs of American English.

Nonphonemic Diphthongs

Listen to these words as you pronounce them:

ear
air
Ayre
or
oar
your
are

All of these words contain diphthongs, but they are nonphonemic diphthongs. They contain blends of two separate vowel phonemes. *Ear* begins with the vowel /ɪ/ (i) and ends with the little unstressed vowel /ɚ/ (ər). All seven of these words end with that same unstressed vowel. These vowel combinations are very common in English, and you should get used to producing them. But remember, these diphthongs contain two separate phonemes.

We will provide Practice Words and Practice Sentences for each of these seven common nonphonemic diphthongs.

/ɪɚ/ (iər)

ear	mere	beer/bier	near
beard	peer	dear	queer
fear	rear	fierce	seer/sear
gear	sheer	hear	steer
cheer	tear	jeer	veer
clear	we're	leer	year

1. Here we go again. How dreary!
2. Speak clearly if you want to appear educated.
3. Others may sneer, but Pam thinks Billy Saltine sincere.
4. Bob has no fear of flying, but we're terrified.
5. Shakespeare wrote some weird plays.
6. The performers staged a fierce war dance with spears.
7. Cheer up! The rest is sheer enjoyment.
8. My dear, you are always in arrears.
9. He merely said he thinks the end is near.
10. His conscience seared, he tearfully repented—again.

/ɛɚ/ (eər)

air	lair	bare	mare
Blair	ne'er	dare	pair
fare/fair	rare	flair	share
hair	snare	chair	spare
care	stare	Claire	wear

1. There is no excuse for such overbearing behavior.
2. What is the air fare to Dallas? I couldn't care less.
3. How do you repair an affair of the heart?
4. Get yourself an affair repairman. But beware of his price.
5. You can't scare me. How dare you try?
6. Mike was not aware that Charlotte was upstairs.
7. It was a daring show, but the dancer barely moved.
8. Don't despair. Someday the government will "promote the general welfare."
9. I want to live where you can dare to be different.
10. Don't stare, but glance at that man standing on the chair.

/eɚ/ (āər)

Ayre	Bayer	gayer	grayer
layer	mayor	player	conveyor
displayer	betrayer	purveyor	portrayer

1. I only know what Sayre told me.
2. The lyrics say, "Gayer than laughter are you."
3. I am a little grayer this year than last.
4. I fell onto the conveyor belt.
5. He is a purveyor of bad news.
6. It doesn't matter who the mayor is.
7. I have found a player piano in working condition.
8. Convinced by the commercials, she would only buy Bayer.
9. There were layers of dust on the old chest.
10. No one respects a betrayer of confidences.

/ɔɚ/ (ôər)

or	quarrel	for	nor
war	dwarf	quart	horse
order	border	morn	warn
warm	north	lord	cord

1. The border guards ordered us out of the bus.
2. I look forward to her warm greeting every morning.
3. They had their worst quarrel standing on a corner.
4. I didn't forbid you; I just warned you of the results.
5. Why do nations resort to war?
6. I'm short on cash. Can you put in a quart of gas?
7. I don't even know what quarter horses are.
8. The warden is lord of this manor.
9. The resort is north of the city.
10. After the stormy fight, he showed remorse.

/oɚ/ (ōər)

Most Americans, but not all, would pronounce these words with /oɚ/ (oər). You may discover that in your idiolect or your dialect, the pronunciation is /ɔɚ/ (oə r).

oar	more	bore	pour
door	roar	abhor	deplore
gore	shore	core	tore
lore	store	implore	wore

1. The gold is stored at Fort Knox.
2. After the game, I was hoarse and had a sore throat.
3. I have been bored all through this course.
4. Fun? Of course, the matador was gored.
5. The crowd roared when he tore into the opposition.
6. I adore the color, but why would she paint the door green?
7. I've told you before I know where everything is stored.
8. The bartender refuses to pour any more after four drinks.
9. She wore out the record before you came.
10. I can't afford to go into that store again.

/Uɚ/ (ooər)

boor	tour	Coors	your
lure	pure	jury	Europe

moor	endure	poor	ensure
sure	mature	allure	adjure

1. There is no cure for boorishness.
2. He may be poor, but he is rich in assurance.
3. He was a poor choice for the jury.
4. I won't go to Europe on a conducted tour.
5. How can we assure that only mature audiences will see it?
6. You're just expected to endure it.
7. Why do impure substances have such allure?
8. I can't be completely sure, but I think it's secure there.
9. I adjure you: Stay pure!
10. Such fury! I'm sure it must be phony.

/ɑɚ/ (äər)

are	mar	bar	par
darling	part	far	shard
hard	smart	jar	star
char	start	car	tar
card	partner	lard	yard

1. You may not be smart, but you drive a hard bargain.
2. I hate to start going to bars again.
3. Darling, I'll leave the door ajar.
4. I don't want to mar the party, but I hate all forms of cards.
5. Are you sure that lard works better than Crisco?
6. The star of the show took a hard fall right on stage.
7. Don't start. I haven't got a partner!
8. Fill the jar with oil, and the urn with charcoal.
9. Art can't go much farther.
10. He darted into the crowd as the rally started.

Nonphonemic Triphthongs

Triphthongs are simply three vowels blended together. If you take a phonemic diphthong and add another little vowel to it, you have a nonphonemic triphthong. The little vowel /ɚ/ (ər) can be added to all three phonemic diphthongs.

We will provide Practice Words and Practice Sentences for three nonphonemic triphthongs.

/ɑʊɚ/ (ouər)

hour	glower	bower	power
cower	sour	dower	shower
Gower	tower	Howard	devour

1. I'm sure she was glowering at Howard.
2. She said I was a tower of strength in her hour of need.
3. The spiders' relationship turned sour and she devoured him.
4. Why are you cowering? I have no power over you.
5. Mr. Brower was showered with gifts at his promotion.

/ɑɪɚ/ (iər)

ire	mire	buyer	pyre
dire	pliers	fire	sire
flyer	inspire	hire	desire
cryer	tire	lyre/liar	wire

1. He was hired by the law firm of Muck and Meyer.
2. I have no desire to see another of his tiresome plays.
3. Why was he fired? His complaints raised the boss's ire.
4. You can't fix a tire with pliers!
5. Dimitri tried to inspire me by playing on his lyre. Even in dire circumstances, don't call anyone or anything a liar.

/ɔɪɚ/ (oiər)

Boyer employer destroyer

1. Is one who annoys an "annoyer?"
2. If so, then one who enjoys is an "enjoyer."
3. He was stationed on a destroyer in the navy.
4. In my judgment, Boyer is the best candidate.
5. My employer will not give me a raise.

16

Sound Changes

In Chapters 2 through 9 and 11 through 15, we talked about the forty-two individual phonemes of the language. In everyday speech, however, we do not talk a sound at a time—first one, then the next, and so on in a one-by-one sequence. Sounds, as we have said, are made by movements, and each sound is produced by a set of movements. Those sets of movements overlap in connected speech.

When we speak, there are simultaneous movements much of the time. We start the next sound before the last sound is finished, or we perform the movements for two sounds at the same time. (Remember some of the consonant combinations we discussed in Chapter 9, for example.)

As you would expect, a sound uttered all alone is one thing, but that sound uttered in combination with other sounds in connected speech will be different. That sound will have to adjust to the other sounds around it. Or, to be more exact, the movements required to make a sound will have to be modified to accommodate those movements required for the sounds that precede, follow, and overlap the sound.

"The easiest way out" is a natural tendency among human beings, and it applies to articulation of speech sounds. Speaking, like any other form of human physical activity, requires coordination. Some movements are easier to perform and easier to combine (perform simultaneously) than others. If we have a choice, we will choose the easier set of movements. That is what sound change in the language is all about.

At this point, we must warn you that some changes have gained social acceptance (and thus become "Standard") and that others have not. You must learn which sound changes are "Standard" and which are not. You will find that the difference is not in the *kind* of change (there are standard and nonstandard assimilations for example), but in the specific change itself. These differences you must simply learn on an individual change basis. (The omission of the first r when pronouncing *February* and the omission of the g when pronouncing recognize are both dissimilations, but the first is "standard" and the second is not.)

We will look briefly at three kinds of sound changes in our language: assimilation, dissimilation, and vowel gradation.

Assimilation

If a sound changes because of the influence of a neighboring sound, that change is labeled *assimilation*. Assimilation, of course, has to do with adjusting—fitting in. Adjustments must take place if sounds are to fit into their environment more easily.

Assimilation is not necessarily "sloppy speech"; rather, it is a regular attribute of socially acceptable speech patterns. It is true that some assimilations are considered lazy, or uneducated, or nonstandard. Assimilations do occur, however, that are customary and acceptable. Indeed, failure to use these standard assimilations sounds affected and pedantic.

Of course, omission of a number of sounds and assimilation of the sounds remaining is careless and nonstandard. For example, /dɪdʒʊit/ is now acceptable for "Did you eat?" but /dʒit/ (jēt) goes too far and is unacceptable.

There are two kinds of assimilation in language: (1) complete and (2) partial, or incomplete. Full, or complete, assimilation involves absorbing or incorporating a sound into an adjacent sound. Partial, or incomplete, assimilation involves a sound becoming more like an adjacent sound. Both forms of assimilation occur in American English.

We will look at both complete and incomplete assimilation briefly.

Complete Assimilation

Full or complete assimilation occurs when a sound in absorbed into an adjacent sound. In full or complete assimilation, the original sound disappears; it loses its identity. It does not just change its nature, it loses its nature. It is no longer heard—in any form.

Pronounce the following material as you would in ordinary conversation:

this shore
less sure
miss sugar
horse shoe
his shirt
Nothing is sure.

What happened to the /s/ or /z/ at the end of each word before the word beginning with /ʃ/ (sh)? Did you discover that the /s/ or /z/ disappeared? That is an example of full or complete assimilation. The /s/ or /z/ has been absorbed by its neighbor /ʃ/ (sh).

Many of our present "silent letters" are visible relics of complete assimilations that occurred long ago. We have preserved the earlier pronunciations in the spelling, long after the sound represented has disappeared into its neighboring sound by means of full or complete assimilation. Pronounce the word *cupboard*, and look at its spelling. The /p/ has been completely assimilated into the /b/; the /p/ has disappeared; the *p* letter is now silent.

Some morphemes retain the assimilated sound in the morpheme unit, and the completely assimilated sound magically reappears when a suffix is added to the root word, changing the syllable arrangement. Pronounce the following list of words, and check for the complete assimilation:

autumn
damn
column
hymn
malign
deign
benign

What sound was completely absorbed into its neighbor? In the first four words, you should have discovered that the /n/ was gone; the *n* is now a silent letter in those words. And in the last three words the /g/ has disappeared; g is a silent letter in those words. But the /n/ and /g/ have not disappeared forever. Note this reappearance, as you pronounce these words, based on the roots you have just pronounced:

autumnal
damnation
columnist
hymnal
malignant
dignity
benignancy

If you are not sure about the pronunciation of any of these words, look them up in your dictionary. What did you find as you uttered these words aloud? That's right. The /n/ and /g/ are back! So the morpheme never lost the sound; the sound remained part of the meaning unit, but it disappears (is completely assimilated) in certain contexts.

Incomplete Assimilation

Partial, or incomplete, assimilation refers to those sound changes in which a sound is modified, or adapted, under the influence of an adjacent sound. In partial, or incomplete, assimilation, a sound changes to accommodate (or adjust itself) to a neighboring sound; the assimilated sound tries to become more like its neighbor.

Partial assimilations, which account for most of the sound changes in your speech, are classified into three types according to the direction of influence. If a sound influences the sound that follows it, the assimilation is called progressive; if a sound influences the sound that comes before it, the assimilation is said to be regressive; if two sounds influence each other to produce a third, the assimilation is reciprocal.

Progressive Assimilation

The names of the kinds of assimilation are based on the *direction* of the influence. If the influence goes forward (that is, it progresses in the word), then the assimilation is said to be *progressive.* If the influence goes forward, then the first sound influences the second sound (the sound that comes after it).

In the word *low*, the /l/ is fully voiced; /l/ is a voiced consonant, as you know. But check your pronunciation of the word *flow* aloud. How has the /l/ changed? It is no longer *fully* voiced. It has undergone an assimilative change. And what caused or influenced this change? The voiceless /f/ that preceded the /l/. Because the first sound (/f/) influenced the second sound (/l/), and the second sound adapted itself to be more like the preceding sound, we have an instance of progressive assimilation.

The past tense, plurals, and possessives offer the best examples of progressive assimilation in English. After the vowel was dropped from the pronunciation of most words in the past tense, the tense was indicated by the voiced /d/. The words *planned, called*, and *leered* are pronounced /plænd/ /kɔld/, and /lɪɚd/. If the sound preceding the past-tense ending is voiceless, however, progressive assimilation occurs and the /d/ becomes /t/. Note that the words *passed, hoped, flunked, coughed*, and *lashed* all end in /t/.

The same kind of assimilation takes place in forming plurals and possessives. The ending /z/ is changed into /s/ after voiceless sounds. Compare the pronunciation of *cubs* and *cups*, *beads* and *beets, pigs* and *picks, elves* and *elf's sheathes* and *sheath's.*

Regressive Assimilation

When a sound is influenced by the sound that follows it, *regressive assimilation* has taken place. In this case, the influence goes backward in the word; it regresses. It is the first sound that gets influenced and the second sound that does the influencing.

In the word *fill*, the /l/ is fully voiced. But note what happens when you add the voiceless sound /θ/ (th). Pronounce the word *filth* and compare it with your pronunciation of the word *fill*. How has the /l/ changed? What accommodation did the /l/ in *filth* make? Well, anticipating the voiceless sound /θ/ (th) immediately following, the /l/ lost some of its voicing (its vocal vibration). The /l/ adapted itself to be more like the following sound.

Look at another example. Pronounce the word *sin*. Listen to the final sound in the word, and feel where the tongue goes to make the final sound (/n/). Now pronounce the word *sink*. Listen to that word as you pronounce it, and check on the sound that comes before the final /k/. Is it the same sound you had in *sin*? If not, what change has it undergone? What adaptation did it make? Try *sink* out aloud again—just to be sure. You have found, of course, that the sound preceding /k/ in the word *sink* is not /n/ but /ŋ/ (ng). The /n/ has changed, influenced by the coming /k/. Because the third nasal—/ŋ/ (ng)—is articulated at the same spot as the /k/ and /g/, it takes less effort to form /ŋ/ (ng) before /k/ than to form /n/. The /n/ has undergone regressive assimilation and become /ŋ/ (ng). Pronounce the words *sink, sank, honk,* and *flunk*; they all contain /ŋ/ (ng) rather than /n/.

When the letter *n* ends a syllable and the next syllable begins with /k/ or /g/, there is a good deal of variation in the use of /n/ and /ŋ/ (ng). Some of your friends may pronounce *banquet* /bænkwɪt/ and others /bæŋkwɪt/, just as some may say /ɪnkʌm/ and others /ɪŋkʌm/ for *income*. The only principle that can be observed here is that when the letter *n* ends a syllable before a syllable beginning with /k/ or /g/, the sound will usually be /ŋ/ if the next syllable is unstressed and final in the word, as in the words *Congress* and *ankle*.

Let us look at another example. Pronounce these pairs of words and phrases aloud:

nine	ninth
well	wealth
bread	breadth
at	at this time

What happened to the /n/, /l/, /d/, and /t/ in the second word or phrase? What change did each of these sounds undergo? How was each of them different the second time you pronounced them? The first time, hopefully, each of the sounds /n/, /l/, /d/, and /t/—was an alveolar sound—made by pressing the tongue tip to the alveolar ridge. The second time, each of the sounds was probably made in a different place; this time, the tongue was on the teeth—anticipating the position of the coming /θ/ (th).

In regressive assimilation, you anticipate the coming sound and get ready for it. This anticipation modifies or changes the sound being uttered.

Reciprocal Assimilation

Reciprocal is another word for mutual. If anything is mutual, of course, it is a matter of give-and-take. That is what reciprocal assimilation is all about: two sounds influence each other. The result is a third sound, different from the other two, that replaces the two original sounds. If two sounds influence each other and produce, thereby, a third sound in their place, *reciprocal assimilation* has taken place.

If **/z/ and /j/ (y)** come together, they may undergo reciprocal assimilation and become /ʒ/ **(zh)**. Check your pronunciation of the following words:

vision	leisure	division
usual	seizure	precision
usury	pleasure	derision
usurer	measure	delusion
azure	treasure	incision
casual	lesion	collision
visual	illusion	occasion
version	intrusion	explosion
conclusion	adhesion	occlusion

If the **/s/ and /j/ (y)** come together, they may undergo reciprocal assimilation and become **/ʃ/ (sh)**. Check your pronunciation of the following words and note the reciprocal assimilations:

fission	profession	sure
mission	confession	glacier
issue	conscience	precious
passion	conscious	delicious
pension	anxious	ocean

If **/t/ and /j/ (y)** come together, they may undergo reciprocal assimilation and become **/ʃ/ (sh)**. Pronounce the following words aloud, and note the reciprocal assimilations:

nation	mention	ration
notion	attention	patient
emotion	detention	infectious
election	caution	reflection
action	fractious	rejection
sanction	inclination	cautious

If **/t/ and /j/ (y)** come together, they may undergo reciprocal assimilation and become **/tʃ/ (ch)**. Note the assimilations in the following words as you pronounce them aloud:

actual	lecture
natural	question
nature	righteous

virtue	picture
virtuous	puncture
digestion	tincture
ingestion	instinctual
congestion	manufacture

If **/d/ and /j/ (y)** come together, they may undergo reciprocal assimilation and become **/dʒ/ (j)**. Pronounce the following words aloud and note the reciprocal assimilations:

gradual	adulation
graduate	module
educate	modulation
education	soldier

Because we do not speak a word at a time, but blend our words in successions of syllables called phrases or thought groups, assimilations may occur between words as well as within words. Abutting consonants can produce assimilations—interverbally as well as intraverbally! Check to see if you pronounce the following examples with assimilations at the marked spots:

as *y*ou know
I miss *y*ou.
Ea*t* *y*our words.
Woul*d* *y*ou try?

Dissimilation

Assimilation, a sound change in which a sound becomes more like an adjacent sound, occurs more often than any other kind of phonetic change. Dissimilation is, in a sense, the opposite of assimilation. Dissimilation is a sound change in which a sound becomes *less* like neighboring sounds; it is change to be different from the neighbor instead of conforming to the neighbor.

Dissimilation occurs when a word contains a repeated sound or at least two very similar sounds, and one of those repeated or similar sounds changes into a different sound or disappears. In assimilative changes, you remember, the two sounds were right next to each other; they were adjacent sounds. This is not so in dissimilative changes. The two sounds involved here will *not* be adjacent, but they will be in the same word.

Dissimilation is a complicated process, and usually there are other factors at work in addition to the repetition of the same or similar sounds. Let's look at two examples. If you pronounce February aloud, you will probably discover that you do not pronounce the first r. Instead, we say *feb yoo e ri* (/ˈfɛbjuˌɛri/). Why? Well, for one thing, we have an instance of dissimilation. The two /r/s in nearby syllables give us trouble, so the first one bows out. Another influence is that we learn the names of the months, and we recite them "January, February . . . ." What could be more natural than for /feb yoo/ . . . to follow /jan yoo/ . . . ! Is it a case of pronunciation based on analogy (comparison)? Or is it dissimilation? Or both? Probably.

The other good example of the complexity of dissimilation is found in our pronunciation of the word *government*. Try that word out loud to check on how you pronounce it. Be sure to say it as you regularly do. What do you discover—pronouncing it as you look at the spelling of the word? That's right. The first *n* is missing. Not because you are a slovenly speaker, but because two syllables in a row ending with /n/ are difficult for anyone. Could there be another explanation for the missing /n/? Could it be an instance of *assimilation* rather than dissimilation? *Complete assimilation*, with the /n/ absorbed by the following nasal sound /m/? Or could it be called either complete assimilation or dissimilation? Again, probably.

At least we should now understand what dissimilation is. It is our effort to avoid tongue-twisters where the same sound is repeated or a similar sound occurs. Some examples of dissimilation are accepted as standard, and some are not. Both of those we just mentioned (*February* and *government*) are standard. But the pronunciation of *liberry* for *library* (a clear case of dissimilation) is nonstandard. *Supprise* for *surprise* does not raise hackles in educated, cultivated circles, but *sekketary* for *secretary* certainly will. Both, of course, are examples of dissimilation, but one is considered standard and the other is not. You will just have to use your ears and your dictionary to be able to distinguish between those dissimilations that are socially acceptable and those that are not.

Vowel Gradation

In our discussion of the individual phonemes of American English, we discussed the fact that vowels have strong forms that appear in stressed syllables and that we weaken the vowels in unstressed syllables. This is a very important concept, which we will explain in detail.

If English is not your first language, you may have difficulty understanding why /ɑ/ (ä) is not always /ɑ/ (ä). In your first language, a vowel may always be the same—no matter what kind of syllable it appears in. But that is *not* so in English.

Let us look at some words and see how vowels can be strong in stressed syllables and changed to weaker vowels in unstressed syllables. Note these words:

Strong Vowel	**Weaker Vowel**
be	between
add	*adore*
purse	pursue
sub	submit
owe	*obey*
day	debris
calm	combine

The vowel in the word *be* is /i/ (ē)—the long, tense, high front vowel. The first vowel in the word *between*, however, is not that same vowel. Instead, the vowel will be shortened and weakened in that syllable (because it is unstressed) to /ɪ/ (i)—the short, lax, high front vowel.

The vowel in *add* is /æ/ (a), but in *adore*, the first vowel is schwa (/ə/). The vowel in *purse* is /ɝ/ (ûr), but in *pursue*, the first vowel is /ɚ/ (ər). The vowel in *sub* is /ʌ/, but the first vowel in *submit* is /ə/. The vowel phoneme in *owe* is the diphthong allophone [oʊ], but in the unstressed first syllable in *obey*, the pure vowel allophone [o]—much shorter—is used. In the word *day*, we use the diphthong allophone [eɪ] in American English, but use the pure vowel allophone [e] for the first syllable in *debris*. The vowel in *calm* is /ɑ/ (ä); the vowel in the first syllable of *combine* is schwa (/ə/).

If you do not weaken the vowels in unstressed syllables, you will distort the sounds, mispronounce the words, and alter the English rhythm of the phrases. You must use the lower grade (or weaker grade) of vowels in the unstressed syllables and the higher grade (or stronger grade) of vowels in the stressed syllables.

Most vowels in unstressed syllables are reduced to schwa, although /i/ (ē) may become /ɪ/ (i) and /u/ (o͞o) may become /ʊ/ (oo). The first syllable in the word *above*, for example, is not /æ/ (a) but /ə/. The vowel in the second syllable in the word *beautiful* may be either /ɪ/ (i) or /ə/. The vowel in the first word of the infinitive *to be* may be either /ʊ/ (oo) or /ə/.

Because we have so many unstressed syllables in our speech, schwa (/ə/) is the most commonly used of the vowels. As we have said, not every unstressed syllable is pronounced with schwa. But schwa is certainly important because it is used so much.

Let us look at a three syllable word—*regulate*. The stress is on the first syllable, so that vowel is the stressed vowel /ɛ/ (e). The /ju/ (yo͞o) in the second syllable will be reduced in grade (or rank) to second-class status; it will become /jʊ/ (yo͞o) or perhaps to /jə/ (yə). The /j/ (y) must be maintained, however. That vowel cannot be reduced to /ʊ/ (o͞o) or /ə/ alone. The /j/ (y) of the original /ju/ (yo͞o) survives. The last syllable is also an unstressed syllable, or at most it has a kind of secondary stress. In that third syllable, the [e] (ā̆) allophone rather than the diphthong allophone [eɪ] (ā) will be heard.

To help you understand the principle of ranking or grading vowels, let us turn our attention to an important group of words in our language: *form words*. Each form word exists as a stressed form (to emphasize the idea inherent in the word) and as an unstressed form (which simply states the idea implied in the word, without giving it special prominence). There are two forms, then, for each of these words: one stressed (using stressed vowels) and one unstressed (using the unstressed vowels: /ɪ/ (i), /ɨ/, ᴜ (oo), /ɚ/ (ər), /ə/, [e] (ā̇), and [o] (ō̇)).

Form words are necessary for the form, or syntax, of our sentences but not for the central ideas. These words are articles, prepositions, conjunctions, auxiliary verbs, linking verbs, and pronouns. Because the meaning is implied in the word itself, no stress on the word is necessary—unless you intend to emphasize the implicit meaning and make it explicit. For example, the word *and* implies addition. If there is no reason to emphasize the concept of addition, you would use the weak form of the word; if, however, you wanted to underscore that idea, you would use the strong form. In the phrase *bread and butter*, you would ordinarily use the weak form [n] for *and*, but if you wanted to emphasize the fact that adding butter was unusual, you would use the strong form [ænd].

Let us look at one other example. The word *the* is a pointing word; it means *one*. Usually it is not necessary to stress the idea of oneness or uniqueness, so we usually use the weak form of this word. We say: [ðə bᴜk], *the book* or [lænd əv ðə fri], *land of the free*. *The* in those phrases is an article, pointing to the noun—not drawing attention to itself. So we use the weak form of the word [ðə] (*th*ə). (Note that in the phrase *land of the free*, there are two idea words, thought-bearing words: *land* and *free*. Those two words are made to stand out by the use of the stressed vowels in them, among other techniques. Note also that the preposition *of* is a form word and is pronounced using its weak form in this phrase, not its strong form [ɑv] (äv).) Contrast the vowel in *the* in the phrase *land of the free* and the vowel you would use in the word *the* if you read this sentence aloud: "I'm going to *the* theater tonight." This time, to emphasize the *the*, you use the strong form of the word and say [ði] (*the*), not [ðʌ] (*thu*). Bob King said that with some irony more than once during his college days. The word *the* was emphasized, not to indicate that he was going to the most prestigious theater in town (a possibility when you emphasize the *one* idea), but that he was really going to *the* theater in town—the *only* one! A special warning about the article *the*: it has two weak forms. Before words beginning with consonants, it weakens to [ðə] (*th*ə). Before words beginning with vowels, it weakens to [ðɪ] (*thi*). Compare your pronunciation of the *the pear* and *the apple*.

It is important for you to master the use of form words, because we use them so often. In the exercises, work to blend the phrases together smoothly, and use the weak form of the form words.

Materials for Practicing Unstressed Forms

Articles

a	Have a ball. Run a risk. It's a game.
an	It's an old story. He's an eager applicant.
the	Here comes the bride. Where are the others? The team lost the final game. The orgy followed.

Prepositions

at	She collapsed at the dance. Meet me at nine o'clock.
for	Ask for an extra one. Please sing "Tea for Two."
from	It's a souvenir from China. We work from dark to dawn.
into	The attorney is looking into the case. He will take it into court.
of	I'm not tired of school. It's the principal of the thing.
to	Are you ready to go? Give it to me.

Conjunctions

and	Life and death. A girl and a boy. Joy and pain. Forever and ever.
as	She's as pretty as a painting. It's almost as expensive!
but	But you said you would! Everyone's going, but no one's staying.
or	I want only one or two of them. You may take either or both.
than	There are more than I wanted. He said nothing other than that.

Auxiliary Verbs

am	I am speaking at the meeting. Then I am staying home.
are	We are reading *War and Peace*. Most are reading the Classic Comic version.
can	He can read Sanskrit. Do you know what she can do?
could	I could have performed all night. I wish I could go.
do	How do you do? Do you want to attend?
does	Does it work? When does she perform again?
had	He claimed he had already paid. The cashier had made a mistake.
has	He has been to the farm. John has learned his lesson.
have	We have seen him often. We should have gone.
must	You must practice. Russ thought he must leave early.

shall	We shall do our part. Where shall we go?
should	What should I do now? You should go home.
was	It was going well, Why was he suspected?
were	We were running all the time. They were provoked.
will	Who will take my place? Anyone will be able to do it.
would	I would rather do it myself. Why would they ask me?

Linking Verbs

am	I am tired of these chores. I suppose I am too lazy.
are	We are ready for anything. They are hostile.
was	It was a serious matter. Nick was eager to stay.
were	They were happy to escape. All of them were pawns.

Pronouns

he	How could he do it? I think he erred.
her	I gave her all I had. Someone told her the supply was limited.
him	Explain it to him. Make him pay his share.
his	You shouldn't have told his wife about it. She resented his running around.
some	I need some help. Give me some money.
that	He believed that he was perfect. Everyone else thought that he should be perfected.
them	I saw them at the bar. Take them home or find them a taxi.
us	Give us your number. She tried to ignore us.
you	I'm working, you know, at the grill. Have you looked for another job?
your	I'll take your place. Always do your best.

Practice Sentences for Strong and Weak Forms

Each of the following sentences contains a strong and a weak form of the same word. Use vowel gradation to achieve the distinction.

1. I can crush a can with my bare hands.
2. I will *not* leave you a cent in my will.
3. I want some time to sum it all up.
4. I could see the cow chewing on her cud.
5. I don't want to be number two!
6. But you're not the butt of all jokes.
7. I am not afraid to fly on Pan Am.
8. Marines are entitled to R and R.
9. Does Duz really clean better?

10. I would prefer a desk made of wood.
11. Sing a hymn to Him.
12. Ann refused to see an old boy friend.
13. The article reviewed "Of Thee I Sing."
14. You must admit the room was musty.
15. How do you know he went to O. P. U.?

17

Pronunciation of Words

When spoken, a word is a verbal symbol which stands for an idea; it "means" something. A word can stir up associations (meanings) in the mind of a receiver.

Sounds (phonemes) do not *have* meaning or *represent* meaning or *stir up* meaning; they *affect* meaning. If you substitute one phoneme for another in a word, the change can change what the word is and what the word represents. Replace /i/ (ē) with /e/ (ā) in the word *meat* and the word is changed to *mate*. Spoken alone, however, the sound /i/ (ē) does not mean anything.

Syllables are defined as a sound or group of sounds uttered on one chest pulse. Words are made up of syllables—sounds uttered on these little chest pulses of exhaled air. Syllables, removed from the word in which they appear, do not mean anything either. (Of course some words are only one syllable long, but it is the *word* that conveys the meaning, not the syllable.) Pronounce the word *wonderful*. How many little pulse units is it broken into? Three: *won-der-ful*. Pull out the middle syllable (although we really cannot pronounce an unstressed syllable alone), and see if *der* means anything. Of course it does not. Syllables are not the units that represent ideas. Words are.

From studying Chapter 1, you know that words are constructed of little meaning units called morphemes. The morphemes are the building blocks of which words are made. But morphemes, like syllables, cannot stand alone (unless, of course, the word is made up of only one morpheme). We use /z/ to represent the idea of more than one (plural) and attach that morpheme to words ending in a voiced sound. But the morpheme /z/ uttered by itself would be meaningless to a listener. However, say *words* (/wɝdz/ or *wurdz*), and a listener will get the idea.

The point is that words are the symbols we use to convey our meanings. And distortions of words—mispronunciations—may interfere with the process of communication. If a sender deviates much from the customary way of pronouncing the word, and the word received differs very much from a listener's expectations of what that word should sound like, misunderstanding may easily take place. The listener may associate a completely different meaning with the word, and the mispronunciation becomes a barrier to understanding.

Because the pronunciation of words is so important to effective and efficient communication, we will analyze the two basic elements of word pronunciation.

Elements of Pronunciation

Pronunciation is the way words are uttered. In pronouncing words, there are two basic elements involved. The two component elements are:

(1) selection of sounds, and

(2) the degree of stress given to the various syllables in the word.

To pronounce a word in the conventional, or customary, way, you must select the sounds currently used by speakers of the Standard (or Status) Dialect, and you must use the syllable stress pattern in current usage.

Thus, you could *mispronounce* a word in two ways. Either you can use ''incorrect'' sounds in the word's formation, or you can put the stress on the wrong syllable or syllables. We will look at each of the two elements and problems related to them in more detail.

Selection of Sounds

Because the earlier chapters on Articulation have dealt with sounds—the customary way to produce them and the common deviations associated with them—this section is, in a sense, a review. We will be focusing on the material in a different way, however, because we will be looking at the entire word.

Four types of sound changes affect the pronunciation of a word. Put another way, there are four kinds of problems related to selecting sounds that result in the mispronunciation of a word.

(1) omission of a sound or sounds;

(2) addition of a sound or sounds;

(3) distortions or substitutions of a sound or sounds;

(4) transposition (reversal) of sounds.

Let us look at each of these problems in turn.

► *Problem 1:* Omissions

Leaving out sounds (remember we are not talking about the letters of the words as they are spelled, but the sounds of the words as they are pronounced) is one of the most common forms of mispronunciation.

Consonants in the middle of words—especially if there are two consonants together—are certainly in danger. Pronounce this list of words. Do you leave out any of the consonants in the middle of the words? Are you tempted to omit any of the consonants?

center	winter	enter	entertain
antidote	anecdote	handle	holder
wonder	wonderful	under	understand
atlas	Atlanta	Easter	mister
recognize	exactly	headless	after
Mazda	handling	obvious	obfuscation
subvert	softer	actual	arctic
picture	accent	accelerate	accessories
skeptical	draftsman	lumber	friendly
falter	twenty	plenty	already
almost	outspoken	outstanding	outgoing

The list could be endless. In fact, *endless* should have been on the list of tempting words. Review chapters 3 through 15 for problems of omission. Read the lists provided for you in those chapters aloud again, checking for the omission of middle consonants.

Consonants at the ends of words are also in danger of being omitted. Here are just a few examples to remind you of this problem. If you review chapters 3 through 15, you will find many more examples of such tempters.

last	missed	hand	planned
hold	kept	dreamed	plant
banked	Colt	sagged	act
fact	clasp	grasp	kicked
rubbed	polled	ask	risk
wrist	held	rest	wrapped

Consonant combinations—both blends and clusters—afford ample opportunity for omissions. At the beginning, in the middle, and at the ends of words, consonant combinations often get cheated by omitted consonants. A thorough review of Chapter 9 should be useful. Here is a list of words just to remind you of this problem.

statistics	throw	through	skeptical
screaming	straight	structure	specific
splutter	sprinkle	sobs	hurts
words	pacts	feasts	holds
hands	tenths	fifths	unmasked
tasks	tents	colts	roads
shelves	thrives	swerves	blends

swiftly abruptly gifts concepts
acts facts wooden shoes wouldn't
shouldn't hadn't didn't wasps

Vowels between consonants are often in danger of being left out—especially if the consonants can then be combined into a blend, or the consonants then become abutting consonants (one ending a syllable and the other beginning the next syllable). Listen to your pronunciation of these words to check for this problem. If the vowel is in an unstressed syllable, don't overcompensate and make the vowel a strong vowel!

support parade delicate relevant
suppose believe belong palatial
bereaved alimony satirical regular
Italy anonymous particular elevator

Two vowels separated by a hiatus (a tiny pause to separate consecutive vowels) offer a challenge and often cause a problem. Usually, people leave out the second of the two vowels, but sometimes it is the first of the two vowels that is omitted. Either way, the omission completely changes the word. The omission of one of the vowels makes the distorted word shorter by giving it one syllable less than it normally has. Pronounce these words aloud and check to be sure you get in all the vowels. (Do not, however, turn weak vowels into strong ones in the process!)

poem ruin museum liable
violet Iowa intuition McKuen
Owen jewel society riot
quiet geography sociology sodium
hilarious delirium memorial violate

Dissimilation accounts for some omissions. We discussed this phenomenon in Chapter 16, "Sound Changes." The omitting of a repeated sound (or related sound) is called *haplology*. Haplology usually results in the loss of an entire syllable, so we refer to this kind of omission as "telescoping." If a whole syllable disappears, it seems to slide inside another syllable and disappear like one segment of a telescope pushed inside the next one. If two syllables in a row have the same sound (or a related sound), there is a danger of omitting one of the sounds or of omitting an entire syllable. *Probably* may turn into *probly, attitude* into *a-tude, and constitution* into *constution*.

Dissimilation can occur without the loss of a syllable, although this is less common. An example would be the pronunciation of the word *library* as *liberry*.

As you pronounce the following words aloud, check to see if you are tempted to omit a sound or even a whole syllable.

probably	institute	institution	constitute
constitution	restitution	substitute	substitution
frustrate	frustration	temperature	attitude
irrepressible	candidate	Mississippi	catatonic
necessity	titillation	fastidious	necessary
similarly	anonymity	immemorial	particularly

Problem 2: Additions

Another frequent error in pronunciation is the *addition* of sounds. In Chapters 3 through 9, we noted several consonants that commonly get added to words where they do not belong. We will not repeat all those additions here, but we will remind you of a few of the most common ones.

The "NG Click"—adding /g/ or /k/ in words like *singer* and in phrases like *Long Island* is not uncommon. If you have this problem, we urge you to eliminate the extra /g/ or /k/.

The "Intrusive R"—adding /r/ in order to separate vowels (instead of using hiatus to do so)—is not uncommon in greater New York and parts of New England. It occurs in words like *gnawing* and phrases like *saw it*. We encourage you to remove the added /r/ from "the idear of it" and "lawr of the land."

Oncet for *once, twicet* for *twice, acrosst* for *across, sumpthing* for *something, how wit is* for *how it is, and I yam* for *I am* are all examples of mispronunciations caused by the addition of consonants.

Spelling leads some people into mispronunciations. As you know, letters in the spelling of a word do not always indicate sounds. Trying to be precise can lead people to add sounds to words (and thus mispronounce them) in an effort to say the word as it is spelled. Putting an /h/ in *honest, a /b/ in subtle, an /l/ in calm* and *palm* (and other such words), /n/ in *kiln, and /ps/ in corps* are all examples of such additions.

Vowels can also be added to words. Because we are used to having vowels between most consonants of separate syllables, we can be tempted to insert a schwa between the final consonant of one syllable and the initial consonant of the next syllable. For example, *athlete* becomes *athalete*. Here are some words that present this problem for some speakers. Read the words aloud, and check to be sure you do not insert an extra vowel.

athlete	athletics	ably	airplane
amazement	bracelet	burglar	business
capably	chimney	evening	lively
lovely	nestling	nimbly	rivalry
tablet	ticklish	toddler	ugly

You may be tempted to insert a schwa between the /l/ and /m/ when the blend /lm/ is final in a word. Check your pronunciation of these words:

elm	helm	film	realm

You may also be tempted to insert a schwa between the /o/ (o) and the /n/ in words ending in /on/ (on). You might even be tempted to add /w/ and schwa both between the /o/ and /n/. Check your pronunciation of these words. (For further examples, see pp. 281-282.)

bone	cone	groan	Joan
known	shown	stone	won't

Some speakers pull consonant blends apart and insert schwa between the two consonants. The blends /tr/, /dr/, /br/, /bl/, /pr/, and /pl/ seem to offer the greatest temptations. Pronounce the following lists of words. Each contains a consonant blend in which some speakers insert a schwa.

try	treacherous	monstrous
foundry	laundry	wondrous
brace	bright	umbrella
bleed	blight	bloated
prince	unproved	pretty
please	plead	plenty

Consonant clusters are sometimes broken up so a vowel (usually schwa) can be inserted. *Asks* [æsks/ (asks)] can become *askus* [/æskəs/ (askəs)] or *askis* [/æskɪs/ (askis)], for example.

We have a number of words in the language that end in /ɪə s/ (iə s). *Devious* is one example. Perhaps, by analogy, some speakers mispronounce some words ending in /əs/ by adding /ɪ/ (i) or /j/ (y). Of course, the *-ious* words come from words that ended in *-y* or whose roots ended in that sound. A person filled with *envy* would be *envious*. But a fault that would make you *grieve* would be *grievous*—not *grevious*. Check your pronunciation of the following words. They all contain /əs/—not /ɪəs/ (iəs) or /jəs/ (yəs).

bulbous	contagious	disastrous	facetious
gorgeous	genus	grievous	heinous
membranous	mercurous	mischievous	momentous
monstrous	outrageous	righteous	stupendous

Some of you might be wondering about such words as *contagious*, *gorgeous*, and *outrageous*. Why only /əs/ and no /ɪ/ (i)? A review of the material on sound changes (assimilation) should give you the answer. In any case, as the words are pronounced today, they do not contain that /ɪ/ (i).

In the South and Midwest, some speakers add /ɚ/ (ər) in the words *wash* and *Washington*. This addition is considered nonstandard, and we suggest you remove the added /ɚ/ (ər).

Problem 3: Distortions and Substitutions

In Chapters 3 through 15, we discussed the common distortions of all the phonemes of American English. We offer here a list of a *few* of the common distortions and substitutions we examined. We urge you to review any problem areas.

(1) dentalization of lingua-alveolar consonants;
(2) unvoicing of consonants—especially at the ends of words;
(3) raising of the tongue on /θ/ (th) and /ð/ (*th*);
(4) substitution of /b/ for /v/;
(5) substitution of /r/ for /l/—and *vice versa*;
(6) substitution of /n/ for /ŋ/ (ng);
(7) retraction of /ɔ/ (ô) and /ɑɪ/ (ī);
(8) nasalization of vowels and diphthongs;
(9) diphthongation of vowels;
(10) substitution of /i/ for /ɪ/;
(11) substitution of /ɪ/ for /ɛ/;
(12) raising the /æ/ vowel;
(13) substituting a nasalized vowel for an oral vowel + a nasal consonant;
(14) substituting a strong vowel when a weak one is appropriate.

All of these and many other distortions and substitutions were discussed at length in Chapters 3 through 15. It should be enough here to remind you that all these distortions and substitutions of sounds result in the mispronunciation of the words involved.

An added reminder: Be careful on the word *pronunciation* itself! Some speakers mispronounce the word by substituting /ɑʊ/ (ou) for /ʌ/ (u) in the second syllable. The word is *pronunciation*—not *pronounciation*.

Problem 4: Transposition of Sounds

Reversing sounds is another means of mispronouncing a word. Switching the sounds, of course, turns it into a different word—which may or may not mean something. The word that suffers this indignity most often is probably *relevant*. Look at the word, and think of how you ordinarily pronounce it. Are you tempted to say *revelant*? And what about *irrelevant*? Do you reverse the /l/ and /r/ there? The scholarly name for sound reversal is *metathesis*.

The little word *asked* is metathesized frequently. Since *asked* occurs often in conversation, people will definitely notice if you reverse the sounds. In fact, this particular sound reversal irritates many listeners. Let's look at it carefully.

The word *asked* has only four sounds: /æ/ (a), /s/, /k/, and /t/. In that order! The problem occurs when many people reverse the second and third sounds. Then *asked* becomes *axed*. Indeed, the same speakers may also say *ax* [/æks/ (aks)] for *ask* [/æsk/ (ask)].

When students say to one of us, "Don't ax me," we assure them that we have no intention of cutting anyone down with a hatchet, ax, or any other dangerous weapon. Even then the students may not hear the distinction between *ax* and *ask*. They are so used to the reversal of sounds, it sounds right to them.

Sometimes letters are reversed in the mind and the sounds follow. This would account for turning *perspiration* into *prespiration*, *hundred* into *hunderd*, children into *childern*, and *pronounce* into *pernounce*.

Turning the word *escape* into *ekscape* is not quite sound reversal because the /k/ reappears in the second syllable—after having been switched with the /s/. *Excaping* is not acceptable. *Escaping* is.

Syllabic Stress

The first element of pronunciation we discussed was the selection of sounds to include in the word. You must choose the right sounds and produce them in the conventional way if the word is to be pronounced "correctly." (Of course, "correctness" has to do with acceptability—with what is expected and respected.)

You can still mispronounce a word even if you have selected all the right sounds to go into it. There is another element in pronunciation that is very important in English. That element is the *stress* we give the different syllables in a word.

Unlike some other languages in which syllables get level or equal stress, American English is characterized by differences in the amount of stress on syllables. It is difficult to define exactly what stress is. It is much easier to tell you how stress is achieved than to tell you precisely what it is. Stress is the giving of emphasis or prominence; it is the process of making a sound or group of sounds stand out. All of the syllables in a word do not get equal prominence or attention; those differences are differences in stress.

Although we have talked about stressed syllables and unstressed syllables (and vowels) in earlier chapters, there is actually no such thing as an *un*stressed syllable. All syllables get *some* stress or attention—or they would not be heard at all. The difference we were calling attention to earlier was a difference of degree: more stressed and less stressed. The so-called unstressed syllables are given less attention and prominence than are the "stressed" syllables.

Indeed, there are three degrees of stress in American English. These various levels have been labeled primary (for the greatest stress), secondary (for less attention than primary but more than tertiary), and tertiary (the lowest or weakest stress of the three). It is the tertiary stress that we have been referring to as unstressed. A one-syllable word will receive, when spoken alone, primary stress. In connected speech, its stress would depend on its meaning, its function in the sentence or phrase, and the syllables around it. A two-syllable word, spoken alone, will probably have one syllable with primary stress and one syllable with tertiary stress. (The exceptions are two-syllable words that have equal primary stress on both syllables; these are called spondee words.) Some words may have enough syllables to contain primary, secondary, and tertiary stress in the one word. Let us examine these three levels of stress in a little more detail.

Most people think of primary stress as an accented syllable. That syllable gets the highest attention we accord syllables. Say the word *stand* out loud. That word received primary stress. You used primary stress; since the word stood alone it had to stand out.

Now say out loud the word *standard*. That word has two syllables. The two syllables divide between the /n/ and /d/ in the middle of the word. So we have two syllables: *stan-dard*. Which of the two syllables gets more attention? Which stands out more as you say the word? That is correct: *stan* does. (Note that you used a strong vowel in that syllable, but a weak /ɚ/ (ər) in the second syllable.) In that two-syllable word, we had the first syllable receiving primary stress and the second syllable receiving tertiary stress.

Now try the word *perform* out loud. Here again is a two-syllable word. Which receives the primary stress this time? Right again. It is the second syllable: *form*. The first syllable contains the little /ɚ/ (ər) vowel, and the syllable gets tertiary stress. Perhaps you should think of the three levels of stress as a kind of class system. Primary is first-class treatment, secondary is second-class treatment, and poor tertiary gets third-class treatment.

We mentioned that some two-syllable words (and phrases) contain two syllables of equal stress. And we mentioned the word *spondee*. That word comes to us from poetics, the analysis of poetry. If the rhythm has two strong beats in a row, the foot containing those two consecutive strong beats is called a spondee. Try this command out loud: *Stand back*. Which is the syllable that is stressed more? Which is the syllable that is stressed less? The answer probably is that you gave equal stress to both syllables in that phrase. Both are important ideas and of equal importance; both receive primary stress. The rhythm of the phrase *stand back*, therefore, is spondee: equal primary stress. The following words and phrases are also examples of spondee. You should be able to think of other examples.

bookcase	ice cream	handmade	archfoe
quite so	left hand	toolbox	strongman
no show	black bird	jack knife	well done

So far, we have given examples of words containing primary and tertiary stress, but none containing secondary stress. We are now ready to do that. Such examples will have to contain three or more syllables.

If you pronounce *polka dot*, you will note that it has three syllables: pō-kə-dät. You should also note that each of the three syllables gets a different amount of attention paid to it. The first syllable gets primary stress; the second syllable gets tertiary stress; and the third syllable gets secondary stress—more stress than the second syllable, but less than the first. Pronounce it again—just to be sure you hear the difference.

Pronounce the following words. Check to see if you can determine which syllables receive which level of stress.

dictionary	secretary	education
dormitory	institution	president
accident	generally	accuracy

Now, after you have checked on your own pronunciation of these words and determined what level of stress you use on the various syllables in the words, we will give you the customary stress patterns for those words. We will represent the words both in dictionary symbols and in IPA phonetic transcription. In the dictionaries, primary stress is indicated by an accent mark in thick, heavy type *after* the stressed syllable; secondary stress is indicated by a lighter accent mark; tertiary stress is indicated by the absence of a stress (or accent) mark. Hence, the word *avalanche* would be represented this way: av**′**ə lanch′. In IPA, the stress marks go *before* the syllable receiving the stress. The mark for primary stress is a short vertical line above the line of symbols; the mark for secondary stress is a short vertical line below the line of symbols; tertiary stress is indicated by the absence of a stress mark of either kind. Hence, the word *avalanche* would be represented this way in IPA: ˈæv əˌlæntʃ.

Here are the sounds and stress patterns for the nine words.

Regular Spelling	**Dictionary Diacritics**	**IPA Symbols**
dictionary	dĭk′s̮hə nĕ′rē	ˈdɪk ʃə ˌnɛ rɪ
secretary	sĕk′rĭ tĕ′rē	ˈsɛk rɨ ˌtɛ rɪ
education	ĕ′jo͞o kā′s̮hən	ˌɛ dʒʊ ˈkeɪ ʃən
dormitory	dôr′mə tō′rē	ˈdɔɚ mə ˌto rɪ
institution	ĭn′stĭ to͞o′s̮hən	ˌɪn stɨ ˈtju ʃən
president	prĕz′ə dənt	ˈprɛz ə dənt
accident	ăk′sĭ dənt	ˈæk sɨ dənt
generally	jĕn′ər ə lē	ˈdʒɛn ə rə lɪ
accuracy	ăk′yə rə sē	ˈæk jə rə sɪ

Do these stress patterns match your own? Can you now tell the difference between primary, secondary, and tertiary stress?

Thus far we have talked about what stress is and noted three different levels of stress on the syllables in English words. But how is stress achieved? What do we *do* to stress a syllable and to make these differences in degree of stress? There are three factors involved in stressing a syllable:

(1) increase in loudness,
(2) higher pitch,
(3) longer duration.

The amount of stress a syllable gets, then, depends on how much volume we give the syllable—how loud we make it; how high the pitch is when we utter the syllable; and how long we make the sounds in the syllable (and, hence, the relative length of the syllable itself).

Check for yourself and see if these three factors are not the cause of stress changes. Read the list of nine words out loud again. *Listen* to the words as you utter them. Can you tell that the syllables with primary stress are louder, higher (in pitch), and longer than the other syllables? Can you tell that the syllables with tertiary stress (third-class status) are the lowest in volume and pitch and the shortest in duration time? Can you discern that the syllables with secondary stress are in between on all three factors, or variables? We hope so, because you must be aware of these differences if you are to be able to control them.

Shifts of Stress

Every word uttered has a pattern of stresses, depending on the amount of stress given to each syllable in the word. On some words, the stress pattern can be changed to indicate meaningful differences. Generally, we may shift the stress around in the word for one of four reasons:

(1) to underscore the contrast implied in similar words;
(2) to indicate, in a two-syllable word, the difference between its use as a noun or adjective and as a verb;
(3) to indicate, in words of three or more syllables, the difference between the word's use as a noun or adjective and as a verb; and
(4) to underscore the meaning implied in a form word.

Let us look at each of these kinds of shift of stress.

Underscoring Contrast

We may alter the usual stress pattern of a word if we want to underline the difference between that word and another word that is very similar.

Ordinarily, for example, we stress the second syllable of the words *ofFENSE* and *deFENSE*. Note the stress pattern on those words used in this sentence: "He's charged with an offense, and I'm his defense attorney." In sports, however, when there is one team for one purpose and another team for the other purpose, we put the stress on the first syllable of each word. Note this sentence: "Mark plays both on *OFfense* and *DEfense*." And the crowds at the games yell, "DE-fense, DE-fense!"

Another example: A judge might say, "I said REmand, not DEmand." And still another: One student might tell her friend, "I'm taking BIology, not GEology."

The purpose of the changed stress in each instance was to call attention to the contrast built into the two words, to point up the difference between two similar words—indeed, to make that difference the center of attention.

Noun or Adjective and Verb Contrast in Two-Syllable Words

When we shift the stress to underline the meaning of a word and point out its contrast with a similar word, we do not change the word's meaning. But it *is* possible to change the meaning of a word by changing the stress pattern.

Many two-syllable words receive stress on the first syllable if they are used as nouns or adjectives, but they receive stress on the second syllable if they are being used as verbs. This shift in stress will affect the vowels in the syllables, of course, because the duration (and strength or weakness) of the vowel in the syllable is one means of indicating its relative degrees of stress.

Let us look at the word *perfect*, for example. If the word is used as an adjective to describe someone or something, the word is stressed on the first syllable. The vowel in the first syllable, then, is /ɝ/ (ur). The vowel in the second (weakly stressed) syllable is /ɪ/ (i) or [ɨ]. But what happens when the word is used as a verb—if you want to talk about trying to *perfect* something (or someone) that (or who) has a few flaws. Then the stress shifts. The primary stress is put on the second syllable, and, in the process, the vowels are changed. The vowel in the first syllable would then be /ɚ/ (ər), and the vowel in the second syllable would be /ɛ/ (e).

We have prepared a list of two-syllable words that illustrate this shift in stress. Read each word aloud twice: once as a noun or adjective, with stress on the first syllable, and then as a verb with the stress on the second syllable.

absent	abstract	address	annex
blowup	breakdown	castoff	collect
combat	combine	compact	compound
concert	conduct	conflict	conscript
console	consort	construct	content
contest	contract	convert	convict
decrease	defect	desert	detail

digest	discharge	discount	entrance
extract	ferment	frequent	imprint
increase	inset	insult	invert
misprint	misrule	misquote	object
upset	perfect	permit	pervert
present	produce	progress	project
protest	rebel	recess	record
recount	refuse	reject	research
subject	survey	transfer	traverse

Noun or Adjective and Verb Contrast in Words of More Than Two Syllables

There are some words of more than two syllables that also shift stress to indicate the difference between the word used as a noun or adjective or as a verb. These words end in *-ate* or *-ment*. When the word is used as a verb, there is a secondary stress on the final syllable (*-ate* or *-ment*). When the word is used as a noun or adjective, this stress is weakened to tertiary stress. This shift in stress changes the strength and length of the vowel in that final syllable. For verbs, the *-ate* is /et/ (āt) and the *-ment* is /mɛnt/ (ment); for nouns and adjectives, the *-ate* is /ət/ (ət) and the *-ment* is /mənt/ (mənt).

The following list of words illustrates this shift in stress in words of more than two syllables. Read the words aloud, pronouncing each word twice—once as a noun or adjective and once as a verb. Note the shift in stress each time.

advocate	affiliate	aggregate	animate
associate	certificate	conglomerate	congregate
consummate	degenerate	delegate	deliberate
pontificate	postulate	segregate	complement
compliment	implement	ornament	regiment

Underscoring Meaning in Form Words

In the section on vowel gradation (Chapter 16), we discussed form words at some length. Form words are those words that are necessary for the form of our sentences but that do not contribute major ideas.

Ordinarily, form words get only tertiary stress in connected speech. In the phrase "I will go," for example, the first word-syllable gets secondary stress because it is an idea word, but not the major idea in the phrase. The second word-syllable, a form word (a helping or auxiliary verb), gets tertiary stress because the meaning of the word is clear and does not need to be stressed. The third word-syllable gets primary stress because it is the major idea in the phrase.

Try that phrase out loud: "I will go." If you are making a simple statement of the fact, you will not give anything more than tertiary stress to the word *will*. If you have been contradicted or you have had doubts about going or if you have been forbidden to go, you may want to stress the idea implied in the word *will*: intention, choice, and determination. If the idea is:

> [I had thought I wouldn't, but ...] I *will* go; or
> [You say I won't, but ...] I *will* go; or
> [There may have been some doubt, but ...] I *will* go; or
> [You may forbid me to, but ...] I *will* go,]

then the word *will* assumes a special importance. It is now an important idea word. To stress its importance and give the word its proper prominence, we raise the word *will* to primary stress.

All form words can be stressed in this way. If you *do* stress a form word, you indicate that the inherent idea of the word is especially important. Again, review the material on strong and weak forms in the previous chapter.

One word of warning: The only danger is that you may use the wrong strong vowel in the process of restressing the word. The strong form of *the* is not /ðʌ/ (*th*u), and the strong form of *a* is not /ʌ/ (u). The stressed forms of these form words are /ði/ (*th*e) and [eɪ] (ā). Also, the strong form of *was* is not /wʌz/ (wuz), but /wɑz/ (wäz).

Hints on Stress

We cannot give you hard-and-fast rules for stress patterns in American English. The guidelines are only general. Your ear (and the dictionary's record of current acceptable usage) must be your guide. We can pass on this observation: stress in English tends to be recessive (early in the word), and strong and weak stresses seem to alternate in our words and sentences.

Pronounce the word *wonderful*. Listen to the stress pattern in the word. Where is the heaviest stress? That is correct: it is early in the word, on the first syllable. Try the word *charitable* aloud. Where is the primary stress in that word? On the *char*, the fourth syllable from the end. These examples demonstrate the general statement that stress tends to go early in the words in English. (British English carries this principle much further than American English does. In British English, for example, the words *dictionary* and *secretary* have their primary stress on the first syllable. In American English, of course, we give that first syllable only secondary stress and put the greatest (primary) stress on the next-to-last syllable in the word.) The problem is that, although this generalization about recessive accent is true, we have already looked at many words stressed on the last syllable or near the end of the word. That is the reason we only talked about the *tendency*; the generalization is certainly not a universal rule to guide your pronunciation.

We have a basic rhythm in English based on alternating strong and weak stresses in our syllables. The pattern is not rigid (spondee breaks the pattern, for example), but it is present in our words and sentences. Listen to the words *absolutely, elevator, stationary, satisfactory, legislator,* and *comprehension*. Can you see the regularity of the pattern? Can you detect any exceptions to the alternating of stronger and weaker stresses? Read the following sentence aloud, just as you would say it in conversation: "I hope to go to the movies tonight." If the stresses were absolutely regular, the rhythm would be very monotonous!

One "problem" that we must face is that some words in the language have more than one acceptable pronunciation. The word *adult*, for example, can be pronounced with the stress on either syllable. The word *abdomen* can be stressed with primary stress on either the first or second syllables. Do you put the primary stress on the *ver* or the *tise* syllable in the word *advertisement*? Either is acceptable; both are commonly heard. Your authors put the primary stress on the first syllable in the words *comparable* and *chastisement*, but many American speakers put the primary stress on the second syllables of those words. One last example is the word *infantile*. What kind of stress do you give the last syllable—secondary with the diphthong /ɑɪ/ (i) in it, or tertiary with the consonant blend /tl/ and no vowel (unless possibly the little schwa)? Both are standard pronunciations of this word. If we gave you a list of the words in American English with more than one acceptable pronunciation, the list would be rather long.

Determining Current Usage

How do you decide on the pronunciation of a word when you are unsure of its current pronunciation? In the long run, your ears are your best guide. Listen to what educated, cultivated, prominent leaders are saying. They set the styles for acceptable usage (and they also follow the styles). They are a good gauge of what pronunciations to use.

The **most** dependable source of information about how to pronounce a word at any given time is a current, reputable dictionary. The dictionary is not a sacred text, but it *is* a record of current usage. Carefully used, it is an invaluable aid to deciding how to pronounce a word. There are several good dictionaries available, and you should develop the habit of using yours regularly. Of course, if you use a dictionary, you must understand the diacritical marks and the stress-marking system. Every dictionary has its own system for representing sounds and stress, and you can make intelligent use of your dictionary only if you understand its particular symbol system. Each dictionary fully explains its system and gives key words to guide you on what symbols represent what sounds. Before you look up *any* word, you must study that explanation and master it.

There is a special dictionary that gives only pronunciations—no meanings of words or histories of words: *A Pronouncing Dictionary of American English* by John S. Kenyon and Thomas A. Knott. The pronunciations are represented in the International Phonetic Alphabet, and regional variations of pronunciation are noted. It is an invaluable aid and, combined with a good, standard dictionary, will provide you with essential tools to develop correct pronunciation.

18

Rhythm and Melody

Every language has a music of its own, based on its rhythms and melodies. If you heard a group of people talking in French, Swedish, Chinese, or American English, you would be able to hear the musical differences in the languages being spoken. We call these elements of language *prosodic features*. (The word *prosody* has descended from a Greek word that means "an accompanied song.") Languages have two musical, or prosodic, elements or features: *rhythm* and *melody*.

Rhythm

We have defined rhythm as the pattern created by recurring, stressed beats. In connected speech, these beats occur in three kinds of units: the syllable, the foot, and the phrase. To understand rhythm and the patterns of stresses that create rhythm, we must look at each of these units individually.

Syllable

A syllable is a sound or group of sounds uttered on one chest pulse. That means the syllable is produced on air pushed out by the external chest muscles. The syllable is the basic unit in rhythmic patterns. We discussed syllabic stress in Chapter 17 as an element of word pronunciation. Now, we will look at these variations in stress of syllables as part of a total rhythmic pattern. First, however, we must look at syllables themselves a little more closely.

Syllables, as we noted in Chapter 2, have three basic component parts: a beginning consonant or consonants, a vowel or diphthong, and a closing consonant or consonants. The syllable pulse, then, like most movement, consists of two strokes—a beat stroke and a back stroke. The beat stroke starts the pulse, and the back stroke stops the pulse.

Although there can be three component elements in any syllable, a syllable does not necessarily have all three. There are four types of syllables, if we classify them on the basis of their components:

Pattern	**Sample Word**
O V O	*Oh*
C V O	*Ho*
O V C	*Oak*
C V C	*Coke*

O stands for nothing. *V* stands for vowel. *C* stands for consonant (or consonants). Consonants start and stop syllables, and vowels and diphthongs provide the quality (resonance, sonority, or carrying power) of syllables. (The one exception, you will remember, occurs in the case of syllabic consonants, such as /l/ and /n/ which provide the carrying power or resonance of the syllable—in words such as *bottle* and *button*.)

In addition to the three degrees of stress given to syllables in words spoken alone, there is another degree of stress possible. This stress is greater than primary stress, and for lack of a better term we call it superstress. We will represent the four degrees of stress with these symbols:

tertiary secondary ′ primary **′** super **X**

Syllables are separated from each other by tiny breaks or pauses. These breaks are called *juncture*. Read aloud the following pairs of words and phrases. In each pair, the difference will not be the succession of sounds (the sequence of the sounds), but where the syllables are divided by juncture. In other words, the sound sequence is the same in both words or phrases in a pair. The difference in meaning is achieved by grouping the sounds differently into syllables.

I scream	ice cream
nitrate	night rate
this tile	this style
my tie	might I?
weak aim	we came
a nice house	an ice house
note rust	no trust
weak rave	we crave
you dare	you'd air
how sin	house in
day time	date I'm
fee tin	feet in
height I'm	high time

node out	no doubt
made A	May Day
Ho prayed	hope raid
Walsh out	wall shout
gross kills	grow skills
Weese prayed	we sprayed

These junctures (syllable breaks) affect the rhythm in the flow of speech, and obviously they affect the meaning. Here are a few sentences containing juncture contrasts:

1. Might I have my tie back?
2. I have no doubt the surgeon got the node out.
3. The date I'm taking will only go out in the day time.
4. Miss Tate did not deliberately misstate her position.
5. Will Miss Reed rest before she gets redressed?

In some languages, stress patterns are almost always regular. In French, for example, stress is put on the syllable at the end of a word of phrase. This regularity makes the rhythmic pattern fairly predictable.

In English, on the other hand, the stress pattern is quite variable. Almost any syllable has a chance of being stressed. To illustrate the variety of stress patterns in words in American English, look at the possibilities in words of one to eight syllables in the list of syllabic stress patterns that follow. (We are noting stress in words spoken alone, not in larger units.)

Number of Syllables	Stress Pattern	Key Word
1-syllable words	ˈ	joke
2-syllable words	ˈ ˘	stupid
	ˈ ˊ	bureau
	ˈ ˈ	bookstore
	˘ ˈ	above
	ˊ ˊ	tattoo
3-syllable words	ˈ ˊ ˘	grasshopper
	ˈ ˘ ˘	syllable
	ˈ ˘ ˊ	envelope (noun)
	˘ ˈ ˘	awarded
	ˊ ˈ ˘	Titanic
	˘ ˈ ˊ	piano
	˘ ˘ ˈ	undertake
	ˊ ˘ ˈ	afternoon

Number of Syllables	Stress Pattern	Key Word
4-syllable words	′ ˘ **′** ˘	education
	′ ˘ ′ ˘	liberating
	′ ˘ ˘ ˘	charitable
	′ **′** ˘ ˘	insidious
	˘ **′** ˘ ˘	oblivion
	˘ **′** ˘ ′	eradicate
	′ **′** ˘ ′	incarcerate
	˘ ˘ **′** ˘	understanding
5-syllable words	˘ **′** ˘ ′ ˘	obliterated
	˘ **′** ˘ ˘ ˘	uncomfortable
	˘ ′ ˘ **′** ˘	consideration
	′ ˘ ˘ **′** ˘	edification
6-syllable words	˘ ′ ˘ **′** ˘ ˘	dependability
	′ ˘ ′ ˘ **′** ˘	interdigitation
	′ ′ ˘ **′** ˘ ˘	unprovability
	′ ˘ ˘ **′** ˘ ˘	interdependency
	˘ ′ ˘ ˘ **′** ˘	internalization
7-syllable words	′ ˘ ′ ˘ **′** ˘ ˘	constitutionality
	˘ ′ ˘ ˘ **′** ˘ ˘	inseparability
8-syllable words	′ ˘ ′ ˘ ˘ ˘ **′**	internationalization

Foot

The foot is a larger unit than the syllable. While syllables are produced by little pulses of pressure from the intercostal chest muscles (the short muscles between the ribs), the foot is produced by an *abdominal* pulse (or push).

Feet may be composed of various numbers of syllables. A foot can be only one syllable long: "No!" for example. Or a foot can be an entire sentence: "I will go." The foot can contain any number of syllables, so long as only one of those syllables receives primary or super stress. Hence, each foot will contain one strong, rhythmic beat. It is on this strongly stressed syllable that the abdominal muscles give their little extra push.

In English, the feet are fairly even and consistent in length. There is almost uniform time between the primary or super stresses. Our language, when spoken, has a fairly steady beat because of the equal time from heavy beat to heavy beat. Say this sentence out loud, and pat your foot on the heavily stressed syllables: "I have *sworn* upon the *al*tar of *God* e*ter*nal hos*til*ity against *all* forms of *ty*ranny over the *mind* of *man*." Did you find that the strong beat made by the stressed syllables was pretty regular? Was your foot patting steadily?

In feet with many syllables, some syllables must be shortened (spoken more quickly) to keep the feet relatively even in length—to keep the strong beats regular. This shortening and weakening of syllables reduces the stress on these syllables and changes the vowel sounds in them. In feet with one syllable or few syllables, the syllables will be lengthened. We stretch out the sounds—especially the vowels and diphthongs. This lengthening increases the stress.

Pauses at the end of feet can be short or long. This variation in the length of pauses is another means we use to keep the strong beat regular and the feet even in length.

When we stress a syllable, we increase the force, or intensity; raise the pitch; and increase the duration, or length, of the syllable. Stressing syllables is a means of giving some syllables more prominence than others. Just as some syllables in a word are more important than others, so also some words in a sentence are more important than others. We give these more important words extra prominence or attention through *emphasis*. We stress a syllable, but we emphasize a word in a foot or phrase. Emphasis in feet and phrases is achieved by centering attention on the stressed syllable of the word to be emphasized. These important words usually come at the beginning or end of the foot. This stress on top of stress creates the super degree of stress that we talked about earlier. We need only three degrees of stress for the pronunciation of a word. But we need this new category of stress to describe the effect of emphasis. We move to thought-bearing words when we speak. They are mountaintops of attention surrounded by weak-syllable valleys.

A change in emphasis changes the rhythm. We can illustrate this principle with a simple sentence. The sentence is made up of one phrase, and that one phrase is made up of only one foot. There are four words in the sentence, but shifts in emphasis yield at least five possibilities for various rhythms. Pronounce each of these variations aloud. Listen to what the shifts in emphasis do to the rhythm.

´ ˘ ´ ´
I will not go.
× ˘ ´ ´
I will not go.
´ × ´ ´
I will not go.
´ ˘ × ´
I will not go.
´ ˘ ´ ×
I will not go.

Emphasis conveys extra meanings—underscoring the idea built into the word *emphasized*. A speaker shifts emphasis from word to word to communicate his or her intent and feelings. Speakers use emphasis to point out what is important to them.

When you are the speaker, you will need to be able to control these shifts in emphasis and these changes in rhythm to communicate your own intentions and feelings. When you are a listener, you need to understand the implications of these shifts in emphasis and rhythm to be able to interpret the speaker's meaning correctly.

Phrase

A *phrase* is a thought group, a sense group, a unified idea that can hang together. From the physiological point of view, it is a breath group, uttered on one stream of outgoing breath.

A phrase is made up of feet. It can contain various numbers of feet. A phrase could be only one foot long, such as: "No!" It can also contain many feet. Look at these examples (in which the diagonal line separates the feet of the phrase).

How could I / possibly / do / such a thing?

Will you go / to the theater / tonight?

It's been / such a difficult / year.

What / a big / one!

A sentence may contain more than one phrase. Note these examples (in which double diagonals separate the phrases and single diagonals separate the feet).

That he / is really / guilty // is far / from clear.

// . . . and that government / of the people // by the people //

and for the people // shall not perish / from the earth.

The beat created by the strongly stressed syllables stays relatively steady (regular) throughout the phrase. Read aloud each of the preceding examples, and pat your foot on the strongly stressed beat of each foot. You should find that the beats are separated by about equal time.

Melody

A *melody* is a tune—a succession of pitches that form a pattern. When we speak, we do not utter every syllable on the same tone or pitch; the pitches vary from syllable to syllable and word to word. Because we do not speak in a monotone (all on one pitch), we have *intonation* (a succession of different pitches that creates melody). If you do not use the usual melodies when you speak, you will have a "foreign accent."

The melody patterns of sentences in one language will be different from those of another language. Each language has its own distinctive "tunes" for thought groups and sentences. In fact, those melodic patterns are an important and integral part of the language itself. Our ears tell us that dialects of the same language also vary in intonation patterns from other dialects.

A detailed analysis of intonation (or melody) in American English is outside the scope of this book. We will, however, give you some basic information about this important element of our language. To do so, we must discuss three basic elements of melody: (1) phrase terminals (sometimes called clause terminals), (2) levels of pitch, and (3) intonation contours.

Phrase Terminals

At the ends of phrases and sentences, we indicate extra information about the content of the phrase or sentence through the use of pitch. How we end the phrase or sentence alerts the listener to the speaker's intentions and private meanings. If the pitch slides up at the end of the phrase, the speaker is uncertain, and the statement is incomplete. If the pitch slides down at the end of the phrase, the speaker is certain, and the statement is complete and final. If the pitch is kept level and is sustained at the end of the phrase, the speaker is not finished with his idea; there is more to come. If the pitch slides up and then back down again—or if the pitch slides down and then back up again—the speaker is expressing irony (saying one thing but meaning another) or is hinting at a double meaning.

There are, then, four possible phrase terminals in English: a rising pitch terminal ↗ which indicates uncertainty or incompleteness; a falling pitch terminal ↘ which indicates certainty, completeness, and finality; a sustained pitch terminal ⟶ which indicates nonfinality; and a circumflex pitch terminal ⤴ or ⤵ which indicates a double meaning (*double entendre*). Look at these examples:

(You asked if I were sure.) I know. ↘ (I am sure.)
(You falsely said I was sure.) I know? ↗ (I am not sure at all.)
I know ⟶ (for who could doubt his word?) he is innocent.
(You may believe something different, but . . .) I know. ⤵

Each of these phrase terminals ended the same phrase "I know." Each changed the meaning of the phrase and indicated how the listener should interpret the message. The words in parenthesis were never said; they were implied—by the pitch moves of the terminals.

Pitch Levels

If you listen to someone else speak, or if you listen carefully to your own speech patterns, you will discover that you do not say each syllable on exactly the same pitch. The pitch varies from syllable to syllable. (Indeed, as we saw with phrase terminals, it is possible to change the pitch during the utterance of the syllable.) Do these pitches matter? Do they change the meaning? Some of these pitch changes are very significant to listeners in English, and others are far less important.

Generally, scholars have noted four levels of meaningful difference in pitch. These four levels are not exact frequencies; rather, they are relationships established by each speaker in his or her own voice range. There are four levels of pitches, each higher or lower than the other levels. How high is the highest level? We can't tell you; it depends on a person's voice. How low is the lowest level? Again, it depends on the range of the speaker's voice. We can tell you that in American English, a speaker will use four different pitch levels. These pitch levels are relative from speaker to speaker. It is the *relationships* of the four levels that are important, as the listener decodes meaning.

Here are the four levels, with 1 representing the lowest level and 4 representing the highest pitch level. Note the use of each of these levels.

4	Special Emphasis	4
3	Primary Stress	3
2	Home Base; Normal, Modal Pitch; Weak Stress	2
1	Finality, Certainty	1

Each syllable we utter can be placed in one of these four levels. Perhaps we should have said each syllable can be classified into one of these levels. Listen to this short sentence as you say it aloud. Listen to the pitch changes, and decide which category each syllable would fit into:

I hate him!

We classified level 2 a home base, and that is where this phrase would start, because the first syllable does not get heavy stress. (Note that stress and pitch are interdependent.) How did you say the second word-syllable? Did you just give it emphasis? If so, it went up to level 3. Or did you really punch it? Then you probably pushed it up into level 4. What happened on the final word-syllable? The pitch of this last syllable was lowest of all, was it not? Was it even lower than when you started the sentence (in level 2)? Did the last syllable have a pitch change while you uttered the syllable, with the pitch dropping down from where you started in the beginning of that last syllable? That is the phrase terminal; it is the falling terminal.

Let us graph another simple sentence, looking at the level of each of the syllables (or words—because each word is one-syllable long).

Here is the sentence: "I don't want one."

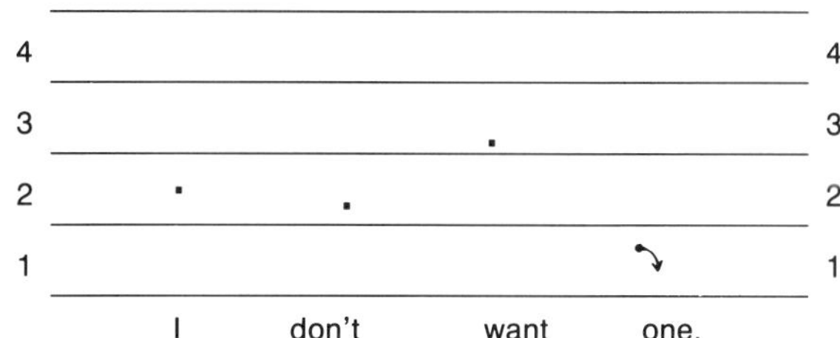

Here there is a difference in pitch between the first two words. The second is lower than the first, but it is still within the range of pitch variation recognized as level 2. The third syllable, however, is the syllable that gets primary stress or attention in this phrase, and it shifts gears up to level 3. The final syllable, at the end of the sentence, is in level 1. It has its little tail on it—the phrase terminal, the falling terminal of finality and certainty.

Contours

We have already moved into the subject of contours. It is almost impossible to discuss pitch levels and not discuss the patterns they make. Pitch levels make no sense alone; they mean something only in terms of a relationship. What matters is the melody (contour) created by a succession of pitches together with phrase terminals.

We cannot list in detail all the possible melodies in the language. We do want to give you some of the most common contours. These patterns will include pitch levels and phrase terminals. Try the sentences out loud to see if your pronunciation of them follows the contour (pitch pattern) given.

Contour 1: Statements of Fact and Commands

Statements of simple fact and imperatives (commands) usually follow this contour:

Contour 2: Statements of Doubt

Statements of wonder, amazement, and doubt usually follow this contour:

2 2 3

He's doing that!

Contour 3: Statements with Phrases in Series

Sometimes we have a sentence in which we give a series of phrases—a kind of list. Each phrase in the list gets one kind of contour—until the last one. The pitch pattern of the first phrases in the series indicates (with a rising or level phrase terminal) that the series is not yet over, and the contour of the last phrase in the series indicates (with a falling phrase terminal) that the series is at an end. Look at these possibilities:

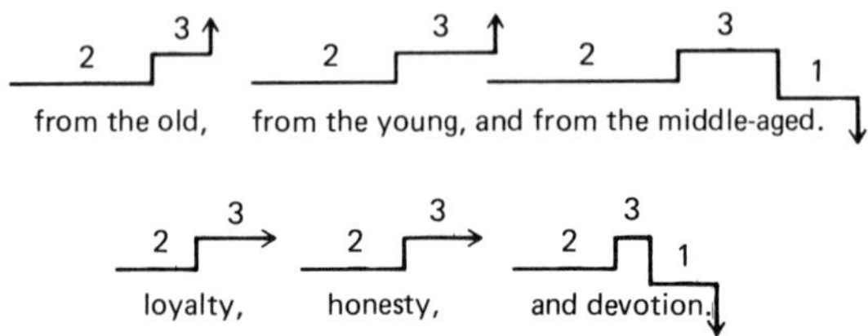

2 3 2 3 2 3 1

loyalty, honesty, and devotion.

Contour 4: Questions Starting with Interrogative Words

Some people have the mistaken notion that every question in English has a melody with a high last pitch level and a rising terminal. This notion is, as we said, mistaken. We have many questions that have a different contour completely. If you ask someone for specific information—questions beginning *what, where, when, why,* or *how,* for example—you will use the same contour we used for statements of fact and for imperatives (commands).

2 3 1

Where is it?

Contour 5: Questions with Yes or No Answers

If you ask a question that can be answered with either yes or no, the contour will end with level 3 and a rising terminal.

2 3

Is he ready?

Contour 6: Maybe This or Maybe That Questions

Sometimes we ask questions that offer choices to our listeners. We ask them if they like or dislike one thing or another; or we ask them if they want to do one thing or another; or we ask if they feel one way or another. By choosing a certain melody, we can offer them the chance to accept or reject either or both of the alternatives we offer. (By choosing a different melody, as we will see in a moment, we can try to make them choose *between* the two alternatives we give them.)

By using the same contour for both phrases, we express doubt about both choices and leave the listener free to accept either or both of the things we suggest. Read the following sentence out loud, paying attention to the intonation pattern.

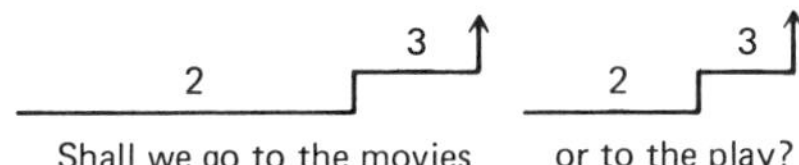

Contour 7: Either This or That Questions

Again, we ask a question and give the listener a choice. This time, by changing the intonation pattern in the second phrase, we indicate that the two choices are the only alternatives the listener has. Remember, we do not tell listeners explicitly, that we are limiting their choices to the two stated choices. We tell them nonverbally with our pitch levels and phrase terminal. We indicate the boundaries of their alternatives with the contour of the melody—the intonation pattern—we use.

Note the difference (from Contour 6) when the question is asked using this intonation pattern:

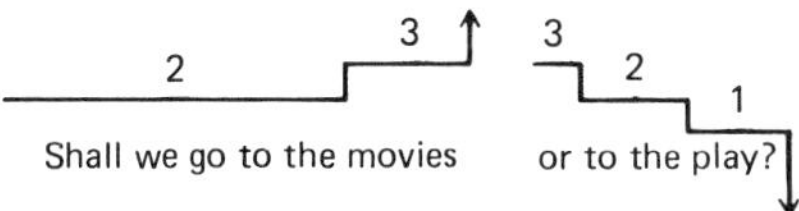

In this chapter, we have examined briefly the musical elements of American English. We discussed the three kinds of units (syllable, foot, and phrase) that create our rhythmic patterns. Then we discussed the three basic components of melody (or intonation): phrase terminals, pitch levels, and contours.

If English is your first language, you may take these prosodic features for granted. If, on the other hand, English is not your first language, you may need to give careful attention to these elements.

19

Special English Problems

If English is not your first language, you face some special problems. We have mentioned some of those problems as we have dealt with individual phonemes of American English. As you have read this handbook and looked at the possible problems associated with each phoneme, we hope you have identified the problems you have encountered in speaking English.

To assist you, we have prepared a brief list of problems you may face. To understand that list (and the Allophone Chart which follows), you need to know the symbols we are using. The first four symbols are our arbitrary choices. The others are standard phonetic subscripts and superscripts added to phonetic symbols to give additional information about the way a sound has been produced. Here are the symbols and their meanings:

Symbol	**Meaning**
>	turns into (or becomes)
?	confusion
–	omission
V	vowel

Subscripts (under phonetic symbol)

o	devoicing or unvoicing of a voiced sound
v	voicing added to a voiceless sound
	dentalizing a sound

Superscipts (above phonetic symbol)

⊥	raising the tongue from usual position
⊤	lowering the tongue from usual position
⊢	retracting the tongue from usual position

˧	pulling the tongue in front of usual position
~	nasalizing a sound
h	strong aspiration (puff of air)
c	weak aspiration
=	no aspiration

Here is a brief list of problems we noted:

Reference	Problem	Explanation
p. 59	/b/ > /β/	substituting voiced bilabial fricative for /b/
p. 60	/p/ > /f/	substituting /f/ for /p/
p. 61	/p/ or /b/ ?	voicing confusion on /p/ and /b/
pp. 66-67	- /t/ & /d/	omission of /t/ and /d/
pp. 67-68	[t̪] & [d̪]	dentalized /t/ and /d/
p. 71	/d̥/	unvoiced /d/
pp. 80-81	/g̊/	unvoiced /g/
p. 89	[l̥] or [ɫ] ?	confusion of light and dark /l/
pp. 89-90	[l̪]	dentalization of /l/
pp. 91, 198-199	/l/ or /r/ ?	confusion of /l/ and /r/
p. 102	/v/ > /w/	substituting /w/ for /v/
p. 102	/v/ > /b/	substituting /b/ for /v/
pp. 108-109	[θ˔], [ð˔]	raising /θ/ and /ð/
pp. 110-111	/θ/ > /s/	substituting /s/ for /θ/
pp. 110-111	/ð/ > /z/	substituting /z/ for /ð/
pp. 118-119	- /h/	omission of /h/
p. 126	[z̥]	unvoicing of /z/
p. 136	[ʒ̊]	unvoicing of /ʒ/
pp. 142-143	/tʃ/, /dʒ/	incomplete closure: /tʃ/, /dʒ/
p. 146	[dʒ̊]	unvoicing /dʒ/
pp. 146-147	/dʒ/ > /j/	substituting /j/ for /dʒ/
p. 155	V/m/ > ṽ	substituting nasalized vowel for oral vowel + /m/
p. 163	V/n/ > ṽ	substituting nasalized vowel for oral vowel + /n/
pp. 170-171	V/ŋ/ > ṽ	substituting nasalized vowel for oral vowel + /ŋ/
pp. 171-174	/ŋ/ + /g/ or /k/	''NG click''; adding /g/ or /k/ to /ŋ/
pp. 182-183	/w/ > /v/	substituting /v/ for /w/
pp. 189-190	/j/ > /dʒ/	substituting /dʒ/ for /j/

pp. 194-195	[ř]	trilled or flapped /r/
pp. 240-241 pp. 244-245	/i/ or /ɪ/ ?	confusion of /i/ and /ɪ/
pp. 250-251	[eɪ] > [e]	substituting [e] for [eɪ]
p. 264	/æ/ > /ɑ/	substituting /ɑ/ for /æ/
pp. 274-275	/ɔ/ > /o/	substituting /o/ for /ɔ/
pp. 280-281	[oʊ] > [o]	substituting [o] for [oʊ]
pp. 286-287	/ʊ/ > /u/	substituting /u/ for /ʊ/
pp. 297-298	/ʌ/ > /ɑ/	substituting /ɑ/ for /ʌ/
pp. 298-299	/ʌ/ > /u/	substituting /u/ for /ʌ/
p. 303	/ə/ > ?V	substituting strong vowel for /ə/

Allophones

In Chapter 1, we said that you must learn the phonemes (the sound families) of a language. That statement implied that you must learn the variations of a phoneme. You must get to know all the members of each sound family; and you must learn when to use each one.

We have already discussed a few allophones in connection with the production of specific phonemes. Now we will provide more information on allophones—first a chart and then some explanation.

Allophone Chart

Consonants

Phonemes			Explanations
/p/	**and**	**/b/**	
[p^h]		[b]	strongly exploded
[p^c]		[b]	weakly exploded
[p=]		[b]	unexploded
		[b̥]	devoiced
/t/	**and**	**/d/**	
[t^h]		[d]	strongly exploded
[t^c]		[d]	weakly exploded
[t=]		[d]	unexploded
[t̬]			voiced
		[d̥]	devoiced
[t̪]		[d̪]	dental

/k/	**and**	**/g/**	
[k^{h}]		[g]	strongly exploded
[k^{C}]		[g]	weakly exploded
[k =]		[g]	unexploded
		[g̥]	devoiced
/ʍ/			no variations
/f/	**and**	**/v/**	
[f]		[v]	
		[v̥]	devoiced
/θ/	**and**	/ð/	no variations
/s/			no variations
/s/	**and**	**/z/**	
		[z]	
		[z̥]	devoiced
/ʃ/			no variations
/ʃ/	**and**	/ʒ/	
		[ʒ]	
		[ʒ̥]	devoiced
/h/			
[h]			
		[ɦ]	voiced
/tʃ/			no variations
/tʃ/	**and**	**/d**ʒ/	
		[dʒ]	
		[dʒ̥]	devoiced
/tʃ/	**and**	**/m/**	
		[m]	
		[m̥]	devoiced
/tʃ/	**and**	**/n/**	
		[n]	devoiced
		[n̥]	
		[n̪]	dental
/tʃ/	**and**	/ŋ/	
		[ŋ]	
		[ŋ̊]	devoiced

/l/		
	[ᶅ]	light /l/
	[ɫ]	dark /l/
	[l̥]	devoiced
	[l̪]	dental
/w/		
	[w]	
	[w̥]	devoiced
/j/		
	[j]	
	[j̥]	devoiced
/r/		
	[r]	without much friction
	[ɹ]	with friction
	[r̥]	devoiced

Vowels

/i/		
	[i]	
	[ɪ]	in unstressed syllables
	[ə]	in unstressed syllables
/ɪ/		
	[ɪ]	
	[ɨ]	medialized
/e/		
	[e]	in unstressed syllables
	[eɪ]	in stressed syllables
/ɛ/		no important variations
/æ/		
	[æ]	
	[a]	tongue slightly lower; a regional variation
/ɑ/		
	[ɑ]	
	[ɒ]	a regional variation
	[ɔ]	after /w/, before /ɚ/ or /r/

Phoneme	Allophone	Notes
/ɔ/		
	[ɔ]	
	[ɒ]	a regional variation
/o/		
	[o]	in unstressed syllables
	[oʊ]	in stressed syllables
	[ɔ]	before /ɚ/ and /r/—in some regional dialects
	[ə]	in unstressed syllables
/ʊ/		no variations
/u/		
	[u]	in stressed syllables
	[ʊ]	in unstressed syllables
	[ə]	in unstressed syllables
/ʌ/		no variations
/ə/		
	[ə]	
	[ɪ]	
	[ɨ]	
	[ʊ]	
	[o]	
/ɝ/		
	[ɝ]	the most common form
	[ɜ]	a regional variation
/ɚ/		
	[ɚ]	
	[ə]	a regional variation

Don't decide the allophone chart is too confusing and refuse to examine it! It makes sense if you just look for patterns.

Look at the stops, for example. The voiceless stops are very similar in their pattern of aspiration. (Only voiceless consonants have *aspiration*—a puff of voiceless air.) /p/, /t/, and /k/ are all **strongly aspirated** if they begin a stressed syllable. Pronounce these examples out loud:

pear	compare	port	report
tire	retire	two	into
cute	acute	cause	because

/p/, /t/, and /k/ are all **weakly aspirated** if they come after /s/ in the same syllable, or if they begin an unstressed syllable. Pronounce these examples out loud:

spare	stare	scare
spy	sty	sky

In American English, /p/, /t/, and /k/ are all **unaspirated** (no puff of air) at the end of a word or phrase. Pronounce these examples aloud:

wrap	rat	rack
tape	rate	take

These sounds are **usually unaspirated** if the next sound is a consonant. Pronounce these examples out loud:

cupcake	utmost	actor
capful	boat show	back seat

The voiced stop consonants (/b/, /d/, /g/ do not have aspiration, but they do vary in the amount of the explosion on their release. The pattern is as follows.

Strong explosion at the beginning of stressed syllables

buy	abide	bound
abound	door	adore
day	today	go
ago	get	forget

Weak explosion at the beginning of unstressed syllables

before	rabbit	beside
rubber	delay	candid
devote	Sunday	garage
beggar	goatee	biggest

No explosion at the ends of words and phrases

rub	blood	rug
grab	wood	dog

And, no explosion before other consonants

crabgrass	good food	big league
rubdown	advantage	logjam

Here is another pattern: Voiced sounds lose some of their voicing at the ends of words and phrases. They also lose some voicing before voiceless consonants and after voiceless consonants in a blend or cluster. There is really no need be concerned or to practice this very much; it will come automatically. Note these examples:

lobster	codfish	big heart
five times	somehow	sincere
try	sly	snake

Yet another pattern: The sounds made with the tongue tip on the gum ridge are all made on the teeth before the two *th* sounds. /t/, /d/, /l/, and /n/ all have a dental allophone that is used before the *th* phonemes in such words as *breadth*, *health*, and *ninth*.

When /t/ comes between vowels in the middle of a word and that /t/ begins an unstressed syllable, we add some voicing to the /t/ in American English. This allophone is not a /d/, but it sounds a lot like a /d/. This allophone would be heard in words such as *pretty*, *city*, *butter*, *batter*, or *matter*.

We have already mentioned two of the most important allophones that might give you trouble if English is not your first language. The diphthong allophone of /o/ (ō) heard in stressed syllables and the diphthong allophone of /e/ (ā) heard in stressed syllables have already been discussed.

We are limiting our attention here to those allophones that will be noticeable to the average listener. The best guide to making these distinctions is your ears. Listen to cultivated speakers of American English and model your speech after them.

Rhythm and Intonation

If American English is not your first language, you will have to learn new rhythm and melody patterns. We have devoted a Chapter 18 to this subject. We suggest you ask your instructor to let you know when you are ready to work on those two elements of the language.

Pronunciation

Chapter 17 deals with the pronunciation of words. It should help you understand some common pronunciation problems—especially syllabic stress. You will have to learn how we divide words into syllables, since the system may be different from the one used in your first language. You will then have to learn our stress patterns.

The best guide to pronunciation is the speech of educated people in your community or area. Listen and imitate. The second best guide is a good dictionary.

Some Specific Hints

If Your First Language is Spanish

The advice we have given so far in this chapter is quite general. We now want to address the problems you may face if your first language is Spanish.

We have encountered **twelve problems associated with consonants.**

(1) lack of firm closure and sufficient explosion on the stop consonants—/p/, /b/, /t/, /d/, /k/, /g/.
(2) dentalization of /t/, /d/, /n/.
(3) raising the tongue up behind the teeth on /θ/ and /ð/.
(4) adding /ɛ/ before /s/.
(5) substituting a voiced bilabial fricative [β] for /v/.
(6) substituting /f/ for /v/ at the ends of words.
(7) substituting a trilled or flapped /r/ for an American English /r/.
(8) substituting /s/ for /z/
(9) substituting /ʃ/ (sh) for /ʒ/ (zh).
(10) substituting /ʃ/ (sh) for /tʃ/ (ch).
(11) substituting /dʒ/ (j) for /j/ (y).
(12) substituting a nasalized vowel for an oral vowel plus a nasal.

► *Problem 1:* Lack of firm closure and sufficient explosion on the stop consonants

When discussing the stop consonants, we have pointed out that the stops must stop completely. To make any of the six stop consonants in American English [/p/, /b/, /t/, /d/, /k/, /g/], you must *firmly* close off the breath stream and hold it closed for a second. For /p/ and /b/, for example, we must *press* the lips together.

In addition, the stop/plosive consonants in English are much more explosive than those sounds are in Spanish. We hold the articulators closed for an instant, build up air pressure, and then release it in a little explosion. On the voiceless stops [/p/, /t/, and /k/], there is a little puff of voiceless air. We call that puff of air *aspiration*. This aspiration is much stronger in English than in Spanish. On the voiced stops [/b/, /d/, /g/], there is no aspiration, but there is a good plosive release.

► *Problem 2:* Dentalization of /t/, /d/, /n/

Spanish has a /t/, /d/, and /n/, but they are not articulated in the same place as /t/, /d/, and /n/ in English. These consonants in Spanish are made with the tongue on the back of the upper front teeth. These consonants in American English are made with the tongue tip on the *upper gum ridge*. That difference in placement of the tongue makes a difference in the sound. Be sure your tongue tip goes to the upper gum ridge (the alveolar ridge) and *firmly* touches the ridge to make these sounds. See pp. 71-72 for practice material.

Problem 3: Raising the tongue up behind the teeth on /θ/ and /ð/

In most dialects of Spanish, [θ] (th) does not exist at all. You may be tempted, then, to put your tongue behind the upper front teeth and make a Spanish form of /t/. That changes the sound completely and will sound like a /t/ to English speaking listeners.

Here are a few word pairs. The first will sound a lot like the second if you make this substitution.

thin	tin	wrath	rat
thank	tank	path	pat
thick	tick	both	boat

Review the instructions for producing /θ/ (th) on p. 106. Be sure to put the tongue tip under the upper front teeth. Think of putting the tongue tip between the upper teeth and the lower teeth. Look in a mirror. You should be able to see the tongue between the front teeth when you make this sound.

The sound [ð] (*th*) is used in Spanish only for /d/ between two vowels. This sound does not occur at the beginning or end of words. In English, we use /ð/ (*th*) at the beginning, in the middle, and at the ends of words. You may be tempted to use the Spanish form of /d/ (with the tongue up behind the upper front teeth) instead of the English /ð/ (*th*)—especially at the beginning and ends of words. If you do, it will probably sound like you are substituting /d/ for /ð/ (*th*).

Here are a few pairs of words. The first will sound a lot like the second if you make this substitution.

they	day	than	Dan
those	doze	father	fodder
other	udder	mother	mudder
breathe	breed	soothe	sued
writhe	ride	lathe	laid

As with the /θ/ (th), you must put your tongue *under* the upper teeth to produce ð. Look in a mirror as you produce this sound. You should see your tongue between the teeth.

Problem 4: Adding /ɛ/ (e) before /s/

Since many words in Spanish begin with *es*, you may add /ɛ/ (e) before /s/ at the beginning of English words. Many words in English begin with /s/ only. There are a few Spanish words beginning with *es*:

escala	escena	escuela	espanol

Here are some English words. The first word will be changed into the second word (a different word completely) if you add /ɛ/ (e) before the beginning /s/:

state	estate
say	essay
steam	esteem
sex	Essex
stir	Esther
strange	estrange
sense	essence

▶ ***Problem 5:*** Substituting a voiced bilabial fricative [β] for /v/

The /b/ in Spanish is not exactly the same as the /b/ in English. We have already alluded to this fact. The lips are brought close together, but there is little, if any, explosion. And there is not the same firm closure on the Spanish /b/ that we have in English. The sound is changed (or almost changed) from a stop to a fricative. We have already discussed the problem this creates for producing English /b/. Since *v* and *b* are pronounced the same in Spanish (at least in most dialects of Latin American Spanish), you may use that same sound for /v/ in English. It is not exactly an English /b/, but it will sound more like a /b/ than a /v/ to English speaking listeners.

In these pairs of words, the first should not sound like the second.

very	berry	vow	bow
vest	best	vote	boat
vase	base	vent	bent

Review the instructions for producing /v/ on p. 100. Be sure your upper front teeth firmly touch your lower lip!

▶ ***Problem 6:*** Substituting /f/ for /v/ at the ends of words

When /v/ is the last sound in a word, many whose first language is Spanish do not voice (vibrate) the sound. This "devoicing" turns /v/ into /f/. That substitution not only changes the sound, it often changes the word! Here are a few pairs of words. If you substitute /f/ for /v/ at the end of the word (if you do not get good voicing on that final /v/), you will turn the first word into the second.

leave	leaf
have	half
alive	a life
save	safe
prove	proof
grieve	grief

Be sure to make the final /v/ a *voiced* sound.

▶ *Problem 7:* Substituting a trilled or flapped /r/ for an American English /r/

The r in Spanish is made differently from the /r/ in English. The Spanish r is made by flapping the tongue tip against the upper gum ridge. The rr in Spanish, as you know, is trilled—touching the tongue tip to the upper gum ridge a number of times. We do not have the Spanish r or rr sounds in English. If you use them instead of the English /r/, listeners will understand you, but they will notice your "accent." Review pp. 193-194 and practice the English /r/. Remember that, in English, your tongue tip does not touch the gum ridge to produce /r/.

▶ *Problem 8:* Substituting /s/ for /z/

In most dialects of Spanish, the letters s and z are both pronounced /s/. Both *sangre* and *zapato* would begin with /s/, wouldn't they? In some dialects of Spanish, however, the letter s is pronounced /z/ before a voiced consonant. How would you pronounce the word *mismo*? Is the s an /s/ or a /z/? Even so, the /z/ is not a common sound in Spanish. Another point of confusion: the /z/ sound is often spelled s in English. Look at the words *is, was, cousin, robes*. All those s's are /z/!

In English, the /s/ is voiceless, but the /z/ is voiced. The vocal cords vibrate on /z/. /s/ hisses; /z/ buzzes. This difference is important—marking the difference between many words. Here are some pairs of words. The first contains /z/; the second contains /s/. The first should not sound like the second.

zoo	sue	zip	sip
zinc	sink	zeal	seal
zone	sewn	eyes	ice
lies	lice	his	hiss
buzz	bus	prize	price
lazy	lacy	razor	racer

▶ *Problem 9:* Substituting /ʃ/ (sh) for /ʒ/ (zh)

In most dialects of Spanish, there is no [ʒ] sound. There is no /ʃ/ (sh) in Spanish either—except as the last half of *ch*. Still, /ʃ/ (sh) seems easier to say (it doesn't have voicing), and it gets substituted for the voiced consonant /ʒ/ (zh). Review the section on /ʒ/ (zh) on pp. 133-140.

▶ *Problem 10:* Substituting /ʃ/ (sh) for /tʃ/ (ch)

The Spanish language contains the /tʃ/ (ch) sound. Think of words such as *chico* and *mucho*. The Spanish language does not contain /ʃ/ (sh). English has both! Many Spanish speakers confuse /ʃ/ (sh) and /tʃ/ (ch) in English and substitute the first for the second. What happens, actually, is there is no firm closure at the beginning of the /tʃ/ (ch). The stop portion [t] is left out, and only the [ʃ] (sh) is left. This substitution, of course, changes the sound and often changes the word.

Here are some pairs of words. The first contains /tʃ/ (ch); the second contains /ʃ/ (sh). The first word should not sound like the second.

chair	share	match	mash
shop	chop	watch	wash
cheap	sheep	march	marsh
choose	shoes	much	mush
cheese	she's	leech	leash

Problem 11: Substituting /dʒ/ (j) for /j/ (y)

In Latin American Spanish, the letters *y* and *ll* are both usually pronounced *y*. In some dialects, however, these letters are pronounced [dʒ] (j)—especially at the beginning of words. If you bring this interchange into English, you will confuse your listeners.

/j/ (y) and /dʒ/ (j) are completely separate phonemes in English. You cannot substitute one for the other. Review the material on /j/ (y) on pp. 186-193. Note how /j/ (y) is produced. The tongue tip is behind the lower front teeth. /dʒ/ (j), on the other hand, starts with the tongue tip on the upper gum ridge.

Use the *y* in *vaya* and *ayudar* for the /j/ (y) sound in English. Here are some pairs of words. If you substitute /dʒ/ (j) for /j/ (y), the first word will sound like the second. It should not.

yet	jet	yell	jell
yolk	joke	yellow	Jell-o
year	jeer	yam	jam

Problem 12: Substituting a nasalized vowel for an oral vowel plus a nasal

/m/, /n/, and /ŋ/ (ng) all exist is Spanish—but the patterns are different from those in English. /m/, for example, occurs in Spanish only at the beginning and in the middle of words—never at the end. In English, /m/ can occur in all three places in a word.

/n/ is made in a different place in English and Spanish. /ŋ/ (ng) is rare in Spanish, but it does occur—before /g/ and "hard *c*" ([k]), even though it is spelled *n*. Think of the words *vengo, tengo*, and *banco*.

Re-read Chapter 9 for a discussion of the three nasal consonants in English. Particularly note the discussion of this problem associated with each of the three nasal consonants. (See pp. 155, 163, and 170-171.) Remember, you must get good closure at the point of articulation for each sound, good humming up through the nose, and a long duration (time) for each of these sounds.

The problem for most Spanish speakers comes at the ends of English words. Since /m/ does not occur at the ends of words in Spanish, many speakers just nasalize the last vowel and leave off the /m/ on English words. They transfer that same pattern over to final /n/ and /ŋ/ (ng).

Pronounce these words out loud, and listen to see if you get a good, long /m/ consonant on these words. Also, look in the mirror to be sure the lips close **completely** while you hum the final /m/ through the nose.

time	dime	room	bloom
come	some/sum	game	tame
same	blame	them	him/hymn
lamb	ham	jam	dam

We have encountered **nine** common problems related to vowels.

(1) confusion of /i/ (ē) and /ɪ/ (i).
(2) inadequate duration and tension on /i/ (ē).
(3) substitution of /ɑ/ (ä), /o/ (ō), or /u/ (oo) for /ʌ/ (u).
(4) substitution of /u/ (o͞o) for /ʊ/ (oo).
(5) substitution of /ɔ/ (ô) for /o/ (ō).
(6) substitution of /o/ (ō) for /ɔ/ (ô).
(7) substitution of /ɑ/ (ä) for /ɔ/ ô).
(8) substituiton of [e] (ā̍) for [eɪ] (ā).
(9) substitution of [o] (ō̍) for [oʊ] (ō).

Problem 1: Confusion of /i/ (ē) and /ɪ/ (i)

Where Spanish has five vowels, English has fourteen. You have to learn to make new sounds in English. You also have to learn to hear and make distinctions unnecessary in Spanish.

There is an /i/ sound in Spanish, but it is made with the tongue about half-way between where the English /i/ (ē) and /ɪ/ (i) are made. In other words, the Spanish vowel is higher and tenser than the lax high front vowel /ɪ/ (i) in English. **But** it is not quite as tense or as high or as long as the tense high front vowel /i/ (ē) in English.

The /i/ (ē) in English is *almost* the same as the *i* in stressed syllables in Spanish. Think of the sound in the words *dia* and *vino*. In English, though, /i/ (ē) is an even longer sound, and it is more tense. The tongue is more tense and the muscles of the jaw also are more tense. The tongue is lifted up just a little more for the English /i/ (ē) than for the Spanish one. Just remember: English /i/ (ē) is tighter and longer!

Try these words out loud:

east	eat	easy	even	eager
seal	peel	reach	brief	seed

Review the material in Chapter 11 on these two sounds. The /ɪ/ (i) causes even more problems than the /i/ (ē) does. You must learn to drop the tongue from the position you are used to using for *i* in Spanish, to relax the tongue and the jaw muscles. Here are some word pairs. The first word, containing /ɪ/ (i), should not sound like the second word, containing /i/ (ē).

is	ease	itch	each
rich	reach	hit	heat
mitt	meat	sin	seen/scene
been	bean	rid	read/reed

Problem 2: Inadequate duration and tension on /i/ (ē)

Although we have already mentioned these factors in the problem we just discussed with you, we want to point it out again. Think of the /i/ (ē) in English as being double-long. It's as if the sound were not a pure /i/, but /ii/! Stretch it out. Hold on to the /i/ (ē) in English. That's the kind of sound it is. Put your thumbs under your jaw bones—one on each side. Say /i/ (ē). Feel the muscles under the jaw tighten up. The /i/ (ē) is *tense* sound. Work on it.

Problem 3: Substitution of /ɑ/ (ä), /o/ (ō), or /u/ (o͞o) for /ʌ/ (u)

The vowel /ʌ/ (u) does not occur in Spanish. You may be tempted to substitute another vowel in its place. We have encountered at least three substitutions for this English vowel.

Some speakers substitute /ɑ/ (ä) for /ʌ/ (u). That changes the sound and often changes the word. The first word in these pairs should not sound like the second:

duck	dock	luck	lock
come	calm	cup	cop
sum/some	psalm	color	collar

Some speakers substitute /o/ (ō) for /ʌ/ (u). That also is confusing for English speaking listeners. The first word in these pairs should not sound like the second word:

loves	loaves
does (verb)	does (female deer)
done	Doan
come	comb

Some speakers substitute /u/ (o͞o) for /ʌ/ (u). The speaker was probably misled (as in the case of words spelled with *o*) by the fact that the words are spelled with *u*. The following words have a *u* spelling, but the sound is /ʌ/ (u).

sun
run
instruction
construction
production

Problem 4: Substitution of /u/ (o͞o) for /ʊ/ (oo)

The vowel /ʊ/ (oo) does not occur in Spanish. For that reason, many whose first language is Spanish substitute the familiar vowel /u/ (o͞o) in its place. This deviation changes many words and confuses listeners. See pp. 285-288 for a discussion of /ʊ/ (oo). /ʊ/ (oo) is more relaxed and shorter than /u/. The lips are not as puckered, and the tongue is not raised quite so high in the back of the mouth. If you say /u/ (o͞o) and then /ʊ/ (oo) one after another several times while you keep your thumbs under each side of your jaw, you should feel the muscles under the jaw relax for /ʊ/ (oo) and tighten more for /u/ (o͞o). Here are a few pairs of words. The first, with /ʊ/ (oo), should not be turned into the second, with /u/ (o͞o).

full	fool	look	Luke

Problem 5: Substitution of /ɔ/ (ô) for /o/ (ō)

This is not a common problem, but it does occur. If you substitute the /ɔ/ (o) for the /o/ (o), you may very well change the meaning of the word. Look at the following pairs. Be careful not to change the first word [containing /o/ (ō)] into the second word.

scold	scald	bold	bald
mole	mall	foal	fall
coal	call	owning	awning
loan	lawn	hole	hall

Problem 6: Substitution of /o/ (ō) for /ɔ/ (ô)

Since the /ɔ/ (ô) does not occur in Spanish, this substitution is not uncommon. Be careful, because it can change the meaning of a word. *Jaw* should not sound like *Joe*, and *bought* should not sound like *boat*. See pp. 273-278 for a discussion of the /ɔ/ (ô) phoneme. Review p. 274-275 for words contrasting /ɔ/ (ô) and /o/ (ō).

Problem 7: Substitution of /ɑ/ (ä) for /ɔ/ (ô)

If you substitute the Spanish (and English) vowel /ɑ/ (ä) for the English Vowel /ɔ/ (ô), you may substitute one English word for another. *Caller* should not sound like *collar*, and *caught* should not sound like *cot*. Remember the lips are more rounded and the tongue raised higher in back on /ɔ/ (ô) than on /ɑ/ (ä). Here are a few pairs of words. The first should not become the second.

stalk stock naught not taught tot

Problem 8: Substitution of [e] (ā̆) for [eɪ] (ā)

As we have said before, the phoneme /e/ (ā) is usually a diphthong in English. In stressed syllables, it is *always* a diphthong. We add an /i/ (ē) tail (at least think of it that way) on to the [e] (ā) to make it long. In Spanish *e* represents the pure vowel [e]. You may be inclined to substitute that sound for the "long A" of English. But Spanish also has the diphthong we use in stressed syllables. It is spelled *ei* or *ey*. Think of the words *rey* and *reina*. That is the sound you need for all accented syllables with /e/ (ā) in English.

Problem 9: Substitution of [o] (ō̆) for [oʊ] (ō)

This is the same kind of problem we have just discussed. Both /o/ (ō) and /e/ (ā) use a diphthong allophone in stressed syllables in American English. Although this diphthong [oʊ] is a lot like the *o* in stressed syllables in Spanish, it is longer and has a *u*-like tail on it. The lips and tongue both move to make this diphthong. You must remember to stretch the /o/ in stressed syllables in English to make it long enough. Look in a mirror and watch the lips as you say /o/ (ō) in the following words. At the beginning the lips will be tense and very round (looking like the letter *o* itself). While making the /o/, they will close down even tighter and rounder—making a smaller circle.

old	own	oak	oats
open	only	blow	grow
throw	no/know	so/sew	show

If Your First Language is Chinese (or a Language of Southeast Asia)

We have encountered **eleven problems associated with consonants.**

(1) /r/ - /l/ confusion.
(2) omission of final consonants.
(3) substitution of /ts/ or /s/ for /tʃ/ (ch).
(4) substitution of /d/ for initial /ð/ (*th*).
(5) substitution of /v/ for final /ð/ (*th*).
(6) substitution of /s/ for initial /θ/ (th).
(7) substitution of /f/ for final /θ/ (th).
(8) substitution of /s/ for /z/.

(9) substitution of /w/ for initial /v/.
(10) substitution of /f/ for final /v/.
(11) substitution of nasalized /ɔ/ (ô) for /ɔŋ/ (ông).

▶ ***Problem 1:*** /r/ - /l/ confusion

This is a major problem for people whose first language is one of the languages of the Orient. /r/ and /l/ are separate and distinct phonemes in English. Your first language probably did not have a phoneme exactly like either the English /r/ or /l/. Bringing the sound you are familiar with into English and substituting it for /r/ and/or /l/ confuses listeners.

Review the material on /r/ (pp. 193-194 and pp. 198-199) and /l/ (p. 91). Work with your instructor to produce clear, accurate, distinct /r/ and /l/ consonants in English.

▶ ***Problem 2:*** Omission of final consonants

Since all syllables in your first language end in vowels, it is quite understandable that you would tend to omit the final consonants in English. However, it is important that you learn our syllable patterns and pronounce all final consonants (on words and syllables). Almost all the words in your first language are monosyllabic (one-syllable), and that will also be a factor. Be careful to sound the consonants that end syllables in the middle of English words as well as at the ends of words. Here are some pairs of words. The first word ends in a consonant. It should not sound like the second word.

deep	D.	feet	fee
leak	Lee	robe	row
load	low	league	Lee
wife	Y.	save	say
house	how	rose	row
pinch	pin	loathe	low

▶ ***Problem 3:*** Substitution of /ts/ or /s/ for /tʃ/ (ch)

The /tʃ/ (ch) phoneme may give you trouble. You may be inclined to substitute the consonant /s/ or the blend /ts/ for it in English words. Since the /ts/ blend never starts a word in English, we cannot give you contrasting English words for /ts/ and /tʃ/ (ch). Here are some words beginning in /tʃ/ (ch). Review the material on that sound on pp. 141-142. Be sure that you are producing it correctly. Seek the help of your instructor. Check your pronunciation of these few words:

China Chinese chin chip cheap

Now check again, pronouncing these pairs of words. The first begins with /tʃ/ (ch), and the second begins with /s/.

chin	sin	chip	sip
cheap	seep	choke	soak
chain	sane	chow	sow
chuck	suck	cheek	seek
chop	sop	chock	sock
cheese	sees	chill	sill

Problem 4: Substitution of /d/ for initial /ð/ (*th*)

The two *th* sounds in English pose a challenge. You are likely to substitute one sound [d] for /ð/ (*th*) at the beginning of words and another sound at the ends of words. The same is true for the /θ (th) phoneme in English. Review the material on /ð/ (*th*) on pp. 106-117, and practice using the materials on p. 112, contrasting /d/ and /ð/ (*th*).

Problem 5: Substitution of /v/ for final /ð/ (*th*)

If you put in any consonant at all at the end of words ending in /ð/ (*th*), you will probably use /v/. The /v/ is made with the upper teeth on the lower lip, while the *th* sounds are made with the tongue between the teeth. Use a mirror to be sure you put your tongue between your teeth to produce the /ð/ (*th*).

Problem 6: Substitution of /s/ for initial /θ/ (th)

Be careful that you do not substitute /s/ for /θ/ (th) at the beginning of words. That is not an uncommon substitution. Here are a few pairs of words for you to check. The first word begins with /θ/ (th) and the second word begins with /s/. The first word should not sound like the second.

thick	sick	thin	sin
thaw	saw	theme	seem
thigh	sigh	thing	sing
thank	sank	thought	sought

Problem 7: Substitution of /f/ for final /θ/ (th)

Check to see whether you substitute /f/ for /θ/ (th) at the ends of words and syllables. These are two separate phonemes in English. Substituting one for the other can change the meaning of the word. Remember the /f/ is made with the upper teeth touching the lower lip. The /θ/ is made with the tongue between the upper and lower teeth. Read these words ending in /θ/ (th) aloud:

oath	path	both	math
birth	death	earth	broth

▶ *Problem 8:* Substitution of /s/ for /z/

This is a common substitution. In English, these are separate phonemes. Read the following pairs of words to check on whether you replace /z/ with /s/.

With /z/	With /s/
his	hiss
laws	loss
peas	peace
fuzz	fuss
lose	loose

▶ *Problem 9:* Substitution of /w/ for initial /v/

Since there is no /v/ in your first language, it is natural that you might substitute a familiar sound in its place. Review the material in this handbook on /v/ on pp. 100-105. To check to see if you make this substitution, read the following pairs of words aloud.

With /v/	With /w/
vine	wine
vain	wane
vet	wet
vest	west

▶ *Problem 10:* Substitution of /f/ for final /v/

/f/ might be easier for you to say at the end of a word than /v/. It does not require voicing. In any case, we have heard this substitution, and you should check to see if you substitute /f/ for /v/ at the ends of words and syllables. To check to see if you make this substitution, read the following word pairs aloud.

With /v/	With /f/
save	safe
wave	waif
strive	strife
prove	proof
have	half

▶ *Problem 11:* Substitution of nasalized /ɔ/ (o) for /ɔŋ/ (ong)

In English, all vowels are oral (the air comes only out of the mouth). There are three nasal consonants—hummed through the nose. You may be inclined to use the nasalized vowel [ɔ̃] (a vowel made with part of the air coming through the nose) instead of an oral vowel followed by the nasal consonant /ŋ/ (ng). Check your pronunciation of the name of the city Hong Kong. Have your instructor show you the difference between a nasalized vowel and an oral vowel plus nasal consonant. Re-read the material on nasal consonants in Chapter 7 and on nasality in the voice section.

We have encountered **three common problems related to vowels.**

(1) substitution of /e/ (a) for /ɛ/ (e).
(2) substitution of /u/ (o͞o) for /ʊ/ (oo).
(3) substitution of /i/ (ē) for /ɪ/ (i).

Problem 1: Substitution of /e/ (ā) for /ɛ/ (e)

If English is not one's first language, substituting familiar vowels for unfamiliar vowels is very common. This problem is an example of this phenomenon. Review the material in this handbook on /ɛ/ (e). Get the amount of relaxation of tongue and jaw muscles required to produce the sound.

Problem 2: Substitution of /u/ (o͞o) for /ʊ/ (oo)

This is another example of substituting a familiar vowel for an unfamiliar one. Review the material on /ʊ/ (oo) on pp. 285-288. Learn to achieve the amount of relaxation of tongue and jaw muscles required to produce this sound. /u/ (oo) is more tense, and the lips are more puckered than they are on /ʊ/ (oo).

Problem 3: Substitution of /i/ (ē) for /ɪ/ (i)

Here again, we have an example of substituting a familiar vowel for an unfamiliar one. Review the material on /ɪ/ (i) on pp. 244-245. In this case also, you substitute a more tense, higher (in tongue position) vowel for a more lax, lower vowel.

In this chapter, we have examined briefly some of the special problems you may face if English is not your first language. We reviewed a list of possible problems and referred to chapters in this text where those problems were discussed. Then we turned our attention to special problems for speakers whose first language is Spanish and Chinese (or a language of Southeast Asia). We trust that this chapter will help you to speak American English more clearly and correctly.

Part II

Voice

Voice Glossary

Abduct: To pull away from the midline; referring to the opening of the vocal cords.
Adduct: To draw toward the midline; referring to the closing of the vocal cords.
Alexander Technique: A system centered around re-training habitual, inefficient movement patterns or posture into stress free body use.
Alignment: The coordination of the body for better or more efficient posture.
Amplitude: Largeness of range; directly related to intensity of sound and to resonance.
Aphonia: Loss of voice due to the failure of vocal cord vibration.
Arytenoids: Pair of triangular shaped cartilages to which the vocal cords are attached; involved with the opening and closing of the vocal cords.
Assimilation nasality: The result of nasal resonance being carried over from the nasal sounds in a word to the neighboring non-nasal sounds within the word.
Auditory feedback: The aural reception and discrimination of your speech as it reaches your ear immediately after speaking.
Aural: Pertaining to your sense of hearing.
Central Nervous System (CNS): The brain and the spinal cord.
Clavicular: A type of breathing involving the use of the clavicles, or collar-bones, to raise the rib cage during inhalation.
Denasality: A type of vocal quality that lacks sufficient nasal resonance during speech.
Diaphragm: Dome-shaped muscle that separates the thoracic cavity from the abdominal cavity; involved with respiration.
Duration: Measurement of time consumed between produced sounds and/or the measurement of time consumed between words and phrases.
Exhalation: One phase of respiration; air is expelled from the lungs.
Glottis: Opening between the vocal cords.
Gross abdominal muscles: Large muscles in the abdominal cavity used actively during the phase of exhalation.
Hyoid bone: A horseshoe-shaped bone at the top of the thyroid cartilage; the larynx is extended from this bone.
Hypernasality: A type of vocal quality that has excessive nasal resonance during speech.
Hypertension: Having excessive tension.
Hypotension: Having insufficient tension.
Kinesthetic: "Muscle sense"; your perception of how the muscular action of your body "feels."

Labial: Pertaining to the lips.
Laryngeal tone: The sound initiated at the larynx as the vocal cords begin to vibrate in phonation.
Laryngitis: Hoarseness of voice due to inflammation of the vocal cords.
Laryngopharynx: Throat area behind the larynx.
Lingual: Pertaining to the tongue.
Loudness: Intensity of sound.
Muscle tonus: Pertaining to adequate muscle tension for effective muscle functioning.
Nasal: Pertaining to the nose.
Nasopharynx: Extension of the throat area behind the nasal cavity.
Negative practice: Deliberate practice of wrong techniques in order to increase your awareness of correct techniques.
Oropharynx: Extension of the throat area behind the oral cavity.
Otolaryngologist: A medical doctor who specializes in the diagnosis and treatment of ear, nose, and throat problems.
Overtone: A sound frequency that is produced in addition to the fundamental tone.
Paralanguage: Extralinguistic features of voice, including vocal range, resonance, and tempo.
Pharynx: Throat area comprised of three sections: laryngopharynx, nasopharynx, and oropharynx.
Phonation: The process of producing vocal tone as a result of breath being vibrated between the vocal cords.
Resonance: Amplification and modification of sound.
Resonators: Three areas for amplifying and modifying the basic laryngeal tone for speech: the laryngeal cavity, oral cavity, and nasal cavity.
Respiration: A process involving breathing for life sustenance and for speech.
Soft palate: Extension of the hard palate; involved with production of nasal versus oral sounds.
Support of tone: Involves the use of the gross abdominal muscles as the breath stream is emitted during phonation.
Tactile: Pertaining to the sense of touch.
Thorax: The upper part of the torso of the body; houses the lungs.
Thyroid cartilage: [9]''Adam's Apple''[9] & large cartilage of the larynx.
Trachea: The windpipe.
Velum: The soft palate.
Vocal cords: Known as vocal bands; vocal folds; ligaments that produce ''voice'' when set into vibration.
Voice: Sound produced when vocal cords are set into vibration; added characteristics include resonance, loudness, and pitch.

20

Basic Principles

The basketball game and the yelling are finished, and so is your voice. The viral cold is gone, and so is your voice. The party "did you in," and your voice is "done in." Do any of these conditions sound or feel familiar? They are not uncommon experiences. Your voice, which was always there when you needed it, has suddenly deserted you. Why?

In the following pages, you will learn how to identify a serious voice problem as opposed to a temporary or passing one. You will learn how to take care of your voice on a daily basis, so that physical abuse is minimized. You will be taught how to produce your voice with ease and efficiency. You will be shown how to use the skills necessary for the production of a voice that is an extension of you, of the image you want to project—you at your best. You will be taught how to transfer the learned skills to the daily use of your voice, so that these learned skills become automatic and your new voice is you! You will not "take on" a new voice. Rather, you will start with the voice you have now. You will learn new ways of using good vocal skills so that the result will be a voice that is produced easily, efficiently, and is your instrument for more effective communication.

If you go back and re-read the preceding paragraph, you will notice the repeated use of the words, "how-to." The use of these words was deliberate. Because the focus of this handbook is on you, the student, our approach emphasizes your deliberate, concentrated involvement with all of the information, instructions, and exercises. You will improve by **doing**!

In some parts of the following chapters, you will be given basic information about the anatomy of the vocal mechanism. This is done to clarify the movements, the function (physiology) of the involved organs. In our experience as teachers, we have found that students learn faster if they know the "why" behind the instructions. When the rationale supports the action, skill acquisition is quick, progressive and lasting.

Here are a few more goals. You will also be taught how to:

1. Manage your practice time efficiently.
2. Get the most benefit from your practice time.
3. Take care of your voice (vocal hygiene).
4. Recognize medical, physical and emotional factors which can affect your voice.
5. Involve and control your body as you produce voice.
6. Vary the pitch of your voice for more vocal (emotional) color.
7. Adjust the volume of your voice to specific speaking situations.
8. Control the rate of your speech for greater clarity, meaning and impact.

Understanding Your Voice and You

Historically, the term *voice* can be traced back to approximately 500 B.C.—the time of Pericles, the Greek orator. Aristotle, who was born in 384 B.C., declared that "the art of delivery has to do with voice." Over 2,000 years later in his book, *The Voice of Neurosis*, Paul J. Moses wrote, "Voice is the prime expression of the individual." Dominic Barbara, a practicing psychiatrist in New York City, stated in *Your Speech Reveals Your Personality* (1957), "Your voice is you." These references are cited to support the concept that your voice is an extension of you. It is your personal instrument for communicating your ideas, intentions, attitudes and feelings. Your voice is as personal and distinctively yours as your religious beliefs, your political loyalties, and your fingerprints. Your listeners recognize you by your voice and receive messages from you and about you from your voice. You manipulate it, intentionally or unintentionally.

A conversation on the telephone is a good example of how your voice conveys your message(s)—sight unseen. On the telephone, most listeners can very quickly identify or interpret your message of happiness, anger, seriousness or illness through your voice and speech without the benefit of visual stimulation. While the listener's response may or may not be what you expected or wanted, they will respond. Even silence is a response.

All voices are not alike, even though we all use the same organs to produce voice. There are infinite varieties of vocal sound, infinite varieties of *quality* of voice—that vocal sound that is distinctly yours. Many factors contribute to these differences. Heredity, environment, personality, paralanguage, and skill all play a role in influencing your distinct quality.

Heredity determines the size and anatomical structure of our bodies. Physically, you are what you are from your ancestors. The color of your eyes or hair and your skeletal frame are observable examples. The structure and physiology (function) of the larynx is no exception. One reason your voice sounds as it does is related, in no small degree, to your genetic history. The Kennedy family illustrates this point. A Kennedy "sounds like a Kennedy." Do you sound like someone in your family? When answering the telephone in your home, are you often mistaken for another member of your household? Have you been told, "you sound just like your mother/father?"

Environment is an important factor influencing your voice. You tend to sound like the people around you. Your family, friends, school, local community, and the part of the country from which you come all help shape your voice. Speech and voice are "caught" rather than "taught." We learn verbal and non-verbal communication by interpersonal contact and imitation—especially in our formative years. The voices that surround us (our environment) are a powerful influence on our speaking voices.

Personality and *emotionality* are psychological factors which play important roles. Your psychological makeup contributes to your basic vocal quality, and your emotional fluctuations "color" your voice. Psychological studies support the relationship between *personality* and *behavior*. The voice patterns you use are *vocal behavior*. What kind of person you are and how you are feeling at the moment are going to influence the voice you produce and use.

Paralanguage is closely related to the factors just discussed. *Para* means "extra" or "beside" in Greek, and involves elements of the spoken message that are in addition to the language of the message. Paralanguage tells the listener how to interpret the main word message, but is always nonverbal. There are two elements of paralanguage that a student of human speech communication should note: the audible (what the listener hears) and the visible (what the listener sees). The audible element of paralanguage is produced by the *voice* of the speaker; the visible element is produced by the *body* of the speaker. In this handbook we are concerned with the *vocal* aspects of paralanguage—those aspects of the use of voice that convey meaning, apart from the words spoken. We convey meaning with our voices (pure sound) when we sigh, scream, grunt, groan, giggle, and make other nonword sounds. We also convey meaning with pitch changes (making our voices higher or lower), rate changes (speaking faster or slower), volume changes (speaking louder or softer), quality changes (changing the "sound" of your voice), and articulation changes (changing how we make speech sounds). These paralanguage "meaning markers" affect our voices and the way we are perceived by other people in interpersonal communication.

The final factor influencing these basic variations in voice quality is *skill*. Individuals vary in the degree of their control over the speech mechanism, and this variance in control produces perceptible differences in vocal output. You were born into your environment with your own degree of speech proficiency, but any native skill can be developed and extended. Under conditions that encourage the growing child to function productively in all areas—physically, intellectually, and emotionally—the speech proficiency should also progress. Far too frequently, skill in this area is not encouraged at early ages and is even hampered.

We mentioned previously that you learned to speak and to use your voice as a result of a combination of factors. Consider some possible situations. If a young child develops a lisp (the reasons for this articulatory defect are complex) and the parents either think the sound is cute or are unable to recognize the articulation problem, then the child's skill in speaking is hindered. If the vocabulary level in a child's home or in the community is on a low level, then the child's opportunities for learning to use a meaningful vocabulary are limited. If a child grows up in a home where the attitude is "Speak when spoken to," or "Speak only when you have something important to say," then the child can develop possible psychological problems that can influence his communication pattern. One of these handicapping conditions could be an ineffective use of voice. Proficiency in voice production cannot be treated as if it were an entity outside of oneself.

In the following pages a very personal part of you will be considered—your voice. Because "your voice is you," any change or any improvement is going to involve more than mechanics. Your voice reflects you in your many moods, your thinking, and your behavior patterns—all of those factors that add up to form your personality. In these pages you will acquire the knowledge and the skills necessary for good voice production. Then you will be told how to use this "good" voice production. However, much of the value of all of this knowledge will be lost if you do not develop self-awareness as quickly as possible.

Remember, improvement in your voice is directly affected by your articulation improvement. Therefore, the information and advice given to you in the remaining pages of this chapter apply to *both* voice and articulation progress. To bring about changes in both your voice and/or your articulation, you must work on:

1. Self-awareness
2. Auditory discrimination (hearing)
3. Productive practice

Developing Self-Awareness

Self-awareness refers specifically to your physical condition, your fluctuating emotional states, and the day-by-day progress in your improvement program. On days when you are fatigued, your practice will be less effective. The very fact that you have less physical energy to expend is reason enough not to be able to practice. However, physical fatigue also affects your mental state, so the problem is compounded. Mentally you are in no mood to work, and physically you are unable to work. Tired muscles do not respond easily to physical stimulation, and if the muscles are *forced* to function, the result could be increased muscular tension. This hypertension will certainly not produce the kind of response you want.

You will discover also that on days when you have experienced an emotional upset, practice might be virtually worthless. The fact that your emotions affect your physical condition, your powers of concentration, and your attitudes contributes to a highly complicated picture of why you are unable to practice when you are tense, anxious, or worried. If you are emotionally upset, your body reacts—your breathing is affected, muscles become tense, and coordinated muscular action is hampered. Concentration during this period is almost impossible because your thoughts are on your worries. Your attitude toward the practice session will either be "I couldn't care less" or "I'm going to acquire this skill—or else." In this highly charged atmosphere, either attitude could interfere seriously with productive practice.

On the brighter side, however, you will become sensitive to days that are potentially good for work. These days can be discovered only on a highly individual basis. For some of you it will be days when you are physically well and emotionally at ease. For others, it will mean days when attitudes are optimistic. Whatever the conditions, you can encourage profitable practice on days when the vocal mechanism is functioning well (for example, no colds, hoarseness, or allergy irritations) and when mental concerns are minimal. Remember, such days do not always just "happen." More often than not they must be encouraged to happen.

We have referred frequently in this book to the psychological aspects of the speech process. At this point we would like to assure you that not all changes in attitude and in application are spontaneous or deliberate. You may be a person who feels very hostile in the initial stages of the improvement program. Do not force yourself to reconsider or to reevaluate your feelings or position immediately. Let knowledge, time, and experience help you on the way to self-acceptance.

There are several basic requirements for a voice improvement program. These three are absolutely necessary:

1. An awareness and a knowledge of the problem itself.
2. A willingness to change or improve.
3. A resolute attitude toward a planned practice program.

Usually a person is made aware of a voice problem after an examination by an otolaryngologist or a qualified speech pathologist. Sometimes a person becomes aware of the voice problem because of physical discomfort, or because of remarks made by friends, or simply because of a recording or taping of the voice. What is important is for you to learn to recognize the *exact* sound of your voice. You should try to develop as quickly as possible auditory discrimination—the ability to hear your own voice accurately. This is really another form of self-awareness. You must become aware of your present method of producing voice and of the changes in your voice production as you try new vocal techniques. Before you can improve your voice, you must learn to *listen*. Remember, your voice will improve in direct proportion to how much you are aware of your voice problem. Become "voice," or "sound," conscious.

Developing Auditory Discrimination

How well are you able to analyze the sound of voices at this early stage? Experiment with the following suggestions:

1. Face a corner of a carpeted room. Cupping a hand behind each ear, pull the ears slightly forward and begin to speak into the corner. The voice that reaches your ears will be fairly close to your voice as other people hear it. Become acquainted with it.
2. Have a "new listening experience" the next time you listen to your favorite disc jockey or television program. Can you *put into words* the descriptions of the voices you are hearing?

Let us take a close look at some of the factors that will specifically aid you in monitoring and controlling your own voice production. The Central Nervous System (CNS) coordinates and directs the speech act. The CNS functions like a computer. The more information you feed into a computer, the more precise and inclusive will be the information returned. The CNS acts in approximately the same manner. The more stimuli fed into it, the more precise and inclusive will be its control over the nerve stimulation and muscle action involved in the speech act. The CNS reacts to visual, tactile, kinesthetic, and aural stimulation. This means that for maximum control and awareness of your use of voice, you must be able to (1) *see* what you are doing; (2) *feel* what you are doing by using touch; (3) *sense* what you are doing; and (4) *hear* what you are doing. Musicians and athletes depend on this kind of awareness and control.

As you practice the suggested voice exercises in this handbook, look at yourself in a mirror (visual) and note how the articulators are moving. Are they active? Is the lower jaw too rigid? Are the back teeth clenched? Using your hand, spread the thumb and middle finger to cover the lower jaw area. Feel (tactile) the muscular action of the jaws and the muscular action under the lower jaw bones. Is this area hypertense? Is it too lax?

Along with the visual and tactile approach, become aware of the kinesthetic (muscle) sensations you experience as you practice. As you feel the muscular action tactually, close your eyes and try to perceive that muscular action. Can you recognize *how it feels?*

Now you are ready to encourage the aural (hearing) sense. Try the following suggestions to help you check on *how well you hear your own voice*:

1. How does your voice sound to you? (a) Do you like the sound? If you like the sound, why do you like it? If not, why not? (b) Does the sound project the image you want? e.g., do you sound much younger? Do you sound harsh, brash or without feeling? Do you think you sound warm and accepting? (c) If you were interviewing this "voice" for a job, would you hire this "voice?"
2. Record your voice. Give your name, the date and the time of day. Read aloud with meaning a paragraph which you have rehearsed. Then, say aloud some sentences or phrases you might use in daily conversation, while on the telephone with friends, or at your office or school. Repeat these sentences, deliberately showing feelings of anger, pleasure or surprise. Play back the recording and evaluate your use of voice. What accounts for the differences? Was it the words you used, or the way you said the words, or a combination of both?

Auditory discrimination will develop in a very specific way. In the initial stage, you will hear differences to only a small degree. This can be discouraging, but be persistent in your efforts. In this initial stage you will become sensitive to the voices and speech of *other* people—your friends, classmates, parents—to anyone but yourself! Your *hearing awareness* will become so sharp that the sound of your favorite disc jockey or TV personality will annoy you. "How can he make so much money? **That voice! That speech!** The second stage of development will be related to you, directly. You will begin to hear yourself *after* you have produced the poor voice or incorrect articulation. This is the most frustrating stage of all because the sound is out, it was wrong, and there's no going back. The third stage is the gratifying stage. As a result of persistent, concentrated practice, you will *initiate* the production and placement correctly and sustain the "new." **You are now on the way to permanent change(s)!**

Practice Sessions

Voice and articulation improvement involves retraining muscle action, but you must not force this action. Rather, you must firmly *encourage* the desired muscular response. This kind of practice should not be continued for any long span of time. Muscles used in a new or different manner tend to get tired, and long periods of practice can cause varied reactions. One of these reactions is related to aural fatigue. When you undertake your new improvement program, your aural feedback will be unreliable. As you practice you will be able to detect some changes in the quality of your voice or speech, but the ability to discriminate will be short-lived.

As you attempt a new skill, aurally and kinesthetically, you will be aware of differences. If the muscles tire and revert back to their old pattern of movement (tired muscles tend to do exactly this), you probably won't notice that the voice or speech produced has your ''old'' quality. Short periods of practice help to avoid this danger. In the beginning, work about five minutes at a time, but plan on frequent periods of practice. Short, but repeated, periods of work are highly beneficial. Two minutes out of every waking hour is ideal. Plan on *daily* practice; skipping days between sessions only retards your progress. Also, be inventive about your time to practice. Do not rely on an allotted ''hour'' for improvement skills, because this time seldom materializes. Rather, make use of odd periods during the day. You will never *find* time to practice; you must *make* it. Practice in your car while driving to work or driving to school; practice as you walk across campus; practice as you dress in the morning or before you retire (if you are not too fatigued). It is better to plan for a specific time to try a new skill, but the reinforcing of that skill can be done during odd periods of the day.

A word about so-called *negative* practice. Periodically in the exercise, you will be asked to practice the *wrong way*—negative practice. **What???** No, we haven't lost touch with reality! Synonyms for the word negative are opposing, contrary, not acceptable. We will ask you to practice the *wrong* way deliberately as a means of highlighting the correct way. If you can do the exercise incorrectly and then immediately manipulate the skills and do the exercise correctly—**you've got it! Trust us!**

Whatever your approach, it is important for you to *progress*. Do not allow irregular practice periods to be responsible for spasmodic progress. Relearning and retraining can be the beginning of boredom and dissatisfaction.

Skill Stimulators

1. *Visual stimulation*
   Practice before a mirror. Watch yourself. What do you **see**? Adjust the skills according to what you **see**!

Practice all skills correctly and don't forget **negative practice**!

2. *Tactile stimulation*
   Touch! As you practice, put your hand on your diaphragm, throat,

jaws or wherever the place of concentration. How does it *feel*? Do you *feel* a difference as you manipulate the skills?

3. *Kinesthctic stimulation*
   Close your eyes! Using tactile stimulation (see No. 2 above), try to evaluate the learning and change taking place *in your mind*. What is your perception of what is taking place?

Be assured that if you follow these instructions regarding your practice sessions, you *will* improve.

Let's take a final look at some Do's and Don'ts regarding your practice sessions.

Don't practice:

1. when you are tired.
2. if you are ill.
3. while you are upset, "hyper," or feel distracted.

Do practice:

1. for short, frequent periods of time.
2. using visual, tactile and kinesthetic stimuli.
3. with your tape recorder (see p. 413).

We have stressed before that this is a "how to" handbook. Therefore, we ask you to follow very specific directions in your improvement program. **All**, we repeat, **all** of the exercises recommended in the following chapters are to be practiced in **three** different body positions—*standing, sitting, walking*. You are to do each exercise **three** times in **three** different positions. These tested directives are crucial to the accomplishment of your final goal(s).

Is this really necessary? Yes! Follow our rationale. You stand, sit or walk during most of your waking hours. Periodically there might be the urge to crash on the couch. Since you use your body in different positions all day, it makes little sense to practice in only one position. You're going to have to apply and to transfer the techniques to all body positions eventually. Why not at the start? Trust us! It works!

In the following chapters you will be taught the necessary facts and skills for voice improvement in this order:

1. Achievement of basic skills
   a. Relaxation techniques
   b. Body involvement and control
   c. Efficient breathing (respiration)
   d. Vocal cord vibration (phonation)
   e. Amplification/modification of the breath stream (resonance)
2. Application of basic skills to:
   a. Quality of voice
   b. Volume
   c. Pitch

d. Rate

3. Development of refined vocal skills
4. Transference of refined vocal skills to everyday speech.

We want you to be aware that this section of the handbook on Voice Improvement has its limitations. The information, instructions and exercises are directed toward the correction and improvement of *functional* voice problems (problems related to the voice production). The text is not necessarily meant for the Speech Pathologist who periodically is involved with *organic* voice disorders (problems caused by physical disorders).

Let's begin!

References

Aristotle, *Rhetoric*. Translated by Lane Cooper (New York: Appleton-Century-Crofts, 1932) 3.1, 1404a, p. 37

Moses, Paul J. M.D. *The Voice of Neurosis* (New York: Grune and Stratton, Inc., 1954) p. 1.

Barbara, Dominic, *Your Speech Reveals Your Personality* (New York: Charles C. Thomas, 1957), p. 40.

21

Body Readiness

"Stand up straight!"

"Why do you slouch all the time?"

We can hear the groans? These reprimands have followed most of us throughout a good part of our lives. Someone in your family or perhaps a teacher has probably attempted to change the way you hold and use your body. Think back—did you resent this "intrusion" on your body? Your reaction may have been one of anger or outright defiance! Sorry! We are going to have to "intrude" if we are to help you achieve a better body for a better voice.

Your Body Affects Your Voice

Have you ever thought about how you look to others when you walk, sit or stand? How do *you* feel about your body? What image do you have of yourself? The same responses can be heard around the world! "I know I have terrible posture." "All my life I've been told not to slump; to stand up straight." Sound familiar? These are just a few samples of the remarks most of us have heard sometime in our lives. Fortunately, today's world promotes awareness of our bodies. "America the Beautiful" currently centers on weight reduction, body building, corrective plastic surgery, energizing activities—all in the interest of better health and the image we project. Why do we talk about this in a section on voice improvement?

Your body is directly involved with your voice. Yes, you read correctly! Stated more specifically—the way you *use* and *control* your body is directly related to:

1. The quality (sound) of your voice.
2. The physical production of your voice.
3. The skills you apply when you use your voice efficiently.
4. The skills you manipulate to convey your vocal message with meaning, feeling, and with the image you want to project.

How can we improve our posture? Can it really affect our voice? There are some answers in a system of movement called the Alexander technique.

The Alexander Technique

This technique was the brainchild of F. Matthias Alexander a 19th century actor and reciter of Shakespeare's work. In his career on the stage, Alexander began to develop severe hoarseness and eventual loss of his voice. Unable to receive help from doctors or vocal coaches, he began to study himself for flaws in his own voice production. Much to his surprise, he discovered that the problem seemed to stem from how he was using his own body. Every time he began to speak Alexander noticed that his neck stiffened and tightened about his shoulders. He concluded that something about this movement was causing his voice distress.

Check Yourself

Do you feel as if your head is scrunched down into your shoulders? Do your neck and/or shoulder muscles ache frequently? Look at yourself in a mirror. Does your posture look ''at ease'' and open? Mentally note those areas that you feel are tight.

Today's world can be demanding, fast-paced, impersonal, taxing and fatiguing. People react to these ''vibrations'' with varying kinds of behavior. When pressures become too great, many people become ''hyper,'' anxious and overtense. Others withdraw and cease, or refuse, to function. No matter what the symptoms are, what matters is that these forms of behavior are anxiety-based. Hypertension may become a way of life, a habitual experience. Usually a personal price is paid physically, physiologically, and/or psychologically. The price paid can be in the form of a heart attack, an ulcer, migraine headaches, back pains or—a voice problem. Your body is physically reacting to stress. Why the voice reaction? An ''Achilles' Heel'' refers to a person's weak spot, whether physical or psychological. When a part of the body breaks down, that particular weakness can be interpreted as a signal for help.

Alexander's Solution

Alexander discovered that his habitual pattern of movement involved a restriction of his vocal mechanism. His tendencies to pull down at the back of the neck, to lock the shoulder muscles, and to lift the chin and chest left him gasping for breath. Try this simple posture check. With chin held high, chest and shoulder rigid and abdomen tight, try breathing deeply. Can you? Of course not!

Many of us consider military posture (see Fig. 1a) to be the model for good posture. After all, didn't Aunt Suzy tell you to throw your

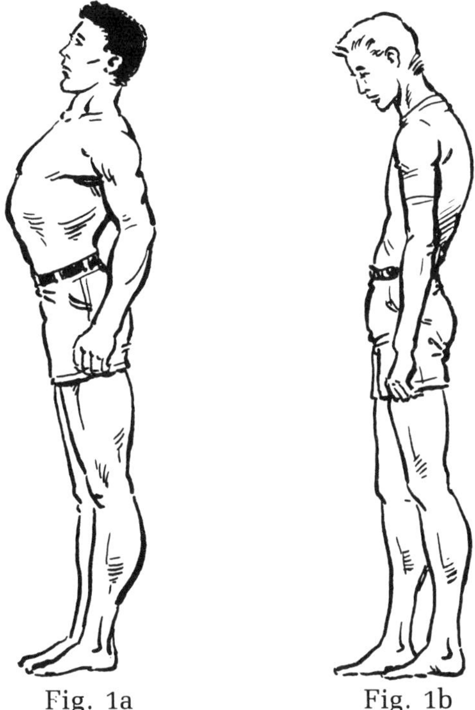

Fig. 1a Fig. 1b

shoulders back, pull your stomach in, and, for heaven's sake, to lift up your head? Didn't you do that for about three minutes and then return to a good slouch, either after Auntie left the room, or because it hurt too much to keep up? Since this posture is harmful for the body, let's find a better way.

The Slouch vs. the Ouch

For many people, the opposite of the military "ouch" is the "slouch" (see Fig. 1b). Seemingly it feels more comfortable to collapse, sag and hunch over—particularly when you are experiencing tension in your shoulders or upper back. Is the slouch position related to the problems Alexander discovered in himself? How does either posture interfere with your production of a good voice?

The Military Posture vs. Slouch Potato Look

You're in the Army now if you:

hold in your abdomen, chest out, and chin up
throw the shoulders back
tighten everything
lock the knees (jammed back)

You're a slouch potato if you:

bow your head
slump your shoulders
collapse your chest
round your back

Do these two posture stereotypes appear to be direct opposites? Not necessarily. Because they are stereotypes, you may not demonstrate all of the positions of the military posture or all of the positions of the slouch. Rather, you may use parts of each. It is not uncommon to have tight shoulders and a bowed head. You may have locked knees and a collapsed chest.

Check Yourself Standing

Stand in a normal comfortable position for you. What do you see? What do you feel? Compare your body alignments to the above two stereotypes. Which one is familiar? Try to mimic each of the points above. How comfortably can you breathe?

Whether you are excessively holding your chest up, letting your head and neck slump or doing any of the above ''don'ts'' of body use, you will find that these postures **restrict** vocal production because:

1. You can't breathe efficiently
2. The larynx is depressed
3. Vocal quality is affected

Voice is produced in the larynx. How you control and use your body dramatically affects the functioning of your larynx. This is the concrete reason we **must** help you to use your body efficiently and effectively. We repeat, we have found that students learn faster if they know the rationale (the why) behind our instructions.

Check Yourself Sitting

For your next exercise, use the ideas learned so far to explore how you sit. Our analysis will be very similar to examining standing posture habits.

Do you:

slump at your desk?
fool aching shoulders and neck muscles?
slouch into the couch?
take superficial breaths?
have to cross your arms, legs, or feet to feel comfortable?

Remember, the first rule of this journey into more productive body use is to observe without negative self-criticism. Use these initial exercises to discover where you are. Only then can you choose to make corrections.

Alexander Applied

When Alexander noticed his habitual tensing of the neck muscles, he learned to re-educate these patterns. As a result of many years of experimentation, not only did his difficulty with vocal hoarseness disappear, but his ability to project was so remarkable that he began to teach what he had realized. Several of the basic principles of his work are important to vocal training. For a complete experience of the Alexander technique, we highly recommend seeing a qualified teacher. A professionally trained practitioner uses gentle hand manipulations to physically guide you. For the time being, however, even attempting the following basic practical suggestions will help enormously. Don't forget that you will be applying what you learn to the three positions: standing, sitting and walking. Comfortable work clothes are an asset here. Ready?

Stand with your feet approximately a hips width apart and parallel.
Rock back and forth, toes to heels until you feel centered and balanced on both feet.
Unlock—gently release the knees (neither jammed back nor very bent)
Now you are grounded.

Classic Alexander Directives

Let the whole head move up and let the whole body follow!!

Let the Whole Head Move Up

1. Imagine a string attached to the top of your head.
2. Let your head float upwards.
3. Do not jut your chin.
4. Relax the back of your neck; do not tense up.
5. Look straight ahead.

Let the Whole Body Follow

1. Gently lengthen your spine.
2. Do not overextend your chest.
3. Do not curve the lower back.
4. Keep your arms, hands and shoulders relaxed.
5. Try to align your ears over your shoulders, hips, knees and ankles.
6. Don't sink into your hips, keep your knees unlocked.
7. Turn your head from side to side as you take a breath. Exhale.
8. Your body is now "open"—not tensed or slouched.

Check Yourself

Use a mirror for visual feedback. The mirror will tell you if your:

1. *feet* are not parallel.
2. *knees* are locked (to retrain your leg muscles will take time)
3. *shoulders* are tense.
4. *head* is tilted.
5. *chin* is raised or lowered too far.
6. *hands* are clenched.

We urge you to be patient with yourself. It helps to remember that *habitual is not always natural or normal*. Habits are learned! Finally, don't strain. The Alexander method is more about a direction of movement of the body, as opposed to a rigid position. Think more of *easing up*, rather than being straight. In time, this technique will help you experience increased energy and well being.

Sitting Positions

In a favorite chair, assume a familiar and/or habitual sitting position. Think about how this position *feels*. If you were to remain in this position for a lengthy period, would you remain comfortable? If not, why not? What part(s) of your body might begin to ache or feel cramped?

Do you have different sitting positions in various settings? Do you sit differently at school than at parties or at work? How does the kind of chair affect your sitting position?

In these initial exercises, try to get some sense of how you typically like to position yourself in a chair. **Remember to observe, not judge.**

1. Basic Sitting Position

If you use a hard back chair, the following suggestions will help you. Sit in the chair and place your feet flat on the floor. Apply the classic Alexander directives. Let the whole head and torso of your body move upward. See p. 421 for specific skills.

Can you lean back in the chair and still not destroy your attempts to minimize tension, aches and pain? Of course you can! You can use the back of your chair for support, and even cross your arms and legs.

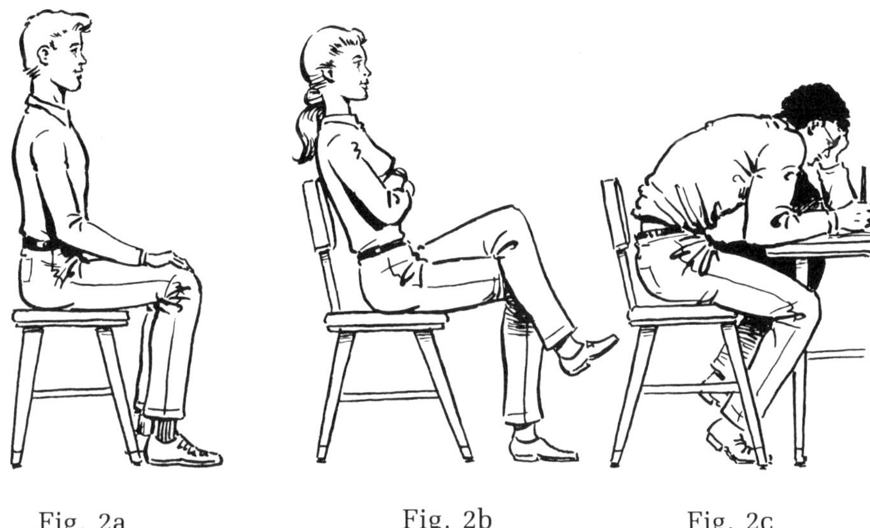

Fig. 2a Fig. 2b Fig. 2c

Warning—**Don't** raise your shoulders or duck your head forward. As long as you keep the chest, neck and shoulders open and unrestricted, you will be able to produce good vocal quality (see Fig. 2b).

2. Sitting at a desk

Observe your typical posture while reading or writing at a desk. Most of you place your elbows on the desk and let the shoulders hunch up. Ouch! We bet that you can't keep that up for long without some twinges. The key factor to being comfortable while sitting at a desk is the *position of the chair* and the *proper use of your hip joints*. Most of you pull the chair in close, lean on your arms, duck your head and round your back (see Fig. 2c).

Try this:

1. put your chair at an appropriate distance from the desk (experiment).
2. place your feet on the floor.
3. review the *basic sitting* techniques. see p. 422.
4. bend at the hips and let this movement bring you toward your desk.
5. keep your head and neck free. Note: letting the bend come from the hip joints protects the back and allows the chest and throat areas freedom.
6. place your arms wherever necessary, don't hunch the shoulders, and proceed with your activity.

Important!!

The Alexander method is not meant to create a frozen upward sitting position. By using the hip joints to bring the upper body comfortably and conveniently close to your reading or writing position, you can minimize (even eliminate) back and eye strain. These directives will also work for you when eating at the table.

Walking

Slowly walk across the room. Change the tempo to a fast walk. How would you characterize your particular walk? Do you slink? Shuffle? Sway? Do you have a "macho" walk? Do you hold your nose high? Do you sink into your hips?

Because we frequently talk as we walk, it is essential to apply the principles of good body mechanics to walking.

Let's review and advance.

1. *Align* your body.
2. *Maintain* an upward movement of your body as you walk forward.
3. *Move* your gaze about; avoid looking down at the ground.
4. *Relax* your shoulders; swing your arms gently.
5. *Walk* with your feet parallel.

Your style of walking is an intensely personal expression of self. You have often read in this handbook, "your voice is you"; "your speech is you;" now—"your walk is you." We also predicted that in the process of change, a little of "you" would have to change. This change is necessary if you are going to achieve your best voice.

Fig. 3a

Fig. 3b

It's difficult at first to alter the way you walk. You recall—"habitual is not necessarily natural or normal." Some aspects of the "cool" walk may need to be adjusted (see Fig. 3a). A groovy slouch cannot supply adequate muscles tonus to support a well projected voice. The student racing down the hall with an armload of books, nose to the ground and shoulders pulled up around the ears, could be creating vocal problems (see Fig. 3b). Obviously you, too, may have to unlearn a few of your walking habits for better body readiness.

Check Yourself

Become aware of the action of your feet as your weight shifts from heel to toe and the knee lifts and bends with each step. Walking with your feet parallel may seem uncomfortable at first. It is, however, anatomically correct and movement efficient. It is helpful to remind yourself that the upward release of the body must include the head, neck, back and *hips*. Its interesting to note our tendency to pull down, tighten up and restrict our physical movement when actually we want to move forward!

Sitting to Standing to Walking

Try these movements as you use differently styled chairs (folding chair, kitchen stool, plush couch).

From a sitting position—stand.
From a standing position—sit.

Did you apply the new movement patterns learned so far or did you regress back to your old ways? Did you push yourself out of the chair by placing your hands on your thighs or on the arms of the chairs? Did you lift your chin high and tighten your shoulders as you got up or down?

The solution to this movement problem? Use the legs and hip joints more, the arms and shoulders less. What do we mean? Follow these steps:

1. Sit in a chair. Review all basic Alexander technique directives (see pp. 422-423).
2. Place your feet comfortably apart.
3. Bend at the hips leaning forward.
4. Using the legs for power, not the arms, come up to a standing position.
5. Keep your shoulders and neck free of tension during this process.
6. Use your hands for *balance* as you stand up, by placing them on your thighs or the arms of your chair.

Most of us use excess energy when standing up or sitting down. Be careful not to lift your chin up nor to tense with the muscles at the back of the neck while moving. To sit down from a standing position, review the basic techniques in your mind. Then, once again, bend at the hips, keeping the head and neck free and aligned with the back as you sit. Practicing quality body readiness and movement will help make these new habits a daily reality.

Why are we being so exact, so demanding? You're probably thinking, "I've been moving since birth. Why hasn't anyone pointed out these details before?" The sad truth is inefficient movement habits are quite common. We tend to ignore them until the voice, the back, or the shoulders begin to protest. You cannot have good vocal quality without the help of proper body alignment and adequate muscle tonus. **Your body must support your voice!**

A Review

Do:

Observe To progress, you must first analyze your needs.

Think Words like gentle, ease up, and release should be in your vocabulary as opposed to be straight, stand tall.

Apply Align your ears with your shoulders, hips, knees and ankles as much as possible.

Experience Visually, tactually and kinesthetically be aware of expansion both in your chest and across your back.

Use Negative practice is helpful. Take a break from good posture. Deliberately slump, change positions.

Don't:

Hold a position. Think direction and quality of movement.

Pull your chin up throw your shoulders back or lock your gaze.

Tighten your neck muscles.

Slouch or sink into your hips when walking.

Lean on your desk with your shoulders up and your back hunched over.

Clench your fists or hold your elbows in tightly.

Relaxation

Do you have a feeling of being "in over your head?" Do you feel under stress or hyperactive? At such times, have you been told to "relax"? The implication of this useless advice is that hypertension can be turned on and off like a faucet! The truth is, relaxation must be learned. It must be *experienced*!

Up to this point you have been taught about body posture. You have been made aware of various body positions which profit from minimized muscle tension. Now we will take you into the wonderful world of **relaxation**.

Relaxation Exercises

The Passive Stretch

Stand upright with feet comfortably apart. Slowly, drop the head forward and continue to bend until you are leaning over rag-doll fashion. Your arms should be very relaxed and your head should feel heavy.

Make sure that your knees are slightly bent to protect the lower back. Do not reach for the floor with your fingertips. Hang forward only to the extent that there is no strain. Imagine yourself to be as loose as a child's favorite Raggedy Ann or Andy doll.

Hang loose for a minute or so and then slowly begin to straighten into a standing position. Have the feeing that you are "rolling" back up. Keep these points in mind:

1. Your head and arms should be as limp as possible throughout the entire exercise.
2. Do not raise your head until the very end.
3. Avoid tensing the shoulders and neck.
4. Give yourself a gentle reminder to "let go." Periodically shake out your arms and head a bit.
5. Enjoy the relaxing sensation.

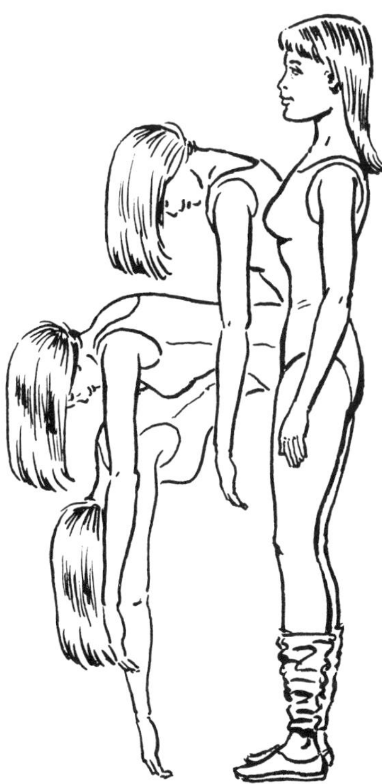

Fig. 4

Take a minute to breathe and to congratulate yourself on your new found ability to let go of muscular tension.

If you teach this exercise to a friend you can check each other's progress in the following manner. When hanging forward in the initial position, let your friend test your tension level by a slight shaking of each arm. If you're on target in this exercise, there will be no resistance to your partner's touch. You can apply this procedure to the head as well, being sure to apply only minor pressure in your push. Taking time to learn and to master this passive stretch will help insure productive movement patterns. Good work!

Check yourself:

Is it easier to feel aligned in the upright position now that you've experienced this exercise? Are there still areas of your body that tighten up unnecessarily? This is called chronic tension as opposed to appropriate muscle tones.

Full Body Relaxation

Yes, you've earned it. Find a comfortable and private place. Tell yourself this is a time for you. It's impossible to "give unto others" if you haven't given to yourself. Put on peaceful music, if you'd like. Set aside the concerns of your day. Since this exercise can take a half hour, have a blanket near you in case of chill. Remember, this is an exercise in **conscious relaxation**

1. Lay on a mat or bed.
2. Roll your head lazily in a side-to-side movement a few times.
3. Tense all the facial muscles: wrinkle your forehead, pucker lips, cheeks, etc. Relax and let go. Create a few "horror" faces until all the muscles have had a workout. Then, be still.
4. Bring the shoulders up to the ears and then release. Repeat.
5. Tense your right fist, lower and upper arm as tightly as you can. Release. Repeat with the left arm and hand.
6. Tense your right foot, lower and upper leg and hip. Remember to really tighten that leg and then, experience the sensation when you stop. Repeat with the left leg.
7. Lift the right arm and then the left arm a few inches off your bed. Let each flop back down.
8. Lift and drop each leg, one at a time, and notice how different the movements of lifting and letting go are.
9. Settle back and adjust your body if you need to be comfortable. Can you feel the change in your body from when you started?
10. Allow your mind to float off to a pleasant environment.
11. Permit yourself to relax deeper still. Feel each breath bringing you greater peace and contentment.

Do not throw off the cover and spring into action. Instead we suggest:

1. Gently open your eyes, moving your hands and feet a bit.
2. Roll over onto your side, resting your head on one outstretched arm, the other hand placed in front of your chest on the mat.
3. Bending your knees slightly towards the chest, pause for a few moments in a fetal position.
4. Raise yourself to a sitting position using your hands and arms and keeping the neck muscles loose. Lift your head. Do you feel refreshed?

Sit Yourself Down

The previous exercise, Full Body Relaxation, can be done in a seated position. Find a favorite chair and take yourself through the entire procedure. It works.

If you have only a few minutes for relaxation, *abbreviate each stage.* This also works!

Negative Practice

For a full explanation of this type of reinforcement exercise for skill mastery, see p. 414. The following negative practice exercises are to be applied to the material in this chapter.

Standing:

1. Stiffen everything.
2. Slump. Really cave your chest in and lower your head.

How does it feel?

Sitting:

1. Try sitting very tall in a straight back chair.
2. Slump, crossing your arms and legs.

How does this feel?

Walking:

1. Lifting the chin and tensing your arms and shoulders, walk cross the room.
2. Sinking into your hips, stare at the floor and walk.

In all these exercises, it is most important to feel the extremes of tension and release. Find a posture in between these two extremes where you feel adequate muscular support without the slump or stiffness. Don't, however, try to hold one ''correct'' position.

Concluding Suggestions

Don't be confused into thinking that proper posture requires you to be able to balance a book on your head. You can always lean back in a chair, stand more on one leg, or have your elbows on the table—**if** you follow the essentials.

Keep the chest comfortably open and shoulders down. Let the head move up a bit so the neck isn't compressed. If you want to balance more on one leg than the other, don't sink into your hips. Allow yourself to be your actual height and width. That's all! Enjoy.

Information

American Guild of Teachers of the Alexander Technique
931 Elizabeth St.
San Francisco, CA 94114
(415) 282-8967

Available at bookstores:

Folon, Lilias — "Rest, Relax, and Sleep" (audio cassette)

Miller, Emmett, M.D. — "Ten Minute Stress Manager." (audio cassette)

"Rainbow Butterfly." (audio cassette)

Carmelita Tillotson
Co-Director Chrysalis Center for Well Being
Wilmington, Delaware 19808

22

Production Processes

Is your body now ready to function efficiently? Are you sure that you can use and control your body with confidence? Will it do what *you* want it to do? Do you still feel awkward when you try to follow the suggestions from Chapter 21? Perhaps the five "W's" from the field of journalism might help you to understand the processes involved with learning and change. All of the following must take place if you are going to improve your voice or speech.

Who: You, the student
What: Your voice or speech improvement
Why: Innervation process
Where: Phonation process
When: Respiration/Resonance/Articulation/Audition processes.

You are going to be asked to create *change* consciously. This is going to require a willingness to pay attention to *process* rather than to product. You are not going to *take on* skills, rather you will be made aware of *total body functioning*.

The Innervation Process

Speech is body actions made audible and these actions don't just happen! Our bodies act as we tell them to act. There is a complicated system of message sending and message receiving inside our bodies. We call this inside-the-body communication *intrapersonal* communication. The brain sends messages to parts of our bodies, ordering those parts into action. It receives messages about the progress of that action. Part of that incoming information comes from inside your body and part of it comes from the world outside your skin.

Innervation is the name given to the process of stimulating activity in the body by the nerves. *Innervate* (coming from *in* + *nerve* + *ate*) is the verb meaning "to stimulate activity by nerves"; innervator is the noun. The innervators are the nervous systems that do the stimulating (intrapersonal message carrying) inside our bodies.

The Central Nervous System (CNS) is specifically involved in the speech act. Its role is one of direction and coordination. The laryngeal branch of the tenth cranial nerve (vagus nerve) is the specific innervator of the vocal process. The human nervous system can be divided into the Peripheral and the Central Nervous Systems. The PNS is both sensory and motor, depending on its specific function at the time. The sensory neurons of the PNS are concerned with the transmission of impulses initiated by an *external* stimulus that can be either visual, tactile, or auditory—or all three combined. The motor fibers of the PNS are responsible for getting nerve impulses to areas of the body where they stimulate muscle action. The CNS directs and coordinates all of this activity.

Now, what does all of this have to do with your voice improvement program? Let us zero in on a change of muscle action as it is related to voice production. You see Jim coming toward you (visual stimulation) with outstretched hand (tactile stimulation) and he says, "How are you?" (auditory stimulation). The PNS and CNS coordinate to decode, interpret, and formulate your reply. Monitored nerve to muscle stimulation results in the reply, "I'm fine." Your reply becomes auditory feedback (stimulus) to your PNS and the process starts all over again.

Skill Stimulators!

1. *Visual* stimulation.
   Practice before a mirror. Watch yourself. What do you **see**? Manipulate the skills according to what you **see**! Practice all skills correctly and don't forget **negative practice**.
2. *Tactile* stimulation.
   Touch! Put your hand on the part of your body you want to **move**! How does the movement *feel*? Can you **feel** a difference?
3. *Kinesthetic* stimulation.
   Close your eyes as you practice! Using tactile stimulation (see No. 2), try to evaluate the learning and/or change taking place *in your mind*! What is your perception(s) of what is taking place?

The Phonation Process

Your voice is initially produced in the larynx, which is commonly called the voice box. Its anatomy and physiology are determined by heredity and environment. For example, your skeletal frame can include a smaller or a larger-than-average-sized larynx. Also, the length of the vocal cords can vary, measuring anywhere from seven-eighths of an inch to one and one-fourth inches in length. Notably, the female vocal cords are shorter in length, thus accounting for the generally higher pitch of the female voice. The larynx, about the size of a walnut, rests on top of the trachea (windpipe) and is made up of nine cartilages bound together by ligaments and membranous tissue. There is one bone in the larynx, the hyoid bone from which the larynx is suspended. The bone is to the larynx what the basketball hoop is to the net extending from it. The hyoid bone is at the top of the larynx and from this bone extends the cartilaginous framework.

It is relatively unimportant for you to know the names and location of all of the parts of the larynx. We will discuss those parts of the larynx that have a direct bearing on your manipulation of this organ. You should become acquainted with the following parts of the larynx.

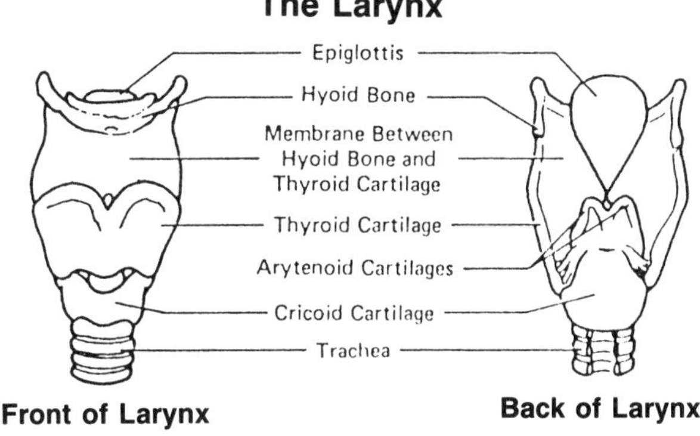

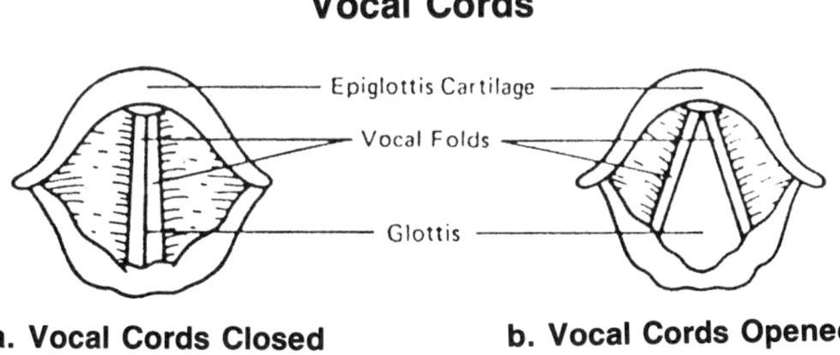

Figure 22.1. *Front and rear views of the principal cartilages of the larynx and diagrammatic representation of the vocal cords showing attachments to cartilages of the larynx.*

1. Hyoid bone: the larynx is suspended from this bone.
2. Thyroid cartilage: forms the shape of the larynx; the vocal cords are attached to the center of the front, inside wall of this cartilage.

3. Cricoid cartilage: forms the last section of the larynx, directly attached to the trachea (windpipe).
4. Arytenoid cartilages: a pair of pyramid-shaped cartilages to which the vocal cords are attached at the rear of the larynx.
5. Vocal cords: a vibrating body that produces basic laryngeal tone as breath passes between them.
6. Glottis: the opening between the vocal cords.

The vocal cords are housed within the larynx and are attached at its front just under the notch of the thyroid cartilage, the larger of the two cartilages. The cords stretch across the larynx and are attached at the rear to two small pyramid-shaped cartilages, the arytenoids. The opening between the cords is called the glottis, through which passes the exhaled breath stream as it comes from the trachea. The vocal cords open and close with a rhythmic motion that is the result of two forces: Innervation (nerve stimulation) by the laryngeal nerve and air pressure.

The vibration of the cords gives your voice its fundamental vocal tone, or basic laryngeal tone. This laryngeal tone is influenced by the physical structure of your larynx and is established by two actions: the vibration of the outgoing breath stream and the amount of tension within the muscles of the larynx and within the vocal cords themselves.

The main biological functions of the larynx are to prevent food from entering the trachea (windpipe) and to protect the lungs. The vocal cords also act as a valve during any form of physical exertion by controlling the air as it is being released from the lungs. To review, the organ of voice production is the larynx and the vocal cords are the vibrator.

Phonation Alerts!

1. Be aware that when you are *breathing for life* (not speaking), the vocal cords are slightly abducted (open) at the midline to allow the breath to escape from the trachea.
2. During a *gasp or quick intake* of breath, the cords are held wide apart.
3. On a *whisper*, the vocal cords are closed at the anterior (front) portion and held apart at the posterior (rear) portion. *This is a strained position.* **Do not whisper!** If you are suffering from a cold or from any other physical discomfort, speak softly so that the cords can vibrate evenly at the midline. This is their normal position for speech. See photographs of the vocal cords in action, Fig. 22.2.

The phonation process is under your direct control to a certain degree. You can learn to increase or decrease muscle tension in the laryngeal-pharyngeal areas. You can also learn to manipulate the closing (adduction) of the vocal cords to achieve a harder attack or a softer attack. What makes all of these skills so difficult for you to master is the fact that you cannot see what is happening *inside* of the larynx. Nor can your teacher or speech therapist point to a particular muscle in the laryngeal area and say, "Move *that* muscle." A case in point is the

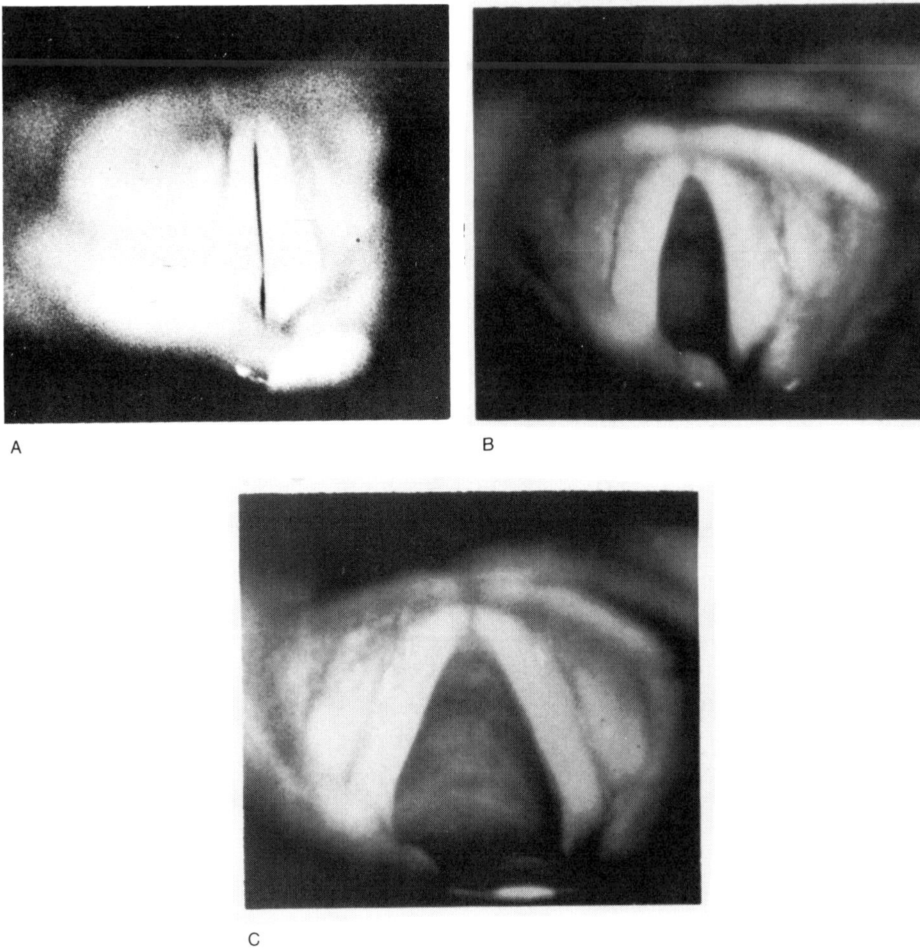

Figure 22.1 *Position of vocal folds (a) during phonation; (b) during whispering; and (c) during a quick intake of breath.* (Courtesy of Bell Laboratories.)

difficulty often experienced by students who have developed vocal pathology (nodules, polyps) on the vocal cords. Growths cannot be seen, but the otolaryngologist says that they are there. Practice periods to alleviate something that cannot be seen can be very upsetting. If vocal pathology developed on the *outside* of the throat where it could be *seen*, much time and anguish could be saved!

The vibratory process demands refined muscle control if you want to use your voice effectively. Refined muscular control is essential in maintaining adequate muscle tonus in the pharyngeal-laryngeal areas. In your voice improvement program, if you are going to make the most of the vibratory process, you must acquire:

1. Over-all body relaxation.
2. Relaxation of the specific muscles in the pharyngeal and laryngeal areas.
3. Adequate muscle tonus in the pharyngeal and laryngeal areas during phonation.
4. Central breathing and control of exhalation.
5. Controlled breath emission.
6. Effective abduction and adduction of the vocal cords during phonation.

We will not describe exercises for the control of refined muscle action of the phonatory process at this time. Rather, the various exercises and techniques will be found in following sections where they will be applied to the specific voice problems under consideration.

The Respiration Process

Just as you must have breath to live, you must have breath to speak. The process of respiration has two phases—inhalation and exhalation. On inhalation you take in air (oxygen), and on exhalation you expel the air (carbon dioxide). Let's take a look at the ways breathing for life and breathing for speech are alike and how they are different.

Breathing for life:

1. You breathe for your very existence.
2. The phases of inhalation and exhalation are about equal in length (the amount of air taken in by the lungs is about equal to the amount of air expelled when you exhale).
3. The phase of inhalation for life is an active phase whereas the phase of exhalation is a passive phase.
4. The entire process is *involuntary* and controlled by the brain stem.
5. Respiration for life is *smooth flowing*. The smooth flow of air is interrupted only when you are engaged in a physical activity or by emotions such as anger, fear, or joy.

Breathing for speech:

1. You need breath to produce voice and speech.
2. The phases of inhalation and exhalation are **not** equal in length (the phase of exhalation can be extended for as long as you wish).
3. The two phases are both active phases.
4. The entire process is *voluntary*.

5. Respiration for speech is not smooth flowing.

Let's explore breathing for speech a little more. We told you that the control is *voluntary* (the cerebrum or cerebral cortex is the control center). The phases of inhalation and exhalation are *not equal in length*, but vary according to the physical and/or semantic demands of the speaker. We speak in phrases (thought groups), and we must inhale between these phrases. Running out of breath forces you to stop and take another breath which can interrupt the thought groups. This interruption, no matter how small, can affect communication. You can control the process to eliminate confusion.

Breathing for Voice Production

Because breath vibrated in the larynx is the basis for voice production, ineffective breathing habits, or inadequate breath control, can be partially responsible for almost all voice quality defects. It is important in your voice improvement program to check very carefully for efficient respiration. There are various types of breathing patterns: the clavicular, the thoracic and the thoracic-abdominal (or central breathing). We believe that the thoracic-abdominal is best suited to speech needs.

The torso of the body is divided into two cavities:

1. the thoracic (chest) cavity which extends from the clavicles to the waistline.
2. the abdominal cavity which extends from the waist to the pelvic area.

These two cavities are separated at the midriff by the diaphragm, a dome-shaped muscle attached to the edges of the lower ribs. In a relaxed position it looks like an open umbrella, opening upward toward the thoracic area and forming the floor of this cavity. The thorax, or chest, is composed of the rib cage, which is made up of the sternum (breastbone), twelve pairs of ribs and the spinal column. The lungs are housed in the chest cavity. All of the ribs are attached to the backbone, but the attachments in the front vary, forming a structure capable of considerable movement. The last two pairs of ribs are floating ribs, the next four pairs are attached to each other by cartilage, and the upper six pairs of ribs are joined to the sternum. The arrangement of the musculature makes possible three movements of the thoracic cavity that are important in inhalation:

1. a slight upward and forward movement.
2. a back to front expansion.
3. a side-to-side expansion.

An additional action is elongation of this cavity as a result of the downward movement of the diaphragm during the phase of inhalation.

In capsule form, this is what happens when we inhale (take a breath) and exhale (expel the air):

Inhalation

1. Air enters through the nose and mouth and then passes through the trachea (windpipe).
2. The air fills the lungs which are housed in the rib cage. **Note**: the lungs fill with air only in so far as the rib cage is expanded.
3. The diaphragm contracts (flattens) as the lungs are filled, making the chest cavity longer.
4. The flattening of the diaphragm causes the soft organs (viscera) of the body to be pushed downward and this causes a slight protrusion of the abdominal cavity. **The inhalation phase is completed!**

Exhalation

1. Immediately the opposite action begins.
2. The abdominal muscles contract (tighten), pushing the soft organs back into position.
3. The diaphragm assumes its domeshaped position (relaxed).
4. The rib cage returns to its relaxed position as the air is forced out of the lungs.
5. The air passes through the trachea and then passes between the vocal cords. **The exhalation phase is completed!**

Now you are ready to check your own breathing habits.

1. Lie on a flat surface (preferably the floor), place a light book or magazine on the diaphragm and *relax*. Do not think about your breathing pattern. Just close your eyes and do nothing. After a few minutes, take note of the gentle rising and falling motion of the book. Apply your knowledge of what you read here in the previous paragraphs. As you take a breath, the book will rise. As you exhale, the book will be lowered. Notice the related coordinated movements of the thoracic and abdominal cavities.

2. Now stand up. Check your posture. Be as relaxed as you were in the position on the floor. Keep in mind *body alignment*. (See pp. 421-422). Place your hands on your chest and breathe quietly. Does this cavity function with a rising and falling motion? It should do so. Now place your hands over the abdominal wall with light pressure of the fingertips on the broad bands of muscle that make up the front wall of the abdomen. Again, breathe quietly. Is there a protrusion of this area when you take a breath? Is there an inward motion on exhalation? If so, you are breathing efficiently.

3. From a standing position, with feet apart, drop from your waist

toward the floor. Hang loose! Practice diaphragmatic breathing. As you take a breath your body will tend to swing forward slightly upward. This position should help you to learn to breathe correctly. Exhale and repeat.

Control of the Respiration Process

In breathing for speech, central breathing is considered the most efficient because it uses the gross abdominal muscles in exhalation. These muscles are effective in controlling the outgoing air stream so that it can be emitted smoothly and evenly. This kind of breath emission is necessary for a firm, well produced voice. The breath must not be allowed to gush out. Neither must tension be allowed to develop in the thoracic cavity by pushing on the thoracic muscles in exhalation. More important, no hypertension must develop in the pharyngeal area in an effort to emit the breath. The breath must be controlled by a strong, steady push by the gross abdominal muscles. This results in what is known as *support of tone*. Specifically, this skill involves the *use of muscles of the abdominal cavity to exert a controlled muscular pressure in order to support a steady stream of breath between the vocal cords.* To further clarify the technique:

On inhalation: thoracic muscles tense, diaphragm tense, abdominal muscles relaxed.

On exhalation: abdominal muscles tense, diaphragm relaxed, thoracic muscles relaxed.

Try the following exercises to help you recognize the various types of muscular action that can take place on exhalation.

1. Place one hand on each side of the chest area, with your fingertips almost touching at the line of the sternum. Take a big breath and then gently push with your hands on the chest cavity as you exhale. Feel the muscular action in this area as the air is expelled from the lungs. You should feel a relaxation of these muscles.

2. Now place one hand on each side of the midriff, with your fingertips meeting at the front. (You are now directly over the diaphragm). Again, take a breath, but this time deliberately push in on the muscles in this area as you exhale. You are now using the diaphragm and the chest cavity on exhalation.

3. Effective central breathing demands even more muscular control than the preceding exercises. You are now ready to feel the action of the gross abdominal muscles in effective exhalation. Place one hand on each side of the abdominal cavity, fingertips almost touching. This is the area of the viscera, the soft organs of the body. You might recall from your reading in this chapter that on the phase of inhalation, the muscles in this area tend to extend out. So as you exhale, concentrate

on pushing in (tensing) the gross abdominal muscles. With this kind of muscular action, as the vocal cords vibrate, the breath will be released in a steady, firm stream. The end result should be a strong, firm, basic laryngeal tone.

When speaking, if the occasion demands a lot of breath for a lengthy sentence or a strong breath to express a vivid emotion, the extra breath need not come from inhalation but rather should be the result of *controlling breath on exhalation*. If you feel that you must take in more breath on inhalation, remember that it is not done by gasping with an *inward* movement or a *pulling in* of the abdominal cavity as you take the breath. A clavicular breather is often guilty of this kind of incorrect muscular action.

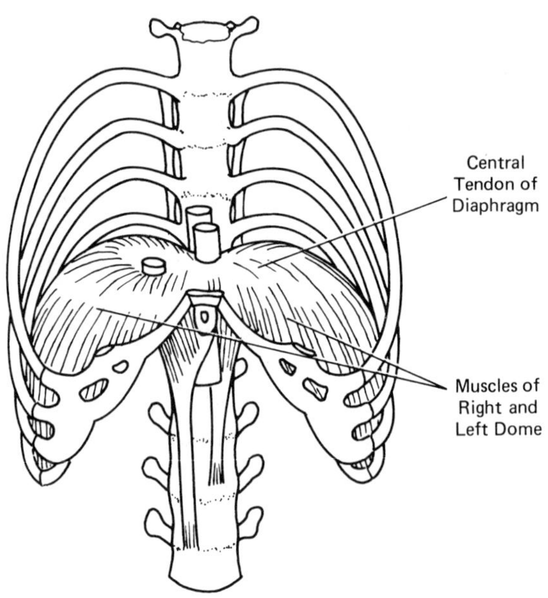

Figure 22.3 *Anterior view of the diaphragm.*

In clavicular breathing the clavicles (collarbones) are used to help raise the thoracic cavity on inhalation, so that instead of the *correct expansion* action outward there is a limited *lifting* action of this cavity. The result is unsatisfactory because the lungs can be only partially filled with air. Hypertension in the thoracic muscles limits the expansion of this cavity, thereby limiting the amount of air to be taken in.

More serious is the effect such breathing has on the larynx. In an effort to raise the thorax by using the clavicles, the extrinsic muscles of the larynx are strained. This results in hypertension of these muscles and the voice quality is directly affected. Usually the quality is *breathy, thin* and sometimes *strident*, the latter depending on the amount of resonator hypertension. The pitch of the voice is also adversely affected. Because of the shallow intake of breath with clavicular breathing, the speaker has to rely either on added strain in the thoracic or pharyngeal areas to sustain the voice or must resort to quick intakes of air. This gasping for breath is distracting to the listeners and certainly interferes with meaningful phrasing. The speech becomes "choppy."

You may now be aware that you do not consistently utilize diaphragmatic action when you speak. (Remember that you do so *automatically* in breathing for life). If this is so, then you must acquire this skill and make it habitual. Central breathing (thoracic-abdominal) is necessary for good voice production.

Margaret Greene, in her book, *The Voice And Its Disorders* (the "Bible" of many voice therapists) says: "The paramount importance of correct breathing in speech and song cannot be overestimated. Permanent improvement in the voice cannot possibly be achieved without improvement in respiration." We have discussed the importance of the action of the diaphragm during breathing for both life and speech. We want to stress here that in central breathing, which directly involves the thoracic and abdominal muscles and the diaphragm, *you will not actually feel the movement of the diaphragm during respiration.* What you will feel is the movement of the outer wall of your midriff section, along with the movement of the abdominal muscles.

The following exercises should help you develop more control over the outgoing breath stream as you speak. When you practice, make use of all possible sensory help—visual, tactile, kinesthetic and aural.

Skill Alerts!

1. Check your posture and body alignment.
2. Be aware of adequate muscle tonus.
3. Aim for central breathing.
4. Avoid hypertension in the throat area.
5. Strive for a steady, even flow of breath on exhalation.

Exercises for Control of the Respiration Process

1. Standing with feet firmly on the floor, place your hands over the abdominal cavity and take a deep breath. Count from one to six as you exhale. Begin the count at the *peak of inhalation*. Do not allow any breath to escape before you say the number one. Concentrate on expelling all of your breath by the time you reach the last number. Do this exercise on one intake of breath. During this practice take note of the movement of the gross abdominal

muscles. There should be a gentle muscular action *inward* as you exhale.

2. Repeat exercise number one (1), trying for different ranges of breath control.
    a. Count from one to eight.
    b. Count from one to ten, etc.
    c. Your goal is one to twenty!

   This exercise is designed to make you aware tactually and kinesthetically of the fact that *you* are in control of your breath as you speak. At this stage of voice improvement, do not let the phase of exhalation *just happen*. Be deliberate in your control.

3. The following paragraph is composed of sentences that grow progressively longer in length. Using the same approach as in exercises one (1) and two (2), read the sentences in the paragraph with an intake of breath on the first word of the sentence and plan complete exhalation at the period. You might find that the amount of intake of air will have to be varied slightly as the sentences become longer. However, the important technique is the control of the exhaled breath.

   Begin now. Notice your posture. During practice aim for central breathing. Do you know the meaning of this? Take a breath through your nose and exhale through your mouth with pursed lips. Begin to speak at the peak of inhalation with no escape of air before you phonate. During exhalation attempt to control the breath stream so that you will have enough breath to complete the sentences. It is important that you feel a push from your gross abdominal muscles as you try to control the outgoing breath stream. This muscular control is important in effective voice production because this control will help you to maintain a firm, steady stream of breath as you speak.

There is one additional skill which you should master in order to have effective control of the entire respiration process. On exhalation, as breath passes between the vocal cords, you must develop a free-flowing emission of breath **out** of the mouth. The breath must **not** be held back in the throat as you speak. After mastering the techniques of effective inhalation and control, the next step is to work on *breath emission*. Throaty, raspy, and strident voices particularly benefit from emphasis on this skill.

Exercises for Effective Breath Emission

1. Hold the palm of your hand about four inches away from your mouth. Place your other hand over the diaphragm area. With an open, relaxed oral cavity and the tongue low and forward in the

mouth (Do not retract the tongue!), let the breath be emitted on the palm of your hand as you say the word, "ha." Do not *say* the word. Take a breath and just let the breath flow out of the mouth and do an *unvoiced*, "ha." Watch that you do not say, "huh." *Open* your mouth for a good /ɑ/ (ä) sound—/ha/. Do this exercise with your eyes open and then repeat the exercise with your eyes closed (kinesthetic stimulus). Get the feel of *free-flowing breath out of the mouth*. Now transfer this feel to speech. Try exercise number 2.

2. Hold the palm of your hand about four inches away from your mouth. Place your other hand over the diaphragm area. Count from one to ten, taking a breath for the individual numbers. On each count, gently push the air stream out of the oral cavity and against the palm of your hand. There will be, of course, more breath on some numbers than on others because of the nature of the sounds produced (plosives will emit more breath than nasals). As you are doing this exercise, attempt to feel muscular action in the abdominal cavity. If the voice begins to sound too breathy, try for more oral resonance by allowing the breath and sounds to resonate a little longer in the oral cavity. Work for a "round" feeling in the mouth. Keep in mind a relaxed pharyngeal cavity and put the tension on the gross abdominal muscles.
3. Now try phrases and sentences. Let your practice material be pragmatic and meaningful, similar to the examples below.
   a. Good morning!
   b. What's for breakfast? Lunch? Dinner?
   c. I'll be home at six tonight.
   d. Is your term paper finished?
   e. I have a meeting tonight, so you'll have to eat without me.

Check yourself! Have you

1. learned to use diaphragmatic action in breathing for speech?
2. learned to increase and control the outgoing breath stream?
3. learned to emit breath from the mouth rather than holding it back in the pharyngeal area?
   Note: Many people speak as if they are walking backwards or away from people. Talk as if you are walking **forward**! Think "up and out." This approach can change your attitude and voice!

The Resonation Process

Resonance can be defined as the amplification and modification of sound. Resonance of voice simply means the development and reinforcement of the basic laryngeal tone as it leaves the larynx. This tone is originally a rather weak one and needs to be amplified. The amplification takes place in three cavities: the laryngopharynx (larynx-throat), oropharynx (mouth-throat), and nasopharynx (nose-throat). All three kinds of vocal resonance are necessary for good voice production. Pharyngeal and oral resonance help to increase the mellow, rich tones of your voice. Nasal resonance, apart from being needed in the production of the nasal consonants of American English, is necessary to give your voice needed brightness.

The resonance system is so structured that what affects one resonance area necessarily affects, to some extent, the other two areas. Therefore, you must be aware that concentration on improving one kind of resonance will noticeably improve the resonance process in general. However, for a clearer understanding of resonance in voice production, we will discuss the three kinds of resonance separately.

The physics of sound tells us that the shape and size of the resonator, the size of its opening to the outer air, and the surface texture of the resonator are all influencing factors in determining the quality and amount of resonance produced. Because the size and shape of your nasal, oral, and pharyngeal cavities can be manipulated, and because the size of the openings of these cavities can be varied, the fundamental tone of your voice can be reinforced. Generally speaking, the larger the resonating cavity, the lower the frequencies produced. An illustration of this might be the comparison of three musical instruments: the violin, the cello, and the bass fiddle. Notice how the "sound" (frequencies) get *lower* as the *size* of the instrument (resonator) gets larger. Similarly, within limits, the larger the opening of the resonating cavity to the outer air, the higher will be the frequencies produced. By keeping these basic sound-production principles in mind, you can encourage a more mellow, more vibrant, and a fuller voice by using your resonators effectively.

Let's transfer all of this information to your voice production.

Skill Stimulators

1. **Open your mouth** when you speak, concentrating specifically on your back jaws. Your enlarged oral cavity (mouth) *increases* the lower frequencies which eventually affect the quality and pitch of your voice.
2. **Move your articulators** when you speak. This increased movement opens the front of your mouth and increases the higher frequencies which, again, can affect the quality and pitch of your voice.
3. **Minimize tension** in your face, in general, and in the nasal, oral and laryngeal cavities specifically.

Tension Alert

1. Tension in the resonating cavities results in a rigid surface and a rigid surface minimizes a mellow vocal quality.

2. Relaxation of the three resonating cavities (nose, mouth, larynx) is *necessary* because sounds bounced off of tense (hard) surfaces do not benefit from the "cushion" effect of relaxed (soft) surfaces.

Kinds of Resonance

We previously explained that the pharynx (throat) can be conveniently divided into three areas—the laryngopharynx, the oropharynx, and the nasopharynx. You probably recall that the term *pharynx* applies to that area behind the larynx, continues upward behind the oral cavity, and extends still farther upward behind the nasal cavity (see Figure). This entire pharyngeal area, including the back wall of the throat, is all intricately involved with resonance. Familiarize yourself with the various kinds of resonance because your voice improvement program could very well depend a great deal on your knowledge and understanding of resonance balance.

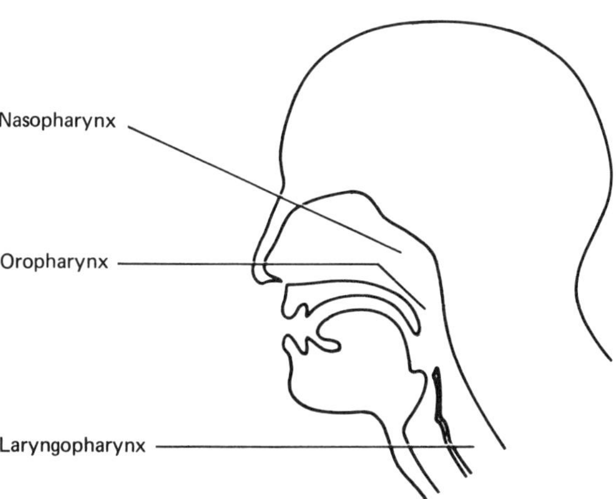

Figure 22.4 *The principal resonators.*

Laryngopharyngeal Resonance

Laryngopharyngeal resonance takes place the moment the fundamental tone of your voice is produced. At the onset of the vibration of the vocal cords during voice production, this fundamental tone is immediately amplified or modified in the laryngopharyngeal area. It is of extreme importance that the muscles in these two areas are neither too tense nor too lax during voice production, but rather that they should have just enough muscle tonus to encourage the amplification or modification of the fundamental tone of your voice.

Oral Resonance

Oral resonance is involved with the amplification or modification of your voice *in your mouth*. Because the oral cavity is more easily manipulated than the laryngeal or nasal areas, your voice improvement program must rely heavily on the manipulation of this cavity. Because effective oral resonance depends on how effectively the oral cavity is used, you should concentrate on control in this area.

To develop oral resonance:

1. *Work* on correctness and clarity of articulation.
2. *Move* your articulators when you speak.
3. *Open* your mouth when speaking, stressing relaxed lower jaws and opened back teeth.

Oral resonance is so basic to voice production that it can be said to be a necessary component of every characteristic of voice (volume, pitch, and rate). On the other hand, lack of adequate oral resonance contributes to many defective qualities of voice (throatiness, stridency, raspiness, thinness, and nasality).

Nasal Resonance

Nasal resonance is necessary for good voice quality. Breath vibrated by the vocal cords and resonated in the nasal cavity contributes a brightness, or brilliance, to the human voice. Proof of this can be found when you have a cold and nasal resonance is either minimized or restricted entirely. The result is a muffled, dull vocal quality—a quality that can interfere with intelligibility of speech. Because the cold has irritated the membranous tissue in the nasal cavity, you are unable to breathe through your nose and, therefore, are unable to resonate in this cavity. This lack of nasal resonance specifically causes distortion or substitution of the m (m), n (n), and (ŋ) sounds.

Let's look at the other side of the coin. Perhaps you have reacted to a T.V. personality with, "So nasal! I can't stand to listen to that voice!" Too much nasal resonance is as distracting as too little.

Later on in this section of the handbook you will be taught about hypernasality, hyponasality and assimilation nasality. For now, let's look at generalities so that you will be more aware of you and your voice.

You must now be conscious of the involvement of the soft palate in the production of both speech sounds and good voice. As you try to achieve an "open" oral cavity for improved oral resonance in your voice, you should detect deliberate movement of the soft palate as you produce nasal sounds. Take a minute to reinforce the kinesthetic sensation.

1. Using a mirror as a visual aid, open your mouth wide, trying for an open throat, and inhale a large amount of air. Gasp *inwardly*, with a prolonged intake of breath. You will experience a "drafty"

sensation inside the mouth and you will see the velum (soft palate) move upward and then immediately relax with a downward motion. Repeat this several times, slowly with your eyes closed.

2. Now quicken the pace. Using the mirror again with the same physical positioning of the mouth and throat, pant hard on an *intake* of breath, repeating rapidly. The velum will move vigorously. You can be assured of this action by the quick, jerky movements of the uvula, which terminates the soft palate.
3. To reinforce the visual and kinesthetic sensations in the movement of the soft palate, try the following: use your mirror to see the opening and closing of the nasopharyngeal areas. Say a prolonged ng /ŋ/ sound. Follow it with a prolonged a /ɑ/ sound. Note how the soft palate lowers on the ng /ŋ/ sound (opening the nasopharynx) and raises on the a /ɑ/ sound (closing off the nasal passages).

The Articulation Process

We have defined the term *articulation* as the process by which the outgoing air stream is divided into distinguishable speech sounds. Do you know someone who speaks through clenched back teeth and tight jaws with the sounds running into and over one another? This kind of articulation is technically called *overassimilation* (see Chapter 16, Sound Changes). On the other end of the spectrum is the person who explodes each sound and/or word with a clarity and precision that is painful to listeners' ears. As a student interested in speech improvement, listen intently to articulation.

Your ability to use your articulators with precision and accuracy affects not only the sounds you speak but also your voice production. As teachers of speech, we are constantly and consistently amazed at what happens to the *voices* of our students in our *articulation* classes. We assure you that all of the skills you have mastered as a result of your work in the articulation section of this handbook have prepared you for developing a better voice.

The Audition Process

Audition describes the physical process of hearing. When people talk to you, your ears receive the sound waves. The sound waves set your ear drums into vibration, the vibrations travel through the middle ear and then are translated into nerve stimulation in the inner ear. The stimuli are then received by the brain via the Central Nervous System and you hear the message.

As you speak you hear yourself. This ability to hear your own voice and speech is called "feedback." However, *hearing* yourself doesn't mean that you *listen* to yourself. Hearing involves the reception of sound waves by the *physical* hearing organ—the ear. Listening involves a deliberate *mental* interpretation of the message received by the ear. When you receive feedback, don't be content to just hear—learn to listen. Try not to listen negatively but do listen critically. Ask yourself: How does my voice sound to me? What am I doing well? What needs correction? (See p. 413 on Auditory Discrimination.)

Skill Alerts:

1. Tape yourself at the very beginning of your improvement program.
2. On the tape use various forms of oral communication. The following is a possible format:
   (a) give your name, date, time of day.
   (b) read aloud eight to ten sentences from any narrative (editorial, sports column, textbook).
   (c) talk for eight to ten sentences. Plan this before you tape. Think through what you are going to say. This is called extemporaneous speaking. Don't write out the material. Try to have a certain amount of spontaneity when you speak.
3. Keep this tape as a point of reference.
4. Continue to tape yourself every two to three weeks. *Hear* and *listen* to the material.
5. Compare the tapes.

Concluding Suggestions

In this chapter you have been told about the six processes involved in speech production.

1. Innervation—nerve stimulation
2. Phonation—vibration of the vocal cords
3. Respiration—breathing for life and speech
4. Resonance—amplification and modification of the sound of your voice
5. Articulation—the phonemes you produce
6. Audition—hearing and listening

Do you have a specific voice problem? Are you interested in over-all voice improvement because you want to sound better? Do you want to project an image of a better you? The following chapters will help you. We've arranged the material so that it targets specific areas. You will improve! Be persistent!

23

Quality

The telephone rings. You pick up the receiver and your ears tell you that this is your friend, Mike. No, it's Bill! You're startled! How did you fail to recognize Bill's voice? Momentarily he sounded so much like Mike! Bill explains that he has a cold.

We spend our lives identifying sounds which help us to recognize our surroundings, the immediate circumstances, and people. We are able to identify these individual sounds because of their differences in *quality*.

There are, as we have already noted, four characteristics of voice: quality, loudness, pitch, and rate. These characteristics of voice can be changed or varied. Loudness, you remember, has to do with variations of loud and soft, pitch with variations of high and low, and rate with variations of fast and slow. Quality? We have a lot of adjectives to describe the variations in quality—mellow, pleasant, harsh, hoarse, nasal, and thin—to name a few.

It is more difficult to define the voice characteristic **quality** than it is to define the other three voice characteristics. Consider the "sound" difference between two musical instruments—a trumpet and a violin. If a note were played with the same amount of loudness and held for the same amount of time, would you recognize a difference in sound between a trumpet and violin? Of course you would. That difference in sound is known as **quality**—the distinctive, characteristic sound made by the sound producer.

Why do these two instruments sound so different? The violin and trumpet are constructed of different materials, and they have different kinds of resonating chambers. Your voice quality is different from anyone else's because *you* are constructed differently and *your* resonators are different.

Vocal quality is affected by many factors including: your anatomy (body structure), your physiology (how your body functions), and your feelings (your fluctuating emotional states).

Vocal quality is also affected by the *processes* involved in speech production: respiration, phonation, resonance, and articulation. Vocal quality is also dramatically influenced by these *characteristics* of voice: loudness (increased/decreased vocal energy), pitch (highness/lowness of your vocal range) and rate (fast/slow speech). This handbook has individual chapters on each of these topics. In this chapter, we will explore the specific effects on your vocal quality.

How many times have you heard someone say, "He has such a pleasant voice. He should be on radio or T.V." What is "pleasant" to one person may not be pleasant to another. Do you like the leading lady's sexy voice in your favorite "soap" or do you think she sounds forced and artificial? Quality of voice is in the ear of the listener, just as beauty is in the eye of the beholder. There are no "standards" of vocal quality.

The sound of your voice is a reflection of you and is highly individual and personal. Your voice can communicate a lot about *you* to *you*. As you speak, are you aware of your voice quality? To check yourself, consider these questions:

1. How does my body and my face look (visual)?
2. Is my body tense (visual, tactile)?
3. Are the muscles in my throat bulging as I speak (indicating physical strain)?
4. How does my voice sound? (auditory)

Your voice quality also communicates messages about you to your listeners. To analyze the messages your listeners hear, think about these questions:

1. Does my voice quality support, and confirm the message I am trying to communicate?
2. What is my voice saying about my physical state?
3. What is being conveyed about my emotional state?
4. Does my voice quality project my attitude about the content of my message?
5. Does my voice quality reflect my feelings about my relationship with my listeners?

Listeners *will* receive a message from the quality of your voice. Will it be the one you intended to convey? More importantly, are you *aware* of the kind of message your listeners received?

Try these sentences. Can your vocal quality alter the meaning of the words?

1. I love you.
2. Come on! Let's go!
3. That outfit makes a statement.

4. Why were you gone so long?
5. You think I should support you.

Your goal, as you deal with voice quality, is to become aware of your distinctive voice, to gain more control over it, and to produce the best possible quality to convey your messages—both in content and image.

Problems of Voice Quality

In this section we will consider the following troublesome vocal qualities: hoarse, breathy/husky, throaty, thin, harsh/strident, raspy, and hyper/hyponasality. We will first describe the characteristics of each of these qualities. Think about these characteristics and whether any of them apply to your voice. We will offer suggestions and/or exercises to help you learn to control possible problems which might result from these characterisitics. The important step after practicing these exercises is to incorporate the new skills into everyday speech. The most important goal is to retain those skills and use them daily—the skills you learn in this course should last long after the instructor is no longer there to remind you to **use** your new voice.

► *Problem 1:* The Hoarse Voice

The term "hoarse" covers many different kinds of sounds and/or conditions. In general, the hoarse voice sounds rough, strained, gratey, and somewhat breathy. Volume is usually inadequate and the pitch range narrow. Sometimes the voice breaks and no voice comes out at all.

If you are hoarse most or all of the time, you should visit an otolaryngologist to see if there is a medical reason. If your hoarseness is only temporary, how can you manage and correct it? Here are our suggestions:

1. Vocal rest when prescribed by the physician or speech therapist.
2. Integrate good posture with body alignment. See pp. 421-424.
3. Work for adequate muscle tonus. See pp. 419-420.
4. Achieve habitual central breathing. See pp. 437-438.
5. Develop a firm, steady stream of breath on exhalation. See pp. 439-442.
6. Achieve gentle adduction of the vocal cords using the intrinsic muscles. See pp. 441-442.
7. Release the breath out of the mouth. See pp. 442-443.
8. Increase oral resonance. See p. 443.

The hoarse voice is affected by faulty closure of the vocal cords. To learn to control this vocal deficit, you need to understand the principles of closing (adduction) and opening (abduction) of the vocal cords. How do we control the muscles in the larynx if we can't see them or reach in and touch them? Exercises that involve pushing, pulling, and lifting close our vocal cords by using the correct (*intrinsic*) muscles. The intrinsic muscles are located *inside* the larynx. We do **not** want to use the muscles located on the outside (*extrinsic*) of the larynx. The extrinsic muscles support the position of the larynx in the throat. If we do use the extrinsic muscles, the quality will be strained.

The following exercises have been used successfully by our students. They are easy to do and can be practiced any place and any time. We think you will experience real feelings of accomplishment as you try them. Your voice will become stronger and firmer. Trust us!

Exercises for Adduction of the Vocal Cords

Pressing/Humming Exercise

1. Stand tall, body aligned. It helps to stand against a wall.
2. Clasp the palms of your hands together in front of your chest, at the level of the sternum (breastbone).
3. Have your crossed thumbs *facing* your chest. Do not interlock your fingers.
4. Your forearms should form a *straight line* across your chest. Shoulders level.
5. Gently press your palms together. The "push" should be coming from your *forearms*.
6. **Your vocal cords are closed using the intrinsic muscles!**

We told you it would be easy! Now you have to vibrate the vocal cords (voice) while the correct muscles are involved. Later, this skill will be transferred to your daily production of voice so that faulty production is minimized—*physiologically*.

Hum on the sound /n/. Remember, do not hum on /m/ because the lips close (bilabial nasal sound) and the breath cannot escape out of the mouth.

1. Follow steps one through six as explained in the above section.
2. While you are pressing your palms together, take a breath (use central breathing).
3. At the peak of inhalation, hum on /n/ as you exhale your breath.

   Take any pitch. Try to hum in mid-range. Hum gently and softly. Hum on the pitch for three or four seconds, taking a breath **on each attempt**. Do **not** hum with a great deal of intensity (loudness). Do not allow the hum to fade away. Try to keep the hum consistent in volume and firmness. Watch that the hum does not acquire a vibrato. If the sound begins to vibrate excessively, concentrate on pushing from your midriff (the diaphragm area). Continue this exercise with your eyes open. Repeat it with your eyes closed (kinesthetic sensation). Try to experience a feeling in the laryngeal area of **firmness**. This firmness is the gentle adduction of the vocal cords.

4. Release the push on the palms of your hands as you exhale, through pursed lips, any unused breath.

That's it! This exercise is basic to producing a *clear* voice. Remember, practice while looking at yourself in a mirror (visual stimulation to the CNS). Practice with your eyes closed (kinesthetic stimulation to the CNS). In addition, practice the exercise in the three positions: **standing! sitting! walking!** A warning—doing the pushing and humming when walking is the hardest!

The following are variations of the basic exercise.

Squeezing/Humming Exercise

Stand tall with your feet slightly apart. Place your hands and arms across your chest, your left hand gripping your upper right arm and your right hand gripping your upper left arm. Slowly squeeze your crossed arms and hands simultaneously with a good amount of pressure so that your chest cavity is noticeably tightened. Keep your chin level (do not look down) during this exercise and try to "feel" the tightening in the laryngeal area. Your vocal cords are being made to close! Repeat the squeezing action rhythmically three or four times with your eyes open. Alternate with your eyes closed to increase the kinesthetic stimulation to the CNS.

1. Take a breath, squeeze your crossed arms, and at the peak of inhalation begin to hum on any comfortable note for three to four seconds.
2. Continue to hum as you exhale your breath, maintaining the squeezed position of the chest.
3. Do this exercise with your eyes closed (kinesthetic stimulation to the CNS).

Push ups/Humming Exercise

Are you feeling in top shape today? Try the following modified version of a push up. Lie on the floor with your face turned to one side, your legs together, your hands placed next to your shoulders with your fingers pointed forward and your palms down. Push up off the floor until your arms are fully extended and your torso is supported by your hands and knees. Your back should be straight. Take a breath and gently exhale the breath as you lower your torso to the floor. Relax! Repeat this action three or four times. By this time you must know and realize that the "pushing" action up off the floor closed your vocal cords.

If you really feel in top shape, repeat the exercise with the following version. As you push up off the floor until your arms are fully extended, support your raised torso **by your toes only**. Your back should be straight. Take a breath and gently exhale the breath as you lower your torso to the floor.

1. Start the push up and reach the position of fully extended arms.
2. While in that position, take a breath and at the peak of inhalation begin to hum for three to four seconds.
3. Stop the hum and exhale as you lower your torso to the floor.
4. Do not continue this exercise for any length of time if you feel strain or fatigue.

Pushing/Humming Exercise

Stand tall in a doorframe with the palms of your hands flat against each side of the frame. Push firmly against each side of the door frame. Notice how the abdominal muscles, the diaphragm area and the chest cavity all tighten. Hold the pushing position from three to five seconds (this action forces the vocal cords to gently close). Release the pressure and relax! Now add the following:

1. Push against each side of the door frame.
2. Take a breath (be sure of central breathing) and at the peak of inhalation begin to hum on a comfortable note. Continue humming for three to four seconds.
3. Continue to hum as you exhale your breath.
4. Repeat this exercise three to five times, alternating with eyes open (visual stimulation to the CNS) and then with your eyes closed (kinesthetic stimulation to the CNS).

Bouncing/Humming Exercise

Stand comfortably away from a wall two to three feet. Fall against the wall with your hands extended and the palms flat on the wall at about eye level. Keep your elbows slightly creased (**not** extended, but within the body line), and keep your heels off of the floor. You should have the feeling that if the wall were suddenly removed, you would fall flat on your face. In this leaning position, gently bounce up and down on the wall, keeping your palms flat **on** the wall. Try to feel a gentle tightening in the larynx. That is the adduction of the vocal cords. Close your eyes to add kinesthetic feedback. You are now encouraging vocal cord adduction so necessary for a firm, clear tone during phonation.

Some precautions:

1. The distance you stand away from the wall is determined by your height (the taller you are, the farther away from the wall).

2. Your elbows **must be slightly creased** and turned to the floor. These two positions insure that the *pushing* action is being done by your *forearms* and **not** by your shoulder or neck muscles.
3. Do not stand up on your toes as you lean on the wall. Using the metatarsal (ball) of your foot encourages you to *lean*.
4. Keep your eyes on the wall in front of you. This frees your larynx to function. Looking down at the floor limits the vibratory action of the vocal cords.

Add humming.

1. You are leaning on the wall. Take a breath (be sure you are using central breathing).
2. At the peak of inhalation, begin to hum on /n/. Hum while the palms of your hands are being *pushed against the wall*. This *pushing action* of the forearm muscles insures the efficient closure of the vocal cords.
3. Hum for three to four seconds.
4. Stop the humming as you ''bounce'' off the wall and are back on your heels, standing tall. Exhale the remaining breath. Relax!

Exercises Substituting Speech for Humming

You must *transfer your new skills into speech* as quickly as possible. You have now mastered the basic skills suggested so far in a *clinical* setting. You have learned correct *posture* and *body alignment*. Having learned *central breathing*, you can now *control the outgoing breathstream*. It is *firm*. You have mastered *vocal cord closure*. Now you must move on!

Using any of the humming exercises as a point of reference, let's add speech.

1. Instead of humming, say the numbers one through five when you push, press, and squeeze. As you press your palms together, take a breath, then say the number ''one.'' Take another breath and say, ''one, two.'' Remember to push the breath out of your mouth. Think ''up and out.'' Take an additional breath and say, ''one, two, three.'' Repeat the process until you can recite all the numbers through five.
2. A challenge! Use the action to close the vocal cords as you say ''one.'' *Repeat the number(s) without the pushing action*. First take a breath and say the numbers without pushing. Do the two numbers sound alike? Can you *retain* the closure and sound *without* using the pushing action?
3. Move on to more challenging material. Using the sounds /n/ and /m/ as catalysts to close the vocal cords, attempt to continue the clarity and firmness of vocal quality as you use the words and

sentences in the articulation section of this handbook. See pp. 158-160 and 166-167.

Now try the following sentences:

1. The mean man met his match on the rim of the mountain.
2. Much money is manipulated on the stock exchange.
3. Semantics is a science which analyzes the emotional content of the words we use in conversation morning, noon and night.
4. The minister in his sermon to the congregation screamed many warnings concerning sin and damnation.
5. John needed consultation in order to manage his finances more efficiently.
6. Politicians tend to spend much of their time making promises, promises and more promises.
7. Nan needed more money than she counted on for her expedition.
8. I find that I cannot count up to 999 without becoming frustrated.
9. "The rain in Spain falls mainly on the plain," is a line from a song long to be remembered by the many fans and enemies of Professor Higgins.
10. "Taxation without representation" had much meaning for our ancestors during the American Revolution.

Exercise to Transfer Skills to Daily Speech

The next step in skill acquisition is the daily use of your new clear and firm voice in conversation. Make a list of ten words, phrases, and sentences that you use daily. For example:

1. What time will you be home for dinner?
2. Good morning, Mary.
3. How long will you be gone for lunch?

Begin by practicing in isolation the words in the sentences that contain an /n/ or /m/ sound. Then work on the entire sentence, attempting to maintain the clarity and firmness of your voice throughout the entire sentence.

► *Problem 2:* Breathy/Husky Quality

The breathy/husky vocal quality (asthenic or weak voice) lacks sound (vocalization) and volume. It has a whispered quality and sounds as if there were an /h/ between sounds and/or words. Some people think this voice sounds sexy, but consistent use of this quality can actually damage the vocal cords. In addition, this quality has limited volume and an inability to make the voice "carry." The pitch range is low and there is frequent fading.

How do we correct this vocal quality?

1. Vocal rest if there is vocal pathology.
2. Integrate good posture with body alignment.
3. Work for adequate muscle tonus. See pp. 419-420.
   Note: This deviant vocal quality, possibly more than any other, needs the feeling of having *your body under your voice*.
4. Achieve habitual central breathing. See pp. 437-438.
5. Develop a firm, steady stream of breath on exhalation. See pp. 439-442.
6. Acquire a **firm** adduction of the vocal cords. See pp. 441-442.
7. Increase oral resonance. Minimize laryngeal resonance.
8. Use an adequate volume level.

It is not easy to develop a *firm* body, to use more effort during respiration, and to increase the energy level on phonation. If you recognize the danger to your vocal cords and *want* to change, it can be done. Practice and work to

1. develop a *firm* body.
2. use more effort during respiration.
3. increase the energy level on phonation. You must *want* to change, so a large part of the voice therapy management is *attitudinal*.

► ***Problem 3:*** Throaty Quality

A throaty quality sounds heavy and thick. The throaty voice sounds as if the tongue were "getting in the way." It lacks clarity and brightness. The throaty voice usually has a low pitch range and is frequently accompanied by a heavy or indistinct articulation pattern. The words sound "muffled."

Sometimes this quality is caused by medical problems, such as enlarged tonsils or adenoids. Correcting the medical problems alone, however, will not necessarily correct the faulty voice quality. If you continue to use the same muscle actions you used before, you will continue to talk with a thick and throaty voice quality. You need to learn how to use your vocal muscles differently.

Faulty voice production involving the position of your tongue also causes the throaty quality. The position of your tongue can adversely affect oral and laryngeal resonance. If your tongue is retracted (pulled back), it "sits on the hyoid bone of the larynx" (see Figure 22.1) and limits the action of the laryngeal muscles. The result is a thick, muffled sound.

The tongue has great mobility. Since the tongue constantly changes both its shape and its position (and, therefore, the size of the oral cavity), it is a very important articulator. Correcting the throaty quality simply requires practice to take advantage of the tongue's inherent mobility.

Correcting this problem requires:

1. Correction of the retracted tongue while producing the various phonemes. Look in the mirror (visual stimulation). Is your tongue tip away from the back of your lower front teeth while you are speaking? We hope not. If it is, then check the articulation section of this book for the proper placement of your tongue on all front and medial vowels. (See pp. 238-267 and 295-315 or Chapters 11 and 13).
2. Increased labial (lip) and lingual (tongue) movement while speaking. Stress the phonemes /t/, /d/, /n/, /l/ to help you increase the mobility of the tip of your tongue (see pp. 71-72). Stress all of the bilabial consonants to increase your labial (lip) movement.
3. Development of adequate muscle tension of the tongue on all vowel production. Take particular note of the difference between the tense and lax vowels of American English. (see p. 236).
4. Increased oral and nasal resonance. Concentrate on acquiring an open oral cavity with unclenched back teeth. Decreased laryngo-pharyngeal resonance will add more brilliance and brightness to your voice. Particularly work on the nasal sounds (see pp. 150-176) and on all of the back vowels and diphthongs (see pp. 268-294, 316-334 or Chapters 12 and 14).
5. Increased effort to get the exhaled breath stream (breath emission) **out of the mouth**. Think and talk "forward."

► *Problem 4:* Thin Quality

Have you ever been told, "You sound so much younger than you look," or "You sound so young, you must not have had much experience. Sorry, you just are not suited for this job." The thin voice sounds young and weak. It has an immature vocal sound with a narrow, usually high, pitch range. The voice frequently fades at the ends of phrases and sentences and lacks adequate volume.

To correct this quality, work on the following:

1. Integrate good posture, body alignment, and adequate muscle tonus.
2. Acquire effective diaphragmatic breathing (see pp. 437-438).
3. Learn to sustain the breath until the end of the sentence. Use the appropriate abdominal muscle support. Do not use the laryngeal muscles (see pp. 439-442).
4. Practice back vowel production. This work opens your back teeth, enlarges the size of the oral cavity, and results in an increase of the lower overtones. The result is a more mature, resonant (not thin) quality.

5. Learn how to increase volume muscularly without involving the pharyngeal muscles (see pp. 469).

Problem 5: Harsh and Strident Qualities

The harsh voice and the strident voice have much in common. Even though they sound somewhat different, the underlying causes are very similar. The harsh quality has a low pitch and sounds hard, strained, abrasive, and loud. The strident quality has a high pitch and sounds sharp, metallic, and abrasive. Both men and women can have either problem, but the harsh quality is more common in men and the strident quality more common in women. These voice qualities are "problems" for two reasons: both grate on the ears and nerves of listeners, and both convey the impression of excitability, hostility, and aggressiveness.

To correct both of these problems, follow these instructions:

1. Relax laryngeal and throat muscles.
2. Acquire an "open oral cavity and unclenched back teeth." Work on back vowels and diphthongs.
3. Reduce "energy" during phonation; try to be less aggressive when communicating your ideas and feelings. Learn to take it easy.

For the Harsh Vocal Quality:

4. Work for a gentle adduction of the vocal cords without hypertension of the tensor and adductor muscles (see pp. 442-443).
5. Develop control of the outgoing breath stream on exhalation; keep the breath going; do not continue to phonate as you squeeze out the last amount of breath (see pp. 441-442).

For the Strident Vocal Quality:

6. Work for adequate muscle tonus in the nasopharynx, oropharynx, and laryngopharynx. Relax! Your pitch range will lower noticeably.

Problem 6: Raspy and/or Glottal Fry Quality

The raspy or gravelly voice quality is sometimes referred to as "glottal fry." The glottis is the space between the vocal cords, and glottal fry refers to the sound the vocal cords produce when the vocal muscles are hypertense. Remember that voice is produced by releasing breath from the lungs and vibrating it between the vocal cords. There is a *delicate balance* between the actual vibrating of the vocal cords and their resistance to the exhaled breath and the pressure beneath the vocal cords needed to produce voice. When an imbalance in these forces occurs, the vocal cords are affected, and this voice quality results.

Some people deliberately induce this quality when they try to lower the pitch. Usually the problem is confined to the ends of phrases and sentences, because the speaker fails to support the tone adequately to the end of the phrase or sentence. The voice "drops back" and "fries" at the glottis.

There are three reasons to correct this problem: (1) it feels unpleasant, (2) it sounds unpleasant, and (3) it can harm the vocal cords. To manage (or correct) this problem, follow these instructions:

1. Achieve relaxation of the muscles in the larynx and throat areas (see pp. 427-428).
2. Make central breathing a habit so that the exhaled breath can be used efficiently (see pp. 437-438).
3. Emphasize the emission of breath **out of the oral cavity during phonation**. Think "up and out." Feel as if you have no throat, only a diaphragm and an oral cavity.
4. Keep the breath flowing out of your mouth as you come to the end of a phrase or sentence. Try not to *squeeze out* final sounds as you near the completion of the exhalation phase. Keep your body under your voice! Be aware that this control of breath does not interfere with dropping pitch at the end of a sentence. You can successfully drop pitch and simultaneously continue the flow of breath out of the oral cavity.
5. Practice steps 3 and 4 with one hand about three to four inches away from your mouth. Experience the emission of breath out of the oral cavity tactually and kinesthetically (repeat steps 3 and 4 with your eyes closed).

▶ *Problem 7:* Glottal Shock

Glottal shock is not a vocal quality, though it affects vocal quality. This problem is limited to the initial release of breath (at the beginning of a word). The vocal cords become hypertense and "explode" the initial breath release. There is a little "pop" sound. Usually this problem occurs on words beginning with vowels, especially the back vowels and the diphthongs /aɪ/ (i), /aʊ/ (ou), and [ɑ] (a).

What is so wrong with beginning words with this kind of shock/attack? Well, it gets you off to a bad start. If you begin with too much tension, it becomes difficult to achieve adequate muscle tonus in the vocal cords which is crucial for smooth voice production. If glottal shock is a problem for you, master the following skills:

1. Acquire a smooth release of breath out of the glottis as you begin to phonate. (See the following exercises).
2. Be **tactually** and **kinesthetically** aware of the hypertense action at the glottis when you begin to speak. Place one of your fingers on the larynx while you deliberately exaggerate the glottal shock sound. Feel the hypertension!

3. Do not rely on your **ear** for the correction of this problem. It is difficult for an untrained ear to hear this sound (at the initial stages of awareness).
4. Do not use glottal shock as a means of emphasis (hitting particular words hard) as you communicate meaning. There are other devices (pauses, pitch changes) that are not inherently injurious to the vocal mechanism. (This advice is only for those of you with glottal shock problems).

Exercises for the Correction of Glottal Shock

1. Avoid a sudden, tense, explosive movement of the vocal cords on initial vowels by stressing a relaxed adduction (closing) of the cords. Producing the sound /h/ accomplishes this for you. With open, relaxed jaws, say a prolonged /h/ sound. Look at yourself in the mirror (visual stimulation). Check to see if your neck and jaws are relaxed during the production of /h/. Repeat /h/ several times. Close your eyes for increased kinesthetic sensation and repeat the /h/.
2. Now move to the trouble sounds, the vowels. See pp. 117-120 for lists of words beginning with the /h/ sound. As you say the word, **prolong** the initial /h/ sound and then complete the word. Check all the muscle action in the neck and jaws. Were you able to g-l-i-d-e easily from the /h/ sound into the following sounds? If so, then try the accompanying word, which does **not** begin with /h/. (Avoid a sudden explosive action). Concentrate on emitting the breath easily. For example, howl-owl. A word of caution. Don't overchallenge yourself. Try the exercise sentences only when you feel you have acquired a smooth adduction of the vocal cords on initial vowels.

► ***Problem 8:*** Hypernasality/Hyponasality

Problems related to nasal resonance fall into two categories **hypernasality** and **hyponasality**. Hypernasality is too much nasal resonance in the voice (talking through your nose), and hyponasality, or denasality, is insufficient nasal resonance. These resonance problems are directly related to the action or inaction of the soft palate and its interaction with the oral cavity. In producing effective nasal resonance, the soft palate moves down and forward, allowing the exhaled breath to be resonated in the nasal cavity. Nasal resonance is basic to the production of the three nasal sounds of /m/ /n/ /ŋ/ (See Chapter 7).

Hypernasality is the result of the soft palate being lowered during the production of nasal and non-nasal sounds. There is no appreciable soft palate action to close off the opening to the nasopharyngeal cavity (see Figure 23.1). As a result, the entire articulation-voice pattern is colored with excessive nasal resonance.

Hyponasality occurs when the soft palate is raised and held up against the back pharyngeal wall during the production of most or all sounds during speech. Seemingly, the soft palate gets "stuck" in a fixed position against the back pharyngeal wall and the resulting voice quality lacks brilliance and brightness. Your voice sounds as if you have a cold and your nose is congested.

Both hypernasality and hyponasality can be corrected by following these instructions:

1. Relax the larynx and throat areas (see pp. 427-428).
2. Acquire habitual central breathing. (see pp. 437-438).
3. Open (relax) the back jaws to encourage interaction between the oropharynx and nasopharynx.
4. Develop lip and tongue movement by stressing bilabial sounds, back vowels, and diphthongs.
5. Work on meaningful pitch variation. Let your voice go!

For the Hypernasal Voice:

6. Attain closure of the nasopharynx by (a) swallowing and yawning (experience these sensations kinesthetically).
7. Stress back vowels and diphthongs in practice. Concentrate on emitting the breath out of the oral cavity.

For the Hyponasal Voice:

8. Using a tactile and kinesthetic approach, reinforce your awareness of nasal resonance in the nasal cavity. Place your thumb and forefinger over the bridge of your nose (lightly) and say a prolonged /n/ sound and then change your tongue position for a prolonged /a/ sound. Note the vibration in the nose on the /n/ sound. There should be no vibration in the nose on the /a/ sound.

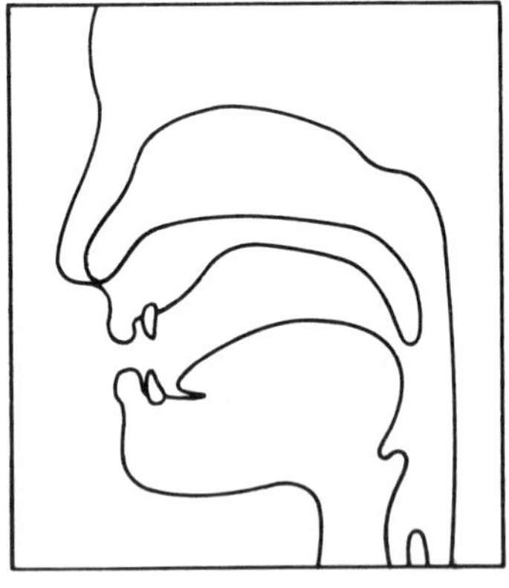

a. Lowered Soft Palate (nasal passage open)

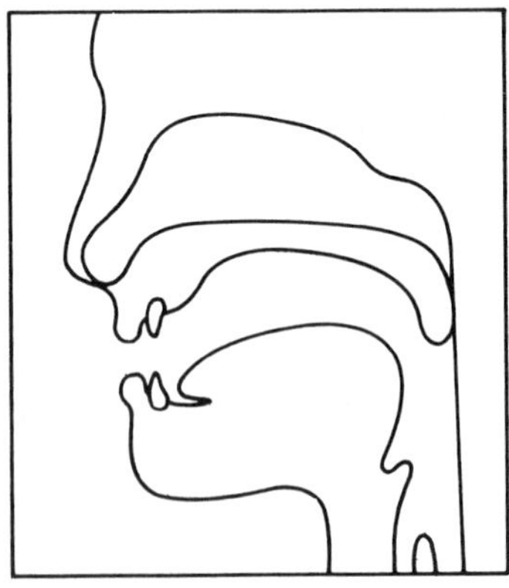

b. Raised Soft Palate (nasal passage closed)

Figure 23.1 *Hypernasality and hyponasality.*

Exercises for Hypernasality and Hyponasality

The following sentences can be used to correct either hypernasality or hyponasality, by slightly altering the focus. Use the sentences in pairs. If hypernasality is your problem, use the sentences *without* nasal sounds in them. Be sure there is no nasal vibration in those sentences. Then, when you read the sentences with nasal sounds in them, be sure there is nasal resonance only on the nasal consonants. Work for good oral resonance on the vowels; prolong the vowels but keep them out of the nose! If hyponasality is your problem, spend more time on the sentences with nasal sounds in them. Prolong the nasal consonants; for increased nasal resonance.

1. The five players asked for a rest period.
2. The nine men on the team demanded a new decision from the umpire.
3. Her favorite period of the day is right after breakfast.
4. Can you imagine having only candy for lunch?
5. Wait for Bill to go with us to the beach.
6. Lying on the sand under the burning sun can be dangerous to one's complexion.
7. The athlete realized he was about to lose the race.
8. The challenger met his match on the rim of the mountain.
9. No doubt, practically all people try to better their lives.
10. Most men want to improve their miserable living conditions.
11. "Pay as you go" could be a good rule to follow.
12. Money and investments can be dangerously manipulated in the stock market.
13. Styles today are triggered by the variety of textiles available.
14. Much of the material was woven in mediocre manufacturing mills.
15. Ideas are like pearls—precious!
16. Can't you find a more meaningful slogan for the advertisement?
17. I could eat food all through the day but my head resists the urge.
18. Nuts are one of my favorite snacks.

There are two additional problems with nasality which we think are important enough to mention. Assimilation nasality is usually more of a problem than nasal twang.

► ***Problem 9:*** Assimilation Nasality

When assimilation occurs, a sound changes to become more like a neighboring sound. Assimilation nasality occurs when an entire word containing a nasal sound is completely nasalized. In other words, the nasal sounds affect the neighboring nonnasal sounds so that these nonnasal sounds are nasalized.

The solution is in the movement of the soft palate. You must control the muscular action of the soft palate. It must move downward for all nasal sounds—allowing for nasal resonance. It must move up and back against the pharyngeal wall for all nonnasal sounds to achieve oral resonance not nasal resonance.

Exercises for Assimilation Nasality

For the improvement of assimilation nasality, try the following pairs of words. The **vowels** in the pairs of words should have the **same amount of** *oral* resonance. Don't let the vowels be affected by the nasal sounds.

at	an
abbey	Aunty
attitude	amplitude
cat	can
it	in
lit	linen
settle	sentinel
cow	now
sow	sound
I	nine

For an extra challenge put the pairs of words into sentences:

1. **At** the World's Fair I noticed **an** attitude of friendliness among the visitors.
2. Westminster **Abbey** will never be the same after **Aunty** Mame's visit last summer.
3. The **cat** ate her dinner out of the tin **can**.
4. I put **it in** the small container on the counter.
5. Only one candle was **lit** on the table which was covered with the pink **linen** tablecloth.
6. Did you **settle** the argument with the **sentinel** about his rounds?
7. **How now** brown cow?
8. The ''oink'' of the **sow sounded** angry as she called her little pigs to meal time.
9. I find that I cannot count up to **nine** hundred and ninety-**nine** without losing count.

▶ *Problem 10:* Nasal Twang

A nasal ''twang'' is a severe case of hypernasality. The problem occurs when hypernasality is compounded by excessive tension in the

along the back pharyngeal wall. This produces a
l "twang."
sal twang, follow the suggestions for correcting
p. 463.) Pay special attention to:

he larynx and throat areas.

avity open and the back teeth unclenched. Develop
nance.

ory discrimination.

ns

talked about improved vocal quality. Some of you
because of vocal pathology (physical problems);
change because of frequent voice problems such
hers of you may want to change to achieve a more
ive voice. Whatever your reason, working to change
it it can also be gratifying. As you change (improve)
tude about yourself will also change (improve) and
ou project to others.

Send to Mary Duelie
SB201/EV118

24

Loudness

"You don't have to shout! I'm not deaf!"
"We can't hear you. Talk louder!"

On initial assessment, loudness (intensity of sound) is seemingly one-dimensional. It would appear that all you have to do is to "talk louder," or "talk softer." That is not so. A closer look at what is involved when we adjust our volume will reveal that loudness is multi-dimensional.

When you speak, obviously you must be heard by your listener(s) or the communication process never gets off the ground. *Your loudness must meet the needs of the listener.* Many times however, it only meets the speaker's needs. For example, if you addressed a group of one hundred people, your volume would be noticeably different than if you were engaged in a conversation at a small party. This seems obvious. But, have you ever been involved in a heated discussion with only *one* person and had the *conversational* loudness become so loud that the words being said were blotted out by the shouting? Or, have you ever asked a favor of someone and had that person say, "What are you asking? I can't hear you." An analysis of these real-life scenes tells us that many things are involved with loudness.

What do we mean by "volume" or "loudness"? Well, intensity of the sound produced is *part* of the answer. Intensity can be measured. How loud is the siren or the train noise? Measure the decibels! But when we talk about loudness with regard to a person's voice, we are not talking about measurements of decibels exactly, but rather about how loud did it *sound*? We are talking about perceptions! How loud somebody's voice sounds to you depends on a number of factors, not just the amount of intensity at the source of the sound.

Factors Affecting Loudness

How loud your voice sounds to your listener and how loud your voice sounds to you is determined by the following factors:

1. *Amplitude of vocal cord vibration.* (How much vibration is produced and how much control is used?)
2. *Physical distance* and *spatial relationship.* (How does physical distance from your listeners affect your loudness?)
3. *Psychological distance.* (How do your feelings about your audience affect your control of loudness?)
4. *The emotional state of the speaker.* (How do your feelings affect your control of loudness?)
5. *The speaker's reaction to ambient noise.* (How do surrounding interfering noises affect your loudness?)

Amplitude of Vocal Cord Vibration

The term amplitude refers to size. Sound travels on waves. The size of these sound wave vibrations depends on the size of your vocal cord vibrations. The stronger the vibrations you set up at the vocal cords, the stronger will be the sound wave vibrations and the louder these vibrations will sound to your listeners.

The force of breath pressure beneath the vocal cords and the elasticity of the vocal cords determine how strong or weak the vibrations will be. When the force of breath pressure beneath the vocal cords increases, the vocal cords tense (tighten). These two combined factors result in increased amplitude and increased loudness. When the force of breath beneath the vocal cords is decreased, causing the vocal cords to become more dense (lax), amplitude decreases, and loudness decreases.

Control of loudness requires control of the exhaled breath stream. Central breathing (diaphragmatic)—not clavicular breathing—helps you to achieve that control. Use diaphragmatic action to support and/or push the exhaled breath stream up the trachea (windpipe) and between the vocal cords. The use of the upper chest or throat muscles to release the exhaled breath results in a hypertense, strained vocal sound.

Not only must you suport the tone adequately to control loudness, but you must keep the vocal cords elastic—capable of many kinds of movements. How do you control vocal cord elasticity? Don't tense the larynx! Put the tension some other place. The tension should be in the midriff area. Use the gross abdominal muscles to support the diaphragmatic action and thus force the air up and out.

A professor of voice therapy had a reputation for being unorthodox. At the opening session, He said: "Kick off your shoes." (The class did, nodding knowingly among themselves.) "Imagine you are at the beach," he commanded. (The class obeyed, wishing they were there!) ''Now close your eyes and with your toes push into the sand. **That**,'' he concluded, ''is where you are going to push for voice production!''The professor had demonstrated emphatically that tension should not come from the laryngeal muscles. In fact, he was not content with support from the diaphragm; he wanted the class to aim at their *feet* for support of tone!

The findings of von Leden and Moore in 1948 confirmed that the glottis *opens more slowly, closes more quickly, and remains closed longer* for increased loudness. If the whole larynx is tense, you lack the control you need for control of loudness.

Physical Distance and Spatial Relationship

Your physical distance from your listeners will affect the amount of loudness required for communication. The ability to project your voice efficiently and effectively is a real asset. This projection, however, must be done without vocal strain.

Psychological Distance

Just as physical distance can affect your loudness, so too can psychological distance. These terms refer to the *perception* you have of your relationship(s) to your listener. When you speak with people, do you feel close or distant, comfortable or threatened, over-whelmed or in control? Do you prefer communicating on a one-to-one basis, in a group, or as a part of a larger organization? How does the physical presence of people affect you? Many people use the telephone to settle differences because the physical presence of the listener makes the situation more difficult to handle. In any of these circumstances, is your loudness affected? Does your perception of your feelings get in the way of control? Are you even aware that your volume changes in different situations?

The Speaker's Emotional State

Emotions plays a vital role in our human relationships and in our vocal management. How you feel at any given moment (happy, sad, preoccupied, worried, enthusiastic, hopeful, discouraged. . .) can affect all the aspects of vocal production and use, including loudness. Are your emotions controlling you or are you controlling your emotions? Your emotions **can** take over and, unless you are vocally disciplined, communication can break down. Your listeners can become so overwhelmed by *how* you are communicating that *what* you are saying loses not only its meaning but also its impact. Be alert! Be aware! Be in control!

Ambient Noise

All of us face situations where we have to talk to others in noisy surroundings. A busy street, a crowded restaurant, or a party are all instances of environments with ambient noise. When you are confronted with such a situation, how do you handle it? Do you try to "talk over" the noise? Do you ignore it? Do you increase the loudness of your voice to compensate for the ambient noise, or do you decrease your loudness? Whatever your approach, you must minimize vocal strain in the process. If you tend to shout over any noise around, you must acquire the skills needed for increasing loudness without vocal strain. (Vocal strain can lead to vocal abuse, which can then lead to vocal pathology.) If you tend to decrease your volume when confronted with surrounding noise, your task is to learn to decrease the volume without allowing your voice to drop back in your throat.

Problems of Loudness (or Volume)

We said earlier that, when speaking, you should achieve "adequate" or "appropriate" volume without vocal strain. The goal is to produce just the right amount of volume to present an effective message.

We will discuss three problems related to loudness: (1) too little volume (the too soft voice); (2) voice fading; and (3) too much volume (the too loud voice). We will outline each of these problems in the following way:

1. We will assess acoustic symptoms. (How does your voice sound?)
2. We will examine the causes of the problem. (Why do you have this problem with loudness?)
3. We will establish goals. (How should your voice be produced to achieve adequate volume?)
4. We will suggest specific skills needed to achieve your goals. (What should you do in order to achieve effective volume control?)
5. We will provide exercises designed to help you develop the skills you need. (What exercises or techniques will develop the needed skills?)

► *Problem 1:* Inadequate Loudness (the too soft voice)

Acoustic Elements

1. minimal audibility
2. periodic breathiness
3. voice fading
4. inadequate oral resonance

Causes

1. poor respiration habits
2. inadequate support of tone
3. minimal subglottal pressure
4. minimal use of the oral cavity as resonator

Skills

1. habitual central breathing
2. support of tone
3. increased physical energy
4. increased oral resonance.

Reminders for all exercises:

achieve good posture

use central breathing

Reduce laryngeal tension. Do not use the laryngeal muscles to push the exhaled breath between the vocal cords. Keep the laryngeal area very relaxed. If you tense up in this area, the voice will become high pitched and strained. Let the breath out of your mouth as you speak. This will help minimize tension in this area.

Exercise 1

a. Hold the palm of your hand about four inches away from your mouth.
b. Place your other hand over the midriff area.
c. Count from one to ten, taking a breath on each individual number.
d. On each number, gently push the air stream out of your mouth against the palm of your hand.
e. Lift from the abdominal muscles for additional energy.
f. Don't allow your voice to get breathy. Don't let extra air escape. Say the numbers.
g. Work for an open, round feeling in your mouth.

Exercise 2

Repeat exercise 1, except: say each number three times.

a. The first time, use a conversational volume. Imagine the person is standing next to you.
b. The second, *slightly increase* the volume. Imagine that the person is about ten feet away. Important: Be sure to feel a definite push on the gross abdominal muscles as you increase the volume. If you are doing this exercise correctly, you will have no change in pitch. If your pitch rises, it means you are involving and tightening the pharyngeal and laryngeal muscles.
c. The third time, greatly increase the volume. Imagine the person is across the room from you. Be sure you increase the volume without strain in your voice.

Exercise 3

Repeat Exercise 2, except use sentences which take you through your daily routine. All of us have a familiar day-to-day "patter." What do you repeat frequently? By using these sentences for practice, you will more quickly encourage transference of loudness skills to your conversational speech. Remember, say the sentences three times as above. Perhaps you say:

1. When is your next class?
2. Can't meet you for lunch today.
3. I'll be late tonight.
4. Go ahead without me.
5. What time is the meeting?

Problem 2: Voice Fading

Acoustic Elements

1. minimal audibility at the ends of phrases and sentences
2. breathiness at the ends of phrases and sentences
3. lower pitch at the ends of phrases and sentences

Causes

1. poor respiration habits
2. inadequate support of tone—especially at the ends of phrases and sentences
3. minimal use of oral cavity for resonance

Skills

1. habitual central breathing
2. control of gross abdominal muscles
3. increased physical energy
4. increased oral resonance

Exercise 1

a. Achieve good posture and put your hand on your diaphragm.
b. Take a breath and begin counting, adding one number for each breath group: One. One, two. One, two, three. One, two, three, four. One, two, three, four, five. Continue until you reach ten. Concentrate on having the *last* number in each group sound as loud as the first number. Keep the breath supported to the end.

Exercise 2

Using the same techniques as in Exercise, 1, although this time use words instead of numbers. See Exercise 3 above for some ideas to transfer this skill to your daily speech.

▶ *Problem 3:* Too much volume (the too loud voice)

Acoustic elements

1. excessive loudness
2. harsh, raspy, or throaty voice quality
3. narrow pitch range, too high or too low
4. lack of pitch variation

Causes

1. hyperpharyngeal/hyperlaryngeal tension
2. excessive push of breath on exhalation
3. hyperpharyngeal resonance
4. minimal oral resonance

Skills

1. whole-body relaxation
2. relaxation of neck and throat areas
3. habitual central breathing
4. reduced physical energy as you speak
5. increased oral resonance

Reminders:

Achieve good posture.

Reduce laryngeal tension.

Control breath emission. This is your trouble spot! You probably tend to over-energize while speaking. You use too much physical energy during voice production. Reduce it! Don't allow your breath to explode out of your mouth when you speak. Use your oral cavity as your main resonator, not your throat. Open your mouth, and get the sounds up and out.

Vary the loudness. Not every word or sentence is equally important. Increased loudness is a way to emphasize words and sentences, so vary loudness to make important words, phrases, or sentences stand out.

Adapt the loudness to the subject, to the situation, and to your listeners. Take into account your physical distance from your listeners and any ambient noise.

Exercise 1

Read the following sentences in two ways: (1) as if you were speaking to a large group of people and (2) as if you were speaking to only one person in an intimate situation.

1. I am delighted to be with you this evening.
2. This is, indeed, a sad occasion.
3. Tonight is a night for celebration.
4. Together we can do it!

5. Let bygones be bygones.
6. This is your responsibility.
7. What are you willing to do about this?
8. I'm hoping to settle this case out of court.
9. Would you be willing to support this cause?
10. For your health's sake, you should stop smoking.

Concluding Suggestions

Be aware of the relationship of vocal hygiene to loudness. On days when your throat feels raw and sore, or when you are suffering with laryngitis or pharyngitis, be *kind to your voice!* Don't overuse it. Don't abuse it. Keep talking to a minimum. However, do not whisper; you do your voice no favor by whispering. When you whisper, your vocal cords are held in a strained, widely abducted position. The best treatment, if you must speak in these circumstances, is to speak softly, allowing the vocal cords to vibrate gently. If necessary, use an amplifying system as a temporary measure for speaking in public.

25

Pitch

"Hi! Are you coming with us over the weekend?"
"Oh! You're not."
"Well! Why not?"

We want to introduce you to the factors which color and affect your meaning as you communicate your messages. The sentences above could have very different meanings depending upon how they were spoken. One of the best clues to whether the speaker was disappointed, relieved, sad or angry would be in the pitch of the voice.

Pitch refers to the highness or lowness of a sound and to all of the degrees of highness or lowness you hear in the human voice. Your own voice has a basic pitch that is dramatically influenced by your inherited laryngeal structure (anatomy) and how you use this structure (physiology). For example, a child's larynx is smaller than the larynx of an adult, which basically accounts for the childlike vocal quality you've come to recognize and expect. Also, the vocal cords of the female larynx are generally shorter in length (seven-eighths of an inch to one inch in length) than the vocal cords of the male (one inch to one and one-fourth inches). The result is the higher pitch range found in the female voice as opposed to the lower pitch range of the male. Look at the strings of a piano (a baby grand makes it easier). You will see that the strings of the piano that produce the low notes are longer and have more flexibility than the strings that produce the high notes.

Your voice has a pitch range. You can change pitch from syllable to syllable and from word to word as you speak. You can even change pitch during a syllable. It is the pattern of pitches that make up the melody of our speech when we talk (see Chapter 18).

Factors Related to Variations in Pitch

The pitch of your voice and your ability to change pitch depend on many factors, some simple and others very involved. Simply stated, your voice changes pitch with the increase or decrease of the number of vibrations per minute of the vocal cords. However, the length, thickness, and flexibility of the vocal cords significantly affect the frequency of vibration. For example, if you lengthen the cords by tensing them, you get a faster vibration, which results in a higher pitch. We also know that vocal pitch and intensity are so interrelated that it is impossible to isolate one from the other. There is a marked interplay between vocal cord tension and subglottal pressure. Other related factors are:

1. frequency of vocal cord vibration
2. tension of the vocal cords
3. length and thickness of the vocal cords
4. intensity—subglottal pressure

In addition to the four physiological and acoustical factors related to pitch that we have already mentioned, there are other factors that are also related to pitch changes.

1. medical condition of the speaker
2. personality of the speaker
3. vocal color

If you consider all of these factors together, a fairly involved picture emerges, possibly even more involved than that of loudness. Obviously, pitch and its variation are not simple matters.

Before you begin to work on your pitch and pitch variation, it is advisable for you to recheck your basic voice production. Using your voice effectively allows you maximum flexibility of vocal cord vibration and minimizes laryngeal-pharyngeal hypertension. Review the following skills:

1. Relaxation of the laryngeal muscles (see pp. 421-424).
2. Efficient respiration (see pp. 437-438).
3. Controlled respiration (see pp. 438-439).
4. Breath emission (see p. 442-443).

Changes in the pitch of your voice depend on many factors, most of which are very complex. **Take note of all of them.**

Factors That Influence the Pitch of Your Voice

Medical Conditions

Physiology and medical ailments can affect pitch. The endocrine system is sometimes a factor: the adolescent voice during puberty and the female voice during menopause. We have personally been involved with two students with endocrine problems: a male student who weighed around 250 pounds yet had a high-pitched voice and a fifty-year-old female with such a low-pitched voice that in telephone conversations she was addressed as "Mr." If you have a serious problem with pitch, a medical assessment is a must.

On the *physical* (acoustical) side, amplitude of vocal cord vibration and tension of the vocal cords are two factors related to pitch. These areas were discussed in Chapter 24, but a quick review might be beneficial at this time. With increased amplitude and increased tension of the vocal cords, the pitch of your voice will go up. The *physics of sound* tells us that *any* vibrating body (guitar string or piano string) when tightened causes pitch to rise. Your vocal cords react in the same physical way. In some cases the higher pitch is not only desirable but *necessary* (in contact ulcers, a vocal pathology, for example). In other cases the rise in pitch (or lowering of pitch) is indicative of vocal strain.

Personality of the Speaker

Yes, your personality is involved with the pitch of your voice. The anxious, high-strung personality usually experiences hypertension; hypertension frequently causes physical changes. The voice is dramatically affected. With the increased body tension, the vocal cords tighten and U-U-U-P goes the pitch of the person's voice.

Turn the coin over. Some anxieties reveal themselves by withdrawal symptoms. Those affected seem to crawl inside themselves, exhibiting little or no outward emotions. The voice is held back in the throat and becomes raspy, breathy, or husky. People with these kinds of vocal qualities sound as if they are "walking backwards," pulling the voice back with them. The breath gets stuck back in the throat, there is minimal breath emission on phonation, and a poor vocal quality is the result. Pitch is lowered and usually lacks range.

At this point, we ask you to review the material in Chapter 24 dealing with spatial relationships, psychological distance, and emotionality (see p. 468). All of this material applies directly to your pitch control. In addition, your emotional state has a profound effect on your pitch range *at the very moment* of utterance.

In a given situation your feelings (your emotional state) show themselves vocally in different ways. When angry, some people scream, sending their pitch sky high; other people withdraw, taking their pitch down with them. In all such emotional settings, your pitch will react accordingly. However, if you are vocally disciplined, if you are aware of the techniques used to control and to vary your pitch, and if you are able to apply these known techniques, then no matter the emotional setting, you will be better equipped to communicate effectively.

Vocal Color

Vocal color is the "happening" when your voice takes on the mood and meaning (semantics) of the words you are saying. For example, consider the following two phrases:

Isn't it a lovely day!

I feel very fatigued.

The wording of the two sentences strongly suggests a different meaning, and particularly a different mood. The first sentence ("Isn't it a lovely day!") suggests a brightness of vocal quality and a "light" voice, in contrast with the second sentence ("I feel very fatigued") which suggests a heavy mood, lacking in spirit and energy. In order to communicate effectively the meaning of the two sentences, there should be a marked difference in use of voice. *Vocal color can be acquired!*

Vocal color and vocal variety do not come easily. Some of you, instinctively, are able to show your feelings. You fully demonstrate happiness, disappointment or sorrow. You visibly let go! You yell! You cry! You smile! You share your feelings. There might be those of you who draw the line at such outbursts. You hold back. You find it difficult, even painful, to reveal your feelings. If you know that you hold back, then letting the voice "go" will be challenging. For those of you who tend to react emotionally, with ease, you will probably find vocal color and variety less difficult.

Let's clarify again. *Vocal color* applies to the particular emotion(s) involved (your voice takes on that "color"). *Vocal variety* involves the application of the emotionality to the words being used. In short—*how not to sound monotonous.*

Before you attempt vocal variety, let's see if you can deliberately (mechanically) move your pitch up and down. Our approach to this skill is *tactile* and *kinesthetic* rather than *aural*. You will learn to listen later.

1. Place your fingertips on your larynx and swallow. You will feel slight tension. *Become acquainted with this muscle action.* Using the alphabet, say each letter on a different pitch.

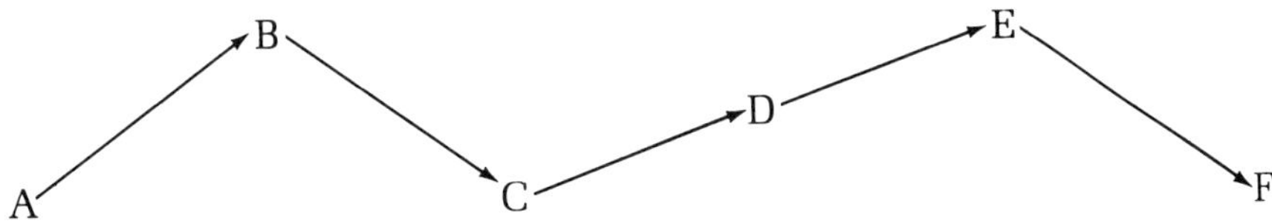

What pitch you use in unimportant. Say one letter high, the next letter lower, the second letter a little lower than the first, and so on. The point is to *deliberately* vary the pitch of your voice.

Feel the difference in muscle action in the larynx as you vary your pitch. Do this exercise with your eyes open and then with your eyes closed (kinesthesia). Try *listening* for the changes in pitch. You might benefit from using the piano keyboard as a guide. Say the letters of the alphabet on different notes, changing the notes indiscriminately. A word of caution: as you practice this exercise, keep in mind open oral cavity and relaxed jaws in order to reduce hyperlaryngeal tension. Concentrate on central breathing.

2. Use the following phrases in the same way as in the first exercise, only this time say *each word in the phrase on a different pitch.*
   a. Come here.
   b. Hello, there!
   c. Sit down.
   d. Where's the fire?
   e. I feel fine.
   f. She's a beauty!
   g. It's time for dinner.
   h. My head really hurts.
   i. Hurry up. You're late!

How did you succeed? Were you able to move your pitch around? If not, keep trying. Use the piano keyboard (the white keys) as a help in making you more aware of your pitch changes. The tape recorder can become your best friend. Tape your pitch improvement sessions. Play back the tape. Listen closely and carefully as you analyze and evaluate your performance.

Check yourself:

You can vary your pitch effectively

1. if your voice is effectively produced so that there is no hypertension in the larynx.
2. if you are breathing efficiently because breath control is necessary for the effective expression of ideas.
3. if there is adequate resonance balance of the basic laryngeal tone. Voices with limited resonance cannot easily acquire vocal color.
4. if there is effective pitch variation.
5. if there is a psychological willingness on your part to express the emotional content of the words you are saying.

Exercises for Acquiring Vocal Color and Pitch Variation

1. Try the following sentences, keeping in mind the *meaning* of the words and the *mood* created by the meaning.
   a. Hello! (Call out cheerfully to a friend across the room.

Concentrate on correct projection and attempt a rising inflection.)

b. How are you feeling today? (Express *concern*. Try a circumflex pitch pattern.)

c. Don't you dare make an accusation! (Express quiet anger. Intentionally use precise diction with a monotonous tone of rising inflection.)

d. Consider the word *goodbye*. Say it with the following meanings: leaving a party of friends at a social gathering; parting in anger; leaving a child with whom you've been playing; anticipating a long departure from a friend.

2. Challenge yourself a little more by moving on to prose. Choose some material that you will enjoy reading, preferably a paragraph that has either colorful language or emotional content. Don't read the box scores of the players of your favorite team!

   a. Examine the material closely for meaning and then decide on the idea(s) and words that you want to emphasize.

   b. Decide on *how* you are going to emphasize them. Are you going to use changes in loudness, pitch, or rate for this? Perhaps you are going to use all three?

3. Move on to extemporaneous speaking. Think through an incident you want to talk about. Plan the incident in your head only. Do not write it out. Turn on your tape recorder and record the incident. Play back the tape. Is your voice beginning to have more pitch changes? If not, repeat the incident. This time make a real effort to move your voice up and down and around.

5. Perhaps you are ready for conversational speech. Invite a friend to help you in this exercise. Don't decide what the two of you are going to talk about beforehand. Turn on the tape recorder and begin talking—about anything. This is easier if the subject matter is of interest to both of you. Talk for about three minutes. Listen to the replay both critically and analytically.

Most books on voice include information on optimum pitch and/or modal pitch. Because this book is not pathologically based, we prefer not to go into this area in depth. However, we want to make some mention of the pitch level at which your voice seemingly functions with the least amount of effort. If you want to find your level of "least effort," try this. Hum up and down the scale. Concentrate on finding a midpoint—that point at which you experience little or no muscle tension in the larynx. When you feel you have reached this comfortable place, hum *down* the scale until you reach a point of *discomfort*. Hum back up the scale approximately five notes. Your optimum pitch can usually be determined within this five note range. The general idea is to speak within this range or, more specifically, to use this five-note range as a basic pitch range for your everyday use of voice. Note that your *modal pitch* is that range of pitch that you use *most*. It may or may not be your optimum pitch.

We prefer *not* to recommend this mechanical way of finding your optimum pitch. It is arbitrary and artificial. Our suggestion to you is to work on achieving over-all effective voice production and then to use this as a firm foundation for encouraging a wide pitch range and variation within that range.

Deliberate manipulation of pitch is to be avoided unless extreme conditions demand it. Voice (like water) will seek its own level when effectively produced. We suggest that stress be placed on (1) an over-all attempt to make the vibratory process work efficiently and (2) a serious, concentrated effort to relate the person to his own voice, physically and psychologically. Certain pathological voice problems require manipulation. However, for most voice improvement cases, pitch manipulation is needless, less than effective, and can even be dangerous. A student with a serious case of huskiness and voice fading registered in one of our voice classes. Our assessment also characterized her voice as having a narrow pitch range (low). She was startled. Her immediate reply was, "I can't believe it! My voice low-pitched? All of my life I've been told about my high, squeaky voice." Questioning revealed that during a recent course in oral reading, the instructor kept hammering away at her to "Do something about that high-pitched voice." The student took it upon herself to talk at a lower pitch and with less volume. The result was a tortured, breathy, husky, low-pitched voice. An otolaryngologist examination revealed the beginnings of pathology (pinhead nodules on both vocal cords).

How do you know if you use pitch variation effectively? How do you know if you use pitch variation ineffectively? Let's take a look at the indicators.

1. *If the pitch of your voice is effective it should*
   a. be appropriate for your sex and for your age.
   b. have pitch range.
   c. be efficiently reinforced by loudness.
   d. be involved with melody and vocal color.
   e. have pitch variations related to the meaning of what is being said (semantics).
2. *If the pitch of your voice is ineffective it can be the result of*
   a. malfunction of the endocrine (glandular) system of the body.
   b. poor use and control of your laryngeal musculature and poor control of loudness.
   c. lack of psychological involvement.
   d. your emotional state at the very moment of utterance.
   e. lack of vocal color and vocal variety.

If your voice quality has any of the following characteristics, note the possible related *pitch problems*:

1. Hoarse (usually low pitched; occasional pitch breaks).
2. Breathy/husky (low pitch; limited range).
3. Thin (high pitch; limited range).
4. Harsh (low pitch; limited range).
5. Strident (high pitch; limited range).

Concluding Suggestions

In review, the common voice problems associated with pitch fall into four categories: too high, too low, minimal range, and a lack of pitch variation. If you have any of these problems, first evaluate your physical condition and determine if the problem is severe enough to require medical attention. Seek help if you are unsure. Next, review the good habits of effective voice production. If your pitch is too high, guard against excessive emotionality. It it is too low, has minimum range and/or little variation, try to become emotionally involved with the material. If your pitch is low, strive for vocal variation and color. If your voice needs more pitch variety, concentrate on the meanings of the words you are speaking.

Review this chapter for specific instructions on how to correct and/or improve any of the pitch problems. Your instructor can suggest practice material.

26

Rate

"Slow down! I can't understand you!"
"Talk faster! I can't wait all day!"

The rate at which you speak is one of the most notable characteristics of your speech. Listeners quickly identify the fast talker or the slow talker. They may not tell you about their impressions or their reactions, but your rate of speech will surely affect their perception or their image of you—however accurate or inaccurate. You may be thinking, "Does it really matter how fast or how slowly I talk?" Yes, it does matter. Your rate of speech affects your intelligibility and your voice.

The term *rate* refers to the number of words you speak per minute. Documented studies show that the so-called normal, or conversational rate of speech is anywhere from 120-140 words per minute. Your rate when reading aloud is slightly faster, with an average of between 150-170 words per minute.

What determines a speaker's rate? Why do some speakers take more (or less) time to utter the same words? The answer lies in duration of sounds, length of phrases, and length of pauses.

Duration refers to the amount of time consumed in producing a speech sound. Continuant consonants, you remember, can be continued. Vowels and diphthongs are uttered with relatively little obstruction; they too can be sustained. The question is: How long do you continue or sustain a given sound. The answer is that sound's duration. Your pattern of sound duration helps determine your rate. If you hold on to sounds longer, your rate (of words uttered per minute) will be slower. If, on the other hand, you cut off the individual sounds more quickly, your rate will be faster.

We do not speak a sound at a time or even a word at a time. We speak in phrases—groups of words representing a thought. We have mentioned this before in discussing breathing for speech. We put words together, pausing before and after each phrase. These thought groups help our listeners to follow our train of thought, and the pauses give us a chance to get our breath. Again, the length of these thought groups/phrases will help determine your rate. If your phrases are longer, your rate will be faster. If you divide your utterance into shorter thought units, your rate will be slower.

Pauses also help determine one's rate of speech. All pauses are not the same length. Usually a pause is longer between clauses and sentences than between phrases. But how long should a pause be at the end of a sentence? That is a very individual matter, and those individual differences in pausing will make your rate faster or slower.

Skill in rate control and variation, like skill in pitch and volume, can be acquired and you can learn to use these skills, but first we have to decide what your needs are. In this chapter you will learn how to

1. Diagnose your rate profile. (How many words do you speak per minute?)
2. Assess your rate profile. (Is the rate too fast? Too slow?)
3. Set goals. (When should I increase rate? When should I decrease rate?)
4. Implement those goals into everyday speech.

We have frequently said that your inherited anatomy and your ability to use gross and refined motor skills play a vital role in forming your individual speech pattern. Your rate of speech is another illustration of these combined factors.

Factors That Influence Your Rate

A fast rate of speaking is found most frequently in the energetic, quick-moving person. Your rate and duration of speaking seem to be related to your overall physiology. Heredity, early environmental stimulation, conditioning, and even the type of education to which you were exposed all were contributing factors to the *pace* of your thinking. Have you ever played the game of charades and been unable to decipher the cues in time to give an answer? Still more frustrating, have you *understood* the given cues and not been able to formulate the answer as quickly as the persons near you because they spoke faster than you?

We want to make the point that none of these ways of functioning has the element of "right" or "wrong." It is not necessarily better to be able to "move" mentally or physically more quickly than the next person. What is important is to be aware of your physical and intellectual pace. *You also have an individual emotional pace*! This emotional pace noticeably affects your rate of speaking. Perhaps you do not demonstrate your emotions as quickly—either verbally or nonverbally—as your friends do. No matter! The goal is to help you to function as comfortably and efficiently as possible where your rate of speech is concerned.

It should now be obvious that *your rate profile is not the result of any single factor*. Rate is multi-dimensional. It is deeply involved with your physical, intellectual, and psychological self.

Physical Factors

Your inherited anatomy (skeletal frame) affects your rate of speech because your physiology (functioning) is related to your anatomy. Your body type can slow you down both physically and emotionally or it can influence your quickness.

Basic physiology is another important physical factor. In daily physical activities, do you usually move quickly, slowly, moderately, or at varied speeds. The answer to this question is highly individual because there are no standards. The same is true for your rate of speech. If you tend to move quickly, your rate of speech will be related. If you move more slowly, your rate of speech may also be slower than average. Your ability to control and to use muscles is based on your knowledge, understanding and acceptace of your individual physiology. The control of your rate in speaking is reflected in your physiological profile, so set your goals realistically.

On the surface, you might question the relationship of respiration to rate control. Studies support the following findings. The average time of expiration in quiet breathing approximately equals the time of inspiration. The ratio is 1:1. The average ratio of expiration to inspiration in speaking is 5:1—five times as much as in quiet breathing. In actual speaking situations, the ratio may rise as high as 10:1. How we control our exhalation affects our rate of speaking.

Physical activity provides an excellent example of the relationship of rate to respiration. After a strenuous game of tennis or basketball, your rate of speech is affected when you try to talk. Either you do not have enough breath to speak so that your rate is slowed down, or you speak with a "staccato" effect as you try to grab for more breath between words. The *ratio of inhalation to exhalation to rate is changed*.

Your physical well being also affects your rate. Your health and your energy level play an important role in your voice production in general, and in your rate in particular. Take note of what happens to your rate on days when you are ill or on those days following an illness. Your body has less energy, because you are taking in less oxygen (good air) and expelling less carbon dioxide (waste products) so, d-o-w-n goes your energy. The brain is receiving less stimulation.

Intellectual Factors

Some people "naturally" seem to be able to think and/or react faster to a given situation. Earlier in this chapter we talked about the fact that this "pace of reaction" was influenced by many things: your heredity, your environment, your particular kind of education.

Mentally we have our pace, also. People differ in the time needed to think over and react to ideas presented to them. They can react spontaneously or after deliberation. Think about your mental "natural pace" for a moment. It is important that you are aware of it because your rate of speech is affected by it. The slow, deliberate thinker usually has a slower rate of speech than the person who thinks and responds more quickly. We emphasize—we are *not* talking about *emergency* replies—those replies which we are forced to make because of threatening circumstances. In this section we are referring to your everyday, across the board, way of communicating.

Psychological Factors

It is practically impossible to separate the kind of personality you are from how you react emotionally in a given situation, so the two areas of personality and the emotional state of the speaker will be considered together with reference to rate control. Your personality determines how you will behave in an emotional setting. Intellectually you can manipulate your behavior, but it is difficult to control your initial emotional reaction. For example, what if you received what you consider to be an unfair grade from a teacher. Your initial reaction might be one of fury ("I'm going to tell that teacher off!"), but intellectually you know that you will be far better off if you calmly discuss the grade with the teacher.

Your perception of your own personality (outgoing, withdrawn, introspective, reactionary) affects your ability to interrelate. Your rate of speech is deeply involved with this interrelationship. Rate is an integral part of you as a person. If you feel strongly about a situation, your rate of speech will be related not only to your feelings about that situation but also to how you express those feelings verbally. Have you ever had someone say to you, "Oh, but I didn't *mean* that. You misunderstood." Your reply, "No, I didn't misunderstand you. You *said*. . . ." If the discussion becomes heated, your rate of speech will undoubtedly be affected in direct proportion. Either your rate will increase and you will begin to speak machine gun fashion (words coming out a mile a minute) or your rate will decrease (depending on your temperament) and you will begin to "bite out your words" through clenched teeth. Your loudness will be affected.

In addition to the physical, intellectual, and emotional factors listed above, *how* we use and speak words also affects our rate. Phrasing is directly linked to rate of speech. By a phrase we mean a group of words that presents a *complete idea*. Phrases are *not* determined by commas. We have often asked students, "Why did you pause at that point?" The reply has been, "Because there's a comma." No! Consider the following sentence, "*I have a blue, yellow, white, red, and green blouse.*" There is no reason to pause after each comma. The commas are for grammatical purposes and for the eye. Take a look at the following:

After I finish eating dinner, I'm going to the movies.

1. After I/finish eating dinner I'm/going/to the movies.
2. After I finish eating dinner/I'm going to the movies.

Version 2 would certainly be considered more meaningful phrasing. You might even say the sentence *without* a pause. Many speakers either overphrase (pause too frequently) or underphrase (continue too long before a pause). Either pattern understandably affects your rate of speech. *Overphrasing slows down your rate* and *underphrasing speeds up your rate.*

Similarly, the way in which we use stress affects our rate of speech. You probably learned about the technique of *emphasis* from your oral reading or public speaking classes. Stress is a form of emphasis, and it involves using greater "force" on words, phrases, and even on complete sentences. However, in your attempt to use greater (or less) force you will necessarily become involved with rate of speech. Greater force generally demands a slower rate; less force usually allows for a faster rate. We would like to repeat an exercise here. *This* time try to be *aware* of how force is affected by rate. Try the following:

I don't feel well today. (Not you, I)
I *don't* feel well today. (Opposite of I *do*)
I don't *feel* well today. (Physical discomfort)
I don't feel *well* today. (I'm ill)
I don't feel well *today*. (Yesterday I was well)

If you are aware that you are on the extreme ends of the continuum of fast versus slow rate of speech, then take the time to consider the following sections so that you will acquire the necessary skill for effective rate control.

Your Rate Profile

Diagnosis

In order to judge if your rate of speaking is too fast or too slow for effective communication, a determination must first be made of the number of words you speak per minute, known as wpm. After an assessment of your rate has been made, goals can be set, and you can learn how to implement the recommendations.

Start with material you can read. In the beginning of this chapter, we said that in reading an average wpm was anywhere from 150-170. Usually your wpm for conversational speech is a little slower. Try the following:

1. Select a passage you can comfortably handle in terms of content and vocabulary. Don't read the box scores from yesterday's baseball games or a chemistry formula.
2. Set up your equipment: a clock with a second hand, a quiet room, and your material. It is helpful to record your reading for an auditory reaction to your rate profile. You are now ready to begin, but first, take a deep breath and relax.
3. Read your selection aloud at a comfortable speed for one minute. Repeat the reading at least twice more. Three times in all. You will now have three minutes of the same passage to evaluate.
4. Determine the total number of words you read during the three readings over a three-minute period. Divide the total number of words by three (the number of minutes). This will give you your average wpm.
5. For an estimate of your conversational speech (this is a little more difficult to do), record a conversation with a friend for two or three minutes. Try to determine the number of words spoken during the allotted time period. Again, divide the total number of words by the total number of minutes and you will arrive at an average wpm. Now this total won't be exactly accurate because the conversational situation was somewhat structured and not entirely spontaneous. However, the recording will give you an approximation of wpm for conversational speech.

Assessment

How did you do? Did you read much faster than the average wpm? Did you read much slower than the average wpm? Perhaps you were right on target. Perhaps your reading wpm was slower than the average wpm and your conversational wpm was faster than the average wpm. Do you think that you have a problem? Whatever the outcome, remember that the numbers we quoted for wpm were *average*. Who is to say what is *average for you*?

Goals

Don't set any goals for your individual wpm in reading or for conversation until you are familiar with the material on "Factors That Influence Your Rate of Speech" Remember, rate of speech is highly individual. However, once you have determined your "natural" speech, you must then head your list of goals with the following:

1. Your rate of speech must not interfere with *intelligibility* of sounds, words and/or ideas.
2. Your rate of speech must be *varied*. There are "fast" words; there are "slow" words. There are ideas which can be "blurted out" as opposed to phrases which benefit from a s-l-o-w delivery.

Try these sentences for *rate variation*. Don't forget *stress*!

1. So sorry.
2. Don't do that again!
3. I prefer the blue tie.
4. What a sight! It's awesome!
5. You've got an attitude. What's your problem?
6. Hurry up! We'll be late for the opening.
7. I need some time before I can make a decision.
8. I can't wait to see what's going to happen at that meeting.
9. Do you really like her costume for the Mardi Gras?
10. Believe me, it's true! I know he still denies the whole thing.

Management/Implementation for the "Too Fast" Speaker

1. Use a tape recorder for this exercise. Write out two or three sentences or phrases that you use daily. Record this material as you would ordinarily say it. Repeat it, only this second time, deliberately slow down your rate by saying "one" between each word of the material. Let the "one" represent one second between each of the words.

   I (one) am (one) going (one) out (one) to (one) lunch (one).

   The object is to take you to the extreme, slow end of the rate continuum; to slow you down as much as is physically possible; to raise your level of awareness regarding the differences in the rate of speaking.
2. Repeat exercise 1, but this time do not say the number one between each word. However, do try to slow down, or at least try to change your pattern of rate. Try to feel the difference in your rate of speaking—no matter what the difference. We are attempting to break through your old habitual pattern of fast rate.
3. As you say the prescribed words and sentences, s-t-r-e-t-c-h the vowel sounds. Resonate them in the oral cavity. This demands more time, so this will help to slow you down. Your too-fast rate of speech will be affected by the prolongation of vowel sounds.
4. Take a closer look at your phrasing. Do you underphrase? Do you tend to go on and on before pausing either for meaning or for a breath? **Stop**! Review the communication situation. Note: (a) your audience; (b) the occasion, and (c) the emotional setting. Do these factors tell you that a relaxed, slower rate is more appropriate?
5. Does everything sound alike in your speech? Do you stress everything? Does every idea sound equally important? Reassess your priorities!

Management/Implementation for the "Too Slow" Speaker

1. Use a tape recorder for this exercise. Write out two or three sentences or phrases that you use daily. Record this material as

you would ordinarily say it. Repeat it, only this second time deliberately speed up your rate. Use the second hand on the clock. Make yourself "beat the clock!" If the sentence originally took you six seconds to say, repeat it in three seconds. The object is to take you to the extreme, fast end of the rate continuum; to speed you up as much as is physically possible; to raise your level of awareness regarding the differences in the rate of speaking.

2. Practice the sentences which appear on p. 488. Do not prolong the vowels. Rather, attempt to run the words and sentences together. Really overassimilate. Don't worry about your speech sounding a little sloppy. We are trying to make you aware of the differences in rate of speaking and to help you break through your old habitual pattern of rate through assimilation techniques.
3. Take a closer look at your phrasing. Do you overphrase? Do you tend to pause too frequently to take a breath? Review respiration (see pp. 436-443). Perhaps you are a clavicular breather. Perhaps you keep running out of breath and this slows you down.
4. Does everything sound alike when you speak? Do you emphasize the important words? Are there high points in your delivery?

Integration of Skills

Before we end this section on vocal skills, try the following material. Can you "get your act together" and integrate all of the skills of:

1. volume (Must be adequate/varied).
2. pitch (Must have a wide range/varied).
3. rate (Speech must be intelligible/rate varied).

Use the following exercise to develop pitch and rate skills:

1. No! They couldn't have given it to him.
2. This is your responsibility; you cannot escape it.
3. Let's get this work done quickly. Perhaps later, when we have time, we can slow up.
4. The people of poverty-stricken Asia need your help. What are you going to do about it?
5. He ran to the corner, peeked around, and seeing the way clear, jumped into his car and took off like a jet pilot.
6. Let's forget old quarrels. Let's put them behind us and work together from here on.
7. The birthrate has increased at an amazing pace—eleven percent in ten years. Just what should we gather from this trend?
8. Have you ever longed for a calm time by the sea? No nagging rush, no day and night grind of unrelenting pressure. Just sleepy peace.
9. Twenty-five points in one game! I told you he was a fine prospect.
10. Pause, if you will, for just a moment; consider the consequences of the course you propose to adopt.

11. Now let's see; we have a long way to go and all the time in the world to get there.
12. You may protest. You may say you're sick to death of heavy taxes, but what are you willing to do about it? Do you really believe, down deep, that anything will be done about them?

Summary

Before we conclude this section on voice, we would like to say that we are not of the **Don't** school of voice improvement:

1. **Don't** scream or yell.
2. **Don't** use your voice too much.
3. **Don't** talk on the telephone.
4. **Don't** attend parties where there is a lot of ambient noise.
5. **Don't** go into smoke-filled rooms.
6. **Don't. Don't. Don't.**

We not only suggest, but we **urge** those of you with voice problems to **learn to use your voice effectively**. We do have our hopes and aspirations concerning your voice improvement program, and we hope these have been clearly stated throughout this section.

Concluding Suggestions

The mental twister "Which is more important, **what** is said or **how** it is said?" can be of real significance at this stage in your speech improvement program. We firmly believe that **what** is said is of paramount importance (in terms of the content of the message, the reasoning, the evidence submitted, and the ethical, personal, and psychological factors involved). We also firmly believe that what is said can be more effective **if it is said with more meaning**, a paraphrase of the adage "You cannot meaningfully communicate what you do not understand." The skills involved with vocal quality, loudness, pitch, and rate must be concerned with this understanding and with willingness on your part to become personally involved with your speech and voice.

We have stressed many times that in any speech improvement program, improvement begins on a mechanistic, or clinical, level. Then the hard work of transference begins, at which time you must work through loaded material, oral reading (the printed page), extemporaneous speaking, and finally spontaneous speech. It *can* and *will* happen! Trust us!

Voice Bibliography

Aronson, A.E. *Clinical Voice Disorders*. An Interdisciplinary Approach. New York: Thieme-Stratton, 1980.

Boone, D.L. *The Voice and Voice Therapy* (3rd Edition). Engelwood Cliffs, New Jersey: Prentice-Hall, 1983.

Brondnitz, F.S. *Keeping Your Voice Healthy*. San Diego: College Hill Press, 1987.

Case, James L. *Clinical Management of Voice Disorders*. Rockville, Maryland: Aspen Systems Corporation, 1984.

Combs, Carolyn, ed. *Vasta Directory of Members*, 1988. (Available from The Voice and Speech Trainers Association, Inc.). 1804 Ravina Road, West Lafayette, Indiana, 47906. To be updated annually.

Fisher, H. *Improving Voice and Articulation* (2nd Edition). Boston: Houghton Mifflin, 1975.

Gelb, Michael. *Body Learning*. New York: Delilah Books, 1981.

Green, M.C.L. The Voice and Its Disorders (4th Edition). Philadelphia: J.B. Lippincott, 1980.

Hahner, Jeffrey C., Sokoloff, Maretin A., Salisch, Sandra L. *Speaking Clearly* (3rd Edition). New York: McGraw-Hill Publishing Co., 1990.

King, R.G. and E.M. DiMichael. *Articulation and Voice: Improving Oral Communication*. New York: Macmillan & Co., 1978.

Mayer, L.V. *Fundamentals of Voice and Diction* (8th Edition). Dubuque, Iowa: William C. Brown, 1987.

McNeil, M.R., Rosenback, J.C. and A.E. Aronson (Eds.). *The Dysarthrias: Physiology, Acoustice, Perceptions, Management*. San Diego: College Hill Press, 1984.

Rickover, Robert. *Fitness Without Stress - A Guide to the Alexander Technique*. Portland: Metamorphous Press, 1988.

Seidler, Ann, and Bianchi, Doris. *Voice and Diction Fitness: A Comprehensive Approach*. New York: Harper & Row, 1988.

Wilson, E.K. *Voice Problems of Children* (2nd Edition). Baltimore: Williams and Wilkins, 1979.

Zemlin, Willard R. *Speech and Hearing Science: Anatomy and Physiology* (2nd Edition). Englewood Cliffs, New Jersey: Prentice-Hall, 1981.

Index